D1391262

CONTRACTS OF EMPLOYMENT LAW, GUIDANCE AND PRECEDENTS

Second Edition

Volume 2:
The Manual

Michael Duggan, Barrister

xpl publishing

Employment Law, Practice and Precedents Series
General Editor, Michael Duggan

© Michael Duggan 2005

Published by
xpl law
31–33 Stonehills House
Welwyn Garden City
Hertfordshire
AL8 6PU

ISBN 1 85811 326 1

All rights reserved. No part of this publication may be
reproduced, stored in a retrieval system, or transmitted, in
any form or by any means, electronic, mechanical,
photocopying, recording or otherwise, without the prior
permission of the publisher.

The moral right of the author has been asserted.

Typeset by Jane Conway

Cover design by Jane Conway
Cover photography by Jon Adams

Printed in Great Britain by Lightning Source

Dedication

To

My Mother and Father

And to my Wife, Michelle, without whose love, encouragement and support I would never get anything done.

And my Sons, Francis, Andrew and Thomas

CONTENTS OF VOLUME 2

Contents of Volume 2: The Manual

Section Three		**Model Terms and Conditions Manual**	**493**
	A	Introduction to the Manual and the Company	495
	B	Job Title and Description/Offers of Employment	502
	C	Scope of Duties and Responsibilities	507
	D	Hours of Work	518
	E	Basic Salary	594
	F	Remuneration and Benefits other than Salary	605
	G	Place of Work and Mobility	631
	H	Preconditions of Employment or Continued Employment	645
	I	Absences from Work due to Holiday	658
	J	Absences from Work due to Sickness and the Provision of Sick Pay	677
	K	Parents	728
	L	Absence for Other Reasons	805
	M	Conduct and Standard of Behaviour at Work	823
	N	Staff Development and Appraisal	844
	O	Employee Representation	851
	P	Public Interest Disclosure	855
	Q	Restrictions during and after Employment	881
	R	Disciplinary Procedures	900
	S	Greivance Procedures	962
	T	Equal Opportunities	984

U   Health and Safety   1012
V   Termination   1024
W   Stress   1036

Section Four   Directors   1047

Index   1077

Contents of Volume 1: The Legal Basis of the Contract and Specific Occupations

Foreword   ix
Updater   xi
Table of Cases   xv
Table of Statutes and Regulations   xxxii

Section One   General Principles of Employment Contracts   1
              1   Introduction   3
              2   The Use of Data   91
              3   Recruitment   151
              4   Right to Statement of Employment
                  Particulars   207

Section Two   A–Z of Different Types of Employment   219
              5   A–Z of Different Types of Employment   221

Index

VOLUME 2

SECTION THREE
MODEL TERMS AND
CONDITIONS MANUAL

Part A	Introduction to the Manual and the Company	495
Part B	Job Title and Description/Offers of Employment	502
Part C	Scope of Duties and Responsibilities	507
Part D	Hours of Work	518
Part E	Basic Salary	594
Part F	Remuneration and Benefits other than Salary	605
Part G	Place of Work and Mobility	631
Part H	Preconditions of Employment or Continued Employment	645
Part I	Absences from Work due to Holiday	658
Part J	Absences from Work due to Sickness and the Provision of Sick Pay	677
Part K	Parents	728
Part L	Absence for Other Reasons	805
Part M	Conduct and Standard of Behaviour at Work	823
Part N	Staff Development and Appraisal	844
Part O	Employee Representation	851
Part P	Public Interest Disclosure	855
Part Q	Restrictions during and after Employment	881
Part R	Disciplinary Procedures	900
Part S	Grievance Procedures	962
Part T	Equal Opportunities	984
Part U	Health and Safety	1012

Part V   Termination   **1024**

Part W   Stress   **1036**

PART A: INTRODUCTION TO THE MANUAL AND THE COMPANY

Precedent A: **Introduction to the Manual and the Company**

    A1: **Introduction**   **495**

    A2: **Alternative introduction**   **498**

Commentary: **Introduction to the Manual and the Company**   **499**

Precedent A1: Introduction

1 The Company is pleased to present this Personnel Manual to you as an introduction to the work that is carried out by the Company and to set out the management structure and basis on which the company operates. You will find enclosed at the back of this Manual a diagram that sets out the management hierarchy and reporting structures from which you will be able to see where you fit into the organization.

2 Whether you are an existing member of staff or a new employee, the document is intended to provide you with information about the activities of the Company as well as details of your terms and conditions of employment. Please read it carefully and keep it safely with your other documents (such as your Letter of Appointment or the individual statement of Terms and

Conditions of Employment) as it forms part of your contract of employment with the Company.

3 The Company provides generous conditions of employment, with particularly beneficial arrangements for items such as holidays, Private Health Insurance and sick pay. In return, we expect staff to be flexible in the way they work, in order to meet our objectives of providing a high level of service to our Customers who wish to use the Company's Services. This means that we all have to concentrate on getting the job done when it is required, balancing this where necessary with time off later. We work on a basis of trust and look to individuals to control their own time as far as possible.

4 The Company also places emphasis on employee initiative, so that we can continue to change to meet the demands of both our Customers and potential customers for the Company's services. We encourage staff development so that wherever possible we can respond quickly and appropriately to every opportunity or problem and we welcome suggestions from members of staff as to how their roles may be improved to further enhance the Company's services.

5 The Personnel Manual sets out the policies of the Company concerning its staff and contains important contractual information relating to your rights and duties at work. The Manual supplements your Terms and Conditions of Employment and the sections that follow this introduction are incorporated into your contract. The Company has the right to vary this Manual from time to time as a result of changes or developments in work or as is reasonably required in order for the Company to carry out its functions. It also may be that, from time to time, legislation requires variations to this manual. When there is a variation in the terms of this Manual you shall be notified as soon as possible of the change by way of issue of new pages to the Manual, which shall then be the terms governing your contract.

6 The rules and conditions in this Personnel Manual apply to all staff, and should be read in conjunction with any Statement of Terms and Conditions of Employment issued under the Employment Rights Act 1996, and with your Letter of Appointment or Conditional Offer of Employment. Your agreement to these conditions is signified by your written acceptance of employment. Should there be a conflict between this Manual and your personal Statement of Terms and Conditions or other written document issued to you, the latter will prevail.

7 The Manual is intended to be a codification of good employment relations practice in accordance with the law as it is currently stated. The Company reserves the right to revise these conditions from time to time as it considers necessary and by reason of changes in legislation. In particular, statutes and related legislation are constantly changing employment obligations and there may be a need to alter this manual from time to time to ensure that it reflects the current state of the law. Any variation of your Terms and Conditions of Employment or to this Manual (which is incorporated into your contract) will be notified to you in writing within one month of the alteration or within such other time period as may be required by statute (the current statutory requirement being one month). These changes will be incorporated into your contract of employment after one month of such notification.

8 You are responsible for keeping this Manual up to date based upon any new pages that are issued to you from time to time. An up to date version of the Manual and a document setting out your pension scheme which you may inspect upon giving notice will be maintained by the Officer of Human Resources/Personnel Manager and if you have any questions about these documents you should address them to _____.

Precedent A2: Alternative Introduction

1 This Personnel Manual sets out important terms and conditions of your employment with the Company. Your letter of appointment together with the Personnel Manual comprise your Contract of Employment ("Contract of Employment") with the Company. This Manual is however, subject to any amendments which will be made from time to time in order to keep it up to date. The Company reserves the right to amend the terms and conditions of employment of all employees whether by amendment to this Manual and to vary the terms in respect of individual employees as necessary. Any amendments will be notified to you in writing one month before such terms and conditions are to be amended.

2 The terms and conditions of employment contained in the Handbook apply to all employees of the Company but where there is any difference between the terms and conditions specified in your Letter of Appointment and this Manual the terms and conditions contained in the Letter of Appointment take precedence.

3 If you are unsure about anything mentioned in your Letter of Appointment or the Manual please contact your Line Manager or the Human Resources Department who will be pleased to answer any questions that you may have.

4 The Company reserves the right to amend its terms and conditions of employment and policies from time to time. Such amendments will be notified in writing to all employees, and this Handbook will be kept updated by the re-issue of the appropriate pages. You will be notified of minor changes of detail by way of a general notice to all employees affected by the change and any such changes take effect from the date of the notice. You will be given not less than one month's written notice of any significant changes which may be given by way of an individual notice or general notice to all employees. Such changes will be deemed to be accepted unless you notify the Company of any objection in writing before the expiry of the notice period.

COMMENTARY TO A: INTRODUCTION TO THE MANUAL AND THE COMPANY

Part A contains two precedents for introductions to the Manual if the Parts contained hereafter are to be consolidated in a Manual. These introductions, to some extent, are an expression of general sentiments as to how the Manual is to operate and the manner in which the employer will treat its employees. They emphasise that the Manual is intended to be a codification of good working practice.

Both precedents also note that the Manual will be subject to change from time to time. It is sensible for such amendments to be produced as issue numbers (e.g. reflected in headers or footers) so that it is clear what is the up to date version of the Manual and for a 'Master Copy' to be available for inspection by the employee.

Whilst the fact that the Manual is subject to variation is mentioned in the precedents (see A1.2–4) it will be important that any flexibility/mobility/variation clauses are brought to the attention of the employee and that the employee is quite clear about the extent to which job functions/hours/workplace and other terms and conditions may be changed, and the Model Terms and Conditions/Manual hereafter sets out a number of Precedents in this regard and the relative effectiveness of such clauses.

It is also common for some form of statement to be included at the outset of the Manual that sets out the employer's/company's objectives and aspirations. A chart setting out the structure of the organisation is also a valuable addition, especially if it shows the channels of communication and reporting channels within the business.

It is important to note that there is a distinction between a Code that lays down standards of good practice but is not meant to have contractual effect and terms and conditions that are intended to be contractually binding. In **Wandsworth London Borough Council v D'Silva** [1998] IRLR 193 the Council had a code of practice on staff sickness which included procedures for monitoring and reviewing different categories of absence. In 1995, the employers notified employees of certain changes to the code, one of which related to the level at which short-term absence would be reviewed, and the other to the period of long-term absence prompting referral to a director, which could result in redeployment or termination. These changes meant that redeployment or termination may be considered after shorter periods of absence. The staff objected to those changes. They maintained that the code formed part of their contractual terms and conditions of employment and that, accordingly, the employers were not entitled to make changes unilaterally. The Council argued that the code was not contractually binding and, in any event, could be unilaterally altered because of a provision which stated:

> "as adopted by the corporation and supplemented by its rules and other conditions as may be determined by the authority ... From time to time variations in your terms of employment may occur, and these will be separately notified to you or otherwise incorporated in the documents to which you have reference."

The Court of Appeal held that the ET had erred in holding that the code was contractually binding and could not be altered by the employers unilaterally. It stated that whether a particular provision in an employer's code of practice is contractually binding depends upon whether it should properly be regarded as conferring a right on employees or as setting out no more than good practice which managers were intended to follow. In the present case, it held that the language of the provisions in question did not provide an appropriate foundation on which to base contractual rights. The code did no more than provide guidance for both supervisors and employees as to what was expected to happen in certain circumstances. It did not set out what was contractually required to happen. The whole procedure in its initial stages was designed to be flexible and informal in a way which was inconsistent with contractual rights being created. Therefore, the employers were entitled to amend the provisions unilaterally.

It is clear that in certain circumstances the courts will prepared to construe a manual as having contractual force. This was the position in **DAL & Ors v A S Orr** [1980] IRLR 413. The employers decided to move from a four to a three shift system due to a fall off in orders. The Employees' Handbook made provision for this eventuality. It was held that the employees were not dismissed for redundancy as there had not been a diminution in work but a requirement to work longer hours on the new shift system. The new arrangement was not in breach of contract since the Handbook provided that the employee could alter shift systems and hours. However, where there is a works rule book that sets out in detail how work is to be performed the book may not be regarded as containing the terms of the contract between employer and employee, though the instructions are to be construed and followed in a manner that is reasonable (**Secretary of State for Employment v ASLEF** [1972] 2 QB 455; ICR 7).

In some cases it has been held that conditions placed on a notice board are incorporated (**Petrie v MacFisheries Limited** [1940] 1 KB 258) though the prudent employer will expressly draw the attention of the employee to any conditions (and it should be noted that *Petrie* was before the requirements for section 1 statements).

Where the contract or manual is updated from time to time the original contract will not be destroyed and only the matters specified will be varied (**Allen v Marconi Space & Defence Systems Limited** (CA 31.1.1980).

PART B: JOB TITLE AND DESCRIPTION /OFFERS OF EMPLOYMENT

Precedent B: **Job Title and Description**

B1:   **Terms of engagement**   **502**

B2:   **Job title and description short form**   **504**

Commentary: **Job Title and Description**   **504**

Precedent B1: Terms of Engagement

1   Your employment will be with _____ Limited [the Company] [or which is a Service Company responsible for the employment of staff.]

2   New employees are reminded that employment is subject to receipt of satisfactory references and a medical report if required by the Company. New employees will have confirmed their acceptance of the 'Conditional Offer of Employment' in writing having received their Letter of Appointment.

All job offers are also conditional upon satisfactory proof of entitlement to work in this country.

By accepting employment with the Company you have confirmed that you will be prepared to attend a medical examination if the Company considers it to be necessary.

If the Company wishes you to attend an examination it will nominate a medical practitioner and an appointment will be made that is mutually convenient. Any medical report that is obtained will be confidential to yourself and the Company. If, as a result of a medical report, the Company has any concerns they will be discussed with you by _____ before consideration is given to any further steps that may be required, which may include terminating your employment.

3 The date that your employment began is shown in your Letter of Appointment and Statement of Terms and Conditions of Employment. If previous service with an associated employer is to count as part of your continuous employment, then the date on which that employment began will be shown.

4 When you arrive, you should ensure that you have brought an income tax form P45 from any previous employer. This must be passed to the [Director of Finance] at _____ together with your National Insurance number and details of your bank account. Without this information, your salary may be delayed or subject to higher tax deductions than are necessary.

5 The title of the job which you are employed to do is shown in your Statement of Terms and Conditions of Employment and your Letter of Appointment. You will have received a description of your duties and responsibilities as an Appendix to your Conditional Offer of Appointment, but this description should not be regarded as exhaustive. There will be times when you may be required to undertake additional tasks within your capabilities or be asked to transfer to an alternative job and where this is agreed on a permanent basis it will be confirmed to you in writing. However, you will not be assigned duties or required to perform services which you cannot reasonably perform, or which are inconsistent with the position or status that you hold. You will be subject to the flexibility and mobility terms contained elsewhere in this Manual.

Precedent B2: Job Title and Description Short Form

1 Your job title is stated in your Letter of Appointment or in the Written Particulars of Terms and Conditions of Employment as may subsequently have been varied or amended in writing. The Company reserves the right to ask you to undertake other duties as may from time to time be reasonably required in accordance with the status of the job to which you have been appointed.

COMMENTARY TO B: JOB TITLE AND DESCRIPTION

The job title is likely to be contained in the Letter or Offer of Employment which may contain a brief job description (see Chapter 4). The job title or description should contain sufficient flexibility to enable the employer to alter the job functions of the employee as is considered appropriate. In smaller organizations a certain degree of flexibility is likely to be implied, as is apparent from the examples given in the cases in Part C (see also *Wrongful Dismissal*). The question of job title and scope of duties/status may be inextricably linked and this part should be read in conjunction with Part C. It is important to consider whether the job title is apposite. A person described as a manager may object to being required to carry out the job of a salesman. The impact of the job title may, however, vary depending on the circumstances, size and nature of the business. The job title may be of contractual significance where it was advertised as such and was instrumental in attracting the employee to the position. In some cases the job title may be inaccurate or meaningless but considered by the employee to be a reflection of his status (e.g. it is common to describe employees as Sales Directors when in fact they are not directors at all).

By way of example, in **Joseph Steinfeld & Co Limited v Reypert** [EAT 550/78] the employee was appointed as a 'Sales Manager (Sales Director Designate)' in a job where sales management experience was required. He was asked to carry out clerical duties and left after some time as he did not believe he would be given the functions of a manager in charge of a sales force. The EAT agreed with the employment tribunal that requiring him to carry out clerical duties for a period of eight months was a fundamental breach of contract. It stated:

> "It seems to us that the appointment of someone as a sales manager does involve work of a certain kind. It is not necessary that one should be able to define with precision the exact duties which are performed by such a person; but it is clear that a sales manager is someone who is responsible for the selling staff, who is dealing with sales statistics, marketing research and matters of that kind. He is a person who is concerned with sales and who is exercising a truly managerial role."

See also Part C which considers further the cases under job content, duties and status.

The Precedents

The two precedents contained in Part B are examples of the description of terms of engagement that one may expect to see in a Manual but are equally appropriate for an Offer of Appointment or Terms and Conditions of Employment.

Precedent B1 is the longer form, containing the following:

- a statement of the identity of the employer. This may frequently be a service company;

- a note of where to find the date of start of employment;

- a reminder about P45 and statement of method of payment of salary;

- a statement that the employer may be required to carry out other tasks and a reminder of any other flexibility/mobility clauses that may exist. This clause states that the employee may be required to transfer to an alternative job, consistent with the employee's capabilities, position or status.

Given that the employer is under a duty to check that the employee has the right to work the offer of employment and/or any intitial Statement of Terms and Conditions should contain a statement relating to the production of documentary proof so that there is no breach of the Asylum and Immigration Act 1996, section 8 (see Part M).

Precedent B2 is a short form, setting out the job title and a statement that the employee may be required to carry out other duties, in accordance with the status of the job to which he has been appointed.

A provision that the employee must perform to the satisfaction of the employer may be a good idea since this will be measured by how the employer viewed the individual: see **Diggle v Ogston Motor Company** [1915] 2165; 112 LR 1029 but note that this may not be of any assistance in relation to an unfair dismissal claim where no procedures were followed.

The subjective approach in *Diggle* was adopted in **Wishart v National Association of Citizens Advice Bureaux Limited** [1990] IRLR 393 in which the EAT distinguished between those matters that could be dealt with objectively (such as a medical report) and matters which may lead to subjective decisions (such as references and quality of work). Mustill LJ was of the view that where an offer was subject to satisfactory references,

> "... the natural reading of a communication, the purpose of which is to tell the prospective employee that part of the decision on whether he is firmly offered the post has yet to be made, is that the employer is reserving the right to make up his own mind when the references have been received and studied. Undeniably, it is possible for an employer to make an offer conditional on something to be objectively determined (for example, the passing of a medical examination) but I find it very hard to see that the defendants' letter falls into this category."

Where it is possible to measure the requirements of the job by objective criteria then this must be the best course but it would appear that otherwise *Diggle* is still good law.

PART C: SCOPE OF DUTIES AND RESPONSIBILITIES

Precedent C: **Scope of Duties and Responsibilities**

Precedent C1:	**Scope of duties**	**508**
Commentary:	**Scope of duties and responsibilities**	**508**
	Implied terms	**509**
	Hours of work (see D)	**509**
	Job content, duties and status	**510**
	Express terms	**511**
	Hours of work (see D)	**511**
	Job content, duties and status – list of cases	**511**
	Mobility and re-location – see G	**514**
	Remuneration – see E	**514**
	Limits of flexibility clauses	**515**
	Construction	**515**
	Reasonable behaviour	**515**
	Employee's liability	**516**

Precedent C1: Scope of Duties

1 You will faithfully and diligently perform such duties and job functions in accordance with your post as may be instructed and should at all times use your best endeavours to further the business of the Company. The Company reserves the right to require you to carry out duties of a different nature that are additional to or instead of those specified in your Letter of Appointment provided that you are capable of performing the same and they are consistent with the status of your position.

2 You are required to work to the best of your ability and to use your best endeavours to promote, develop and expand the business of the Company and its interests generally. You will act at all times with consideration for the needs of the Company's customers and your colleagues and comply with the rules, procedures and policies of the Company.

3 If you are engaged to carry out a particular function or trade you must at all times carry out your work to the best of your ability and in a manner which is consistent with the normal standards of skill required by that particular function or trade.

4 The Company is part of a Group and you therefore agree that you may be transferred to any Group Company and may be required to be employed by any Group or Associate company or seconded to such Company. In the event of such transfer or secondment the terms and conditions of your remuneration will be no less beneficial than they are at present.

COMMENTARY TO C: SCOPE OF DUTIES AND RESPONSIBILITIES

The Letter of Appointment or Offer Letter is likely to set out the scope of duties and responsibilities of the employee as well as the job title. The employer will no doubt wish to build in a certain amount of flexibility so that the employee can be moved to other duties, be given other responsibilities or a change in status, or so that terms and conditions may be varied as the employer considers necessary, for example, by changing hours, work systems or policies such as sickness, disciplinary and grievance procedures to meet the needs of the business. The distinction between contractual and non contractual matters (as exemplified in the *Wandsworth* case) should be borne in mind in this respect. Furthermore, where the employer seeks to unilaterally impose change it is unlikely to be able lawfully to do so unless there is a clear power to this effect. It was said in *Wandsworth* that:

> "Although contracts of employment generally can only be varied by agreement, either party can reserve the ability to change a particular aspect of the contract unilaterally by notifying the other party as part of the contract that this is the situation. However, clear language is required to reserve to one party an unusual power of this sort. In addition, the court is unlikely to favour an interpretation which does more than enable a party to vary contractual provisions with which that party is required to comply. To apply a power of unilateral variation to the rights which an employee is given could produce an unreasonable result, which the courts in construing a contract of employment will seek to avoid."

The cases contain numerous examples where employers have sought to change the terms of employee's contracts, with varying degrees of success. Where the contract does not contain an express term the court will consider the scope of the implied term in the contract of employment. Where there is an express term its ambit will have to be construed, though it should be noted that in certain circumstances the courts may imply a term that the employer invokes the term in a reasonable manner.

Implied terms

The circumstances in which the courts may imply terms have already been set out above. In the context of scope of job functions implied terms have particularly been considered in relation to:

1. Hours of work

This is considered in Part D.

2. Job content, duties and status

Where the employee has performed a particular function or has had a particular status over a period of time, there is likely to be an implied term, in the absence of an express power to vary, which establishes that function or status as a term of the contract. In **South Yorkshire Passenger Transport Executive v Baldwin** [EAT 518/78], Mr Baldwin, employed as a handyman, worked as a substitute charge hand for two nights a week then full time for three months when the charge hand died. Someone else was then given the job. The EAT held that the ET were correct in finding that it had become an implied term of his job, by custom and practice, that he be a relief charge hand and the whole nature of his job had been changed when this was taken away and his pay was detrimentally affected. Compare **Horrigan v Lewisham LBC** [1978] ICR 15 where the conduct of the employee after the contract had been entered into did not lead to a term being implied.

It has been seen that there may be an implied term that an employer will not behave intolerably (or breach trust and confidence) and this may occur where an employer unilaterally changes duties or status. In **Giblin v Seismographic Services (England) Limited** [EAT 305/78] the employers restructured Ms Giblin's job without consultation, which resulted in another employee being given some of her duties. When she complained it was decided to share the duties on an alternating basis but Ms Giblin resigned and claimed constructive dismissal. The EAT held that the ET had not erred in finding there was no breach of the implied term as the employer had sought to repair the situation when the found out the employee objected.

In **Walker v Josiah Wedgewood & Sons Limited** [1978] ICR 744; IRLR 105 Mr Walker had a poor relationship with his newly appointed supervisor, which resulted in an assistant being appointed without consultation, Mr Walker receiving a final warning without justification, not receiving a pay rise and the supervisor placing his secretary in Mr Walker's office and transferring him to an unfinished room. The EAT agreed that the conduct, though unreasonable, was not repudiatory. However, a series of incidents which lead to a demotion and reduction in status may be in breach of the implied term that there be no intolerable conduct on the part of the employer (**J W Carr M & Co Limited v Hammersley** (unreported); **Garner v Grange Furnishings Limited** [1977] IRLR 206) a promotion over the head of an employee may be part of the conduct, as in *Hammersley* but merely promoting another employee is unlikely to be so (**Goodchild v BL (UK)** (unreported)).

A series of incidents which in themselves do not amount to a breach of contract may lead to a breach of the implied term of mutual trust and confidence. It was said in **Woods v W M Car Services (Peterborough) Limited** [1982] IRLR 413; ICR 693 that to constitute a breach of the implied term it is not necessary that the employer intended any repudiation of the contract since the tribunal's function is to look at the employer's conduct as a whole and determine whether it is such that its effect, judged reasonably and sensibly, is such that the employee cannot be expected to put up with it. An employer who persistently attempts to vary an employee's conditions of service with a view to getting rid of the employee or varying the employee's terms of service does act in a manner calculated or likely to destroy the relationship of trust and confidence between employer and employee. Any breach of the implied term is a fundamental breach amounting to a repudiation since it necessarily goes to the root of the contract. (In this case, as a matter of fact there was no breach.)

It is not a loss of status to insist that an employee is supervised where the employer is concerned about his work. The only loss is one of self esteem (**Mensah v London Borough of Islington** [EAT 156/79]). However, a reduction in status does not have to be permanent in order to amount to a repudiatory breach (**McNeill v Charles Crimin (Electrical Contractors) Limited** [1984] IRLR 179).

3. Mobility and relocation

This is considered in Part G.

Express Terms

It has already been noted that express terms will be strictly construed. However, where the express term is absolutely clear there will be no justification for construing it on a more restrictive basis than the term warrants. In **Nelson v British Broadcasting Corporation** [1977] ICR 469, Mr Nelson was employed pursuant to a contract which included a term that stated:

"During the subsistence of this Agreement the employee shall perform such duties and exercise such powers and authorities as may from time to time be assigned to or vested in him ... and the employee shall at all times obey and conform to the reasonable orders and directions and restrictions given by the Board of Governors or the Director-General for the time being of the Corporation or such other person as aforesaid which shall include the right to direct the employee to serve wherever he may be required..."

Mr Nelson was dismissed when the Caribbean service closed down and he refused alternative employment. The Court of Appeal held that he had not been redundant (as the BBC had contended) as the express term made it clear that he was not employed solely for the Caribbean service. Roskill LJ stated that it is a basic principle of contract law that if a contract makes provision in almost unrestricted language it is impossible to imply a restriction as the tribunal had sought to do in this case.

The courts have, however, construed express clauses in a restrictive way, whilst playing lip service to what was said the *Nelson* case.

1. Hours of work

This is considered in Part D.

2. Job content, duties and status

The issues of job content, duties and status have been considered in the following cases (in chronological order):

Goode & Cooper Ltd v Thompson [1974] IRLR 111. Mr Thompson was the general manager of a garage and taxicab business. When it was taken over another manager was appointed and he was told that he would be in charge of the garage workshop and no longer be able to sign cheques or have responsibility for buying in stores. It was held that there "...was a change of status, and a change of such a nature as to show that there was a repudiation of the contract and an intention only to employ him in some very much lower, though undefined, capacity."

Managers (Holborn) Ltd v Hohne [1977] IRLR 230. It was held that Mrs Hohne was effectively downgraded in status as manageress, when she was moved to another office at which there was already a manageress as "she was in effect down-graded in status because in the Regent Street hive there was only room for one Queen Bee, and that was Mrs Falconer."

Coleman v S & W Baldwin [1977] IRLR 342. Mr Coleman was promoted to acting manager with responsibility for buying groceries. When the firm was taken over he was removed from this position and his buying duties were taken away, leaving him with only humdrum duties. It was held that the employer had unilaterally changed the whole nature of the job, which they could not do unilaterally and by way of ultimatum, so that there was a constructive dismissal.

Gronow v GKN (South Wales) Limited [EAT 461/78]. Mr Gronow was employed as a stock control clerk, grade 3, at a time when a job evaluation scheme was introduced and it was a term that he could be reassessed and re-graded. He was upgraded to grade 5 on the basis that he would take a job as divisional planner but this did not happen. After 4 years he was regraded to grade 3. The EAT held that there was no provision in the scheme to reduce to a lower grade in accordance with the scheme. It is clear from this case that if the employer wishes to have the power to downgrade there must be an express provision to this effect.

Glitz v Watford Electric Co Limited [1979] IRLR 89. Miss Glitz was employed in 1974 as a "Copy typist/general clerical duties clerk". In 1977 she was asked to operate a duplicating machine but refused to do so after it gave her headaches. It was held that the operation of the machine fell within the ambit of typist/clerk and she was contractually bound to operate the machine. It was said that "in the context of the case, with a small clerical staff in a small office, the ambit of general clerical duties is wide enough to include the operation of a duplicator."

Peter Carnie & Son v Paton [1979] IRLR 260. Mr Paton was employed to carry out "general garage duties/stores" duties. He engaged in handyman duties, care hire and spent 25% of his time on reception. Although he liked the latter, it was taken away from him as his employers were not satisfied with him. The EAT held that he had been engaged to carry out a variety of jobs of an unskilled nature and that "it is unreasonable, if not absurd, to suggest that an employee who is engaged on general duties can insist on doing only those duties which he likes most". The employer was not bound to keep him on reception duties and the duties could be altered from time to time to meet the needs of the business.

Joseph Steinfeld v Reypert (see Part B).

Ford v Milthorn Toleman Limited [1980] IRLR 30. Mr Ford was appointed as a sales manager and was responsible for "sales, administration, estimating and quoting, keeping an order book, invoicing, monitoring the production development and prices of competitors." He was responsible to the MD and was paid a commission. When he gave notice a number of his functions were taken away and his commission was removed. It was held that the removal of some of his functions amounted to a demotion. Stephenson LJ indicated that loss of job satisfaction may amount to a repudiatory breach of contract.

Pedersen v London Borough of Camden [1981] IRLR 173. The employer advertised for a "bar steward/catering assistant", stressing the primary function as being bar steward. Over a period of four years Mr Pedersen's duties changed to primarily that of a catering assistant. The Court of Appeal held that the ET were correct in construing the letter of appointment by reference to the surrounding circumstances including the job advert and that if the function of bar steward was substantially reduced there was a change of conditions of work which could be a breach of contract.

Cresswell v Board of Inland Revenue [1984] IRLR 190; ICR 508. The introduction of computers was held not to change the nature of clerical work. The employers were employed to do clerical work and "it was recognisably the same job but done in a different way." This case shows that technological advances will not necessarily change the nature of the work.

The employer is not entitled to change the job content and demote merely because the employee has given notice (**Milthorn Toleman Limited v Ford** [1978] IRLR 306; see the Chapter on SOSR in Duggan, *Unfair Dismissal*).

3. Mobility and relocation

This is considered in Part G.

4. Remuneration

This is considered in Part E.

Limits of flexibility clauses

1. Construction

Where there is a flexibility clause it will be for the tribunal/court to construe its meaning. The courts will not seek to expand upon it as the following cases make clear:

SmithKline Beecham PLC v Johnston [EAT 559/96]. The employees were employed on a 40 hour week under a three shift system. The contract provided that the shifts could be changed to 12 hour shifts. The terms were changed so that employees worked under this system for 42 hours. After a re-organisation the hours were again changed to 40. The EAT held that there was no power to vary the hours in this way so as to reduce the employees' basic salary.

National Semiconductor (UK) Limited v Church & Ors [EAT 252/97]. Four employees were engaged to work a total of 25 hours at weekends. The contract provided that "Although you are employed in the shift/position quoted, production requirements may change from time to time and it is a condition of employment that you should be able, with due notice, to change to other shifts/positions." The employers sought to change the conditions so that the employees worked 42 hours during the week on a shift system. It was held that they had been constructively dismissed. The new shift patterns necessitated longer hours. The contract provided that the employees' work could be relocated in terms of time, not in terms of an extension of hours. The EAT stated that "in order for there to be an express term in a contract which entitles the employer to increase the working hours it must be thus, i.e. express". The EAT also recognised that if an employer seeks to unilaterally change the conditions of employment, even within the band of an express term, so as to achieve a result which precludes the employee in practical terms from complying with the change he may act unreasonably and create a constructive dismissal. (See *Akhtar* below.) It is thus necessary that the flexibility clause contemplates the variation that is proposed.

2. Reasonable behaviour and implied terms

Where there is an express mobility clause, there may nevertheless be implied terms that the clause is operated reasonably as in **United Bank Limited v Akhtar** [1989] IRLR 507. An alternative way in which a term may be implied is that the employer does not operate the express clause in such a way as to destroy mutual trust and confidence between the parties. In **French v Barclays Bank PLC** [1998] IRLR 646 Mr French was employed under a contract that contained a mobility clause entitling the employer to transfer the employee to any of the offices throughout the country. There were also terms for financial assistance, including an interest free bridging loan, which was stated to be at the bank's discretion and not part of the contract of employment. Mr French was provided with a bridging loan on relocation but this was withdrawn when house prices fell and he could not sell the house he had moved from. He was forced to sell it to the bank for less than the loan and repay the balance which he did by taking out a further loan. The Court of Appeal held that the employers were in breach of the obligation of mutual trust and confidence in that, having ordered the employee to relocate and given an interest free loan, they then sought to change the terms of the loan to the employee's detriment. The employer was in breach of the obligation in that, once they had exercised their discretion to grant a bridging loan, they were under an obligation to maintain that position. The employer was therefore in breach but was not entitled to damages for distress (on this point see Duggan, *Wrongful Dismissal, Law Guidance and Precedents*).

Employee's liability

It should be noted that, where the employee fails to achieve a standard of reasonable care he may be liable to indemnify his employer for his negligence. In **Semtex Limited v Gladstone** [1954] 1 WLR 945 it was held that the employee was liable to indemnify the employer in respect of negligent driving.

Commentary on Precedent C1

Precedent C.1 ties in and overlaps with the precedents in B. It requires a certain standard of competence and application to the job as well as stipulating for flexibility.

The clause makes it clear that the Employee is expected to perform his duties well and diligently and to achieve a certain standard where he is engaged in a certain function or trade. The following propositions are applicable here:

(1) Where the employee professes to have a particular skill he is taken to have guaranteed a reasonable level of competence. In **Harmer v Cornelious** [1858] 5 CB (NS) 236 two workers were engaged as "first rate

panorama and scene painters". They were not competent and were dismissed after two days. The Court stated that:

> "When a skilled labourer...is employed, there is on his part an implied warranty that he is of skill reasonably competent to the task he undertakes... An express premise or express representation in the particular case is not necessary."

(2) It is a question of fact whether the standard has been achieved. This must be looked at on an objective basis. The test is that of a reasonably competent man and not angels. (**Jupiter General Insurance Co Limited v Schroff** [1937] 3 All ER 67).

(3) However, where the employer is expressed to be the judge of the standard the test is whether the employer honestly believed that the employee was not up to the position and it is a subjective test. In **Diggle v Ogston Motor Company** 84 LJKB 2165; 112 LR 1029 the employee was engaged for one year with a provision that if he performed his duties "to the satisfaction of the directors" his contract could be extended for a further six years. The directors were not so satisfied. It was held, in the King's Bench Division, that it was not necessary for the employer to show reasonable cause for the dissatisfaction. It was for the claimant to prove that "the directors were in fact satisfied with his services or dishonestly professed to be dissatisfied or were at least capriciously dissatisfied."

The clause re-iterates that the employee may be expected to carry out duties of a different nature within the scope of his capability and status (see also Part B).

Where the employer is part of a Group or is the service company for a Group, it is important that it is made clear to the employee that he may be transferred to another Company within the Group in a situation where the Transfer of Undertakings (Protection of Employment) Regulations 1981 would otherwise apply prior to a transfer taking place, so that the employee will not be in the part transferred, if that is the objective the employer wishes to achieve.

PART D: HOURS OF WORK

Precedent D: Hours of Work

D1:	**Normal Hours of Work**	**519**
	D1.1: Normal hours of work; statement for manual	**519**
	D1.2: Normal working hours: weekly statement (1)	**520**
	D1.3: Normal working hours: weekly statement (2)	**520**
D2:	**Overtime**	**521**
	D2.1: Overtime (1)	**521**
	D2.2: Overtime (2)	**521**
	D2.3: Overtime (3)	**521**
	D2.4: Overtime (4)	**522**
D3:	**Flexitime**	**522**
D4:	**Time-keeping**	**524**
D5:	**Shift workers**	**524**
D6:	**Factory Workers**	**525**
	D6.1: Factory worker-shiftwork	**525**
	D6.2: Clocking in procedures	**525**
	D6.3: Factory closure times	**525**
	D6.4: Lay off	**526**

D7:   Retail employment   526

            D7.1:   Hours of Work   526

            D7.2:   Sunday working   527

D8:   Working Time   527

            D8.1:   Working time: exclusion of the
                    48-hour week   527

            D8.2:   Existence of a workforce agreement   528

            D8.3:   Precedent workforce agreement   529

Commentary: The Law Relating to Hours of Work   530

Cross References

Duggan, *Wrongful Dismissal and Breach of Contract* at 3.8 (Express Terms) and 6.9 (Implied Terms).

Precedent D1:   Normal Hours of Work

Precedent D1.1:   Normal Hours of Work

1 Your normal working hours are as set out in your Statement of Terms and Conditions of Employment or as modified and confirmed in writing by mutual agreement. The Company may make reasonable changes in your working hours having regard to [its core 'open for business' hours][its normal opening hours which are   ] and the needs of the Company. You will be given reasonable notice of any changes and you are expected to be flexible. [You will be given [   ] days notice of any changes]. [The Company may vary the hours by changing the work start time by [   ] hours and the work end time by [   ] hours on any particular day].

2   The Company aims to provide a high level of personal service to its clients and you may therefore be required to work additional hours in order to ensure that the needs of the business are met.

3   Your starting and finishing times allow for an unpaid meal break during each working day. You must always take this break, which is a statutory requirement. If you exceed the allotted time, you are expected to extend your working day either on that day or, by mutual agreement with your _____, on some subsequent day. If you need to be away from the office for personal reasons which you do not wish to be counted against your holiday entitlement you are required to make up for lost time and must first seek the agreement of _____.

4   The Company reserves the right to vary your hours of work as necessary to meet its business requirements.

Precedent D1.2: Normal Working Hours

Your normal hours of work are _____ to _____ Monday to Friday. You are expected to work _____ per week. You are entitled to take a lunch break of 45 minutes to be taken between _____ and _____ or at a time to be agreed with your manager. The Company reserves the right to vary your hours of work as necessary to meet its business requirements.

Precedent D1.3: Normal Working Hours

1   Your normal hours of work are as follows

Monday . . . . to . . . .
Tuesday . . . . to . . . .
Wednesday . . . . to . . . .
Thursday . . . . to . . . .
Friday . . . . to . . . .

2   You are entitled to take a lunch break of 45 minutes to be taken between _____ and _____ or at a time to be agreed with your manager.

3   The Company reserves the right to vary your hours of work as necessary to meet its business requirements.

Precedent D2:   Overtime

Precedent D2.1:   Overtime

It is expected that you will be able to finish your work within your normal hours. However, you may be required to work overtime if it is necessary for the proper performance of your duties. Your Letter of Appointment or Statement of Terms and Conditions will set out your entitlement to overtime payments if applicable. You will not be required to work for more than 48 hours per week as an average over a period of 17 weeks. Overtime does not count for the purpose of calculating your holiday pay.

Precedent D2.2:   Overtime

It is not the Company's normal policy to pay overtime to office staff. You are expected to manage your time and complete your work within the normal working day. If you work in an office and it is necessary to work overtime you must first obtain the agreement of your Head of Department in relation to the hours of overtime. If you need to work overtime you will be entitled to time off in lieu with the prior consent of your Head of Department. If overtime is a contractual requirement you will be paid for any overtime you are required to undertake. You will not be required to work for more than 48 hours per week as an average over a period of 17 weeks.

Precedent D2.3:   Overtime

You shall be available, when required by the Company, to work outside your normal working hours. This includes Saturdays, Sundays and public holidays. Overtime may be required at short notice although the Company will try to give you as much notice as possible. If you are entitled to be paid for overtime it will be specified in your Letter of Appointment. You will not be required to work for more than 48 hours per week as an average over a period of 17 weeks.

Precedent D2.4: Overtime

Overtime where applicable is calculated on annual basic salary and will be paid at the following rates:

> Monday to Friday: time and a half
> Saturday: double time
> Sunday: double time

> Statutory public holidays: treble time or, at the discretion of your Manager, double time together with one day's holiday in lieu of the statutory public holiday worked to be taken at such time as is agreed with your Manager.

You will not be required to work for more than 48 hours per week as an average over a period of 17 weeks. Overtime does not count in calculating your basic salary.

Precedent D3: Flexitime

1 The Company's standard hours of work are _____am until _____ pm with a one hour lunch break to be taken between _____ and _____ unless your manager agrees that such breaks may be taken at a different time.

2 The Company operates a flexitime system where it is possible for employees to carry out their duties and to start and leave work on flexitime. It recognises the benefit of flexitime in co-ordinating your time and whilst the essential needs of the office are of paramount importance, if working conditions permit the operation of the system your Manager may permit you to operate on this basis. The flexitime system will comply with the requirements of the Working Time Regulations 1998.

3 Your Manager may approve flexitime or set your schedule at standard hours of operation. If you wish to work flexitime you must obtain prior approval from your Manager.

4 Flexitime operation will operate within the following restrictions:

1. The Company's premises are open to employees (except for certain statutory holidays which will be announced in advance) between the hours of _____. You must attend work on Monday to Friday subject to the rules set out below.

2. The hours when you must be present at work are between _____ and _____ ('the core hours') and you must work a minimum of _____ per day.

3. You are free to arrive and depart at any time provided that you attend within the core hours and provided that:

   (1) you comply with the departmental requirements as laid down by your Manager,

   (2) you must take a break of at least _____ during the day in order that the provisions of the Working Time Regulations are complied with and you will in any event not be paid for this period.

4. At the end of each month no more than _____ hours may be carried forward into the next calendar month and any hours in excess of this will not be carried over nor will remuneration be paid for these hours unless you have been prevented by working requirements from taking off those hours.

5. The operation of flexitime may be suspended at any time by your Manager as the operational needs of the business so require.

Precedent D4: Time Keeping

1 All employees are required to record time actually worked and salaried workers will be expected to complete appropriate time sheets.

2 Hourly paid workers will be required to use the time clock which is located at _____. It will be the responsibility of your Manager to approve your time and he will forward the time sheet or card to Payroll. You are required to clock in when arriving for work and to clock out on leaving work for any reason. You must not clock in or clock out for any other person, or request or permit any other person to clock in or out for you and it will be a disciplinary offence to do so.

3 An employee found tampering or interfering with the time clocks or the time system will be liable to summary dismissal for gross misconduct.

Precedent D5: Shiftworkers

1 The Company operates on a _____ hours _____ days a week basis due to the nature of its business. If you have been appointed to work as a shift worker the hours that you will be required to work will have been set out in your Letter of Appointment. You will be given reasonable notice of the shifts you are required to work and of the times you will be required to take a break from work during your shift.

2 The rates of pay for shiftwork will have been set out in your Letter of Appointment and will vary as follows depending on the hours that you work:

[Rates of Pay for Days and Shifts to be worked]

3 Managers are responsible for drawing up shift rosters to conform with operational requirements.

4 Requests to change shifts must be submitted at least _____ hours in advance whether by your Employer or you if you wish to alter your shift. Changes to shifts among employees will be restricted to _____ shifts per month and may be allowed in order to extend holidays where the employee has _____ days holiday outstanding.

5 Where your hours of work involve night shift work you will be required to undergo an annual medical examination to ensure that you are fit for such work.

Precedent D6: Factory Workers

Precedent D6.1: Shiftwork

The Company operates on a 24-hour/seven day a week basis in order to fully utilise its production process and comply with orders from its customers. You have agreed to work a shift system in order that the business can continue to operate. You will be advised of the shifts that you are required to carry out on a weekly basis and will be given ____ hours notice should these be varied.

Precedent D6.2: Clocking in Procedures

You have been provided with a clocking in number and card and are required to clock in when arriving for work and to clock out on leaving the work premises for whatever reason. You must personally clock in and out. You are not allowed to clock in or out for any other person and it will be regarded as a dismissible offence to clock in for any other person, tamper with clock cards or to in any way interfere with the clocks.

Precedent D6.3: Factory Closure Times

It is the Company's practice to close down the factory for a period of _____ each year in order to carry out maintenance work. You will be required to take part of your annual holiday during this period but the Company reserves the right to require you to work during this period if a skeleton staff is needed. You will be notified of these requirements at least _____ weeks in advance.

Precedent D6.4: Lay Off

From time to time it is necessary to close down the factory or to reduce manpower due to the fact that there is a diminution in the requirements of the business for work of the kind which you carry out due to a shortfall in orders. In that event the Company is entitled to lay you off for a period of _____ days during which you may be paid _____ [will not be paid].

Precedent D7: Retail Employment

Precedent D7.1: Hours of work

1 The hours of work that you will normally be required to carry out are _____ and will normally be during the following hours:

> Monday . . . . to . . . .
> Tuesday . . . . to . . . .
> Wednesday . . . . to . . . .
> Thursday . . . . to . . . .
> Friday . . . . to . . . .
> Saturday . . . . to . . . .
> Sunday . . . . to . . . .

2 You are entitled to take a lunch break of _____ which should be taken at a time agreed with your Manager, and to other breaks as follows:

[SET OUT BREAKS TO BE TAKEN]

3 Your hours may be varied in order to meet particular requirements and you may be required to work overtime in excess of your normal hours upon being given reasonable notice. If you work overtime then you will be paid at the rate of _____.

Precedent D7.2: Sunday Working

It is a condition of your employment that you will work on Sundays. You are entitled to give written notice stating that you object to working on Sundays and this notice must be signed and dated by you. It will become effective three months after you have given notice and after that date you will not be required to work on Sundays unless you decide to withdraw the notice.

Precedent D8: Working Time

Precedent D8.1: Exclusion of the 48 Hour Week under the Working Time Regulations 1998

You have agreed that the limit of an average working time of 48 hours including overtime for each seven day period as set out in Regulation 4 of the Working Time Regulations shall not apply to your employment and you have signed a document to this effect. You may however, give three months written notice to the Company to terminate this Agreement.

Example of opt out in the DTI Guidance

Example of opt-out agreement

I (*name*) agree that I may work for more than an average of 48 hours a week. If I change my mind, I will give my employer (*amount of time – up to three months*) notice in writing to end this agreement.

Signed   _____

Dated   _____

Precedent D8.2: Existence of a Workforce Agreement

There is a workforce agreement in effect whereby the Company and the employees have agreed to opt out of the Regulations in the terms set out hereafter. This agreement came into force on _____ and will remain in force for a period of five years unless it is terminated by either party giving not less than three months notice in writing. The terms of the agreement are as follows:

1) The maximum weekly working time of 48 hours shall not apply [but shall be _____].

2) The reference period of 17 weeks shall be consecutive periods which commenced on _____.

3) The provisions relating to daily rest periods, weekly rest periods and rest breaks shall not apply. Equivalent rest periods shall be permitted to be taken wherever possible.

Precedent D8.3:   A Precedent Workforce Agreement

1 This Workforce Agreement is dated ...... and is made between ...... [the Employer] and the workers listed in Schedule 1   to this Agreement.

OR

2 [This agreement is made between ..... the Employer and the Worker's representatives. All definitions contained in this Agreement may be found in Regulation 2 of the Working Time Regulations 1998 (SI 1998 No. 833) as amended.]

3 This Agreement applies to [the whole of the workforce of the Employer] [OR SPECIFY GROUP] and it is agreed that it will remain in force for a period of [not more than five years after date it is signed] when it will automatically cease to have effect, or until terminated by either party at any time by giving not less than [three months] written notice to the other.

4 Pursuant to the terms of the Regulations the Employees hereby agree with the Employer to opt out of the Regulations to such extent as is set out hereafter.

5 REGULATION 4: WORKING HOURS

The maximum weekly working time (including overtime) of 48 hours for each seven day period shall not apply to the Employees.

[The maximum working week (including overtime) shall be _____ for each seven day period.

6 REGULATION 4(3): REFERENCE PERIOD

The reference period of 17 weeks shall be successive periods as permitted under Regulation 4(3), the first to commence on _____.

7   REGULATION 6: LENGTH OF NIGHT WORK

The normal hours of work in any 24 hour period may exceed 8 hours for night workers.

8   REGULATION 10-DAILY REST PERIOD

Adult workers shall not be entitled to 11 hours consecutive rest in each 24 hour period but will be entitled to a compensatory rest period where appropriate.

9   REGULATION 10: WEEKLY REST PERIOD

Adult workers will not be entitled to a rest period of 24 hours in each seven day period but shall be given a compensatory rest period where appropriate.

10   REGULATION 12: REST BREAKS

Adult workers shall not automatically be entitled to a rest break where they work more than six hours but will be given a compensatory rest period as appropriate.

11   SIGNED BY THE EMPLOYER:

SIGNED by the Elected Representative(s) of the Employees:

or

SIGNED by the majority of the Employees where LESS THAN 20 EMPLOYEES

COMMENTARY: THE LAW RELATING TO HOURS OF WORK

Until 1998 there was no general law in the United Kingdom which dictated the maximum hours that a worker could be expected to work. In fact the United Kingdom continues to have some of the longest working hours in Europe. However, Article 137 (previously 118A) of the European Treaty was utilised to introduce the Working Time Directive as a health and safety measure and this was adopted by other member states on 9 December 1989. The Directive was due to be transposed into national law by 23 November 1996 but an unsuccessful challenge was mounted by the Government (**United Kingdom v Council of Ministers** [1997] IRLR 30) and the Working Time Regulations were in the event introduced to come into effect in October 1998. Since that time there have been a number of amendments to the WTR 1998 which are considered below and in Part I, Holidays. There are currently further proposals for amendment (particularly to the opt out) and the Government's Consultation Document "Working Time – Widening the Gap" was released on 29th June 2004 (see *http://www.dti.gov.uk/er/work_time_regs/consultation.pdf*).

It is therefore necessary to consider all of the Precedents in this book, in so far as they relate to hours of work and holidays, against the backdrop of the WTR 1998.

This section will consider:

(1) Express and implied terms relating to hours of work.

(2) The Working Time Regulations.

(3) Variation of hours of work.

(4) Overtime.

(5) Timekeeping.

(6) Shiftworkers/Factory workers and lay off.

(6) Retail employment

(8) Discrimination in relation to hours of work.

(1) Express and implied terms relating to hours of work.

Express terms

In the absence of statutory restrictions it will be for the employer and employee to agree the hours of work between themselves. **Precedent D1: Normal hours** at **D1.1** to **D1.3** sets out standard provisions relating to hours of work, with a reservation in each case that the employer has the ability to vary the hours of work to meet its business requirements. These precedents assume that the employee is not expected to work more than a 48 hour week. Regard should be had to D8.1 if this is to be the position. Without the power to vary the hours of work, there is likely to be a breach of contract should hours be altered without consent and reference should be made to the section on variation below.

Implied terms

The employee's hours of work are an essential term of the contract of employment. Where the working hours are not specified it will be necessary for the court to imply a term as to normal working hours.

- **Dean v Eastbourne Fisherman's & Boatmen's Protection Society** [1977] IRLR 143; ICR 556. The employee worked as a part time barman, working such hours as were required, being over 21 hours for 86 weeks and less for 18 weeks. The EAT considered the hours that were worked and held that there was a contractual obligation to work the hours required which were normally more than 21 a week.

- **Scott v Victor Blagden (Barking) Limited** [EAT 367/82]. As a matter of practice, a maintenance fitter had worked weekends over the years to carry out major maintenance work. He was dismissed when he refused to work on a Sunday. The EAT held that it had become an implied term, by custom and practice, to work on weekends and to be paid double time.

The Working Time Regulations 1998

The Working Time Regulations came into effect on 1 October 1998. They have been amended several times as set out below and, as well as there being further proposals for change, there are still a number of issues that are working their way through the Courts (i.e. in relation to holiday pay). This section will summarise the effect of the Regulations and provide an 'at a glance' table which can be used to check how the Regulations apply. (The first table at the end of this section.) The following will be considered:

(a) The definitions contained in the WTR 1998.

(b) The 48 Hour week

(c) Night work

(d) Monotonous Work

(e) Daily Rest Periods

(f)   Weekly Rest periods

(g)   Rest Breaks

(h)   The exceptions to the WTR 1998.

The requirements relating to annual leave are considered under holidays, Part I.

(a) Definitions

Regulation 2 of the WTR sets out a number of definitions that are important in understanding the scheme of the Regulations:

Working time: means any period during which the worker is working, at his employer's disposal and carrying out his activity or duties. These three elements must be satisfied in order for the worker to be regarded as working during 'working time'. The DTI have published Guidance Notes which are of some assistance in considering what may be regarded as working time. The following points arise:

• Where the worker is on call but is free to pursue his or her own activities during this time then he is unlikely to be regarded as working unless called out. This will also be the position where the worker is required to be at the place of work 'on call' but is sleeping. The particular circumstances of the case will govern whether someone is regarded as working; for example, shop assistants are likely to be regarded as working even when they are idle because there are no customers in the shop. Where the employee is on call at home he may not be regarded as working (**SIMAP v Conselleria de Sanidad y Consumo de la Generalitad Valencia C303/98** [2000] IRLR 845). In **Landeshaupstadt Kiel v Jaeger** [2003] IRLR 805 the ECJ held that all time spent by a doctor on call in a hospital counted as working time. This has caused considerable concern to a number of Governments and there may be reforms in this area. However, the result is that night watchmen, residential wardens or carers may be on working time when they are on call at work.

- The Guidance Notes state that time spent travelling to and from work is unlikely to be working time as the worker is probably not working or carrying out his duties. However, the worker may work on the train or have to travel for the purpose of the job and this may be working time.

- Working lunch breaks may be working time.

- The Guidance Notes state that if a worker takes work home this will only count as working time if previously agreed by the employer. Difficulties may arise where the worker simply takes work home without express agreement but to the knowledge of the employer and it is prudent for some form of agreement to have been reached so that the position is clear.

- A further grey area is that where the worker has to read reports or literature to keep up to date. It is not clear whether this will amount to working time. It is to be noted that training is catered for.

- Any period during which he is receiving training. Training is defined as work experience provided pursuant to a training course or programme, training for employment or both other than the immediate provider being an educational institution or a person whose main business is the provision of training.

- Any additional period which is to be treated as working time under a relevant agreement. The parties may agree to extend the definition of working time by a relevant agreement but they cannot reduce it.

Workers: the Regulations apply to workers (see the detailed commentary at Chapter 1).

Day: a period of 24 hours starting at midnight.

Mobile worker: means any worker employed as a member of travelling or flying personnel by an undertaking which operates transport services for passengers or goods by road or air.

Night time: is a period of not less than 7 hours which includes the period between midnight and 5am as determined by a relevant agreement, or in default the period between 11pm and 6am, and night work means work during night time.

Nightworker: is a person who as a normal course (i.e. the majority of days) works at least three hours of his normal working time during night time, or works such proportion of his annual working time as may be specified in a collective or workforce agreement. The words 'as a normal course' were considered in **R v Attorney General for Northern Ireland ex parte Burns** [1999] IRLR 315 where it was held that this meant no more than this should be a regular feature of his work.

A relevant   is a workforce agreement (WA), a provision in a
agreement (RA):   collective agreement (CA) or any other agreement in writing that is legally enforceable. It is to be noted that there are four means by which the Regulations may be modified; the above three and, in the case of the 48 hour week, a non-contractually binding agreement (NCBA).

An adult worker: is a person who has reached the age of 18. A 'young worker' is someone who has attained the age of 15 but not 18 and is over compulsory school age.

A workforce   is an agreement between the employer and workers
Agreement: which satisfied the conditions set out in Schedule 1 being:

- it is in writing;

- it has effect for a specified period of not more than 5 years;

- it applies to all relevant members, or particular group of members of the workforce;

- it is signed by the representatives of the workforce or group or, if there are 20 or less employees, a majority.

- before the agreement was made available for signature the employer provided all the workers to whom it was intended to apply on the date on which it came into effect with copies of the text of the agreement and such guidance as those workers might reasonably require in order to understand it fully.

(b) The Maximum Weekly Working Time: the 48 hour week

Regulation 4 of the WTR imposes a contractual duty and may therefore be enforced in the ordinary civil courts (**Barber v RJB (Mining (UK)) Limited** [1999] IRLR 308).

By regulation 4(1) the maximum working time shall not exceed an average of 48 hours for each seven days in any reference period and the reference period is 17 weeks in the course of employment unless:

- A relevant agreement provides for the 17 weeks to be successive;

- the worker has worked for less than 17 weeks in which case it is the period elapsed. This provision will protect temporary workers;

- or (under regulation 23(b)) for objective or technical reasons or reasons concerning the organisation of work, a collective or workforce agreement has substituted a different period being a period not more than 52 weeks.

- or the period can be extended to 26 weeks for a number of special cases set out in regulation 21.

In arriving at the 17 weeks, account is not taken of periods of annual leave, sick leave, maternity leave or periods where the worker has agreed the 48 hour limit shall not apply.

Since the 48 hour week is taken as an average over 17 weeks the fact that the employee is required to work in excess for some weeks will not necessarily infringe the Regulations if, averaged out, the excess is not 48 hours (see **King v Scottish & Newcastle (Retail) North Limited** (Newcastle upon Tyne ET IDS Brief 641). Regulation 4(2) places on the employer a duty to take all reasonable steps, in keeping with the need for health and safety, to ensure that the limit is complied with.

By regulation 5 where the worker has agreed in writing that the limit shall not apply the 48 hour week may be excluded. This may be for a definite period or indefinitely and can be terminable by the worker giving not less than 7 days or more than 3 months' notice. A Collective or Workforce Agreement cannot disapply the 48 hour week; it must be by consent of the worker in writing, whether or not legally enforceable. The ECHJ has confirmed that consent cannot be "given by trade-union representatives in the context of a collective or other agreement" (**Sindicato de Médicos de Asistencia Pública (SIMAP) v Conselleria De Sanidad Y Consumo De La Generalidad Valenciana** [2000] IRLR 845).

Time on call will normally count as working time; See *Sindicato* above and **Landeshauptstadt Kiel v Jaeger** Case C–151/02 [2003] IRLR 804). In the latter case it was held that time counted for doctors on call even if they were allowed to sleep during the period that they were on call. The ECJ stated that the Working Time Directive:

"must be interpreted as meaning that on-call duty (Bereitschaftsdienst) performed by a doctor where he is required to be physically present in the hospital must be regarded as constituting in its totality working time for the purposes of that directive even where the person concerned is permitted to rest at his place of work during the periods when his services are not required with the result that that directive precludes legislation of a Member State which classifies as rest periods an employee's periods of inactivity in the context of such on-call duty"."

(See also **British Nursing Association v Inland Revenue (National Minimum Wage Compliance Team)** [2001] IRLR 659 and **Walton v Independent Living Organisation Ltd** [2003] IRLR 469 in relation to on call for the purposes of the Minimum Wages Act 1998.)

Workers may not be subjected to any detriment if they refuse to consent to the 48 hour week being disapplied (section 45A ERA 1996 and see Duggan on *Unfair Dismissal*).

Calculating the 48 hour week

The formula for working out the average weekly hours of work is set out in regulation 4(6) as follows:

"...a worker's average working time for each seven days during a reference period shall be determined according to the formula—

$$\frac{(A + B)}{C}$$

where—

A   is the aggregate number of hours comprised in the worker's working time during the course of the reference period;

B   is the aggregate number of hours comprised in his working time during the course of the period beginning immediately after the end of the reference period and ending when the number of days in that subsequent period on which he has worked equals the number of excluded days during the reference period; and

C   is the number of weeks in the reference period."

The DTI Guidance gives the following examples:

Example 1

A worker has a standard working week of 40 hours and does overtime of 12 hours a week for the first 10 weeks of the 17-week reference period. No leave is taken during the reference period.

The total hours worked is:

17 weeks of 40 hours and 10 weeks of 12 hours of overtime

$(17 \times 40) + (10 \times 12) = 800$

Therefore their average (total hours divided by number of weeks):

$$\frac{800}{17} = 47.1 \text{ hours a week}$$

The average limit of 48 hours has been complied with.

Example 2

A worker has a standard working week of 40 hours (8 hours a day) and does overtime of 8 hours a week for the first 12 weeks of the 17-week reference period. 4 days' leave are also taken during the reference period.

The total hours worked in the reference period is:

16 weeks and 1 day (40 hours a week and 8 hours a day) and 12 weeks of 8 hours of overtime

$(16 \times 40) + (1 \times 8) + (12 \times 8) = 744$

Add the time worked to compensate for the 4-day leave, taken from the first 4 working days after the reference period. The worker does no overtime, so 4 days of 8 hours ($4 \times 8 = 32$) should be added to the total.

Therefore their average is (total hours divided by number of weeks):

$$\frac{744 + 32}{17} = 45.6 \text{ hours per week}$$

The average limit of 48 hours has been complied with.

(c) Night work and Nightworkers

By Regulation 6 a nightworker's normal hours in any reference period shall not exceed an average of 8 hours for each 24 hours. The reference period is again 17 weeks or such period, if less, that the worker has worked. However:

- there is no provision to extend this up to 52 weeks;

- rest periods are deducted in arriving at the calculation;

An employer shall take all reasonable steps to ensure that the limit is complied with in accordance with the need to protect the health and safety or workers but where the worker has been identified as in work involving special hazards or heavy physical or mental strain the employer *shall ensure* that the limit is complied with (6(7)).

The definition of night work may be modified by a Collective or Workforce Agreement. There remains a question mark over the extent to which a worker on call may be regarded as working.

Regulation 6(5) sets out the way in which night work is to be calculated:

"...a night worker's average normal hours of work for each 24 hours during a reference period shall be determined according to the formula—

$$\frac{A}{(B - C)}$$

where—

A   is the number of hours during the reference period which are normal working hours for that worker;

B   is the number of days during the reference period, and

C   is the total number of hours during the reference period comprised in rest periods spent by the worker in pursuance of his entitlement under regulation 11, divided by 24."

It is important to note that this formula is concerned with the worker's normal hours rather than actual hours. The worker's normal hours will be defined by the ERA 1996 if section 234 of that Act applies. This would mean that overtime would not be included where it is not stated to be normal working hours, an anomaly which seems to go against the intent

of the WTR 1998. The DTI Guidance contains the following examples of
how to calculate night time working:

Example 1

A night worker normally works four 12-hour shifts each week.

The total number of normal hours of work for a 17-week
reference period is:

17 weeks of 4 shifts of 12 hours

$$17 \times (4 \times 12) = 816$$

There are 119 days (17 weeks) and the worker takes 17 weekly
rest periods, as entitled to under the regulations. Therefore the
number of days the worker could be asked to work is

$$119 - 17 = 102$$

To calculate the daily average working time, the total of hours
is divided by the number of days a worker could be required to
work.

$$\frac{816}{102} = 8$$

This equals an average of 8 hours a day.

Example 2

A night worker normally works 5 days of 10 hours followed by 3 days of rest. The cycle starts at the beginning of the reference period (so there are 15 cycles of work). The worker takes 2 weeks' leave and works 6 hours overtime every five weeks. During this reference period, the overtime is worked in the fifth, tenth, and fifteenth weeks. The leave does not affect the calculation of normal hours, but the overtime does.

15 cycles of 5 shifts of 10 hours = 15 × (5 × 10) = 750 hours

6 hours overtime × 3 = 18 = 768 hours (including overtime)

There are 119 days (17 weeks) and the worker takes 17 weekly rest periods, as entitled to under the regulations. Therefore the number of days the worker could be asked to work is:

119 – 17 = 102

To calculate the daily average working time, the total of hours is divided by the number of days a worker could be required to work.

768

$$\overline{} = 7.53$$

102

This equals an average of 7.53 hours a day.

By regulation 6(7) the employer shall ensure that no night worker employed by him whose work involves special hazards or heavy physical or mental strain works for more than eight hours in any 24-hour period during which the night worker performs night work and by 6(8) work shall be regarded as involving special hazards or heavy physical or mental strain if it is identified as such in a collective agreement, or a workforce agreement which takes account of the specific effects and hazards of night work, or if it is recognised in a risk assessment made by the employer under regulation 3 of the Management of Health and Safety at Work Regulations 1999 as involving a significant risk to the health or safety of workers employed by him.

Health assessments for night workers

The employer shall ensure that a worker has an opportunity for a free health assessment before night work is carried out (regulation 7) and a young worker should have a free health assessment as to his health and capacities. The Guidance notes that, as a minimum, the assessment should consist of a screening questionnaire before beginning night work. Where a worker is suffering from health problems and it is possible to transfer him to non night work that is suitable, the employer shall transfer the worker (7(6)). The Guidance states that the employer should take two steps to be sure workers are fit to work nights.

- **"Step 1:**   You ask workers to fill in a questionnaire which asks specific questions about their health which are relevant to the type of night work they will be doing.

- **Step 2:**   If you are not certain they are fit for night work following the questionnaire results, you ask them to have a medical examination."

A model questionnaire is available on the Internet at:

http://www.dti.gov.uk/er/work_time_regs/wtr9.htm

The following is the DTI's suggested questionnaire

SECTION 9: SAMPLE HEALTH QUESTIONNAIRE

This health questionnaire is provided for sample purposes only. Make sure you ask a qualified health professional to help you devise this form.

Are you fit to work nights?

The purpose of this questionnaire is to ensure that you are suited to working at night. All the information you provide will be kept confidential.

TYPE OF WORK/ DURATION OF NIGHT WORK _____

1. **Surname**

2. **First and second name/s**

3. **Sex** _____ **M/F**

4. **Date of birth**

5. **Permanent address**

6. **Job title**

7. **National insurance no.**

8. **Department/clock no.**

Do you suffer from any of the following health conditions? Y/N

Diabetes

Heart or circulatory disorders

Stomach or intestinal disorders

Any condition which causes difficulties sleeping

Chronic chest disorders, especially if night-time symptoms are troublesome

Any medical condition requiring medication to a strict timetable

Any other health factors that might affect fitness at work

If you have answered 'yes' to any of the above questions, you may be asked to see a doctor or nurse for further assessment.

I, the undersigned, confirm that the above is correct to the best of my knowledge.

Signed _____ Date _____

ASSESSMENT

[this gives an indication of whether the worker is fit to work nights or should see a doctor or nurse for a medical examination]

Signed _____ Date _____

It should be noted that there will in any event be duties under the DDA 1995 in respect of reasonable adjustments where a worker's health is affected by the type of work that he is carrying out or by working nights/shifts and that worker has a disability.

There is an obligation of confidentiality so that the assessment cannot be disclosed to anyone other than the worker unless permission has been given to disclose (regulation 7(5)).

Where a registered medical practitioner has advised an employer that a worker employed by the employer is suffering from health problems which the practitioner considers to be connected with the fact that the worker performs night work; and it is possible for the employer to transfer the worker to work to which the worker is suited, and which is to be undertaken during periods such that the worker will cease to be a night worker, the employer is under a duty to transfer the worker to such work.

(d) Work Patterns – Risky work and Monotonous Work

By regulation 8 where the pattern of work:

> "Is such as to put the health and safety of a worker employed by him at risk, in particular because the work is monotonous, or the work rate is predetermined, the employer shall ensure that the worker is given adequate rest breaks."

There is no definition of adequate rest breaks but this duty is likely to overlap with duties under the health and safety legislation in any event. The worker is entitled to take advantage of the minimum entitlements under Regulations 10 to 17 – though it should be noted that these are entitlements and the worker is not obliged to take such advantage of them.

(e) Daily Rest Periods

An adult worker is entitled to a rest period of not less than 11 consecutive hours in each 24 hour period during which he works for his employer. A young worker is entitled to 12 hours though this may be interrupted in the case of activities involving periods of work that are split up over the day or of short duration (reg. 10). This entitlement does not apply to shift workers where they change shift and cannot take a daily rest period between the end of one shift and the start of another (reg. 22(1)). There is then an obligation to provide a compensatory rest period (24(a)) though in exceptional cases if this is not possible the employer should provide protection as is appropriate to safeguard health and safety (24(b)).

(f) Weekly Rest Periods

An adult worker is entitled to not less than 24 hours in each seven day period, which may be two periods of not less than 24 hours in each 14 day period or one period of not less than 48 hours. A young worker is entitled to not less than 48 hours during each 7 day period but this may be reduced to not less than 36 hours and may be interrupted in the case of activities involving periods of work that are split up over the day or are of short duration; and may be reduced where this is justified by technical or organization reasons, but not to less than 36 consecutive hours (reg. 11(8)). In the case of shift workers the entitlement does not apply where the worker changes shift (22(1)(b)). There is then an obligation to provide a compensatory rest period (24(a)) though in exceptional cases if this is not possible the employer should provide protection as is appropriate to safeguard health and safety (24(b)).

(g) Rest Breaks

Where an adult worker's daily working time is more than 6 hours he is entitled to a rest break which, subject to any collective or workforce agreement, shall be not less than 20 minutes, and a young worker is entitled to 30 minutes where the working time is four and a half hours (reg. 12). Payment does not have to be made unless this is agreed. In the case of young workers who work for more than one employer the number of hours must be aggregated (12(5)). The worker is entitled to spend the break away from his workstation if he has one.

(h) Exceptions

Regulations 18 to 27 contain a large number of exceptions and exclusions for particular sectors of employment. The second Table at the end of this section provides a ready means of identifying the modification or exclusions. There are five broad categories:

1. The excluded sectors under Regulation 18 and mobile workers under regulation 24B

As originally drafted (pursuant to the original form of Directive 93/104/EC), the excluded sectors under regulation 18 were very broad, including the transport industry. The Directive had provided that it applied to all sectors of activity except "air, rail, road, sea, inland waterway and lake transport, sea fishing other work at sea and the activities of doctors in training." This exception was interpreted very wide so as to include non-mobile workers such as secretarial staff who happened to work for a transport company: **Bowden v Tuffnells Parcels Express Ltd C–133/00** [2001] IRLR 838, ECJ).

The original regulation 18 was replaced by the Working Time (Amendment) Regulations 2003 to reflect the narrowing of the exclusions by the Horizontal Amending Directive 2000/34/EC. Most of the exclusions therefore ended on 1 August 2003. A number of other directives have been adopted to extend working time provisions to the areas that were previously excluded. The Commission has adopted four sector specific directives to deal with particular activities.

The Working Time (Amendment) Regulations 2003, SI 2003/1684 ensure that all non-mobile workers are entitled to the benefit of the WTR 1998.

Regulation 18 now provides that:

- The Regulations do not apply

    (*a*) to workers to whom the European Agreement on the organization of working time of seafarers dated 30th September 1998 and put into effect by Council Directive 1999/63/EC of 21st June 1999 applies.

    (*b*) to workers on board a sea-going fishing vessel; or

    (*c*) to workers on board a ship or hovercraft employed by an undertaking which operates services for passengers or goods by inland waterway or lake transport.

There are separate Regulations which apply to seafarers and in relation to inland waterways: Merchant Shipping (Hours of Work) Regulations 2002 SI 2002/2125; Merchant Shipping (Working Time: Inland Waterways) Regulations 2003 SI 2003/3049).

- Regulations 4(1) and (2), 6(1), (2) and (7), 7(1) and (6), 8, 10(1), 11(1) and (2), 12(1), 13 and 16 do not apply in these professions:

    Specific services

    (*a*) where characteristics peculiar to certain specific services such as the armed forces or the police, or to certain specific activities in the civil protection services, inevitably conflict with the provisions of these Regulations;

Aviation

(*b*) to workers to whom the European Agreement on the organization of working time of mobile staff in civil aviation concluded on 22nd March 2000 and implemented by Council Directive 2000/79/EC of 27th November 2000 applies.

Doctors

(*c*) to the activities of workers who are doctors in training only until 31st July 2004. The exclusion of doctors in training under regulation 18(2)(c) lapsed on 31 July 2004 from which time the hours are subject to progressive reduction (up to July 2009) (Regulation 25A). The Regulation provides that:

- for the reference to 48 hours there is substituted a reference to 58 hours with effect from 1st August 2004 until 31st July 2007;

- for the reference to 48 hours there is substituted a reference to 56 hours with effect from 1st August 2007 until 31st July 2009

Road Transport

- Regulations 4(1) and (2), 6(1), (2) and (7), 8, 10(1), 11(1) and (2) and 12(1) do not apply to workers to whom Directive 2002/15/EC of the European Parliament and of the Council on the organization of the working time of persons performing mobile road transport activities, dated 11th March 2002 applies. This regulation excludes those activities to which the Road Transport Directive applies. The Directive covers self employed and employed drivers. There is currently consultation ongoing with the Government about reform to include lorry drivers within the regulations. The last date for implementation is 23 March 2005 see: *http://www.dft.gov.uk/ stellent/groups/dft_freight/documents/page/dft_freight_024812.hcsp*

Where the Road Transport Directive applies there is provision that there will be:

- A 48 hours maximum average working week over a 4 months reference period. If the worker works for different employers each employer must "ask the mobile worker concerned in writing for an account of time worked for another employer" and the worker concerned must provide that information, also in writing (*art 4*);

- maximum weekly working time in any week of 60 hours (*art 4*);

- A break of at least 30 minutes after 6 hours work and at least 45 minutes after 9 hours (*art 5*);

- If night work is performed, the daily working time must not exceed 10 hours in each 24 hour period (*art 7*).

There will, no doubt, be much consultation prior to 2005 as to the way in which the Road Transport Directive will be implemented. At present, mobile workers who are not excluded by the new regulation 18 as set out above are subject to the other (specific but partial) exclusions in regulation 24A.

Mobile workers – current position

By regulation 24A in relation to mobile workers:

- Regulations 6(1), (2) and (7), 10(1), 11(1) and (2) and 12(1) do not apply to a mobile worker in relation to whom the application of those regulations is not excluded by any provision of regulation 18.

- A mobile worker, to whom paragraph (1) applies, is entitled to adequate rest, except where the worker's activities are affected by any of the matters referred to in regulation 21(e) (an occurrence due to unusual and unforeseeable circumstances, beyond the control of the worker's employer; exceptional events, the consequences of which could not have been avoided despite the exercise of all due care by the employer; or an accident or the imminent risk of an accident).

Adequate rest, means that a worker has regular rest periods, the duration of which are expressed in units of time and which are sufficiently long and continuous to ensure that, as a result of fatigue or other irregular working patterns, he does not cause injury to himself, to fellow workers or to others and that he does not damage his health, either in the short term or in the longer term (24A(3)).

The position with regard to road transport is therefore that:

- All non mobile workers in the transport industry are covered by the WTR.

- Where the Road Transport Directive does not cover transport workers such as couriers and workers who drive people carriers, taxis or vans the amendments to the WTR required by the Horizontal Directive apply so that the workers are entitled to a 48 hour week, annual leave, regular health assessments to night workers and transfer to day work wherever possible if suffering from a health problem. The protections in relation to night work, daily rest, weekly rest and rest breaks are not extended.

- Where the Road Transport Directive applies the WTR will not apply and the RTD is to be implemented by 2005. Such workers are currently entitled to paid annual leave and health assessments as the sector directive does not cover these points.

- Where Regulation 18 excludes the mobile worker then he is entitled to adequate rest, subject to the exceptions in Regulation 24A.

The following are the relevant sets of legislation in relation to each area:

(1) Road Transport: Road Transport Directive

(2) Air: Aviation Directive 2000/79

(3) Sea: Seafarers Directive 1999/63 & ("(Merchant Shipping (hours of Work) Regulations 2002 SI 2002/2125

(4) Inland waterways: Merchant Shipping (Working Time: Inland Waterways) Regulations 2003 SI 2003/3049

See the second At a Glance Chart at the end of this Chapter.

---

2. Domestic Servants

Regulation 19 provides that Domestic servants in private households are excluded from those areas identified in the first chart below. Domestic servants will cover employees working at domestic establishments who sleep on the premises (see **Re Junior Carlton Club** [1992] 1 KB 166; **Re Wilkinson** [1992] 1 KB 584).

3. Unmeasured working time

An important exception relates to 'unmeasured working time'. To cover the situation regulation 20(1) provides that regulations 4(1) and (2), 6(1), (2) and (7), 10(1), 11(1) and (2) and 12(1) do not apply in relation to a worker where, on account of the specific characteristics of the activity in which he is engaged, the duration of his working time is not measured or predetermined or can be determined by the worker himself, as may be the case for (a) managing executives or other persons with autonomous decision-taking powers; (b) family workers; or (c) workers officiating at religious ceremonies in churches and religious communities.

Regulation 20(2) states that:

"Where, part of the working time of a worker is measured or predetermined or cannot be determined by the worker himself but the specific characteristics of the activity are such that, without being required to do so by the employer, the worker may also do work the duration of which is not measured or predetermined or can be determined by the worker himself, regulations 4(1) and (2) and 6(1),(2) and (7) shall apply only to so much of his work as is measured or predetermined or cannot be determined by the worker himself."

This amendment was made by the Working Time Regulations 1999 in order to cover the situation where the employee did in fact have certain pre-determined hours but also had a measure of choice as to the time during which he carried out his work.

4. Special cases

Regulation 21 contains a list of special cases which are excluded from the Regulations set out in the chart. The special cases cover:

• where the worker's activities are such that his place of work and place of residence are distant from one another or his different places of work are distant from one another.

• where the worker is engaged in security or surveillance requiring a permanent residence in order to protect property or persons.

- where the worker's activities involve the need for continuity of service or production, as may be the case in services relating to reception, treatment or care by hospitals or similar establishments or prisons; work at docks or airports, press, radio, television, postal and telecommunications services and civil protection services; gas, water and electricity services; industries where work cannot be interrupted on technical grounds; research and development activities and agriculture or the carriage of passengers on regular urban transport services

- where there is a foreseeable surge in activity as in the case of agriculture, tourism and postal services.

- where the worker's activities are affected by an occurrence due to unusual and unforeseeable circumstances beyond the control of the employer or exceptional events, the consequences of which could not have been avoided despite the exercise of all due care by the employer or an accident or the imminent risk of an accident.

- where the worker works in railway transport and his activities are intermittent; he spends his working time on board trains; or his activities are linked to transport timetables and to ensuring the continuity and regularity of traffic. This was added by added by SI 2003/1684, as from 1 August 2003.

5. Shift Workers

By regulation 22(1) subject to the compensatory rest provisions of regulation 24—

(*a*) regulation 10(1) does not apply in relation to a shift worker when he changes shift and cannot take a daily rest period between the end of one shift and the start of the next one;

(*b*) paragraphs (1) and (2) of regulation 11 do not apply in relation to a shift worker when he changes shift and cannot take a weekly rest period between the end of one shift and the start of the next one; and

(*c*) neither regulation 10(1) nor paragraphs (1) and (2) of regulation 11 apply to workers engaged in activities involving periods of work split up over the day, as may be the case for cleaning staff.

Under regulation 22(2):

- 'shift worker' means any worker whose work schedule is part of shift work; and

- 'shift work' means any method of organizing work in shifts whereby workers succeed each other at the same workstations according to a certain pattern, including a rotating pattern, and which may be continuous or discontinuous, entailing the need for workers to work at different times over a given period of days or weeks.

6. Mobile workers

See above and regulation 24A.

7. Doctors

See above and regulation 25A. Junior doctors will be most affected by the reforms. The BMA estimates that the changes will require an extra 6,0000 junior doctors to maintain standards (see *The Times* of 19th November 1998) at a cost of over £1 billion.

8. Agreements to modify or exclude

By regulation 23 collective or workforce agreements may modify or exclude certain provisions. For the requirements of these agreements see the Definitions section above. The areas where these agreements may apply are set out in the first At a Glance Chart below. The three precedents D8.1. to 8.3 contain:

- exclusion of the 48 hour week by agreement with the Worker.

- confirmation that there is a Workforce Agreement;

- a draft Workforce Agreement.

9. Annual Leave

Regulations 13 to 16 cover annual leave and this is dealt with under Part I.

Reforms

The position with regard to the WTR does not stand still. Current developments include:

- There is a Consolidating Directive 2002/0131 issued on 24th June 2002 which will repeal and replace Directive 93/104/EC.

- The opt out provision in relation to the 48 hour week is being reviewed. Consultation was stared in early 2004 and there was a deadline for submissions of March 2004. A resolution of the European Parliament of 11th February 2004, para 17 called

    "for the revision, with a view to the phasing-out, as soon as possible, of the individual opt-out ..... ; in the meantime, calls on the Commission to identify practical ways of tacking potential or actual abuses of the opt-out provision including seeking views on how best to strengthen the voluntary nature of the opt-out".

In its Consultation document the Government has suggested 11 possible alternatives/variations on the opt-out and the reader is referred to Chapter 3 of the document.

- There is particular concern among member countries over the decision of the ECJ in **Landeshaupstadt Kiel v Jaeger** whereby time will count even where the employee is sleeping. The Commission wishes to clarify when time will count as working time.

- There is also a proposal to extend the reference period beyond the current 17 weeks.

Ironically, a DTI Survey in August 2002 shows that there has been a rise in the number of hours worked and that one in six now work over 60 hours a week this rate having doubled with women since 1999. (See DTI Press Release P/2002/551).

At a Glance Guide to the Working Time Regulations 1998

An agreement may be reached to add to what is the definition of working time, but not to exclude (Regulation 2)	
Effect of Regulation	Working time defined in Reg. 2 as any period when working, at employer's disposal and carrying out his activity or duties, or receiving relevant training may be added to.
Automatic Exclusion	N/A
Reference Period	N/A
Exclusions & Modifications	May add to definition by RA (2)
Compensatory Rests	N/A

At a Glance Guide to the Working Time Regulations 1998 *(continued)*

48 hours working week (Regulations 4 and 5)	
Effect of Regulation	Working time in the reference period shall not exceed 48 hours subject to automatic exclusions and agreement to exclude (4(1)). Employer is to take all reasonable steps in keeping with the need to protect the health and safety of workers to ensure that (1) is complied with (4(2)).
Automatic Exclusion	1. Excluded Sectors (18) 2. Domestic Servants (19) 3. Unmeasured working time (20)
Reference Period	1. Average worked in 17 weeks (4(3)b). 2. If worked less than 17 weeks then average of period worked (4(4)). 3. Where Reg. 21 special cases the period is 26 weeks (4(5)).
Exclusions & Modifications	1. Employee may agree to work in excess by NCWA (5(1)). 2. Employee may give 7 days notice to terminate agreement to work in excess. By NCBA the notice period may be extended to 3 months 5(2)) 3. May agree 17 weeks to be successive rather than rolling by RA (4(3)(a)) 4. Reference period may be extended to 52 weeks under Reg. 23 by CA or WA.
Compensatory Rests	N/A

At a Glance Guide to the Working Time Regulations 1998 *(continued)*

Night Workers: average hours not to exceed 8 in any 24 hour period: Regulation 6	
Effect of Regulation	Normal hours of work in any reference period that is applicable shall not exceed average of 8 in any 24 hours (6(1)). Employer is to take all reasonable steps in keeping with the need to protect the health and safety of workers to ensure that the limit in (1) is complied with (6(2)).
Automatic Exclusion	1. Excluded Sectors (18) 2. Domestic Servants (19) 3. Unmeasured Working time (20) 4. Special cases (21)
Reference Period	1. 17 weeks (6(3)(b)). 2. If worked less than 17 weeks then average of period worked (6(4)).
Exclusions & Modifications	1. 17 week period may be successive by RA (6(3)(a)). 2. Definition of night time may be defined by RA. 3. CA, WA may modify or exclude or define number of hours to be a night worker (r 23).
Compensatory Rests	N/A

At a Glance Guide to the Working Time Regulations 1998 *(continued)*

Night work where there are special hazards or heavy physical or mental strain	
Effect of Regulation	An employer shall ensure that no nightworker whose work involves special hazards or heavy physical or mental strain works for more than 8 hours in any 24 hour period during which he performs nightwork (6(7)).
Automatic Exclusion	1. Excluded Sectors 2. Domestic Servants 3. Unmeasured Working time 4. Special cases
Reference Period	No reference period
Exclusions & Modifications	As above + definition of hazards or heavy physical or mental strain may be defined in CA, WA (6(8)).
Compensatory Rests	N/A

Night work where there is a right to a health assessment before transfer to night work	
Effect of Regulation	A worker cannot be assigned to nightwork unless the worker has had an opportunity of a free health assessment or one has already been undertaken and there is no reason to believe it is no longer valid and the employer ensures there are free health assessments at regular intervals (7(1)).
Automatic Exclusion	1. Excluded Sectors except for young workers (7(2)). 2. Domestic Servants (includes young workers).
Reference Period	No reference period
Exclusions & Modifications	Cannot exclude or modify this provision.
Compensatory Rests	N/A

At a Glance Guide to the Working Time Regulations 1998 *(continued)*

Night work where there is a duty to transfer to suitable day work for health reasons	
Effect of Regulation	Where a registered medical practitioner has advised that a nightworker is suffering health problems connected with night work and it is possible to transfer to suitable work so the worker will cease to be a nightworker he will transferred accordingly (7(6)).
Automatic Exclusion	1. Excluded Sectors 2. Domestic Servants
Reference Period	No reference period
Exclusions & Modifications	N/A
Compensatory Rests	N/A

Night work: duty to provide for adequate breaks	
Effect of Regulation	Where the work pattern is such as to put the health and safety of the employee at risk, in particular because the work rate is monotonous or the work rate is predetermined the employer shall ensure that the worker is given adequate rest breaks (8).
Automatic Exclusion	1. Excluded Sectors 2. Domestic Servants
Reference Period	No reference period
Exclusions & Modifications	There is no power to exclude or modify this provision.
Compensatory Rests	N/A

At a Glance Guide to the Working Time Regulations 1998 *(continued)*

Daily rest periods of 11 hours in each 24 hour period: Regulation 10(1)	
Effect of Regulation	Adult worker is entitled to a rest period of 11 consecutive hours in each 24 hour period during which he works (10(1)).
Automatic Exclusion	1. Excluded Sectors (for young workers see below). 2. Unmeasured working time (not young workers). 3. Special cases (not young workers). 4. Adult shift workers, changing shifts where he cannot take a daily rest period between the end of one shift and the start of another (r. 22(1)(a)) 5. Minimum period may be interrupted in the case of activities split up over the day or of short duration (10(3)).
Reference Period	No reference period
Exclusions & Modifications	CA or WA may modify or exclude except for young workers (23).
Compensatory Rests	Where a CA or WA excludes or modifies and the worker works through what would be a rest period the employer: 1. shall wherever possible allow him to take an equivalent period of compensatory rest; 2. in exceptional cases where it is not possible, for objective reasons, to grant such a period of rest, afford such protection as may be appropriate to safeguard the worker's health and safety (24).

At a Glance Guide to the Working Time Regulations 1998 *(continued)*

Daily rest period for young workers: Regulation 10(2)	
Effect of Regulation	A young worker is entitled to a rest period of 12 consecutive hours in each period of 24 hours (10(2)).
Automatic Exclusion	Minimum period may be interrupted in the case of activities split up over the day or of short duration (10(3), 22(1)(c)).
Reference Period	No reference period
Exclusions & Modifications	10(2) will not apply where: 1. no adult worker is available; 2. work is occasioned by an occurrence due to unusual and unforeseen circumstances beyond the employer's control or exceptional events, the consequences of which cold not have been avoided with the exercise of all due care by the employer and is of a temporary nature and must be performed immediately (27).
Compensatory Rests	Where the young employer is required to work during a period which would otherwise be a rest period, his employer shall allow him to take an equivalent period of compensatory rest within the following three weeks (27(2)).

At a Glance Guide to the Working Time Regulations 1998 *(continued)*

Weekly rest period of 24 hours in each 7 day period: Regulation 11	
Effect of Regulation	An adult worker is entitled to not less than 24 hours in each 7 day period (11(1)). This does not include reg. 10(1) rest periods unless justified by objective or technical reasons or reasons relating to the organization of work (11(7)).
Automatic Exclusion	1. Excluded Sectors (except young workers) 2. Unmeasured working time 3. Special cases (except young workers) 4. Adult shift workers changing shift and not a weekly rest period between the end of one shift and the start of another (22(1)(b). 5. Adult workers whose work is split up over the day (22(1)(c).
Reference Period	No reference period
Exclusions & Modifications	1. Employer can determine 2 periods of 24 hours in each 14 day period or 1 period of 48 hours in each 14 day period (11(2)). 2. RA may determine when each period of 7 or 14 days is to begin (11(4)(5)(6)). 3. CA, WA may modify or exclude (23).
Compensatory Rests	N/A

At a Glance Guide to the Working Time Regulations 1998 *(continued)*

Weekly rest period for young workers: Regulation 11(3)	
Effect of Regulation	A young worker is entitled to a rest period of not less than 48 hours in each 7 day rest period (11(3)).
Automatic Exclusion	N/A
Reference Period	No reference period
Exclusions & Modifications	The minimum period may be interrupted in the case of activities involving short periods of work that are split up over the day or are of short duration or where it is justified by technical or organizational reasons but not to less than 36 consecutive hours (11(8)).
Compensatory Rests	Where the young worker is required to work during a period which would otherwise be a rest period, his employer shall allow him to take an equivalent period of compensatory rest within the following three weeks (27(2)). He shall be allowed such a period of compensatory rest (25(3)).

At a Glance Guide to the Working Time Regulations 1998 *(continued)*

Rest breaks of 20 minutes in each 6 hour period: Regulation 12	
Effect of Regulation	Where an adult worker's working time is more than 6 hours he is entitled to a rest break of 20 minutes, away from a workstation if he as one (12(1),(3)) — subject to 12(2).
Automatic Exclusion	1. Excluded Sectors (except young workers) 2. Unmeasured working time (except young workers) 3. Special cases (except young workers)
Reference Period	N/A
Exclusions & Modifications	The details of a rest break, duration and terms on which granted may be contained in a CA, WA.(12(2)) CA,WA may exclude or modify (23).
Compensatory Rests	Where a CA or WA excludes or modifies and the worker works through what would be a rest break the employer: 1. shall wherever possible allow him to take an equivalent period of compensatory rest; 2. in exceptional cases where it is not possible, for objective reasons, to grant such a period of rest, afford such protection as may be appropriate to safeguard the worker's health and safety (24).

At a Glance Guide to the Working Time Regulations 1998 *(continued)*

<table>
<tr>
<td colspan="2">Rest Breaks of 30 minutes in each 6 hour period for young workers:
Regulation 12(4)</td>
</tr>
<tr>
<td>Effect of Regulation</td>
<td>Where a young worker's daily working time is more than four and a half hours he shall be entitled to a rest break of 30 minutes which shall be consecutive possible and he shall be entitled to spend it is away from his workstation (12(4)).</td>
</tr>
<tr>
<td>Automatic Exclusion</td>
<td>None</td>
</tr>
<tr>
<td>Reference Period</td>
<td>No reference period</td>
</tr>
<tr>
<td>Exclusions & Modifications</td>
<td>
1. Where a young worker is employed by more than one employer his daily working time shall be determined by aggregating the number of hours worked for each employer (12(5)).

2. 12(4) will not apply where:

(1) no adult worker is available;

(2) work is occasioned by an occurrence due to unusual and unforeseen circumstances beyond the employer's control or exceptional events, the consequences of which cold not have been avoided with the exercise of all due care by the employer and is or a temporary nature and must be performed immediately (27)
</td>
</tr>
<tr>
<td>Compensatory Rests</td>
<td>N/A</td>
</tr>
</table>

Working Time Chart for Different Occupations

At a glance Guide to Sector Protection and Working Time

	48 hour week	4 weeks leave	Night work protection	Weekly rest	Daily rest	Rest breaks
Non mobile workers (subject to certain derogations i.e. offshore workers)	✓ WTR Reg 4(1) Option to opt out in Reg 5	✓ WTR Reg 13 starts on 1 Oct each year if employed before 1/10/98 or their first date of employment if after 1/10/98. Reg 15A(2) accrues at the rate of 1/12 of entitlement at the beginning of each month if employed after 25/10/01.	✓ WTR Reg 6 (8 hours per 24 hours)	✓ WTR Reg 11 (not less than 24 hours in each 7 days)	✓ WTR Reg 10 (11 consecutive hours in each day)	✓ WTR Reg 8 (monotonous work) Reg 12 (20 minutes if more than 6 hours work)

Mobile workers[1]	✓ WTR Reg 4(1) Option to opt out in Reg 5	✓ WTR Reg 13 (See section for non-mobile workers)	N/A Reg 24A(1) Adequate rest Reg 24A(2)	N/A Reg 24A(1) Adequate rest Reg 24A(2)	N/A Reg 24A(1) Adequate rest Reg 24A(2)	N/A Reg 24A(1) Adequate rest Reg 24A(2)
Road-mobile workers not covered by RTD	✓ WTR Reg 4(1) Option to opt out in Reg 5	✓ WTR Reg 13 (See section for non-mobile workers)	N/A Reg 24A(1) Adequate rest Reg 24A(2)	N/A Reg 24A(1) Adequate rest Reg 24A(2)	N/A Reg 24A(1) Adequate rest Reg 24A(2)	N/A Reg 24A(1) Adequate rest Reg 24A(2)
Road-mobile workers covered by RTD (Regulations due to come into force on 23 March 2005)	✓ RTD Art 4.2 Max 48 hours in a 4 month reference period and maximum 60 hours in any given week. No opt outs are permitted	Not specified	✓ RTD Art 3.19 If some work is done at night, will be subject to a 10 hour per day limit.	✓ RTD Art 5.3 45 consecutive hours weekly rest which can be reduced to 36 or 24 if compensated for within 3 weeks.	✓ RTD Art 5.2 11 consecutive hours in each 24 hour period. Possibility of reducing this to 9 hours 3 times per week. 12 hours	✓ RTD Art 5.4/5.5 30 minutes after 6 hours and at least 45 minutes after 9 hours.

1. Workers who simply happen to be working for the transport industry are now covered by the WTAR regulations so the scenario in **Bowden v Tuffnells Parcels Express Ltd** C-133/00 [2001] IRLR 838, ECJ will not arise again.

	48 hour week	4 weeks leave	Night work protection	Weekly rest	Daily rest	Rest breaks
					rest may be taken in 2–3 periods, the last of which must be at least 8 hours.	
Rail (-workers where activities are intermittent, on board trains or linked to transport timetables)	✔ WTR Reg 4(1) Option to opt out in Reg 5	✔ WTR Reg 13 (See section for non-mobile workers for terms)	N/A Reg 21(F) Compensatory rest reg 24	N/A Reg 21(F) Compensatory rest reg 24	N/A Reg 21(F) Compensatory rest reg 24	N/A Reg 21(F) Compensatory rest reg 24
Crew workers on board a civil aircraft flying for the purposes of public transport	CAWTR Reg 9 Work done must not exceed 2,000 hours per year	CAWTR Reg 4 4 weeks paid annual leave	✗ WTR	CAWTR s.10(2)(a) 7 days per month	✗ WTR	CAWTR s.7(2)(a) Adequate rest

Other aviation workers (those who are not excluded in reg 18(2)(b))	✓ WTR Reg 4(1) Option to opt out in Reg 5	✓ WTR Reg 13 (See section for non-mobile workers for terms)	✓ WTR Reg 6 (8 hours per 24 hours)	✓ WTR Reg 11 (Not less than 24 hours in each 7 days)	✓ WTR Reg 10 (11 consecutive hours in each day)	✓ WTR Reg 8 (monotonous work) Reg 12 (20 minutes if more than 6 hours work)
Sea transport	✗ Reg 5(1)(b) only specifies period of rest meaning there are 91 hours left in the working week.	✓ Reg 12 SD	Reg 10 SD No seafarer under the age of 18 can work at night, unless it would interfere with an established programme of training.	Reg 5(1)(b) SD 77 hours in any 7 day period Reg 5(4) adequate rest if rest period disturbed	Reg 5(1)(a) SD 10 hours in every 24 hours Reg 5(4) adequate rest if rest period disturbed	Reg 5(4) SD adequate rest if rest period disturbed
Inland waterway and lake transport	✓ IW Reg 6(1)	✓ IW Reg 11(1)	✓ IW Reg 8 (Permitted hours not specified, but	IW Reg 10(1) Adequate rest	IW Reg 10(1) Adequate rest	IW Reg 10(1) Adequate rest

	48 hour week	4 weeks leave	Night work protection	Weekly rest	Daily rest	Rest breaks
			health check is required when transferring from day work to night work			
Sea fishing	DTI document dated 4/7/03 states that specific regulations on working time will be implemented to cover sea fishing. These have not been implemented yet.					
Other work at sea	✓ WTR Reg 4(1) Option to opt out in Reg 5	✓ WTR Reg 13 (see section for non-mobile workers for terms)	✓ WTR Reg 6 (8 hours per 24 hours)	N/A Reg 21(A) Compensatory rest Reg 24	N/A Reg 21(A) Compensatory rest Reg 24	N/A Reg 21(A) Compensatory rest Reg 24
Young workers (aged 15–18)	✓ WTR Reg 5(1)(b) 40 hours per week maximum	✓ WTR Reg 13 (see section for non-mobile workers for terms)	✓ WTR Reg 6A No young worker is allowed to	✓ WTR Reg 11(3) (48 hours in each 7 day period)	✓ WTR Reg 5(1)(a) Young workers cannot work	✓ WTR Reg 12(4) (30 minutes for every 4 hours worked)

			work in the restricted period (defined in Reg 2 as either 10 pm to 6 am or 11 pm to 7 am) (But see conflict in Reg 7).		more than 8 hours per day)	– consecutive if possible)
Young workers: *Force majeure*	Reg 27 Usual clauses do not apply in exceptional circumstances	✓ WTR Reg 13 (see section for non-mobile workers for terms)	Reg 27 Usual clauses do not apply in exceptional circumstances	✓ WTR Reg 11(3) (48 hours in each 7 day period)	Reg 27 Usual clauses do not apply in exceptional circumstances	Reg 27 Usual clauses do not apply in exceptional circumstances
Young workers where there is a need for continuity/a surge in demand and no adult	Reg 27A(1) Usual maximum will not apply where there is no adult worker and it	✓ WTR Reg 13 (See section for non-mobile workers for terms)	Reg 27A(2) Restriction for youth workers does not apply	✓ WTR Reg 11(3) (48 hours in each 7 day period)	✓ WTR (Reg 5(1)(a) young workers cannot work more than 8 hours per day)	✓ WTR Reg 12(4) (30 minutes for every 4 hours worked – consecutive if possible)

	48 hour week	4 weeks leave	Night work protection	Weekly rest	Daily rest	Rest breaks
worker is available	will not interrupt education & training					
Young workers in a hospital, cultural, sporting, advertising or artistic activities	✓ WTR Reg 5(1)(b) 40 hours per week maximum	✓ WTR Reg 13 (See section for non-mobile workers for terms)	Reg 27A(2) Restriction for youth workers does not apply	✓ WTR Reg 11(3) (48 hours in each 7 day period)	✓ WTR Reg 5(1)(a) (Young workers cannot work more than 8 hours per day)	✓ WTR Reg 12(4) (30 minutes for every 4 hours worked – consecutive if possible)
Young workers in agriculture, retail trading, newspaper/post delivery, catering, hotel/pub or similar establishment & bakeries	✓ WTR Reg 5(1)(b) 40 hours per week maximum	✓ WTR Reg 13 (see section for non-mobile workers for terms)	Reg 27A(3) Restriction for youth workers does not apply, but work between 12am–4am is prohibited.	✓ WTR Reg 11(3) (48 hours in each 7 day period)	✓ WTR Reg 5(1)(a) (Young workers cannot work more than 8 hours per day)	✓ WTR Reg 12(4) (30 minutes for every 4 hours worked – consecutive if possible)

Children (Children are not workers for the purpose of the WTR)	✗ S.18 CYPA 12 hours in any week in which they are to attend school. 35 hours when not at school 25 hours when at school	✗ Must have at least two consecutive weeks without employment	S.18 CYPA Is not allowed to work 7pm–7am.	See maximum working hours	S.18 CYPA Is only allowed to work two hours a day on school days 8 hours per day on non school days or 5 hours per day if under 15.	S.18 CYPA 1 hour per 4 hours worked
Night workers	✓ WTR Reg 4(1) Option to opt out in Reg 5	✓ WTR Reg 13 (See section for non-mobile workers for terms)	✓ Reg 6 WTR (8 hours per 24 hours)	✓ WTR Reg 11 (Not less than 24 hours in each 7 days)	✓ WTR Reg 10 (11 consecutive hours in each day)	✓ WTR Reg 8 (monotonous work) Reg 12 (20 minutes if more than 6 hours work)
Doctors in training	Reg 25A(1) Any reference to 48 hours in	✓ WTR Reg 13	✓ Reg 6 WTR	✓ WTR Reg 11	✓ WTR Reg 10	✓ WTR Reg 8

	48 hour week	4 weeks leave	Night work protection	Weekly rest	Daily rest	Rest breaks
	the regulations to be replaced by 58 hours from 1/8/4–31/7/7 then 56 from 1/8/7–31/7/9	(See section for non-mobile workers for terms)	(8 hours per 24 hours)	(Not less than 24 hours in each 7 days)	(11 consecutive hours in each day)	(monotonous work) Reg 12 (20 minutes if more than 6 hours work)
Domestic services in a private household	N/A Reg 19	✔ WTR Reg 13 (see section for non-mobile workers for terms)	N/A Reg 19	✔ WTR Reg 11 (not less than 24 hours in each 7 days)	✔ WTR Reg 10 (11 consecutive hours in each day)	✔ WTR Reg 8 (monotonous work) Reg 12 (20 minutes if more than 6 hours work)
Security/ Surveillance positions requiring permenant residents	✔ WTR Reg 4(1) Option to opt out in Reg 5	✔ WTR Reg 13 (see section for non-mobile workers for terms)	N/A Reg 21(B) Compensatory rest Reg 24	N/A Reg 21(B) Compensatory rest Reg 24	N/A Reg 21(B) Compensatory rest Reg 24	N/A Reg 21(B) Compensatory rest Reg 24

Cases where an employees place of work and residence are distant from each other, including off-shore workers	✓ WTR Reg 4(1) Option to opt out in Reg 5	✓ WTR Reg 13 (See section for non-mobile workers for terms)	N/A Reg 21(A) Compensatory rest Reg 24	N/A Reg 21(A) Compensatory rest Reg 24	N/A Reg 21(A) Compensatory rest Reg 24	N/A Reg 21(A) Compensatory rest Reg 24
Shift workers	✓ WTR Reg 4(1) Option to opt out in Reg 5	✓ WTR Reg 13 (See section for non-mobile workers for terms)	✓ WTR Reg 6 (8 hours per 24 hours)	Reg 22(1)(B) does not apply if worker changes shift and cannot have the break between the two, subject to compensatory rest under Reg 24	Reg 22(1)(A) does not apply if worker changes shift and cannot have the break between the two, subject to compensatory rest under Reg 24	✓ WTR Reg 8 (monotonous work) Reg 12 (20 minutes if more than 6 hours work)
Workers whose work is split up over the day e.g. cleaners	✓ WTR Reg 4(1) Option to opt out in Reg 5	✓ WTR Reg 13 (See section for non-mobile workers)	✓ WTR Reg 6 (8 hours per 24 hours)	Reg 22(1)C does not apply if worker changes shift and cannot	Reg 22(1)C does not apply if worker changes shift and cannot	✓ WTR Reg 8 (monotonous work)

	48 hour week	4 weeks leave	Night work protection	Weekly rest	Daily rest	Rest breaks
		workers for terms)		have the break between the two, subject to compensatory rest under Reg 24	have the break between the two, subject to compensatory rest under Reg 24	Reg 12 (20 minutes if more than 6 hours work)
Workers whose working time is unmeasured NB. Any work that is capable of being measured will be included in the Regulations: Reg 20(2)	N/A Reg 20	✔ WTR Reg 13 (see section for non-mobile workers for terms)	N/A Reg 20	N/A Reg 20	N/A Reg 20	N/A Reg 20
Armed forces WTR applies under Reg 38 except that complaints	✔ WTR Reg 4(1) Option to opt out in Reg 5	✔ WTR Reg 13 (see section for non-mobile	✔ WTR Reg 6 (8 hours per 24 hours)	✔ WTR Reg 11 (not less than 24 hours in each 7 days)	✔ WTR Reg 10 (11 consecutive hours in each day)	✔ WTR Reg 8 (monotonous work)

may not be made to an employment tribunal unless the internal redress procedures have been followed	Reg 18(3)(a) Except where the characteristics of the job conflict with these regulations	workers for terms) Reg 18(3)(a) Except where the characteristics of the job conflict with these regulations	Reg 18(3)(a) Except where the characteristics of the job conflict with these regulations	Reg 18(3)(a) Except where the characteristics of the job conflict with these regulations	Reg 18(3)(a) Except where the characteristics of the job conflict with these regulations	Reg 18(3)(a) Except where the characteristics of the job conflict with these regulations
Young workers in armed forces	Reg 25(2) Not limited to maximum for young workers	✔ WTR Reg 13 (See section for non-mobile workers for terms)	Reg 25(2) Restriction for young workers does not apply	Reg 25(2) Restriction for young workers does not apply	Reg 25(2) Restriction for young workers does not apply	✔ WTR Reg 8 (monotonous work) Reg 12 (20 minutes if more than 6 hours work)
Agency workers who are not otherwise workers	✔ WTR Reg 4(1) Option to opt out in Reg 5	✔ WTR Reg 13 (See section for non-mobile workers)	✔ WTR Reg 6 (8 hours per 24 hours)	✔ WTR Reg 11 (Not less than 24 hours in each 7 days)	✔ WTR Reg 10 (11 consecutive hours in each day)	✔ WTR Reg 8 (monotonous work)

	48 hour week	4 weeks leave	Night work protection	Weekly rest	Daily rest	Rest breaks
The WTR applies under Reg 36		workers for terms)				Reg 12 (20 minutes if more than 6 hours work)
Freelance workers	✔ WTR Reg 4(1) Option to opt out in Reg 5	✔ WTR Reg 13 (see section for non-mobile workers for terms)	✔ WTR Reg 6 (8 hours per 24 hours)	✔ WTR Reg 11 (not less than 24 hours in each 7 days)	✔ WTR Reg 10 (11 consecutive hours in each day)	✔ WTR Reg 8 (monotonous work) Reg 12 (20 minutes if more than 6 hours work)
Self-employed	The working time regulations do not apply to the genuinely self-employed. However, the line between this and freelance workers is very fine. See **Byrne Bros (Farmwork) Ltd v Baird** [2002] IRLR 96.					
Workers in crown employment (except armed forces)	✔ WTR Reg 4(1) Option to opt out in Reg 5	✔ WTR Reg 13 (See section for non-mobile	✔ WTR Reg 6 (8 hours per 24 hours)	✔ WTR Reg 11 (Not less than 24 hours in each 7 days)	✔ WTR Reg 10 (11 consecutive	✔ WTR Reg 8 (monotonous work)

					hours in each day)	Reg 12 (20 minutes if more than 6 hours work)
The WTR applies under Reg 37 except that the crown cannot be criminally liable	workers for terms)					
House of Lords Staff The WTR applies under Reg 39	WTR Reg 4(1) Option to opt out in Reg 5	WTR Reg 13 (See section for non-mobile workers for terms)	WTR Reg 6 (8 hours per 24 hours)	WTR Reg 11 (Not less than 24 hours in each 7 days)	WTR Reg 10 (11 consecutive hours in each day)	WTR Reg 8 (monotonous work) Reg 12 (20 minutes if more than 6 hours work)
House of Commons staff WTR applies under Reg 40	WTR Reg 4(1) Option to opt out in Reg 5	WTR Reg 13 (see section for non-mobile workers for terms)	WTR Reg 6 (8 hours per 24 hours)	WTR Reg 11 (not less than 24 hours in each 7 days)	WTR Reg 10 (11 consecutive hours in each day)	WTR Reg 8 (monotonous work) Reg 12 (20 minutes if more than 6 hours work)

	48 hour week	4 weeks leave	Night work protection	Weekly rest	Daily rest	Rest breaks
Police service The WTR applies under Reg 41	✔ WTR Reg 4(1) Option to opt out in Reg 5 Reg 18(3)(a) Except where the characteristics of the job conflict with these regulations	✔ WTR Reg 13 (see section for non-mobile workers for terms) Reg 18(3)(a) Except where the characteristics of the job conflict with these regulations	✔ WTR Reg 6 (8 hours per 24 hours) Reg 18(3)(a) Except where the characteristics of the job conflict with these regulations	✔ WTR Reg 11 (not less than 24 hours in each 7 days) Reg 18(3)(a) Except where the characteristics of the job conflict with these regulations	✔ WTR Reg 10 (11 consecutive hours in each day) Reg 18(3)(a) Except where the characteristics of the job conflict with these regulations	✔ WTR Reg 8 (monotonous work) Reg 12 (20 minutes if more than 6 hours work) Reg 18(3)(a) Except where the characteristics of the job conflict with these regulations
Non-trained employees The WTR applies under Reg 42	✔ WTR Reg 4(1) Option to opt out in Reg 5	✔ WTR Reg 13 (See section for non-mobile	✔ WTR Reg 6 (8 hours per 24 hours)	✔ WTR Reg 11 (Not less than	✔ WTR Reg 10 (11 consecutive	✔ WTR Reg 8 (monotonous work)

		workers for terms)		24 hours in each 7 days)	hours in each day)	Reg 12 (20 minutes if more than 6 hours work)
Agricultural workers	✔ WTR Reg 4(1) Option to opt out in Reg 5	WTR Reg 13 Reg 43 schedule 2(1)(a) Leave year commences on 6/4 each year.	N/A Reg 21(C) Compensatory rest Reg 24	N/A Reg 21(C) Compensatory rest Reg 24	N/A Reg 21(C) Compensatory rest Reg 24	N/A Reg 21(C) Compensatory rest Reg 24
Workers in situations where unforeseeable circumstances, exceptional events, accidents or an imminent risk of accident has occurred	✔ WTR Reg 4(1) Option to opt out in Reg 5	WTR Reg 13 (see section for non-mobile workers for terms)	N/A Reg 21(E) Compensatory rest reg 24	N/A Reg 21(E) Compensatory rest reg 24	N/A Reg 21(E) Compensatory rest reg 24	N/A Reg 21(E) Compensatory rest reg 24

	48 hour week	4 weeks leave	Night work protection	Weekly rest	Daily rest	Rest breaks
Workers who have a forseeable surge of activity	✔ WTR Reg 4(1) Option to opt out in Reg 5	✔ WTR Reg 13 (see section for non-mobile workers for terms)	N/A Reg 21(E)	N/A Reg 21(E)	N/A Reg 21(E)	N/A Reg 21(E)
Workers whose activities include a need for continuity of service	✔ WTR Reg 4(1) Option to opt out in Reg 5	✔ WTR Reg 13 (see section for non-mobile workers for terms)	N/A Reg 21(E) Compensatory rest reg 24	N/A Reg 21(E) Compensatory rest reg 24	N/A Reg 21(E) Compensatory rest reg 24	N/A Reg 21(E) Compensatory rest reg 24

(1) RTD — Road Transport Directive
(2) AD — Aviation Directive 2000/79
(3) CAWTR — Civil Aviation (Working Time) Regulations 2004
(4) SD — Seafarers Directive 1999/63 & Merchant Shipping (Hours of Work) Regulations 2002 SI 2002/2125
(5) IW REG — Merchant Shipping (Working Time: Inland Waterways) Regulations 2003 SI 2003/3049
(6) WTAR — Working Time (Amendment) Regulations 2003
(7) CYPA — Children and Young Persons Act 1933

(3) *Variation of Hours of Work*

In the absence of an express term, a unilateral variation of terms is likely to be a repudiatory breach of contract. This is the position where it is sought to change working hours. For example, see:

- **Risk Management Services (Chiltern) Limited v Shrimpton** [EAT 803/77]. The employee applied for a day job as a security guard. After certain problems at work the company decided to put him on night work, as he would be supervised. The EAT held that the employment tribunal was entitled to find that this amounted to a constructive dismissal on the basis that the contract was for a day job only.

- **Brechin Bros v Kenneavy & Strang** [EAT 373 & 374/82]. The employees were given written statements which provided that their hours of work were as set out on a notice board and that any variation would be similarly exhibited. The EAT held that this provision did not have any meaning and that any power to vary a 20 hour week within the framework of 48 hours must be "unequivocally contained in the contract of employment". This was not done so that there was a fundamental breach of contract when the employer sought to change the hours.

It will therefore be necessary to include an express power to vary. It is also important that the terms and conditions make it clear what can be varied.

(4) *Overtime and Flexitime*

Overtime may be obligatory so that the employee has a contractual right to payment. In certain cases some degree of flexibility may be required and the provisions of the Working Time Regulations may need to be considered in so far as they relate to unmeasured time. Where overtime is part of the employee's normal working hours this will have an impact upon calculations for the purposes of holiday under the Working Time Regulations or for the purposes of a redundancy payment.

Precedents as to overtime and flexitime are contained at Precedents D2 and D3.

There are a large number of cases which consider express and implied terms relating to overtime and which give guidance as to the effect of particular wording:

Examples of cases involving express and implied terms:

Express terms

- In **Pearson & Workman v William Jones Limited** [1967] ITR 471 the appellants were paid a redundancy payment based upon a 40 hour week. They had a clause incorporated into their contracts which provided that

  > "The Federation and Trades Unions agree that systematic overtime is deprecated as a method of production, and that when overtime is necessary the following provisions shall apply, namely: No union workman shall be required to work more than 30 hours overtime in any four weeks after full shop hours have been worked...It is agreed that employers have the right to decide when overtime is necessary, the work people or their representatives being entitled to bring forward...any cases of overtime they desire discussed...".

  The Divisional Court held that the overtime was permissive and not compulsory so that the employees were entitled to redundancy based upon a 40 hour week.

- **Martin v Solus Schall** [1979] IRLR 7. Mr Martin's contract stated that "you will be expected to work such overtime as is necessary to ensure continuity of service." He was dismissed when he refused to work overtime. The EAT held that the document he had signed implies that he had accepted the need to work such overtime as was necessary to ensure continuity of service so that this was a contractual obligation.

Implied terms

- **Darlington Forge Limited v Sutton** [1968] ITR 196. The respondent was a furnace man whose statement provided that he work 40 hours per week, though he worked more to cover for other staff. The Divisional Court held that he was only entitled to a redundancy payment based on 40 hours as there was no term in his contract that he work such overtime as was necessary.

- **Horrigan v Lewisham Council** [1978] ICR 15. Where the employee was employed as a driver on a contract that stipulated 40 hours a week, but regularly worked overtime for which he was paid and there was an agreement that he would not be pressed if he had a specific reason for not wishing to work late on a particular day, there was no implied term, to give business efficacy to the contract, that he must work sufficient overtime to complete his rounds. This was so even though he had worked overtime in the past.

- **Lake v Essex County Council** [1979] ICR 577; IRLR 241 (see WTR reg. 20). Ms Lake was a part time teacher, on duty for 19 hours 25 minutes, of which there were three hours forty minutes when she was not teaching. She was to undertake marking and preparation during these sessions but would spend several hours a week preparing classes at home. At the time she could only succeed in an unfair dismissal claim if she had 21 hours a week service. The Court of Appeal held that the extra hours she worked were voluntary and were so unpredictable that they could not be regarded as contractual. "If she chose to do more, it was a voluntary act on her part outside her contractual obligations."

- **Ali v Christian Salvesen Food Services Limited** [1997] ICR 25; IRLR 17. Mr Ali and four others had an annualised hours agreement incorporated into their contracts through a collective agreement, whereby they were paid for a 40 hour week and, at the end of the pay year, would be paid overtime if they had worked for more than 1,824 hours in the year. They were made redundant after six months before the 1,824 threshold was reached. The Court of Appeal held that there was no scope to imply a term that the employees would be paid overtime where the employee had not worked more than the annual hours figure but had worked more than the weekly hours. The collective agreement had not provided for this contingency and to deal with every eventuality would have required an immense degree of elaboration.

Precedents D 2.1 to D2.4 are different examples of overtime precedents. The first three precedents make it clear that overtime will not normally be paid as the employee will be expected to manage his job within his normal working hours. These precedents are for more senior staff where some degree of flexibility can expected. The fourth precedent is more suitable for those on set hours such as factory workers who will be expected to be paid for any extra hours that they put in.

D3 contains a suggested precedent for flexitime. It may be that the employer will wish to make it clear that flexitime is not a contractual right in order that the system may be abolished if the employer finds that it is being abused by employees or is not conducive to the best interests of the business.

(5) Timekeeping

Precedent D4 contains a precedent for timekeeping/clocking in procedures that one would expect to find in the factory environment and other work environments where set hours are of importance. Note the importance of specifying that it is gross misconduct to tamper with clocks or to clock in for any other person. In **Dalton v Burton's Gold Medal Biscuits Limited** [1974] IRLR 45, the dismissal of an employee after twenty years' service was fair where he falsified a fellow worker's clock card. He was fully aware of the fact that such conduct would warrant dismissal.

(6) Shiftworkers/Factory Workers and Lay Off

Precedents D5 and D6 contain a set of precedents for shiftworkers and/or factory workers.

D5 deals with the requirements to carry out shiftworking. Note the requirements of the Working Time Regulations in this respect.

D6.1 contains an alternative shiftworking precedent.

An alternative clocking in procedure to D4 is contained at D6.2.

It is common for factories to have a closure period during the year and D6.3 sets out the entitlement of the employer to require the employee to take holiday during this period.

D6.4 contains important terms relating to the right to lay off and the importance of having an express term is shown by the cases set out below.

Lay Off

The provisions with regard to layoff are included in this section as they are most common in the factory environment though there is no reason, of course, why they cannot apply to any employee.

Express Terms

There may be an express term giving a right to lay off as with Precedent D6.4. The express term may give the employee a contractual right to lay off but the actual lay off may trigger certain statutory consequences. Where there is such a right two issues may arise:

1. The right to a guaranteed payment

    By section 28 of the ERA 1996 there is a right to a guaranteed payment where there is a diminution in the requirements of the employer's business for work of the kind that the employee is required to do or any other occurrence affecting the normal working of the employer's business in relation to work of the kind that the employee is employed to do. Where the worker can turn down work then he is not entitled to a guaranteed payment (**Mailway (Southern) Limited v Willsher** [1978] ICR 511). There are also exclusions in respect of trade disputes or where there has been an offer of suitable alternative work (s.29 ERA 1996). The guaranteed payment cannot exceed five days in any three months and any contractual payments both go to offset the guarantee payment and are counted in calculating the number of workless days in any three months (**Cartright v G Clancy Limited** [1983] ICR 552).

2. Redundancy by reason of lay off or short time working

    In cases where the employee is considered to be laid off because he receives no pay of any kind or there is no work for him to do during that week (section 147 ERA 1996) or where the employee is on short time because he receives less that half a week's pay (section 147(2) ERA 1996):

    *   A redundancy payment may be claimed where he gives notice in writing of his intention to claim and the claim is submitted within four weeks of a continuous period of lay off or short work of four weeks' duration or the end of the period of six weeks' lay off or short time out of thirteen weeks (where not more than three weeks were consecutive) (section 148 ERA 1996).

    *   Where notice of intention has been given, he will not be entitled to a redundancy payment if it was reasonably to be expected that he would, not later than four weeks after service, enter into a period of employment of not less than thirteen weeks during

which he would not be laid off or kept on short time (section 152(1) ERA 1996). However, the employer cannot take advantage of this provision unless he has, within seven days after service of the notice of intention, served a counter notice that he will contest liability to make payment (section 152(1)(b)) and a tribunal may then be asked to determine whether he is entitled to a payment (section 149 ERA 1996).

The contract must then be terminated by the employee giving the contractual period of notice or one week's notice:

- Where no counternotice has been served within seven days after the notice of intention to claim, then three weeks after the end of those seven days;

- Where a counternotice has been served in seven days after the notice of intention to claim, then three weeks after the end of those seven days;

- Where a counternotice has been served in seven days but then withdrawn, three weeks after service of the notice of withdrawal;

- Where a counternotice has been served and not withdrawn and the matter is referred to a tribunal, three weeks after the tribunal has notified to the employee its decision on the reference (section 140,141,156,157 ERA 1996 in particular).

It should be noted that there are various exclusions from the right to claim (see section 141, 156).

Implied Terms

Where there is no express term, there may still be a right to lay off by reason of custom and practice, as the following cases illustrate.

- **Devonald v Rosser & Sons** [1906] 2 KB 728. The employer alleged that they were entitled to lay off Mr Devonald when there were no profitable orders so that the works were closed. The Court of Appeal held that, in order for such a term to be implied, it must be certain and notorious which was not the case here.

- **Browning v Crumlin Valley Collieries Limited** [1926] 1 KB 522. Men were temporarily laid off whilst the mine where they worked was made safe. Greer J held that it is it is was an implied term to give business efficacy to the contract that where the mine had to be closed, through no fault of the employers, the risks would be shared so that the employers would lose production and the employees lost their wages.

- **Jones v Harry Sherman Limited** [1969] ITR 63. In order for there to be an implied term giving a right to lay off the custom must be reasonable, certain and notorious so that, where the employee knew nothing of it and it was unclear how it would operate there was no such implied term.

- **Puttick v John Wright & Sons Limited** [1972] ICR 457. Mr Puttick worked on a job by job basis for 23 years. Between jobs he would do no work or may carry out odd jobs on the employer's premises. He was not dismissed between jobs and, after a long period of not working, he applied for a redundancy payment. The NIRC held that there had been an implied term "empowering the employer to suspend, in the sense of to lay off temporarily, the employee."

- **Waine v Oliver (Plant Hire) Limited** [1977] IRLR 434. Mr Waine had been absent for six months and when he was reported back was told that there was no work for him on the Monday and to report on Wednesday. The EAT held that a right to lay off could not be implied from this one incident and that it is was necessary to look at the custom of the trade in order to ascertain whether there was a right to lay off in the particular industry.

- **Neads v CAV Limited** [1983] IRLR 360. Setters were laid off in a department C19 because work was running low. At the time there was a dispute with another department about machines that were being used and they had been told not to report to work unless they would work normally. A collective agreement, which was incorporated into the contracts provided that "The guarantee of employment for hourly rated manual workers ... is subject to the following conditions ... In the event of a disruption of production in a federated establishment as a result of an industrial dispute in that or any other federated establishment the operation of the period of guarantee shall be automatically suspended." Pain J held that the agreement did not apply as there was work available. There was no general right to lay off without pay. (See also **Johnson v Cross** [1977] ICR 872 on which Pain J relied.)

- **Window Centre Limited v Lees & F Lees** [EAT 742/85]. A working rule agreement provided that if work was temporarily stopped the employee was entitled to a guaranteed minimum weekly pay in lieu for the first week of lay off and the employer could thereafter require him to register as unemployed. The ET and EAT held that this did not give an indefinite right of lay off and that a period of four months and one of nine months were unreasonable and could not be said to be for a temporary period.

(7) Retail Employment

Precedent D7 is a standard clause relating to retail employment. Note that certain procedures must be followed in relation to Sunday working, in the context of Betting Workers/Shopworkers (see Chapter 5.2 and 5.14.).

(8) Discrimination Issues

Issues of indirect discrimination may arise where a female employee is required to work certain hours, which she cannot comply with because, for example, of child care arrangements. This may particularly be the case where a woman is unable to work full time (see Chapter 5 Part Time Workers) as in **Home Office v Holmes** [1984] IRLR 299 or where the woman cannot carry out extra curricular activities as in **Briggs v North Eastern Education and Library Board** [1990] IRLR 181. The imposition of flexible hours into a contract may be discriminatory **Oddbins Limited v Robinson** [EAT 188/96]) as may the requirement to have a particular start time (**Hellewell v Manchester Metropolitan University** [EAT 835/95]).

Similarly, in respect of religious discrimination the requirement to work certain times may be indirect discrimination unless it can be shown to be a proportionate means of achieving a legitimate aim. The ACAS Code gives the following example at paragraph 1.3:

Example

A small finance company needs its staff to work late on a Friday afternoon to analyse stock prices in the American finance market. The figures arrive late on Friday because of the global time differences. During the winter months some staff would like to be released early on Friday afternoon in order to be home before nightfall – a requirement of their religion. They propose to make the time up later during the remainder of the week.

The company is not able to agree to this request because the American figures are necessary to the business, they need to be worked on immediately and the company is too small to have anyone else able to do the work.

The requirement to work on Friday afternoon is not unlawful discrimination as it meets a legitimate business aim and there is no alternative means available.

See **Wetsein v Misprestige Management Services Ltd** [EAT 523/91].

In the context of disability discrimination, it may be that a reasonable adjustment will be to change hours of work where the disabled person cannot comply with the employer's normal hours and the employer should give consideration to this. In **Mansoor v Secretary of State for Education and Employment** [ET 1803409/97] a tribunal found that the respondent had failed to make a reasonable adjustment when it dismissed the applicant because of poor timekeeping. There was evidence that the employee could not get to work at the required time because of his condition, which amounted to a disability. His hours could easily have been shortened or varied but none of these possibilities were acted on by the employer.

Clearly, in considering working hours the employer will need to have the above issues in mind.

PART E: BASIC SALARY

Precedent E: Basic Salary

        E1: Salaries   **594**

        E2: Salaries   **596**

        E3: Collective Agreement for salaries   **596**

        E4: Salary reviews   **597**

        E5: Salary reviews   **597**

Commentary: Basic Salary   **598**

Precedent E1: Salaries

1 The rate of your starting salary and the method and frequency of payment are contained in your Statement of Terms and Conditions of Employment. (Subsequent changes will be advised in writing.)

2 Salaries are subject to annual review on _____ January each year.

3 Salaries are paid monthly in arrears by credit transfer to a bank account so that the money will be available in your bank or building society accounts on the ... day of each month or on the nearest working day beforehand. You agree that if, for reasons beyond the control of the

Company the payment of salary into your account is delayed, this will not amount to a breach of contract on the part of the Company.

4 At or before the time when your salary is paid you will be given a written itemised statement which will detail:

(a) the gross amount of salary;

(b) the amount of any variable or fixed deductions from that gross amount and the purposes for which they are made;

(c) the net amount of salary payable;

(d) where different parts of the net amount are paid different ways, the amount and method of payment of each part payment.

[e) Where your payment includes percentage over and above your salary in respect of advances against holiday entitlement (which you may choose to take in the future) the percentage and amount of such advance holiday payment.]

5 Deductions from salary are made for:

(a) National Insurance, State Pension and Income Tax where applicable, and any other deductions which are or become legally required;

(b) any Additional Voluntary Contributions to the appropriate Pension Scheme from your date of entry;

(c) any other contributions or subscriptions, such as to a Private Medical Insurance scheme, or repayments of loans such as season ticket advances, for which you have been given written authority. Requests for special deductions relating to your individual situation will be considered but the Company reserves the right to refuse such a facility.

(d) Any deductions which the Company has made and which it is entitled to make by virture of any agreement with you.

6 A day's pay will be calculated as annual pay divided by [260]. For calculating hourly rates for overtime purposes, an hour's pay is annual pay divided by 52, divided again by the number of hours worked per week.

Precedent E2: Salaries

1 Your rate of pay is as set out in your Letter of Appointment or your Written Particulars of Terms and Conditions of Employment which may be amended from time to time.

2 Your salary is paid by credit transfer monthly in arrears on _____ in twelve equal monthly amounts. If your employment terminates part way through a month your salary will be calculated on a daily basis.

3 You will receive a monthly itemised salary slip setting out your gross salary, statutory and other deductions and the net sum paid.

Precedent E3: Collective Agreements for Salaries

There is currently a collective agreement in force between the Company and _____ which covers all matters relating to pay which is negotiated from time to time with the union. Your employment is subject to this collective agreement and you are therefore bound by any agreement that is reached between the union and the Company regardless of whether you are a member of the union. You will be notified of any variations in your pay within one month of the same having been agreed with the union.

Precedent E4: Salary Reviews

Salaries are reviewed annually on ____ and any rise is awarded at the absolute discretion of the Company. Whilst the Company always endeavours to reward performance and effort it must be borne in mind that other factors have to be taken into account, including the profitability of the Company, team work and the competitiveness of the industry at the time. Salary increases will normally be announced _____ and will be notified to you in writing. [Your salary increase will remain confidential to you and the Company.] Increases in salary are at the absolute discretion of the Company.

Precedent E5: Salary Reviews

The Company has a policy of reviewing salaries based upon the contribution that the employee has made to the Company. The Company will normally consider the following matters in deciding whether there should be a salary increase for any one individual:

1) The self motivation of the employee and the contribution that has been made to the Company;

2) The current market rates and benefits in the industry. The Company prides itself on offering competitive market rates.

3) The profitability and turnover of the Company.

4) The responsibilities of the employee, including whether the employee has taken on increased responsibilities or duties.

Salaries will only be adjusted upwards. Any salary rises are at the absolute discretion of the Company.

COMMENTARY: BASIC SALARY

The above precedents contain standard clauses relating to payment of salary. The basic salary provisions should not normally cause any difficulties as salary will normally be agreed beforehand (see the next Part in relation to other payments which may cause complications).

Agreed remuneration

The remuneration agreed between employer and employee is subject to the National Minimum Wages Act 1998 (see below).

Where no remuneration has been agreed then the court will imply a term that it be a reasonable remuneration for the services (**Way v Latilla** [1937] 3 All ER 759) and a similar approach will be taken where it is agreed a bonus will be paid but the method of assessment has not been agreed (**Powell v Braun** [1954] 1 WLR 401).

Late payment of wages may be a fundamental breach of contract but this is not necessarily so where the employee knows that salary is on the way and of the reason for late payment (**Adams v Charles Zub Associates** [1978] IRLR 551). Precedent E1 contains provision for late payment.

Varying salary and other benefits: Express Terms

In the absence of any express power in the contract, or the agreement of the employee, any unilateral change in the employee's remuneration will be in breach of contract and can be resisted by the employee. Note that it is likely to be an unlawful deduction under Part II of the Employment Rights Act 1996 to make any deduction without the express consent of the employee (See Part F4). The difference in salary will remain repayable (**WPM Retail Limited v Lang** [1978] ICR 787). Where the employer commits a repudiatory breach of contract by reducing the salary the employee may refuse to accept this and stand by his rights under the contract or resign and claim constructive dismissal.

- **Managers (Holborn) Limited v Hohne** [1977] IRLR 230. The employer repudiated the contract of employment by reducing the employee's status and salary so that she was entitled to claim constructive dismissal and to a redundancy payment.

- **Miller v Hamworthy Engineering Limited** [1986] ICR 846; IRLR 461. The Court of Appeal held that the employers were not entitled to place employees on a three day week, with consequent reduction in salary without consent. It is stated that "...the defendants must show some agreed variation of the contractual terms binding upon the plaintiff".

- **Rigby v Feredo Limited** [1988] ICR 29; IRLR 516. The employer cut the wages of its employees as part of a strategy of survival. Employees of CSEU refused to accept this and continued to work as normal. The House of Lords held that, on the facts, there had been no notice of termination and the employees were entitled to work on under protest and sue on the original terms of the contract. The claims were for the sums due under the continuing contract that had never been terminated. Lord Oliver pointed out that the employer could have chosen to terminate on notice or dismiss out of hand and face the consequences but it chose neither of these options. It continued to employ the employees week by week under contracts which entitled them to a certain level of wages.

- **Burdett-Coutts & Ors v Hertfordshire County Council** [1984] IRLR 91. The Council sent a letter which purported to reduce the salary of its school dinner ladies. The letter stated that "This letter is the formal notice of these changes in your contract of service...". The claimant brought a claim for arrears of wages and a declaration that the Council were not entitled to unilaterally vary the contracts of employment. Kenneth Jones J held that the claimants were entitled to stand and sue on the contract. The letter was not a notice of termination and offer of re-engagement but an attempt to unilaterally vary the terms which was not effective.

The Precedents

The five precedents for salaries contained at Part E are relatively straightforward. Precedents E1 and E2 cover the timing and means of payment and confirm that an itemised pay statement will be sent whilst E3 deals with the position where the salary amount is governed by a collective agreement. E4 and E5 cover salary reviews. The following points should be noted:

- Where the employer awards pay rises to its staff there may be an implied term that the employer will not treat an employee in a manner which is arbitrary, capricious or inequitable. In **F C Gardner Limited v Beresford** [1978] IRLR 63, the employee had not been given a pay rise for two years whereas other staff had received one. She resigned and claimed constructive dismissal. The EAT held that there was such an implied term, stating:

> "if there was evidence to support the finding, that the employers were deliberately singling her out for special treatment inferior to that given to everybody else and they were doing it arbitrarily, capriciously or inequitably, if they did victimise in that sense, one could see it is might well lead the tribunal to say that she had a good claim..."

See also **Deniet & Son Limited v Eagle** [EAT 409/79] where the implied duty of trust and confidence was breached by the employer when the employee was not given a pay rise after a quarrel with a director and other employees were awarded a rise.

- Where there is no right to a pay increase the Court may be reluctant to imply a term that there should be an increase (**Murco Petroleum Limited v Forge** [1978] IRLR 50).

- In the case of employees who receive tips, these may amount to remuneration and would have to be shown on the itemised pay statement (**Nerva v RL & G Limited** [1996] IRLR 461, ECJ at [2002] IRLR 815 (and see Duggan, *Wrongful Dismissal and Breach of Contract* at page 415)

The National Minimum Wage

Useful websites

- See DTI site at

  http://www.dti.uk/er/nmw/index.htm)

  And

  www.lowpay.gov.uk/nmw/index.htm

The National Minimum Wages Act 1998 came into force on 1 April 1999. The Act provides the framework and the detail is fleshed out in the Regulations.

There have been a number of amendments to the Regulations. The complete set of Regulations are as follows:

- The National Minimum Wage Regulations 1999, SI 1999/584 and National Minimum Wage Act 1998 (Amendment) Regulations 1999, SI 1999/583 which were made on 6th March 1999 and came into effect on 1st April 1999.

- The National Minimum Wage (Offshore Employment) Order 1999 which came into effect on 1st May 1999.

- The National Minimum Wage (Increase in Development Rate for Young Workers) Regulations 2000 SI 2000/1411 which came into effect on 1st June 2000.

- The National Minimum Wage Regulations 1999 (Amendment) Regulations 2003 SI 2003/1923 which came into force on 1st October 2003

- The National Minimum Wage Regulations 1999 (Amendment) Regulations 2004 SI 2004/1161, which make new provision for output work and are expected to come into force in October 2004 (See Homeworkers at Chapter 5).

Full consideration of the complicated provisions of the Act and Regulations is beyond the scope of this book. However, the following points may be made:

- The minimum wage from October 2004 is £4.85 for adults over 21 and £4.10 for those aged 18 to 21. A minimum wage for 16 to 17 year olds is introduced at the sum of £3.00.

- A person qualifies for the NMW if he is a worker (See Chapter 1). Trainees on government training schemes are excluded whilst under 19 or during the first twelve months of the training scheme. Resident family workers and resident home helps are also excluded (1999 Regs. r. 2(2)).

- The self employed do not qualify (see **Smith Inland Revenue NMW Compliance Officer v Hewitson** [EAT 17.9.2001] and **Commissioners of Inland Revenue v Post Office Limited** [2003] IRLR 199).

- An employer may be in breach of the NMWA by seeking to switch discretionary payments to basic salary (See **Laird v AK Stoddard Ltd** [2001] IRLR 591; **Aviation and Airport Services Ltd v Bellfield** [EAT 14.3.2001].

- Tips which are paid direct do not count (**Nerva v UK** [2002] IRLR 815) but if they are added as a service charge and paid through a 'tronc' system they will count.

- There are four distinct types of work for the purpose of calculating working time for the minimum wage. The NMWR reg. 14(3) refers to 'time work', 'salaried hours work', 'output work' and 'unmeasured work'. The detail is contained in Part II of the Regulations. These types of work are dependant upon the way that the worker's pay is calculated so that it is possible for the worker to carry out more that one type of work.

- Time work is defined by NMWR reg. 3. This is work that is paid for according to set or varying hours or periods of time and which is not salaried hours work. It will include circumstances in which the worker's pay is set according to a measure of output per hour or other period of time during the whole of which the worker is required to work so that a pieceworker in a factory who is required to clock in and out at specified times will be covered. Time on call may count as timework (**British Nursing Association v Inland Revenue** [2002] EWCA Civ 494, [2002] IRLR 480, [2003] ICR 19; **Scottbridge Construction Ltd v Wright** [2003] IRLR 21).

- Salaried hours work is work done under a contract to do salaried hours under which the worker is entitled to no payment in addition to his annual salary other than a performance bonus (NMWR reg. 4(1)). Overtime or bonus payments will not prevent the work being salaried hours work.

- By Regulation 5 of the NMWR, output work is work which is paid for under a worker's contract that is not time work and which, apart from the national minimum wage, is paid for under the contract wholly by reference to the number of pieces made or processed by the worker or some other measure of output such as sales made or transactions completed. This will cover piecework or commission work

- By Regulation 6, unmeasured work is any work which is not time work, salaried hours work or output work including, in particular, work in respect of which there are no specified hours and the worker is required to work when needed or when work is available. (See **Walton v Independent Living Organisation Ltd** [2002] ICR 1406.)

- Once the type of work has been identified it is necessary to apply the appropriate test to decide what work counts for the purpose of calculating the NMW. The detail of this is contained in Part II and, in particular, regulations 15 to 19 of the 1999 Regulations.

PART F: REMUNERATION AND BENEFITS OTHER THAN SALARY

Precedent F: **Remuneration and Benefits other than salary**

F1:	**Overtime**	**606**
	F1.1: Overtime	606
	F1.2: Obligatory overtime	607
F2:	**Bonus**	**607**
	F2.1: Bonus	607
	F2.2: Bonus	607
F3:	**Commission**	**608**
F4:	**Deductions**	**608**
	F4.1: Deductions from salary	608
	F4.2: Deductions in retail employment	609
F5:	**Pensions**	**609**
	F5.1: Company Pension scheme	609
	F5.2: Employer contributions to personal pension scheme	610

F5.3: Group Personal pension scheme   610

F6: Health care   610

F6.1: Private medical health insurance   610

F7: Shares   611

F7.1: Approved Employee Share schemes   611

F8: Loans   611

F8.1: Educational Loans   611

F8.2: Season ticket loans   611

F9: Cars   612

F9.1: Car/car allowance   612

F9.2: Provision of a vehicle   613

F10: Luncheon vouchers   614

F11: PHI   614

Commentary: Remuneration and Benefits other than Salary 615

Precedent F1: Overtime

Precedent F1.1: Overtime

You will be entitled to be paid overtime for the hours you work in addition to your normal working hours. Overtime will be paid on an hourly basis at the rate of time and a half. For bank holidays and Sundays it will be paid at the rate of double time at the discretion of the Company. The Company reserves the right to vary overtime rates.

Overtime will not be taken into account in calculating your holiday entitlement.

Precedent F1.2: Obligatory overtime

Although your normal weekly hours are [number] you may be required to work overtime up to a limit of [hours] upon being given [period] notice. Such overtime does not count in calculating your holiday entitlement.

Precedent F2: Bonus

Precedent F2.1: Bonus

The Company may award an annual bonus and if you are entitled to such bonus it will have been specified in your Letter of Appointment. The bonus payment is entirely discretionary and the fact that you may have been paid a bonus in previous years does not mean that you are entitled or can have an expectation that you will get a bonus in any particular year. Bonuses are intended to reward exceptional effort which has increased the profitability of the Company. The size and nature of the bonus is at the absolute discretion of the Company.

Payment for the bonus is based upon [SET OUT THE FACTORS THAT WILL LEAD TO PAYMENT – SO FAR AS POSSIBLE THESE SHOULD BE OBJECTIVE]

Precedent F2.2: Bonus

The Company has a discretionary bonus scheme which applies to management and which depends on the Company's turnover as set out the rules of the scheme. **[It may be dangerous to link in bonus to company turnover as the employee will be entitled to payment even when absent (i.e. long term sick/maternity leave)]** If you are entitled to participate in the scheme this will have been set out in your Letter of Appointment. The payment of the bonus depends upon the Company attaining certain targets. However, it must be emphasised that the scheme is entirely discretionary and you are not entitled as a matter of contract or expectation to payment under such scheme. [The bonus is also based upon your contribution – SET OUT].

Precedent F3: Commission

In addition to your basic salary you are entitled to commission on orders as set out in your Letter of Appointment. Commission is only payable on monies received in respect of any order and will be paid in the monthly salary payment following clearance of an order through the Company's bank accounts.

Consider the following as a clause

Should your employment with the Company be terminated for any reason you will not be entitled to any further commissions in relation to any orders where payment has not been received by the Company as at the date of the termination of your employment.

Precedent F4: Deductions from Salary

Precedent F4.1: Deductions from Salary

The Company will be entitled:

1) At any time to deduct by way of reimbursement from your salary any overpayment of wages or expenses that have been paid to you for whatever reason.

2) Upon the termination of your employment to make any such deduction, including deduction in respect of holiday, loans or other advances that have been

made to you and which represent an overpayment at the date of the termination of your employment.

Precedent F4.2: Deductions from Pay in Retail Employment

The Company will be entitled at any time during employment or upon termination of employment to deduct from your wages any cash shortages or stock deficiencies for which you were responsible and any such deduction will be made in accordance with the provisions relating to retail employment contained in Part II of the Employment Rights Act 1996.

Precedent F5: Pensions

Precedent F5.1: Company Pension Scheme

1 You are entitled to join the Company's Pension Scheme and will be subject to the rules of that scheme as are in force from time to time. The Pension scheme may be amended or withdrawn by the Company at any time.

2 A contracting out certificate under the Pensions Schemes Act 1993 is [not] in force in respect of your employment.

3 The rules of the scheme provide that you may be a member if:

1) you are a permanent employee of the Company;

2) you are aged between _____ and _____ years old;

3) you have completed at least _____ years service with the Company.

4) Copies of the scheme are available for inspection at _____ .

5) You are entitled to make additional voluntary contributions to the Scheme to increase your

pension. Advice about this may be obtained from _____.

Precedent F5.2: Employer Contributions to Personal Pension Scheme

If you have your own personal pension plan the Company is prepared to contribute to it at rates which may be obtained from _____. [The Company will pay _____ per annum to a personal pension scheme approved by the Inland Revenue. There is no pension scheme arising from your employment with the Company. (N.B. Stakeholder Pension Schemes Act s.3 below must be considered.)]

Precedent F5.3: Group Personal Pension Scheme

There is a group pension scheme and you are entitled, if you so wish, to join the scheme. Contributions to the scheme will be deducted from your salary and you must inform _____ of the sum that you wish to be deducted from your salary and paid into the scheme. The Company will also pay a percentage into the scheme. These sums are subject to maximums permitted by the Inland Revenue and details may be obtained from _____.

Alternatively

The Company has provided access to a Stakeholder Pension Scheme for your benefit. Full details of the Rules of the Scheme may be obtained from _____.

Precedent F6: Medical Insurance

Precedent F6.1: Private Medical Health Insurance

Private Medical Health Insurance is available for all employees other than employees who are on probation or are temporary. The scheme may be extended to family members for an additional contribution. Full details of the scheme may be obtained from _____.

Precedent F7: Share Schemes

Precedent F7.1: Approved Employee Share Schemes

There is an employee share scheme for which you will be eligible if this was stated in your Letter of Appointment. The membership of the scheme is in accordance with the Trust Deeds and Rules of the scheme for the time being in force.

Precedent F8: Loans

Precedent F8.1: Educational Loans

F8.1.1 The Company may, at its discretion, give an interest free loan to assist you in a course of study for approved professional qualifications that relate to your job and you may obtain information about what courses are approved from _____.

F8.1.2 However, you should note that the Company will only grant such loan on the basis that you expressly agree that any sums advanced will be repaid if you fail to complete the course without sufficient justification or you leave the Company's employment either during the course or within ____ months of completing the course. The Company may also recover any sums advanced if you have been dismissed for gross misconduct.

Precedent F8.2: Season Ticket Loans

The Company will be prepared, at its discretion, to grant you an interest free season ticket loan for an annual season ticket on the following conditions:

1) The loan will be repayable by deductions from your salary on a monthly basis;

2) The loan will be repaid before the season ticket expires or is given up;

3) You will repay the balance of the loan in full if you leave the company's employment;

4) You will sign a document consenting to deductions being made before any loan is advanced to you.

Precedent F9: Cars

Precedent F9.1: Car/Car Allowance

1   Your Letter of Appointment sets out the basis on which the Company will provide you with a vehicle of a make and model determined by reference to the Company's Car Policy in effect from time to time for both business and private use.

2   If your Letter of Appointment so provided the Company will pay for all expenses of the vehicle save for private petrol and any additional costs that you incur in using the vehicle for private purposes.

3   The Company will replace the vehicle as provided for in its Car Policy and you agree that you will run the vehicle in accordance with the Car Policy.

4   Only employees who are aged over 21 (for insurance reasons) and who have a valid licence may drive any Company vehicle. Failure to comply with this requirement could lead to police prosecution as the driver will be uninsured and it will lead to disciplinary action by the Company for misconduct.

5   Employees using Company vehicles must not carry any unauthorised passengers.

Precedent F9.2:   Provision of a Vehicle

1   If you are provided with a vehicle by the Company it will be subject to you complying with the conditions set out hereafter.

2   Care of vehicle: You are responsible for ensuring that the vehicle is properly looked after at all times. You may only retain the vehicle if you have a full driving licence. You have the vehicle at the discretion of the Company and it may change its procedures at any time. Vehicles are insured on a third party basis and the Company may seek to recoup any losses in the event of negligence.

3   Nature of vehicle: You will be entitled to a vehicle in accordance with the terms of your Letter of Appointment and the vehicle may be replaced after ____ miles or at the discretion of the Company. You have no right to a replacement.

4   Car documents: The Company will retain all documents relating to the registration of the vehicle. You are responsible for ensuring that the car has an MOT certificate and a valid licence disc.

5   Personal Use: Your spouse may use the vehicle provided that he/she has a valid licence. Other members of staff may use it provided that they have a licence and are covered by the Company's insurance scheme.

6   Upkeep: You are responsible for ensuring that the car is properly maintained and serviced and that the car is in roadworthy condition. The Company will bear the cost of repairs and service provided that they are not caused by your negligence or default.

7   Motoring offences: You are responsible for the payment of any fines incurred as a result of a motoring offence, including parking fines. You must notify the Company of any serious offence that may result in the loss of your licence or cause the Company any loss.

8   Tax: You agree to bear any tax liability in respect of the use of the vehicle.

9   You may be required to return the vehicle to the Company if you have been absent due to illness for a period of [period] months. [NOTE THAT CONSIDERATION WOULD HAVE TO BE GIVEN TO WHETHER SOMEONE HAS A DISABILITY BEFORE THIS CLAUSE IS UTILISED].

10   Termination of employment: Should your employment terminate for whatever reason, you agree that you will immediately return your vehicle and deliver up the keys to _____.

11   Alternative allowance: You may be entitled to an allowance as an alternative to the provision of a Company vehicle and should contact _____ for details of the same.

Precedent F10: Luncheon Vouchers

Luncheon vouchers are provided by the Company if this was set out in your Letter of Appointment. They are issued at the rate of _____ per day. Vouchers are a taxable benefit and must be declared on your tax return. Vouchers are provided at the Company's discretion and may be withdrawn at any time.

Precedent F11: Permanent Health Insurance

The Company operates a permanent health insurance scheme of which you are eligible to be a member. The Scheme is in the absolute discretion of the Company and may be discontinued at any time. You should also note that it is the decision of the insurer as to whether you qualify for permanent health benefits under the Scheme and the Company has no responsibility or liability for decisions made by the insurer. You are referred to the rules of the Scheme which sets out eligibility.

COMMENTARY: REMUNERATION AND BENEFITS OTHER THAN SALARY

There are a wide range of benefits that may be available to employees other than salary, whether by way of cash payments or benefits in kind, with different tax consequences and consequences should there be a dismissal (These are considered in detail in Duggan on *Breach of Contract and Wrongful Dismissal* at Chapters 3, 6 and 14).

Fringe benefits are often an important part of the employee's remuneration package so that withdrawal of the same may amount to a fundamental breach of contract or found a claim for constructive dismissal. In **McColl v Gael Motors (Dumbarton) Limited** [EAT 63/80] the employee was given the use of a company car to travel to and from work and the company did not object to her using it at weekends. She also received a petrol allowance. When insurance terms were re-negotiated she was no longer able to use the car at weekends. She alleged constructive dismissal. The EAT stated that the withdrawal of a fringe benefit could be of sufficient materiality to amount to a dismissal. In this case, however, the essential element was transport to and from work which was not affected in any way by the proposed variation.

Each of the benefits set out in the Precedents above will be reviewed briefly.

F1: Overtime

A precedent is contained at F1. Further precedents can be found at D2. It is to be noted that overtime will not usually count for the purpose of calculating holiday entitlement (See Part I).

F2: Bonus

Bonus is likely to be expressed to be discretionary and based upon the profitability or turnover of the Company or upon the effort of the individual employee. Although expressed to be discretionary caution should be exercised in this respect as the payment of bonus may become a 'legitimate expectation'. The two precedents in F2 state that the payment of bonus is entirely discretionary. However, in **Kent Management Services Limited v Butterfield** [1972] ICR 272; IRLR 394, it was held that a commission scheme that was expressed to be non contractual nevertheless gave rise to a claim for deduction from wages as there was a legitimate expectation that the employee would be paid.

The bonus payment may in some cases be the most important element of remuneration, as in the City where huge bonuses may be the motivating force of the particular job in question. In such cases it is important that the circumstances in which bonus will be payable are precisely defined. Even where the bonus is expressed to be discretionary, there will be limits as to the manner in which the employer may exercise its discretion, as recent cases have made clear.

In **Clark v Nomura** [2000] IRLR 766, the employee was entitled to participate in a bonus scheme which provided that the bonus was "Not guaranteed in any way, and is dependant upon individual performance and after the first 12 months remaining in employment on the date of payment." Mr Clark was dismissed in February 1997 but was in employment in March 1997 when bonuses were paid. He was not awarded a bonus. It was argued that he was not entitled to a bonus because of his poor performance, which it was asserted included all aspects of his performance. It was asserted that his non-financial performance had been poor. Burton J thought that the exercise of discretion was subject to the fetter of assessment by reference to individual performance, which meant performance of the contract. Whilst profitability for a trader was an important aspect of performance other factors such as corporate contribution, team working, capital usage and due regard to risk were to be taken into account, but in the context of the requirement to make a profit and the actual obligations under the contract. In the absence of any deficiency or variation in individual performance the employee was entitled to be treated equally to other employees. The decision to award Mr Clark a nil bonus was irrational and perverse and irrelevant factors had been taken into account. Burton J stated at paragraph 40:

"Quite apart from the additional contractual straitjacket for the discretion in this case, the employer's discretion is in any event, as a result of the authorities, not unfettered, as both sides have accepted to be the law in this case. Even a simple discretion whether to award a bonus must not be exercised capriciously (**United Bank Ltd v Akhtar** [1989] IRLR 507 EAT, **Clark v BET plc** [1997] IRLR 348 and **Midland Bank plc v McCann** 5/6/1998 unreported EAT) or without reasonable or sufficient grounds (**White v Reflecting Roadstuds Ltd** [1991] IRLR 331 EAT, and **McClory v Post Office** [1993] IRLR 159). I do not consider that either of these definitions of the obligation is entirely apt, when considering whether an employer was in breach of contract in having exercised a discretion which on the face of the contract is unfettered or absolute, or indeed even one which is contractually fettered such as the one here considered. Capriciousness, it seems to me, is not very easy to define: and I have been referred to **Harper v National Coal Board**

[1980] IRLR 260 and **Cheall v APEX** [1982] IRLR 362. It can carry with it aspects of arbitrariness or domineeringness, or whimsicality and abstractedness. On the other hand the concept of 'without reasonable or sufficient grounds' seems to me to be too low a test. I do not consider it is right that there be simply a contractual obligation on an employer to act reasonably in the exercise of his discretion, which would suggest that the court can simply substitute its own view for that of the employer. My conclusion is that the right test is one of irrationality or perversity (of which caprice or capriciousness would be a good example) i.e. that no reasonable employer would have exercised his discretion in this way. I canvassed this provisional view in the course of argument with both counsel, and neither appeared to dissent, and indeed Mr Temple QC in his closing submissions expressly adopted and used a test of irrationality. Such test of perversity or irrationality is not only one which is simple, or at any rate simpler, to understand and apply, but it is a familiar one, being that regularly applied in the Crown Office or, as it is soon to be, the Administrative Court. In reaching its conclusion, what the court does is thus not to substitute its own view, but to ask the question whether any reasonable employer could have come to such a conclusion. Of course, if and when the court concludes that the employer was in breach of contract, then it will be necessary to reach a conclusion, on the balance of probabilities, as to what would have occurred had the employer complied with its contractual obligations, or, as Timothy Walker J put it in **Clark v BET plc** [1997] IRLR 348, assess, without unrealistic assumptions, what position the employee would have been in had the employer performed its obligation. That will involve the court in assessing the employee's bonus, on the basis of the evidence before it, and thus to that extent putting itself in the position of the employer; but it will only do it if it is first satisfied, on the higher test, not that the employer acted unreasonably, but that no reasonable employer would have reached the conclusion it did acting in accordance with its contractual obligations, and the assessment of the bonus then of course is by way of an award of damages."

See also **Manor House Healthcare v Hayes & Skinner** [EAT 1196/99] where a similar test was propounded.

(C.f. **Mallone v BPB Industries** [2002] IRLR 452 on discretion in relation to share options)

Where the employer has a discretionary Scheme and agrees to notify the employee of the Scheme it will be bound until such time as the employer notifies the employee that the scheme has been withdrawn or varied (**Chequepoint (UK) Limited v Radwan** [CA 15.9.2000]).

It is apparent from these cases that, in order to ensure that the exercise of discretion will 'stand up', employers should have regard to the purpose of the bonus scheme and any statement in the Scheme rules (i.e. motivation, reward and retention of employees) and should ensure that there is consistency between employees who perform on a similar level.

Where the scheme stipulates that employees must be in employment at the time that a bonus is paid it may be that the right to a bonus will be lost (See **Peninsular Business Services Ltd v Sweeney** [2004] IRLR 49 and **Brennan v Mills & Allen Ltd** [EAT 418/99]. However, in *Clark* at paragraph 38, Burton J was of the view that a purported summary dismissal to avoid payment of a bonus may be rejected by the employee who may keep the contract alive. (See also **Re: Richmond Gate Property Co Ltd** [1964] 3 All ER 936 – no scope for quantum meruit and **Item Software (UK) Ltd v Fasshi** [2003] IRLR 769 in which it was held that the Apportionment Act 1870 does not assist where the bonus is payable after employment has ended. See now CA at [2004] EWCA 1244.)

There may be a claim for sex discrimination when a bonus is not paid; See **Barton v Investec Henderson** [2003] IRLR 332). The failure to pay bonus because of absence may also give rise to a claim for disability discrimination where the employee is absent due to disability or sex discrimination where the employee is absent due to maternity.

Where the terms of a bonus scheme are contained in a collective agreement they will remain in force if incorporated into the contract, even if the collective agreement is terminated (**Robertson v British Gas Corporation** [1983] ICR 351).

Implied Terms

In the absence of express terms the implied terms may still have a part to play as the following cases show:

*   **Frischers Limited v Taylor** [EAT 386/79]. Where a week's wages had been paid as a Christmas bonus for several years this consistent conduct made it an implied term that the bonus would be paid as part of the employee's remuneration.

- **Noble Enterprises v Lieberum** [EAT 67/98] IDS Brief 623. BP provided money to participating companies, which provided labour for BP explorations, to be paid to employees as an incentive bonus scheme. The companies decided what proportion of the monies should be paid to its employees. When Mr Lieberum resigned on 21st January 1997 he was not paid a bonus. The employer argued that it was discretionary and was, in any event, not payable if the employee was not employed on 30th January of each year. The EAT held that the scheme was contractual in that, once BP had paid monies to the company, the scheme became contractually operative, the consideration from the employee being that a certain standard was achieved. Moreover, there was no evidence that the requirement of being employed at a certain date had ever been drawn to the attention of the employee.

- In **Pendragon PLC v Jackson** [EAT 108/97] IDS Brief 622 it was held that the fact that the employers had inserted a term into a share incentive scheme stating that it was non contractual was an indication that the employer did not intend the scheme to create legal relations so that there was no legally binding obligation to pay out under the scheme.

It may be a breach of an implied term to provide work to refuse to allow an employee to work a shift so that the employee can earn a shift premium or overtime (**Langston v AUEW & Anor** (No 2) [1974] ICR 510; IRLR 182).

F3: Commission

(See further Duggan, *Wrongful Dismissal and Breach of Contract* at pp 396–398.)

For many employees commission may be an important part of remuneration and, in some case, the only remuneration (see 5.15 for a Salesman's contract). Again, in the absence of express terms, implied terms are likely to play an important part. Where the express term of the commission agreement states that commission will be excluded if the employee is not in employment at the date that commission would otherwise be payable then the employee will be bound by this term. This was the conclusion of the EAT in **Peninsula Business Services Limited v Sweeney** [2004] IRLR 49.

It was held in **Steen v Ikon Office Solutions plc**, EAT on 20 May 2003, [EAT/236/02/ILB] that where a clause in an agreement provided that the employee would be paid commission "subject to such conditions and at such times as the company shall notify you in writing from time to time", this meant the employer had to tell the employee not only that there was commission but how it would be paid, when it would be paid, whether and how it had been changed and, if that was the case, that it had been discontinued. The employee did not receive a copy of an amended plan. It was held that he was entitled to commission based upon the old plan of which he was aware.

Implied terms

Where the employee earns part of his remuneration by way of commission there may be an implied term on the part of the employer that the employee be provided with work so that a suspension on basic salary can be a repudiatory breach of contract. In **Re Rubel Bronze & Metal Co Limited v Vos** [1918] 1 KB 315 the employee was suspended during an investigation into allegations of inefficiency on his part. McCardie J held that where an employee is paid by way of commission he must be given an opportunity to earn it.

Where an employee receives advance commission and the employment terminates, or the monies upon which the commission was paid is not forthcoming for some reason, then there will be an implied term that the employee will account for the excess (**Bronester Limited v Priddle** [1961] 1 WLR 1294). The employee will be liable for any secret profits that he has earned during employment, even if they would not have been earned by the employer (**Boston Deep Sea Fishing & Ice Co Limited v Ansell** [1988] 39 ChD 339).

As stated in F3 it is should be made clear that commission will only be payable in respect of payments actually received rather than orders placed. This will have the effect that sums are likely to remain due after the employee has left the employment of the employer and some consideration may be given as to whether there should be a provision whereby any sums received may be set off against any monies that may be owed by the employee.

F4: Deductions from Salary

Part II of the Employment Rights Act 1996 (previously the Wages Act 1986), sections 13 to 27 sets out rights not to suffer unauthorised deductions from wages and there are specific provisions relating to retail employment. Precedent F4 sets out two clauses which permit the employer to deduct certain sums from wages. However, these clauses must be incorporated into the contract if they are to be effective (See 5.14 Shop workers). The provisions of the ERA 1996 will be here summarised.

1. Right not to suffer unauthorised deductions

By section 13 of the ERA an employer may not make a deduction from wages of a worker employed by him unless:

- the deduction is required or authorised to be made by virtue of a statutory provision or a relevant provision of the worker's contract (which means a provision in a contract comprised in one or more written terms given before the deduction or the existence and effect of which has been previously notified in writing); or

- the worker has previously signified in writing his agreement or consent to the making of the deduction.

The employee must be notified individually so that a notice on a notice board will not be sufficient (**Kerr v The Sweater Shop** [1996] IRLR 424). Written consent can include consent given over the internet (**Mondesir v Lloyds TSB Bank PLC** [EAT 19.12.2003).

The employee must have already given consent when the deduction is made so that consent given after, for example a theft, to reimbursement is invalid (**Discount Tobacco and Confectionary Limited v Williamson** [1993] IRLR 327).

Consent cannot be implied (**Watt (MJ) Decorators Ltd v Davies** [2000] IRLR 759).

If there is a variation of the contract then a deduction will not be authorised until the variation takes effect (13(5)) nor will an agreement or consent authorise making the deduction on account of the conduct of any worker before the agreement or consent takes effect (13(6)).

Where the total amount of wages paid is less than the amount properly payable on that occasion the amount of the deficiency is treated as deduction (13(2)) but this does not apply to an error of computation (13(4)).

Where the worker agrees to a deduction he may still be able to argue that the amount deducted was an excessive deduction and claim that the excess is a deduction from wages (**Fairfield Ltd v Skinner** [1992] ICR 836).

Unilateral reductions in wages will be unlawful deductions under Part II of the ERA 1996 (**Bruce v Wiggins Teape (Stationery) Limited** [1994] IRLR 536). It was an unlawful deduction for an employer to hold back tips under the tronc system (**Saavedra v Aceground Limited t/a Terraza-Est** [1995] IRLR 198).

2. Wages and excepted deductions

By section 14, section 13 does not apply to a deduction where:

- it relates to the reimbursement of an overpayment of wages (But note that where the employee innocently receives the money and spends it an estoppel may arise: **Lipkin Gorman (A Firm) v Karpnale Ltd** [1992] 4 All ER 512 and see, for a case of anticipatory reliance: **Commerzbank AG v Gareth Price-Jones** [2003] EWCA Civ 1663).

- it relates to an overpayment in respect of expenses incurred by the worker in carrying out his employment;

- it relates to a deduction in consequence of any disciplinary proceedings if the proceedings were held by reason of a statutory provision (this will not apply to private disciplinary hearings – **Chiltern House Ltd v Chambers** [1990] IRLR 88).

- it relates to a deduction by reason of a statutory requirement to pay amounts over to a local authority;

- it relates to arrangements which have been established in accordance with the contract, the inclusion of which the worker has signified his agreement or consent in writing or with the prior agreement or consent of the worker in writing;

- it is made where the worker has taken part in a strike or other industrial action;

- it is made with proper agreement or consent where there is an order of a court that money be paid to the employer.

Errors of computation will not attract the benefit of the remedies for unlawful deductions (**Morgan v Glamorgan County Council** [1995] IRLR 68) but where the employer wrongly believes that it is not obliged to make a payment and does not make it there may be an unlawful deduction from wages (**Yemm v British Steel PLC** [1994] IRLR 117).

3. Payments to the employer and excepted payments

As with deductions, there is protection for workers in relation to payments that may otherwise have to be made. By section 15:

- an employer may not receive a payment from a worker unless the payment is required or authorised to be made by virtue of a statutory provision or a relevant provision of a worker's contract; or

- the worker has previously signified in writing his agreement or consent to the making of the payment.

The section contains the same restrictions in relation to variations or modifications as section 13.

Payments are, by section 16, excepted where:

- it relates to the reimbursement of an overpayment of wages;

- it relates to an overpayment in respect of expenses incurred by the worker in carrying out his employment;

- it relates to a deduction in consequence of any disciplinary proceedings if the proceedings were held by reason of a statutory provision;

- it is made where the worker has taken part in a strike or other industrial action;

- it is made where there is an order of a court that money be paid to the employer.

Retail Employment: Restrictions on Deductions

There are special protections for retail workers in sections 17 to 22 of the ERA. 'Retail transactions' mean the sale or supply of goods, or the supply of services, including financial services, and 'retail employment' means employment involving:

- the carrying out by the worker of retail transactions directly with members of the public or with fellow workers or other individuals in their personal capacities;

- the collection by the worker of amounts payable in connection with retail transactions carried out by other persons directly with members of the public or fellow workers or other individuals in their personal capacities.

The protection applies to deductions or payments due to cash shortages which cover deficits arising in relation to amounts received in connection with retail transactions and to stock deficiencies arising in the course of such transactions, whether or not a deduction of payment is made on account of dishonesty or any other event in respect of which the worker had any contractual liability.

By section 18(1) where the employer of a worker employed in retail employment in accordance with the powers under section 13 makes on account of one or more cash shortages or stock deficiencies a deduction or deductions from wages payable to the worker on a pay day, the amount shall not exceed one tenth of the wages payable on that pay day. Any deduction must be made in any event within 12 months of when the shortage or deficiency was established or ought reasonably to have been established (18(3)). Where the wages are determined by reference to shortages or deficiencies this will be treated as a deduction so that sections 13 and 18 apply.

There are similar protections for payment contained in section 20. By section 20 the worker should have first been notified in writing of the total amount and required to pay by means of a demand, not earlier than the first pay day following the date when the worker was notified and not later than 12 months after discovery of the shortage. By section 21 the amount to be paid shall not exceed one tenth.

Where the worker receives a final instalment of wages there are no restrictions on the amount of any deduction or payments (section 22). This means that, provided section 13 applies, the one tenth rule is not applicable to a final payment on termination.

Enforcement

A worker may apply to the tribunal where there has been an unauthorised deduction from wages (see section 23 ERA 1996).

The two precedents at F4 contain provisions relating to deductions from salary in relation to retail and non-retail employment.

F5: Pensions

It is likely that the rules of any pension scheme will be in a separate document and the Manual or contract will merely state what entitlement the employee has and refer to the Rules of the Scheme. The precedents at F5 adopt this approach. The employee cannot be required to join a personal or occupational pension scheme and any term to this effect is void (section 160 Pension Schemes Act 1993). It should be noted that, since the rules of the scheme are likely to change from time to time, there may be a duty on the part of the employer to tell the employee of his rights and any matters that may affect the value of his pension (see **Scally v Southern Health and Social Services Board** [1992] 1 AC and page 54 above). However, it was held by the Court of Appeal in **Outram v Academy Plastics** (CA 10.4.2000) that there was no duty owed in tort to the employee by the employer. Moreover, in **University of Nottingham v Eyett** [1999] IRLR 87, the High Court held that there was no implied contractual duty on the part of an employer to advise the employee that if he waited one month before retiring he would be entitled to an enhanced pension. The scope of the implied term still remains unclear and the prudent employer will make it clear that it accepts no contractual liability in relation to advice.

From 8 October 2001 the employer will be under a duty to provide access to a Stakeholder Pension Scheme provided certain conditions are met (see Chapter 4). The employer is under no duty to contribute to the scheme but must administer it by deducting employee's contributions and paying them into the scheme.

F6: Medical Insurance

This clause relates to the provision of health insurance to cover medical bills for hospital, operations, etc. and is likely to be regarded by a senior employee as an important part of the package. Consideration should be given as to whether this benefit is to cover members of the employee's family as well as the employee. It may be that the employer will also wish to have a right to withdraw such insurance if it becomes too expensive and a clause giving the employer such a general discretion may be advisable.

F7: Share Schemes

This benefit will usually be subject to the rules of the particular scheme and the employee will need to refer to the express rules of the scheme in order to ascertain when options may be exercised. Issues have arisen in the cases as to when a scheme may automatically lapse and as to the effect of termination of employment before an option is exercised. These matters will, of course, depend upon the wording of the scheme.

In **Thompson v ASDA MFI Group PLC** [1988] IRLR 340, Mr Thompson, who was employed by a wholly owned subsidiary, Wades Limited, was given an option to subscribe for shares. The option certificate provided that the option would lapse in the event of "the option holder ceasing to be in the employment of the company or a participating subsidiary." ASDA sold all its shares in Wades Limited and wrote to Mr Thompson stating that the shares lapsed when Wades ceased to be a member of the Group. Scott J held that the shares options lapsed when the shares in Wades were sold and it is was not possible to imply any term to the effect that ASDA would not do anything to cause the option to lapse or sell off the participating subsidiaries. There was no breach of duty on the part of ASDA so that it is could not be argued that they could not take advantage of their own acts.

In **Micklefield v SAC Technology Limited** [1990] IRLR 218, Mr Micklefield had the benefit of a share option scheme of the parent company. He was entitled to six months notice of termination of employment. The share scheme provided that the option was not exercisable until three years after grant and that if an option holder ceased to be an executive for whatever reason he would not be entitled and would be deemed to have waived any entitlement by way of compensation for loss of any rights under the scheme. On 19th February 1985 he was granted an option. On 3rd February 1988 he wrote stating that he wished to exercise the option on 19th February 1988. His contract was terminated forthwith on 12th February and he was paid in lieu. It was held that he was not entitled to exercise the option as his contract had terminated before the option became exercisable. Liability was clearly excluded and the clause did not fall within section 3 of the Unfair Contract Terms Act 1977 as it is fell within the exclusion of any contract so far as it is relates to the creation or transfer of securities or of any right or interest in securities. (C.f. **Chapman v Aberdeen Construction Group PLC** [1991] IRLR 505 for the position in Scotland.)

However, where an employee is dismissed in breach of contract the employer may not be able to rely on a clause that provides that the option would lapse in the event of the employee being dismissed following disciplinary action. In **Levett v Biotrace International PLC** [1999] IRLR 375 the Court of Appeal held that an employer was not entitled to rely on its own breach in these circumstances.

The Court of Appeal considered the exercise of share options in **Mallone v BPB Industries Plc** [[2002] IRLR 452. Options were granted by the directors each year in light of the employee's performance. After three years, they matured and could be exercised. The rules of the scheme gave the employer "absolute discretion" to decide the "appropriate proportion" of mature options an employee who left the company for reasons other than misconduct would be allowed to retain. After Mr. Mallone was dismissed because his performance was regarded as having deteriorated, the directors decided that the appropriate proportion in his case was zero, and cancelled all his options. The Court of Appeal upheld finding that this was an irrational decision. Rix LJ stated:

"a valid reason for treating the whole scheme as a sort of mirage whereby the executive is welcomed as a participant, encouraged to perform well in return for reward, granted options in recognition of good performance, led on to further acts of good performance and loyalty, only to learn at the end of his possibly many years of employment, when perhaps the tide has turned and his powers are waning, that his options, matured and vested as they may have become, are removed from him without explanation."

Where the employee had been employed for three years the starting point was 36/36 months as, though the employers in this case had an absolute discretion under the rule, their discretion still remained one to find "the appropriate proportion" and in deciding the proportion it was:

"hard to see why someone who was not being dismissed for misconduct should on the ground of his performance after the vesting of his options be treated just the same as one who was being dismissed summarily for misconduct."

The committee's minutes were silent as to its reasoning, and there was no sign that any regard was had to the fact that the options were granted at a time when the claimant's performance was clearly regarded as excellent. The committee's decision was one which no reasonable employer could have reached.

F8: Loans

Where the employee is provided with training paid for by the employer or the employer pays for the employee to go on a course, there may be a term in the contract that the employee will refund part of the costs of the training if he leaves before a certain period of time. In **Neil v Strathclyde Regional**

Council [1984] IRLR 14 the employee was given paid leave to go on a training course as a social worker. She signed a contract that stated she would stay in employment for two years and would repay "an amount proportionate to the unexposed service period" covering her salary and the cost of training. She resigned after fifteen months and a liquidated sum was claimed. It was held that she was liable to repay the proportionate amount.

Unless the employee has agreed in writing, deductions from salary in relation to a loan that has been made are likely to be unlawful deductions (**Potter v Hunt Contracts Ltd** [1992] ICR 337, EAT).

F9: Cars

Express Terms

The employee may be contractually entitled to a car or a car allowance. Once he has become contractually entitled it will be a breach of contract to take away the benefit unless there is an express power to do so.

- **Knox v Down District Council** [1981] IRLR 452. The National Joint Council conditions of service provided that

    "any officer whose employing authority so resolves that it is essential in the interests of the efficient conduct of the business of the Authority that the officer shall be permitted to use his private car for the carrying out of his official duties shall be eligible for financial assistance in accordance with this scheme".

It was further provided that the Authority may on receipt of an application, subject to the terms of the scheme, authorise the grant of a loan not exceeding the purchase price. The Council turned down an application because of lack of financial resources. The Northern Ireland Court of Appeal held that there was an implied term that, once the conditions had been complied with, the applicant would receive a loan under the scheme.

- In **Keir & Williams v County Council of Hereford and Worcester** [1985] IRLR 505 the Council paid an 'essential user allowance' to certain employees under terms agreed by the National Joint Council, depending upon authorisation by the Council. The NJC Conditions defined essential users as "those whose duties are of such a nature that it is essential for them to have a motor car at their disposal when required", and casual users as "those for whom it is merely desirable that a car will be available when required". An essential user received a greater allowance than a casual user. Keir and Williams were told that their essential user allowance was to cease and that they could use a pool car and therefore would receive a casual user allowance. The Court of Appeal held that once an employee had been given authority to use his car for Council business he was entitled to an essential user allowance. The Council could not take away the essential user allowance in the case of someone who needed to use his car simply because a pool car was available.

It was held in **Ropaigealach v THF Hotels Limited** [EAT 180/80] that the withdrawal of free transport which only cost the employer £1 per week was not so fundamental as to amount to a breach of contract on the part of the employer. On the other hand where employees were provided with free transport in a company car over several years, at a loss in excess of £14 per week and that entailed two hours walking, such provision had become a term by custom and practice so that the employer could not withdraw the same (**Power Lines Pipes & Cables Limited v Penrice** (EAT 29.1.1987)).

F10: Luncheon Vouchers

This is a common perk for office workers and a sample precedent is at F10.

F11: Health Insurance Schemes

The contract of employment may provide that the employee is entitled to the benefit of a health scheme or PHI Scheme which is administered by an insurer and operated at the discretion of the insurer. Whilst there may be a power to dismiss the employee on notice any express terms may be affected by implied terms as the following cases illustrate.

Implied terms

- **Aspen v Webbs Poultry & Meat Group Holdings Limited** [1996] IRLR 521. Mr Aspen was entitled to the benefit of income replacement insurance which applied from 26 weeks after incapacity and continued until death, retirement or "the date on which the group member ceases to be an eligible employee". His contract provided that the Company could dismiss him if he was absent for 183 days in any twelve months due to illness of accident. He was absent on sickness certificates and was given three months' notice of dismissal as the employer thought he was malingering. Sedley J held that there was an implied term that he would not be deprived of his entitlement under the scheme whilst incapacitated for work save for summary dismissal in response to a repudiatory breach of contract on his part. This term could be implied notwithstanding the contract provided for termination after a period of absence. The contract had been entered into during the currency of the employment and was not intended to replace the scheme nor was it is drafted with the scheme in mind.

Where an insurance policy is terminated without notice to the employee and the contract permits this, any sickness benefits will not thereby automatically terminate unless and until the employee is informed that the contract has been varied (**Bainbridge v Circuit Foil UK Limited** [1997] ICR 541; IRLR 305).

It was held in **Briscoe v Lubrizol Limited and Anor** [2002] IRLR 607 that once a claim has been rejected by the insurer the only remedy lay in suing the employer for breach of contract as the insurer did not owe any duty of care to the employee.

It has been held that there may be an implied term that the employer takes all reasonable steps to get the insurer to pay under a scheme (see **Jowitt v Pioneer Technology (UK) Ltd** [2003] IRLR 356 and see Part J). Moreover, the Contracts (Rights of Third Parties) Act 1999 may be a route by which the employee can claim against the insurer.

PHI Schemes normally apply only to existing employees so that any termination of employment may end the right to claim (**Bastick v Yamaichi** [1993] (unreported CA).

(See Duggan, *Wrongful Dismissal and Breach of Contract* at 6.16).

PART G: PLACE OF WORK AND MOBILITY

Precedent G: **Place of work and mobility**

G1: **G1–4 Precedents** 632

    1. **UK** 632

    2. **Head office** 632

    3. **Worldwide** 632

    4. **Miles** 632

G2: **Relocation Policy** 633

    1. **Aim of Policy** 633

    2. **Entitlement** 634

    3. **Precedure for Claiming under the Relocation Policy** 634

    4. **Full Relocation Assistance** 636

    5. **Inland Revenue** 637

G3: **Application Form** 638

Commentary on G: **Place of Work and Mobility** 639

Precedent G1: Place of Work and Mobility

Precedent G1.1:   Your normal workplace is _____.

However, you accept that you will work at any other establishment of the Company within the United Kingdom whether on a temporary or permanent basis as your contract with the Company shall so require for the needs of the business. You also agree that you will make visits to clients or other establishments of the Company throughout the United Kingdom and abroad as may be required.

Precedent G1.2:   You agree that you are employed to work from the Head Office of the Company and that you are prepared to work from the Head Office wherever it may be located. You also agree that you will be mobile and prepared to work from any establishment of the Company to which you may, on reasonable notice, be instructed to move.

Precedent G1.3:   The Company operates [in the following territories] [on a worldwide] basis. You agree that, subject to having been given [days] [reasonable] notice, you will transfer to any of the Company's locations within the area where the Company carries out its activities.

Precedent G1.4:   You agree to carry out work for the Company within a radius of [   ] miles from the Company's premises at _____.

Precedent G2: Relocation Policy

RELOCATION POLICY

1. Aim of Policy

The purpose of this policy is to ensure that:

- Employees who are asked to relocate within the terms and conditions of their employment are given a reasonable period of time to make arrangements for relocation and are able to raise any problems or difficulties that they may have with the proposed move.

- Employees are reimbursed for reasonable relocation expenses as a result of the change in their place of employment.

- New employees who are relocating as a result of being offered employment with the Company are reimbursed for reasonable relocation expenses.

This policy will apply to employees who are requested to relocate and to new employees who are taking up employment with the company and that have to relocate as a result.

Where new employees are required to relocate in order to take up employment their entitlement will be determined individually and set out in the offer of employment or in a separate document.

This policy is not to be regarded as contractual and the Company reserves the right to apply or vary the policy as it appropriate.

Any additional benefits that are payable under this policy are subject to the maximum allowances that may be granted by the Inland Revenue limits from time to time and whatever rules or requirements for eligibility the Inland Revenue or other statutory authorities may have in place from time to time.

2. Entitlement

In order to be entitled under this Policy the relocation must involve a change of the employee's main residence.

Any entitlement only arises in the relevant tax year in which the move took place.

In deciding whether the Employee is entitled to payment for relocation and the level of any payment the Company will take into account.

- The location of the current main residence and work base.

- The location of the proposed new main residence in conjunction with the place of work to which the employee is moving.

- The existing and proposed new travel arrangements, including the distance, method of travel (i.e. rail, car), time taken each day and the cost of such travel.

- The cost to the employee of moving place of work (including whether the employee is to receive a substantial pay rise because of the move).

- The business interests and needs of the Company in the employee relocating.

It will be expected that if the employee is relocating his/her main residence this will be within [number] minutes/hours of the new place of work and/or one way daily travel will be no more than [number] miles or [number] minutes/hours.

Eligibility under this Policy will be decided by .... If you are not satisfied with any decision made under this Policy you may utilise the Company's Grievance procedure.

3. Procedure for Claiming under the Relocation Policy

The following procedure will apply (subject to the terms and conditions of your offer of employment or of your contract of employment):

(1) You must seek approval from [   ] before any expenses will be authorised. This approval must be sought before you incur such

expenses. If you incur expenses without approval then the Company will not sanction them in any event.

(2) If relocation expenses are approved you will be provided with a written offer setting out the level and limit of expenditure. You must return this to [   ] as soon as possible. The offer will set out what items are covered and the period over which assistance will be granted and will become binding once you have signified your acceptable in writing. Payments will not be made until the offer is accepted in writing.

(3) If the offer of relocation assistance on upon change of main residence is accepted, you must commence relocation soon as possible. The Company is may withdraw the offer if there is no evidence that the relocation has begun within [   ] months. If relocation does not take place within [   ] months the offer will be regarded as withdrawn and you will have to make another application.

(4) You must submit proof of expense for all approved expenses and receipts must be provided for individual items of expenditure before payment will be made.

(5) If you have been paid relocation assistance on change of main residence, but leave employment with the Company or your contract is terminated in circumstances where the Company was entitled to terminate your contract because of your conduct.

• within three years of the date on which you were paid relocation expenses the Company shall be entitled to recover all or a proportion of the total monies paid through relocation assistance and which are still outstanding.

or

• Repayment shall be subject to a sliding scale of

[consider putting in percentages over a time period] of

or

• This proportion of the total monies will be reduced by [fraction i.e. 1 24th] for each complete month from date of payment [date of relocation] for reach month remaining of the [two year period].

By signing this Policy you agree that the Company shall be entitled to recover the sums as set out above.

4. Full Relocation Assistance

Relocation assistance may include:

(1) A Disturbance Allowance to cover miscellaneous expenditure incurred as a result of the relocation, such as alterations, carpets, curtains. This will be paid after the exchange of contracts for the purchase of a new property, or at the time of taking out of rental agreement for a long-term tenancy. Redirection of mail and Council tax bills do not qualify under this head. This allowance may be paid up to [ ]% of annual basic salary or the commencement salary for new employees.

   Shift payments overtime and, commissions or bonus payments will not be included in this calculation.

(2) Removals and Storage Costs may be paid. Storage costs may be paid for a period up to [number] weeks. Removal costs shall include

   The Company has a preferred supplier for the purpose of removals and storage. Details will be confirmed by the Human Resources Department.

(3) Legal/Conveyancing Costs may be incurred through a solicitor or conveyancing agent of your choice and legal fees may be paid up to a maximum of £[ ] which will be reimbursed against receipts. If this does not meet the total costs of legal fees the Disturbance Allowance may be set off against the balance.

(4) [Consider whether any loans or capital; sums may be paid and the terms on which they should be paid back.]

(5) The cost of Temporary Accommodation will be paid by the Company, for an initial four-week period, if approved by [   ]. This sum will normally be paid for hotel expenses to the same level as the Company expense' Policy. The reasonable costs of rented temporary accommodation may be paid for a maximum of [number] weeks provided that the accommodation is [distance] miles from the new

place of work. This may be extended beyond [   ]. You must first obtain approval for the rental limits, which the Company will be prepared to pay and beyond which you will not be reimbursed

(6) Travel expenses are likely to include:

- Travel home to the main residence before the move. The cost of weekend return travel will normally be reimbursed equivalent to [SET OUT i.e. second class fare etc.].

- Travel expenses in searching for new main residence which will be paid for up to [   ] visits by you and your family and which will include overnight accommodation where this was unavoidable and has been approved in advance.

(7) Other limited assistance may be offered and inquiries should be made of [   ] before any expenditure is incurred as such sums will not be paid if approval is not obtained prier to expenditure.

5. Inland Revenue

The employee will be liable for any tax incurred in respect of entitlement to expenses which exceeds that allowed on a tax free basis by the Inland Revenue.

Precedent G3: Application Form

DRAFT APPLICATION FORM

Name:

Position:

Salary on commencement of role:

Package Agreed: i.e. Full Relocation/Partial

The following expenses may be claimed to the limit set out in the second column

Disturbance Allowance	
Legal Fees	
Removal Costs	
Pre-location visit(s)	
Rental accommodation	
Other	

1. Relocation must be completed within [   ] months unless otherwise specified in your contract of employment.

2. Payment is to be made and claimed back using the company personal expense claim form, tougher with all invoices.

3. The maximum relocation expenses repayable without a tax liability is currently [£8,500]. Amounts paid to employees in excess of this will be taxable.

4. If you leave the Company [set out clause 3(5) above.

I accept and agree to the contents of this letter and hereby authorise any monies owing in respect of relocation expenses to be deducted from my salary, on termination of my employment.

Signed: _____   HR Department Date: _____

Signed: _____   Head of Function Date: _____

Signed: _____   Employee Date: _____

COMMENTARY ON G: PLACE OF WORK AND MOBILITY

A mobility clause may be of some signifigance where the employer has a number of depots/factories around the country or where it is alleged that the employee may be moved in order to avoid redundancies. In such cases the employer may seek to 'sweeten' the move by providing for relocation allowances or assistance. Where there is no express clause, it may be possible to imply a mobility clause because of the nature of the employee's job (i.e. where it involved travelling or working from site to site). Even where an express clause exists there are certain pifalls to be avoided. It is apparent from the case law that a mobility clause should generally be exercised in the way that a reasonable employer would apply the clause and it is important that a general clause should not be operated in a way that may breach the implied term of trust and confidence. There are many examples in the cases of both express and implied terms and some of them are set out below (For a fuller exposition see Duggan, *Wrongful Dismissal* at 3.12 (Express terms) and Chapter 2 on Trust and Confidence.

Implied Terms

In the absence of any express terms there is considerable scope for the implication of a term. However, such a term will be applied in such way as does not breach the implied duty of trust and confidence (see Chapter 4).

Scope of implication

It is clearly preferable that the employer stipulates the place of work and makes it clear that the employee can be moved as required where a degree of mobility is required. In the absence of an express term there must be an implied term as to the place of work since this is one of the essential terms of the contract of employment.

See (in chronological order):

O'Brien v Associated Fire Alarms Limited [1968] 1 WLR 1916; [1969] 1 All ER 93. The appellants were employed as electricians, installing fire and burglar alarms. The respondents operated nationwide but divided the business into regions and the appellants were employed in the Northwest region, based at Liverpool. During their employment they had only visited customers in the Liverpool area. They were asked to visit a customer in Barrow, 120 miles away and were dismissed when they refused. The Court of Appeal held that the tribunal had erred in finding that there was an implied term that they would work anywhere in the Northwest area. The proper term to imply was that they would work within reasonable or daily travelling distance from their homes. The case illustrates the importance of an express term if the employer wishes to have the power to instruct its employees to be mobile.

Stevenson v Tee-Side Bridge & Engineering Limited [1971] 1 All ER 296. Mr Stevenson was employed as a steel erector. He said at interview that he would be prepared to work away from home, worked at sites in different parts of the country and was paid travel and subsistence. When he refused to transfer from a site near his home because the overtime would not be as good he was dismissed. The Divisional Court held that he could be contractually required to work anywhere in the country. Parker CJ held, taking into account the aforesaid factors, that there was every reason to imply such a term to give business efficacy to the contract. The position may be different where the course of conduct shows that the employee worked within daily commuting distance, as in **Mumford v Boulton & Paul (Steel Construction) Limited** [1970] ITR 222.

Express Lift Co v Bowles [1976] IRLR 99; [1977] ICR 474. Where there was an implied term that the employee would work anywhere in the UK a further term could not be implied that it would be subject to exceptions in certain circumstances, as in the present case where Mr Bowles refused to transfer because his wife was ill. However, it may be that there is an implied term that the employer would not operate an implied condition in an unreasonable fashion as in **BBC v Beckett** [1983] IRLR 43 (and see **Prestwick Circuits Limited v McAndrew** below).

Burnett v F A Hughes & Co Limited [EAT 109/77]. The EAT held that a term could be implied into the contract of a salesman that his territory be changed as management must have an overriding power to make such alterations to the areas and functions of their sales representatives as they may reasonably require.

Little v Charterhouse Magna Assurance [1979] IRLR 19. Mr Little was a senior employee (effectively the Managing Director) on a five year fixed term with no stated place of work. He was entitled to mileage and accommodation expenses. The Head Office moved from Uxbridge to Bletchley. The EAT held that he was contractually required to move to whatever location the company had as its head office.

Prestwick Circuits Limited v McAndrew [1980] IRLR 191. Mr McAndrew was ordered to attend at another factory the following day, which was fifteen miles away even though there was no mobility clause in his contract. It was held that the Industrial Tribunal had not erred in holding that the respondents' conduct in requiring the appellant to change his place of work at short notice amounted to a fundamental breach of an implied contractual term that he would not be transferred to another location except on reasonable notice and, therefore, was conduct justifying the appellant in resigning and claiming that he had been constructively dismissed.

Jones v Associated Tunnelling Co Limited [1981] IRLR 477. Mr Jones worked from 1964 at colliery sites that were within reach of his home. In 1973 he was given a statement of terms that provided his employers could move him as they decided and in 1976 he was given a statement that provided he could be moved between sites. He did not object at the time but in 1980 he considered that he had been constructively dismissed when he was ordered to move. The EAT held that where there was no express term then a term must be implied. The employer had some power to transfer Mr Jones and, based upon the nature of the employer's business, whether the employee had been moved, what the employee had been told when he started work and provision as to expenses, in this case a term was implied that Mr Jones work at any place within reasonable daily reach of his home. Mr Jones had not acquiesced in a variation of his contract when he received the statements of terms and conditions.

Courtaulds Northern Spinning Limited v (1) Sibson (2) TGWU [1988] IRLR 451; ICR 305. Mr Sibson who was employed as a lorry driver, was required to move site after he resigned from the TGWU and they threatened action if he remained at the depot where there was a closed shop. The Court of Appeal held that he could be required to move to a site within daily reach of his home, the depot being the starting and finishing place for his job, so that the employer was entitled to require him to move one mile to another depot. There was no need or justification to import into the implied term a requirement that the request be reasonable. (Cf **Prestwick Circuits v McAndrew**).

Aparau v Iceland Frozen Foods PLC [1996] IRLR 119. In the absence of a mobility clause, the EAT held that it is was not possible to unilaterally transfer a checkout supervisor to a different store. There was no need to imply such a term given the nature of the work or to give the contract business efficacy. It was also held that the employee had not accepted a unilaterally imposed mobility clause merely by continuing to work.

An employee may rely upon the implied term of trust and confidence in relation to a proposed relocation. However, this must amount to a repudiatory breach of contract. In **Brown v Merchant Ferries Limited** [1998] IRLR 682 it was held that the fact that a proposed location left an employee felling unsettled and concerned about his future did not, viewed objectively, amount to a breach of contract as there was no evidence that his position was insecure.

Express mobility terms

The issue of place of work and mobility is likely to be an important one as employers are likely to want to have a large degree of flexibility in being able to move its workforce around as it considers appropriate. It is therefore likely to want to have mobility clauses drafted in the widest possible terms. There has been a considerable amount of case law on the issue of mobility clauses, both in the context of whether or not an employee is entitled to a redundancy payment on the basis that the workplace has closed down, or whether there has been unfair dismissal.

- **Parry v Holst & Company Limited** [1968] ITR 317.

  Mr Parry worked in the construction industry and his contract provided that "an operative may be transferred at any time during the period of his employment from one job to another". He finished one job in South Wales and was asked to transfer to Chard, in Somerset. He was dismissed when he was refused and it is was held that he was not entitled to a redundancy payment. Parker CJ stated that the clause, which was on its face unlimited, permitted the transfer that had been proposed, though he considered it is necessary to decide whether it is would permit transfer in the whole of the United Kingdom.

- **Litster v Fram Gerrard Ltd** [1973] IRLR 302.

The employee was employed at a depot at Swinton. When it closed he was dismissed for refusing to transfer to a different depot in circumstances where his contracted provided that he could be transferred 'from one site to another'. The NIRC held that there was no contractual right to transfer as 'site' should be interpreted as a temporary workplace, whereas a 'depot' was a permanent operation

- **Scott v Formica Limited** [1975] IRLR 104.

A clause which entitled the employer to transfer the employee to different jobs or departments did not enable the employer to transfer to a job where there was a reduction in salary.

- **Wilson-Undy v Instrument & Control Limited** [1976] ICR 508

Mr Wilson-Undy was employed in a labour force which transferred from site to site in the UK. At the time of his appointment he stated that he could only accept the job, which was in daily travelling distance, on the basis that when it ended he would not be transferred due to family commitments. When the employer sought to transfer him he claimed a redundancy payment. The EAT held that it was the common intention of the parties that he would only be employed within daily travelling distance.

- **Barratt (Manchester) Ltd v Ingram** EAT 341/85

A term that an employee could be transferred to another location 'if the needs of the company demanded it' was too imprecise to be enforceable.

- **BPCC Purnell Ltd v Webb** EAT 129/90

The employee was transferred from one pre-press department of a printing company to another pre-press department and stood to lose about £80 per week in earnings. His contract of employment provided stated that 'there will be total flexibility between all pre-press departments'. The EAT did not accept that the provision was subject to an implied term that the express provision be exercised reasonably but agreed that there had been a constructive dismissal as the instruction to move had destroyed trust and confidence (See Duggan, *Wrongful Dismissal*, Chapter 2).

Where the employer purports to vary the contract to include a mobility clause but this does not have any immediate effect, an employee will not be taken to have affirmed the variation merely because he has continued to work for the employee. In a case where the employee worked on for a year after the employer purported to introduce a clause which did not have immediate effect the EAT held that no consent to variation could be implied (**Aparau v Iceland Frozen Foods PLC** [1996] IRLR 119).

A temporary transfer may not be a repudiatory breach if it is for a short or specific time but where an employee is transferred until work picked up, with uncertainty as to how salary will be affected, this may amount to a breach on the part of the employer (**Millbrook Furnishings Industries v McIntosh** [1981] IRLR 309).

Precedents G1.1.–4. contain examples of different scope ranging from limited miles to worldwide mobility and should be tailored to the employment.

Precedent G2 contains a draft relocation policy. It is suggested that such a policy would be useful when relocating an employee some distance as it would point to reasonableness and make it more diffiult to allege that trust and confidence has broken down.

Precedent G3 contains an application form for expenses.

PART H: PRECONDITIONS OF EMPLOYMENT OR CONTINUED EMPLOYMENT

Precedent H: **Preconditions of employment or continued employment**

H1:	**References**	**645**
H2:	**Probationary period and confirmation of Employment**	**646**
H3:	**Car driving licence**	**646**
H4:	**Qualifications**	**647**
H5:	**The right to work**	**647**
Commentary:	**Pre-conditions of Employment or continued Employment**	**648**

Precedent H1: References

1 Your employment with the Company is subject to the receipt of satisfactory references. If any reference is not satisfactory the Company shall be entitled to terminate your employment with immediate effect.

2   The Company may, at its absolute discretion, provide a reference upon request from a prospective employer. It will not provide a general reference but only provide references upon request. The Company will also provide references in respect of any mortgage, financial or other applications upon receipt of a written request from both the employee and the person seeking the reference.

3   The Company does not accept any liability for any references that it may give.

Precedent H2: Probationary Period and Confirmation of Employment

1   There is a minimum probationary period of ___ months for all new employees. This may have been varied by your Letter of Appointment. Moreover, the Company may, at its absolute discretion, extend the period of your probation if it considers this to be an appropriate course to adopt. You will be informed of the reasons for this.

2   Your performance will be continuously reviewed during your probationary period. If at any time during the period your performance is not considered to be satisfactory you will be advised and if there is no improvement you may be given notice.

3   At the end of the probationary period if your performance was satisfactory your continued employment may be confirmed. Your probationary period will count towards your continuous employment.

4   You will have been advised in your Letter of Appointment of what benefits you are entitled to receive during your probationary period.

Precedent H3: Car Driving and Driving Licence

You must have a full driving licence as a condition of your employment. Loss of a licence will result in immediate dismissal unless you demonstrate that you can make satisfactory alternative arrangements. The use of public transport will not be regarded as a satisfactory alternative.

Precedent H4: Qualifications

If your employment is subject to you having certain qualifications, which will have been notified to you in your Letter of Appointment, and you have not yet achieved the qualification because you are awaiting exam results or for some other reason, the employer reserves the right to terminate your employment forthwith, without notice or any compensation, should you fail to achieve the qualification by the notified date.

Precedent H5: Right to work in the United Kingdom

The Company will wish to satisfy itself that you have both leave to be in the United Kingdom which does not prevent you from taking the job that is being offered and that you come within a category of employee where employment is allowed. The Company imposes this requirement on all employees without exception. You will be required to produce documentation that is satisfactory to the Company and will be advised [by HR] [or alternatively list documents as per the list from the Order – see below] of the documents that are needed.

Your employment will not be confirmed until you have produced the documents to satisfy the Company that you are legally able to take the position that is being offered.

COMMENTARY ON H: PRE-CONDITIONS OF EMPLOYMENT OR CONTINUED EMPLOYMENT

H1: References

Where an employer provides a reference in respect of an ex-employee it will be under a duty to take reasonable care in preparing the reference and if a negligent reference is provided that results in the employee suffering loss then the employer may be liable in damages (**Spring v Guardian Assurance PLC** [1994] ICR 596; IRLR 460; **Lawton v BOC Transhield Limited** [1987] ICR 7; IRLR 404) (C.f. **Kapfunde v Abbey National PLC** [1999] IRLR 246 in relation to medical reports provided by a doctor).

In **Bartholomew v London Borough of Hackney** [1999] IRLR 246 it was held that an employer did not act negligently when it stated in a reference that the employee had left the employment whilst being investigated for gross misconduct. The employer was under a duty not to mislead the prospective employer and the reference had not been drafted in a way that was unfair to the employee.

The precedent makes it clear that no liability is accepted in relation to the reference. However, this is unlikely to be effective if the employer knows that he has provided a reference that is not correct. See **Lawton v BOC Transhield Limited** [1987] ICR 7; **Legal and General Assurance Limited v Kirk** [2002] IRLR 124 and **Kidd v Axa Equity & Law Life Assurance Society PLC** [2000] IRLR 301 and see the full commentary in Duggan, *Wrongful Dismissal and Breach of Contract* pages 5–7).

H2: Probationary Periods

It should be noted that an employee who is advised that he will be given a certain position or be promoted after a probationary period may bring a constructive dismissal claim if such is not forthcoming (**D H Russell (London) Limited v Magee** [EAT 201/78]). (Any precedent relating to probationary periods should make it clear that the employer is entitled to give notice at any time during the probationary period and is not bound to wait until the end before it terminates the contract.)

H3: Driving Licences

The nature of the employment may mean that a driving licence is essential. In **Roberts v Toyota (GB) Limited** [EAT 614/80] the employee was employed as an area sales manager. He was provided with a vehicle and it was ascertained at his interview that he had a valid driving licence. He was dismissed after nine years following a conviction for drunk driving and loss of licence for one year. He claimed unfair dismissal. It is was held that there was an implied term that he have a valid licence. The EAT stated:

> "The written contract of employment is fairly comprehensive and includes a provision to the effect that a company car would be provided for use on the company's behalf and for private purposes. It does not specifically state that the employee must be in possession of a driving licence but the provision with regard to the supply of a company car would be meaningless without it."

There was also evidence that the area managers had been told they would lose their job if they lost their licence. Notwithstanding this case, it is prudent to contain a provision that a licence is a condition of employment where this is intended to be the position, particularly where the driving is not as extensive as in the Roberts case. Other cases in which it has been held to be fair to dismiss on the loss of a licence include **Appleyard v Smith (Hull) Limited** [1972] IRLR 19 and **Fearn v Tayford Motor Co Limited** [1975] IRLR 336.

The precedent makes it clear that a licence is essential to the job. It should also be made clear that other alternatives are not acceptable. In Roberts the offer to employ a chauffeur was rejected and this was regarded as acceptable by the Tribunal where it had been made clear that a driving licence was required.

H4: Qualifications

Employers should ensure that they have made it clear any employment or continued employment turns upon obtaining qualifications within a certain time. In **Stubbes v Trower Still & Keeling (a firm)** [1987] IRLR 321 the employer had given articles but failed to state that continued employment turned upon passing the solicitor's exams. The Court of Appeal held that there was no necessary implication that the continued employment turned upon passing the exams. The employer had the means of securing their position through the medium of an express term. The precedent makes it clear that continued employment is subject to the possession of the required qualifications.

H5: *Right to work in the United Kingdom*

It is necessary for the employer to ensure that the employee has the right to work in the United Kingdom. Checks need to be carried out before an offer of employment is firmly made otherwise there is a real risk that an offence may be committed.

Under section 8 of the Asylum and Immigration Act 1996:

> "8. – (1) Subject to subsection (2) below, if any person ("the employer") employs a person subject to immigration control ("the employee") who has attained the age of 16, the employer shall be guilty of an offence if–

> (a) the employee has not been granted leave to enter or remain in the United Kingdom; or

> (b) the employee's leave is not valid and subsisting, or is subject to a condition precluding him from taking up the employment,

> and (in either case) the employee does not satisfy such conditions as may be specified in an order made by the Secretary of State."

It may be a defence under section 8(2) to prove that–

"(a) before the employment began, there was produced to the employer a document which appeared to him to relate to the employee and to be of a description specified in an order made by the Secretary of State; and

(b) either the document was retained by the employer, or a copy or other record of it was made by the employer in a manner specified in the order in relation to documents of that description."

The defence afforded by subsection 8(2) is not available in any case where the employer knew that his employment of the employee would constitute an offence under section 8(1): (8(3)).

By section 8(4) a person guilty of an offence under section 8 is liable on summary conviction to a fine not exceeding level 5 on the standard scale. By section 8(5), where an offence under section 8 committed by a body corporate is proved to have been committed with the consent or connivance of, or to be attributable to any neglect on the part of (a) any director, manager, secretary or other similar officer of the body corporate; or (b) any person who was purporting to act in any such capacity, he as well as the body corporate shall be guilty of the offence and shall be liable to be proceeded against and punished accordingly. Under section 8(6) where the affairs of a body corporate are managed by its members, subsection (5) above shall apply in relation to the acts and defaults of a member in connection with his functions of management as if he were a director of the body corporate.

Section 8A of the Act, which was effective from 2 May 2001, permits the Secretary of State to produce a Code of Practice to provide Guidance on avoiding breaches of section 8 (see SI 2001/1436 at *http://www.legislation.hmso. gov.uk/si/si2001/20011436.htm*).

The Code states that:

- "The best way to make sure that you do not discriminate is to treat all job applicants in the same way at each stage of your recruitment process.

- Don't assume that a foreign national or someone from an ethnic minority has no right to work in the UK.

Treat all people who apply in the same way. Ask all applicants for a document, or combination of documents from the lists below, and ask everybody if they need permission to work. A specified combination of documents from List 2 is just as valid as evidence of right to work as one document from List 1.

- Don't assume a person is an illegal worker if they can't produce a document. Suggest they go to a Citizens Advice Bureau for further advice on what to do.

- Monitor your recruitment practices taking account of equality issues."

There is a complete defence if the employer can show a document in relation to the employee of a description specified by the Secretary of State was produced of which the employer has retained a copy. Until 30 April 2004 the relevant Order was SI 1996/3225. From 1st May 2004 the relevant Order is the Immigration (Restrictions on Employment) Order 2004, SI 2004/755. The changes are explained in Government Publication – 2003/03/16 – Home Office Press Release 120/2004 [*http://www.homeoffice.gov.uk/n_story.asp?item_id=877*] (and see the Government Website at *http://www.ind.homeoffice.gov.uk/content /ind/en/home.html*).

It is important that the employer applies the same requirement to produce papers to all employees or face a risk of a claim for discrimination

(Cf **Olatokun v Ikon Office Systems** [EAT 10 May 2004 EAT/0074/04]). In *Olakotun* an agency worker who moved into a permanent position was given an application form which was a standard form issued to all applicants requiring details of place of birth. Ikon's policy was to request a passport from employees born outside the EU, to avoid an offence under the Asylum and Immigration Act 1996. Ikon requested the employee's passport even though it would not have received protection from the defence as she had already commenced employment. No passport was forthcoming and she was dismissed. The employee appealed, enclosing a letter from the Home Office which outlined her conditional right to work, but did not attend an appeal hearing because the passport had not turned up. The employee then brought a claim of discrimination. It was held by the ET that the fact that a different standard was applied to non-EU citizens as against those from the EU may be discriminatory, but it was sanctioned by the Asylum Act and protection was obtained from section 41 of the Race Relations Act 1976, which states that any act of discrimination will not be unlawful if it is done under statutory authority. Olatokun appealed, but the Employment Appeals Tribunal (EAT) upheld the original decision. Note however, that if all employees had been required to produce the same documents such a claim would be bound to fail.

Paragraphs 19 and 20 of the Code states:

> "19. In order to establish a defence you need to make sure that, before a person starts working for you, you see at least one document which appears to you to be listed in Appendix 1. You should ensure that the document is an original and that it appears to relate to the person that you are intending to employ. You should make either a copy or record of the document or retain it. This last option will normally only be appropriate in the case of Part 2 of a P45. The statutory defence is only established by checking documents before taking on a new employee. There is no requirement to do anything else, even if the person's permission to be in the United Kingdom is not yet permanent. You should not ask existing employees to demonstrate that they have permission to work.
>
> 20. The checks which you need to make to claim the statutory defence are in most cases straightforward and can be built into your normal recruitment procedures. Such checks are not compulsory but they are advisable. If you do not make them you will not have the statutory defence which they provide. But if you make checks you should ensure that they are made in a non-discriminatory manner."

There are two separate lists of documents. The first list contains 'secure' documents where one of the documents will suffice whilst the second refers to less secure documents where it will be necessary for the employer to see at least two documents. The employer must see the original document and be satisfied that they relate to the employee in question. He must take a copy of the document. Article 4 of the Immigration (Restrictions on Employment) Order 2004, SI 2004/755 states:

"4. – (1) The requirements set out in paragraphs (2) to (5) are requirements for the purposes of section 8(2) of the 1996 Act (defence for a person charged with an offence under section 8 to prove that before the employment began any such requirement was complied with).

(2) There must have been produced to the employer either –

   (a) a document of a description specified in Part 1 of the Schedule, or

   (b) one document of a description specified in –

      (i)   each of sub-paragraphs (a) and (b) of paragraph 1 of Part 2 of the Schedule; or

      (ii) each of sub-paragraphs (a) and (b) of paragraph 2 of that Part.

(3) The employer must have taken the steps specified in Part 3 of the Schedule to copy or record the content of any document produced to him in accordance with paragraph (2)

(4) The employer must have satisfied himself that each document produced in accordance with paragraph (2), appears to relate to the employee in question; in particular –

   (a) if a document contains a photograph, the employer must have satisfied himself that the person photographed is the employee in question; and

   (b) if a document contains a date of birth, the employer must have satisfied himself that the date of birth is consistent with the appearance of the employee.

(5) If either –

    (a) the name on a document produced under paragraph 1(a) of Part 2 of the Schedule differs from the name on a document produced under paragraph 1(b) of that Part; or

    (b) the name on a document produced under paragraph 2(a) of Part 2 of the Schedule differs from the name on a document produced under paragraph 2(b) of that Part,

a document must have been produced to the employer explaining the difference."

Part 1 of the Schedule refers to the secure documents, Part 2 refers to less secure documents whilst part 3 sets out those steps to be taken by the employer. The Schedule is reproduced here:

PART 1

Descriptions of documents for the purposes of article 4(2)(a)

1. A United Kingdom passport describing the holder as a British citizen or as a citizen of the United Kingdom and Colonies having the right of abode in the United Kingdom.

2. A passport containing a certificate of entitlement issued by or on behalf of the Government of the United Kingdom, certifying that the holder has the right of abode in the United Kingdom.

3. A passport or national identity card, issued by a State which is a party to the European Economic Area Agreement or any other agreement forming part of the Communities Treaties which confers rights of entry to or residence in the United Kingdom, which describes the holder as a national of a State which is a party to that Agreement.

4. A United Kingdom residence permit issued to a national of a State which is a party to the European Economic Area Agreement or any other agreement forming part of the Communities Treaties which confirms that the holder has rights of entry to, or residence in, the United Kingdom.

5. A passport or other travel document or a residence document issued by the Home Office which is endorsed to show that the holder has a current

right of residence in the United Kingdom as the family member of a named national of a State which is a party to the European Economic Area Agreement or any other agreement forming part of the Communities Treaties which confers rights of entry to, or residence in, the United Kingdom, and who is resident in the United Kingdom.

6. A passport or other travel document endorsed to show that the holder is exempt from immigration control, has indefinite leave to enter, or remain in, the United Kingdom or has no time limit on his stay.

7. A passport or other travel document endorsed to show that the holder has current leave to enter, or remain in, the United Kingdom and is permitted to take the employment in question, provided that it does not require the issue of a work permit.

8. A registration card which indicates that the holder is entitled to take employment in the United Kingdom.

PART 2

Descriptions of documents for the purposes of article 4(2)(b)

Article 4(2)(b)

1. (a) A document issued by a previous employer, Inland Revenue, the Department for Work and Pensions' Jobcentre Plus, the Employment Service, the Training and Employment Agency (Northern Ireland) or the Northern Ireland Social Security Agency, which contains the National Insurance number of the person named in the document; and

   (b) either:–

      (i) a birth certificate issued in the United Kingdom, which specifies the names of the holder's parents; or

      (ii) a birth certificate issued in the Channel Islands, the Isle of Man or Ireland; or

      (iii) a certificate of registration or naturalisation as a British citizen; or

      (iv) a letter issued by the Home Office, to the holder, which indicates that the person named in it has been granted indefinite leave to enter, or remain in, the United Kingdom; or

      (v) an Immigration Status Document issued by the Home Office, to the holder, endorsed with a United Kingdom Residence Permit, which indicates that the holder has been granted indefinite leave to enter, or remain in, the United Kingdom; or

      (vi) a letter issued by the Home Office, to the holder, which indicates that the person named in it has subsisting leave to enter, or remain in, the United Kingdom and is entitled to take the employment in question in the United Kingdom; or

      (vii)an Immigration Status Document issued by the Home Office, to the holder, endorsed with a United Kingdom Residence Permit, which indicates that the holder has been granted limited leave to enter, or remain in, the United Kingdom and is entitled to take the employment in question in the United Kingdom.

2.   (a) A work permit or other approval to take employment issued by Work Permits UK; and

     (b) either:–

       (i) a passport or other travel document endorsed to show that the holder has current leave to enter, or remain in, the United Kingdom and is permitted to take the work permit employment in question, or

       (ii) a letter issued by the Home Office to the holder, confirming the same.

PART 3

Steps which must be taken to copy or record the content of a document produced to an employer

Article 4(3)

1. In the case of a passport or other travel document, the following parts must be photocopied or scanned into a database, using the technology known as "Write Once Read Many" –

    (a) the front cover; and

    (b) any page containing;

        (i)   the holder's personal details including nationality;

        (ii) the holder's photograph and/or signature;

        (iii) the date of expiry; and

        (iv) the information referred to in paragraphs 1 (other than citizenship) and 2 of Part 1 and the endorsements referred to in paragraphs 5, 6 and 7 of Part 1 and paragraph 2(b)(i) of Part 2.

2. All other documents must be photocopied or scanned in their entirety into a database, using the technology known as "Write Once Read Many".

PART I: ABSENCES FROM WORK DUE TO HOLIDAY

Precedent I: Absences from work due to Holiday

I1:	Annual holidays	659
I2:	Public holidays	661
I3:	Shutdown periods in relation to factory workers	661
I4:	Form setting out request for holiday leave	662
I5:	Rolled up holiday pay agreement	662
Commentary:	The Law Relating to Holidays	663

Cross References

Duggan, *Wrongful Dismissal and Breach of Contract* at 3.7. Holidays and 6.8. Holiday Pay.

Precedent I1:   Annual Holidays

1   Your holiday entitlement is set out in your Letter of Appointment [ALTERNATIVELY 'You are entitled to holiday in accordance with the provisions of the Working Time Regulations 1998 or such legislation as may be in force from time to time]. [You are entitled to [20] days holiday pay a year [Inclusive of Bank and Statutory Holidays] [in addition to Bank and Statutory Holidays].

2   Your holiday entitlement is based on your length of service with the Company as follows:

SET OUT YEARS OF SERVICE AND HOLIDAY ENTITLEMENT THIS SHOULD ONLY BE INCLUDED IF THE ENTITLEMENT IS OVER FOUR WEEKS-IT IS NECESSARY TO INCLUDE A PROVISION RELATING TO THE FIRST YEAR OF EMPLOYMENT].

First year of employment

3   During your first year of employment your holiday entitlement will accrue at the rate of one twelfth of four weeks' annual leave for that year (or one and two third days per month), to accrue on the first day of each month.

The amount you may take at any time during your first year is limited to the amount which is deemed to have accrued at the rate of one twelfth. Where the amount that has accrued in a particular case includes a fraction of a day other than a half day the fraction shall be treated as a half day if it is less than a half day and as a whole day if it is more than a half day.

[Where there is a relevant agreement in force and the date on which you commenced employment is later than the date on which (by virtue of the agreement) the first leave year begins you are entitled to a proportion of the four weeks' annual leave of that year remaining on which your employment began. The date the relevant agreement commenced is _____. Where the period of leave includes a proportion of a week that proportion shall be determined in days and any fraction of a day shall be treated as a whole day.]

Annual entitlement

4   Your holiday entitlement commences on the date on which employment began and each subsequent anniversary of that date.

5   You will be paid your basic salary whilst on holiday.

6   It is important to the Company that it is aware of when holiday entitlement is to be taken. Accordingly the following rules apply in respect of obtaining authorisation for holidays:

1) You must obtain prior written permission [*FROM . . . . .*] before you book any holiday.

2) The Company has a holiday booking form which must be used for this purpose.

3) The maximum holiday that may be taken is two weeks, unless special permission is obtained for a longer period. You must give notice of not less than [period] weeks of the dates that you request to take for holiday.

4) It will be expected that two weeks of your holiday will be taken in the summer and any proposal to take holiday at other times must be notified at least the same number of days in advance as the length of holiday that it is proposed to take.

5) If you had already booked a holiday before joining the Company then the Company may, at its absolute discretion, authorise you to take the holiday.

6) Holiday entitlement will not be carried over from year to year without express written permission.

7) You may be required to take any accrued holiday entitlement during your period of notice where you have given notice or the Company has given notice to terminate your employment.

8) Holiday entitlement accrues at the rate of ____ days per month so that, in the event of termination of your employment, outstanding holiday will be calculated on an accrued basis. If you have taken in excess of your entitlement then, upon termination, the Company will be entitled to reimbursement for any overpayment. Accrued holiday is worked out on the basis of a five/seven day working week.

9) Your holiday pay will be based upon your normal salary [an average of salary over the twelve weeks before you take holiday or, where you have not worked twelve weeks, on the average salary over the weeks

that you have worked for the Company. [Overtime will/will not count in working out your salary].

10) If you resign or are dismissed you will be paid for your accrued entitlement up to the date of termination of your employment where there is any money owing to you.

11) You will be paid for all Bank and public holidays. Where you are dismissed for gross misconduct your entitlement to holiday pay will lapse and you will only be entitled to be paid for the last day that you worked and a termination sum of [£nominal amount].

12) Where you have taken in excess of your holiday entitlement so that there is a balance owed by you to the Company this may be deducted from your last salary payment and you will remain liable for the balance of monies that are due in respect of overall holiday payment.

Precedent 12: Public Holidays

You are entitled to the statutory public holidays each year which are:

New Years Day
Spring Bank Holiday
Good Friday
Later Summer Bank Holiday
Easter Monday
Christmas Day
May Day
Boxing Day

Precedent 13: Shutdown Periods in Relation to Factory Workers

The Company shuts down its factory premises during _____. You will be required to take _____ days of your holiday entitlement during this period.

Precedent I4: Annual Leave Request Form

Annual Leave Request Form	
Name	DEPARTMENT: JOB TITLE:
Date of commencement of employment	
Dates for which leave is requested	From _____ to _____ (NB. The first date for which leave is requested must be at least twice the number of days away from the length of the leave that is to be taken i.e. If it is for 1 week the first date must be at least two weeks from the date of the form.]
Signature of employee:	Date submitted:

This form was received by _____ on _____ (Date).

Your leave for the period requested above is authorised.

Your request for leave for the period requested above is refused.

You are required to take your leave for the period from _____ to _____

Precedent I5: Rolled up holiday pay

You are entitled to 20 days holiday pay a year [SET OUT PROVISIONS AS TO FIRST YEAR ETC.]

In order to assist you in planning your holiday and so you may make payments for any holiday sums that you need to pay in advance, the Company is prepared to pay you holiday entitlement with your salary. This will go in diminution or reduction of any holiday pay that would otherwise be paid to you during your holiday leave period.

You will be paid an additional rate of [ ]% on top of your hourly salary which is paid as holiday pay and is paid in addition to your normal salary. Your pay statement each week will itemise the precise sum that you receive for that week as holiday pay. You will be expected to take your holiday in the annual leave year and will be provided with a breakdown of the holiday pay that you have accrued when you make a request to take holiday leave. If you have not accrued holiday pay that will fully cover the holiday leave which you have requested the Company may pay the balance or may require you to take your holiday entitlement at another time.

[IF POSSIBLE SET OUT THE ACTUAL FIGURES IN THE CLAUSE]

COMMENTARY: THE LAW RELATING TO HOLIDAYS

The Working Time Regulations 1998

The terms on which an employee may take holiday leave will be governed by the contract of employment but this will be subject to the requirements of the Working Time Regulations 1998 as amended by the Working Time (Amendment) Regulations 2001 SI 2001/3256, which lays down certain minimum requirements for paid holiday leave. It will be an automatic unfair dismissal to dismiss a worker because he asserted his rights to holiday under the WTR (See **Armstrong v Walter Scott Motors** [EAT/766/02/TC] (19 March 2003).

It should be noted that there is separate legislation in relation to agricultural labourers who have long held rights under Agricultural Wages Orders.

The requirements under the WTR can be modified by a Relevant Agreement. This exclusionary power is of great importance to the employer who does not wish to have to comply with the requirements of the WTR (see also Part D to this Manual) and may be contained in:

- A Workforce Agreement

- A provision in a collective Agreement

- Any other Agreement in writing that is legally enforceable.

Regulations 13 to 16 of the WTR give specific rights in relation to leave entitlement in each leave year. The Regulations as originally implemented gave entitlement to four weeks' leave after working for at least 13 weeks at which time the whole of the period of leave could be taken. This restriction was held to be contrary to the Directive (**R v Secretary of State for Trade and Industry ex p BECTU** [2001] IRLR 559 ECJ) so that regulations 13(7) and 13(8) were repealed and replaced by a system whereby holiday accrues for the first year.

Entitlement

Article 7 of the Directive provides for a minimum of four weeks paid annual leave. The introduction of this right did not allow employers to finance the cost by reducing salaries to cover the holiday period (**Davies v MJ Wyatt (Decorators) Ltd** [2001] IRLR 759) if holiday pay had not otherwise been paid. Existing contractual entitlement will count towards discharging this right on the part of the employer (regulation 17).

The worker will still be entitled to accrued holiday pay even though he or she is on long term sickness absence (**Kigass v Aero Components Ltd** [2002] IRLR 312; ICR 697) (but note this case is being appealed).

However, in **Ainsworth v Commissioners of Inland Revenue** [EAT 4 February 2004] [UKEAT/0650/03/TM] the cases where workers have been entitled to holiday pay during long term absences were referred to the Court of Appeal for clarification. The EAT stated that the Court of Appeal would wish to consider the principles in *Kigass*, *List* and *Farrar*.

These cases are being appealed to the Court of Appeal so that a definitive ruling as to when holiday pay will accrue if an employee is absent due to sickness should be given in due course.

There is no entitlement in English law to holiday for bank or public holidays so that employers will be entitled to include these days as going towards satisfying the requirements of the Regulations.

The Regulations provide that an employee is entitled to four weeks annual leave in each leave year. The leave year begins on such date as may be provided for in a relevant agreement. Where there are no provisions of a relevant agreement and employment began before 1 October 1998 it will be each anniversary of the set October 1998 date. Where it began after 1st October 1998 it will be the date on which that employment begins and each subsequent anniversary of that date (reg. 13(3)). There is separate provision in relation to agricultural Workers (reg. 13(4)).

Where the date on which employment begins is later than the date which, by virtue of Relevant Agreement, his first leave year begins the leave will be a proportion of the four weeks equal to the proportion of that leave year remaining on the date when his employment began (reg. 13(5)). The proportion is to be determined in days and any fraction of a day to be treated as a whole day (reg. 13(6)).

Leave may be taken in instalments *only* in the year in which it is due and it cannot be replaced by a payment in lieu (reg. 13(9)). The Regulations do not permit holiday to be carried over. It will still be possible for holidays to be carried over as a matter of contract for periods over the four weeks holiday required by the Regulations, but the worker must be given four weeks in the relevant leave year and these cannot be carried over. Once employment has ended the worker may claim holiday pay for holiday that has not been taken. This may include back holiday pay for any holiday that was not taken during employment, subject to any contractual provision and to bringing the claim in time. In **Canada Life Limited v Gray and Farrar** [2004] ICR 673 [UKEAT/0657/03/SM], Mr Gray and Mr Farrar were self-employed consultants who had worked for Canada Life under the terms of commission only agreements which did not provide for holiday or holiday pay. Neither of them had taken holiday during the period from 1 October 1998 to 31 October 2002 when they both ceased working for Canada Life or received any holiday pay. The last commission payments made to them were on 20 December 2002 for the final period of work up to 31 October 2002. Both had been told by Canada Life that they were not workers and so were not entitled to payment under the Regulations. They claimed that they were workers and therefore entitled to holiday pay. The Nottingham Tribunal found in their favour and awarded deductions from pay. The EAT noted that Canada Life did not dispute the finding that the two were workers

Canada Life argued that there is no right to holiday pay where the entitlement to annual leave is not in fact exercised, as the right must be exercised in the appropriate leave year and that if it is not then the right to that leave expires, relying on *Kigass*. However, the EAT noted that provision of the WTR on health and safety grounds, had the aim of preventing employers persuading workers to take money instead of holiday and that the position is different where the worker's employment has ended (**List Design Group Ltd v Douglas** [2000] ICR 686).

It was held that Mr Gray and Mr Farrar could properly bring a claim under Employment Rights Act 1996 Part II, when the Working Time Regulations reg. 30 makes specific provision for compensation for breach of those regulations. The EAT, applying its previous ruling in *List Design* held that they could do so as the sums were payable not under the men's contracts but under the Working Time Regulations (i.e. "otherwise" for purposes of ERA 1996 section 27 (1)(a)) and were holiday pay within the definition of wages in the ERA 1996 section 23(1)(a). It was also argued that the claims were time barred in that they related to periods which ended more than three months before their claims had been presented. The EAT rejected this argument on the basis that where there is *a series of deductions or payments the references in subsection (2) to the deduction or payment are to the last deduction or payment in the series*. The non-payments amounted to a series of deductions so that the claims were made in good time. The EAT noted that if Canada Life's arguments were correct an employer who refused to acknowledge a worker's entitlement throughout employment would escape liability for compensating the worker for that breach of his statutory rights.

The *Canada Life* case is likely to be of relevance in other circumstances where holiday money has not been paid, such as where an employee has already accrued holiday entitlement and is not given the opportunity to take leave when she takes time off for maternity leave.

The First Year of employment

A new Regulation 15A was added by the 2001 Regulations. By Regulation 15A(2), during the first year of employment leave will be deemed to accrue at the rate of one twelfth of the amount of four weeks on the first day of each month. Where the amount that has accrued in a particular case includes a fraction of a day other than a half day it will be treated as a half day. Where it is more than a half day it shall be treated as a full day.

However, where the date when the employee commences is, by virtue of a relevant agreement, later than the leave he is to be entitled under a relevant agreement he will be entitled to a proportion of the period of four weeks equal to the proportion of that leave year remaining and proportions and fractions of a day shall be treated as days.

Notices to take leave

By Regulation 15(1) the worker may take the four weeks' leave by giving notice to his employer. The scheme is as follows:

- the worker may give notice relating to all or part of the leave to which he is entitled in a leave year and shall specify the days on which leave is to be taken;

- the notice must be given twice as many days in advance of the earliest date specified as the number of days or part days to which the notice relates.

The employer may require the worker:

- to take leave to which the worker is entitled, notice for which shall be given twice as many days as the earliest day specified in the notice as being the date on which leave must be taken.

- not to take leave in which case the notice must be given as many days in advance of the earliest date to which the notice relates. This means that if the worker gives 10 days' notice to take five days' holiday the employer may give notice five days before that he may not take the leave.

The Notice Provisions may be excluded or varied by a relevant agreement (15(5)).

Payment

A worker is entitled to be paid for any period of annual leave at the rate of a week's pay for each week of leave (regulation 16(1)). Sections 221 to 224 of the ERA 1996 apply for the purposes of determining the amount of a week's pay under the Regulations. The application of the ERA in calculating a week's pay may mean that commission is not included as part of the calculation. In **Evans v Malley Organisation Limited** [2002] EWCA 1834; [2003] IRLR 156 the EAT held that that the applicant's remuneration did not vary with the amount of work done in normal working hours and that, therefore, the amount of a week's pay for the purposes of holiday entitlement under the Working Time Regulations fell to be calculated in accordance with s.221(2) of the Employment Rights Act and, on that basis, did not include commission payments but was based on basic annual salary.

It was held in **Bamsey v Albon Engineering Limited** [2004] EWCA 359 (25th March 2004) [2004] IRLR 457, (See also **Rich v Forbouys Limited** [19.04.2002]) that the value of overtime may be excluded where it was not contractually agreed even if the worker habitually worked the overtime since Regulation 16 provides for calculation by reference to normal working hours. Although the Working Time (Amendment) Regulations 2002 provided that Regulation 6(6) was revoked this had the effect of including overtime in the calculation of night working hours but not for the purposes of calculating holiday pay. The Court of Appeal held that "*where overtime is involved, there must be mutuality of obligation between the employer and the employee for it to be included in the latter's normal working hours*". The employer was not obliged to provide overtime (and the employee was obliged to work only a maximum of 9 hours overtime if requested). As there was no mutuality of obligation the overtime actually worked could not be included as part of Mr Bamsey's normal working hours when calculating the amount of a week's pay for holiday purposes.

The right to be paid applies to the full four weeks entitlement and not to any lesser period that has actually be taken as holiday (**List Design Group Limited v Douglas** [2002] ICR 686).

Rolled up holiday pay

There has been considerable difficulty in cases where workers have been paid at an 'enhanced' rate to cover holidays so that they do not receive holiday pay whilst they are actually on leave. Employers may find it convenient to include an element of holiday pay in the hourly rate which will accrue over the course of the employee's employment. There were, initially, inconsistent decisions from the Tribunals as to whether the worker could then demand full holiday pay when he took holiday that had accrued. In **Chapman v Eurostaff Personnel Limited** (London (Stratford ET)) it was held that the entitlement was to paid leave and this could not be dealt with by paying an enhancement, which had been in place at the time the Regulations came into force, whilst in **Ackerman v Stratton** (Manchester ET) it was held that the practice of making a supplementary payment included in a rate was not acceptable as the worker would not earn the rate whilst on leave and the practice therefore effectively prevented the entitlement to any minimum paid leave. However, in **Davies v M J Wyatt (Decorators) Limited**

(Manchester ET) the ET considered it acceptable for the hourly rate to be reduced as the employees would otherwise have been, effectively, paid twice.

The Scottish Court of Session came down on the side of holding that a worker was entitled to be paid though he had received rolled up holiday pay in **MPB Structure Limited v Munro** [2003] IRLR 350 on the ground that payment by way of rolled up holiday pay would exclude or limit the effect of the WTR. However, in **Marshalls Clay Products Limited v Caulfield** [2003] IRLR 552 the EAT adopted Counsel's submissions as to different scenarios, as follows:

Category 1: Contracts between the worker and the employer which are silent in relation to holiday pay.

Category 2: Contracts which purport to exclude any liability for or entitlement to holiday pay.

Category 3: Contracts where the rates are said to include holiday pay, but there is no indication or specification of an amount.

Category 4: Contracts providing for a basic wage or rate topped up by a specific sum or percentage in respect of holiday pay.

Category 5: Contracts where holiday pay is allocated to and paid during (or immediately prior to or immediately after) specific periods of holiday.

It held that contractual provision for rolled-up holiday pay which identifies an express amount or percentage by way of an addition to basic pay is not unlawful under the WTR as regulation 16(1), does not require holiday pay to be allocated to and paid at the time holiday is taken. A contractual term providing for payment of holiday pay in respect of an express holiday entitlement but accruing throughout the year, (category 4 above) was an entitlement to "contractual remuneration ... in respect of a period of leave" in terms of reg. 16(5), which provides for the offsetting of "any contractual remuneration paid to a worker in respect of a period of leave" against any liability of the employer to make payments under reg. 16(1) in respect of that period. This was held to be the case albeit that it is not at the stage of its payment specifically appropriated to any particular period, and is not paid at the time of such leave, but wholly or partly in advance of it.

However, the EAT stated that there must be contractually a specific sum or percentage allocated to holiday pay in order to ensure that there is payment under reg. 16(1) and/or to prove that there has been payment under reg. 16(5), and to ensure that a specific sum on an accruing basis will have been paid during the year so as to satisfy any entitlement to accrued holiday pay on termination pursuant to reg. 14.

The EAT considered that contracts between a worker and employer which are silent in relation to holiday pay; contracts which purport to exclude any liability for or entitlement to holiday pay; and contracts where the rates are said to include holiday pay, but there is no indication or specification of an amount (categories 1–3) fall foul of the Regulations as, in such situations:

- either there is no "contractual remuneration paid to a worker in respect of a period of leave" to be offset against the statutory entitlement under reg. 16(1), and there is a simple breach of reg. 16(1) and/or

- an entitlement to be paid pursuant thereto; or there is a purported exclusion of such entitlement, which is void pursuant to reg. 35(1)(a);

- or there may be a breach of reg. 13(9)(b), which stipulates that a worker's entitlement to leave cannot be replaced by a payment in lieu except where the worker's employment is terminated.

It was stated that, in order for an agreement as to rolled up holiday pay to be valid:

"(a) The rolled up holiday pay must be clearly incorporated into the individual contract of employment, and thus expressly agreed.

(b) The allocation of the percentage or amount to holiday pay must be clearly identified in the contract, and preferably also in the payslip.

(c) It must amount to a true addition to the contractual rate of pay.

(d) Records of holidays taken must be kept.

(e) Reasonably practicable steps must be taken to require the workers to take their holidays before the expiry of the relevant holiday year."

The matter has now been referred to the European Court of Justice by a Leeds Tribunal and by the Court of Appeal (**Robinson-Steele v R D Services Ltd** (Leeds Tribunal on 9 March 2004) and **Caulfield v Marshalls Clay Products** and **Clarke v Frank Staddon Limited** on 28 April 2004 ([2004] EWCA Civ 422] [2004] IRLR 564)). The Court of Appeal was of the view that the Regulations are not contravened by a contractual arrangement where wages are topped up by a sum that relates to holiday pay, so that holiday pay is not payable when the employee actually takes his or her holiday. Laws LJ was of the view that there was nothing in the Directive which imposed an obligation to make payment at the time holiday is taken. The Court of Appeal stated that the English EAT is not bound by the Court of Session decision in *Munro*, nor would the Scottish EAT be bound by the English Court of Appeal. However, because of the differences between the English and the Scottish Courts, it was felt appropriate to refer the matter to the ECJ.

Termination

Where the worker's employment is terminated during the leave year and the proportion of leave to which he is entitled differs from the proportion which has expired he is entitled to a payment *in lieu* in respect of the leave not taken (regulation 14(2)). The payment due under 14(2) shall be such sum as may be provided for in a Relevant Agreement or, where there is no provision of a Relevant Agreement that applies, a sum equal to the amount that would be due to the worker under regulation 16 in respect of a period of leave determined according to the formula—

$$(A \times B) - C$$

where—

A   is the period of leave to which the worker is entitled under [regulation 13];

B   is the proportion of the worker's leave year which expired before the termination date; and

C   is the period of leave taken by the worker between the start of the leave year and the termination date.

It was held in **Witley and District Men's Club v Mackay** [2001] IRLR 595 that a provision which stipulates that nothing will be paid in the event of dismissal for gross misconduct was not covered by regulation 14(3)(a). The provision in a collective agreement was struck down as being in breach of regulation 35 so that holiday pay was then calculated under the formula. There does not seem to be any reason why a provision could stipulate for a nominal amount to be payable in the event of dismissal for gross misconduct and this is reflected in Precedent I1.

If the worker has already taken in excess of his entitlement then a Relevant Agreement may provide that any payments be paid back (Regulation 14(4)). In the absence of a relevant agreement it is unlawful to seek to recoup overpaid holiday by deducting it from the last salary payment (**Hill v Howard Chapell** [2003] IRLR 19). The contract must therefore always stipulate for overpayment.

Where there are short breaks in employment, for example where the worker is a teacher working only during school terms, it will be necessary to calculate entitlement, as in **Brayshaw v Lambeth Community of Refugees** [EAT 16th December 2003, UK EAT/0713/03/T]. The employee entered into a series of three identical contracts to provide personal services as a tutor in English as a second language for the three terms of the academic year 2001–2002. The first contract started on 10th September 2001 and ended on 17th December 2001. The second started on 7th January 2002 and ended on 15th April 2002. The third started on 22nd April 2002 and ended on 25th July 2002. The Applicant's hours of work were 9.30 am to 12.30 pm on Monday to Wednesday at a salary of £16.25 per hour. The Applicant had only been given three days paid leave. The Tribunal calculated the award on the basis that Ms Brayshaw was not continuously employed but was employed under three separate contracts. The EAT held that the Christmas holiday fell to be included in computing her overall period of employment as she was then "absent from work on account of a temporary cessation of work" within the meaning of the ERA s 212(3)(b). The Easter holidays were included in computing overall employment because ERA s 212(1) provides that "*Any week during the whole or part of which an employee's relations with his employer are governed by a contract of employment counts in computing the employee's period of employment*". Both the week beginning 15th April and the week beginning 22nd April 2002 counted in computing her period of employment. The calculation of holiday pay had to be worked out in accordance with the default formula set out in the WTR, namely (A _ B) – C, where A is the period of leave to which the worker is entitled, B is the proportion of the worker's leave year which expired before the termination date, and C is the period of leave taken by the worker between the start of the leave year and the termination date. The EAT calculated that:

> "..... applied to the present facts, and expressed in terms of days, we proceed on the basis that that formula is (12 × 87.12%) – 4, or 6.45 days. Ms Brayshaw was paid at the rate of £48.75 per day, and so we find that she was entitled to £48.75 × 6.45, or £314.43, by way of payment in lieu of leave".

This was in contrast to the £146.25 awarded by the Tribunal on the basis of three separate contracts.

It was held in **Merino Gomez v Continental Industrias del Caucho SA** [ECJ] 18 March 2004; [2004] IRLR 407 that a women is entitled to her statutory holiday in addition to any maternity leave to which she may be entitled.

In the case of part time workers, the entitlement may be pro-rated (though the Regulations are silent on this point). The Guidance notes state at Chapter 7 that the entitlement will be pro-rated so that for example:

"A part-timer who works three days a week and is still in his or her first month of employment would be able to take one day's leave. The annual entitlement of 12 days (four weeks times three days a week) multiplied by 1/12 equals one day."

Where the employee is entitled to a number of paid holidays per year the week will normally be based on five days equaling one week (**Taylor v E Midlands Offender Employment** [2000] IRLR 760; **Leisure Leagues UK Ltd v Maconnachie** [2002] IRLR 600).

Contractual entitlements

Where the employee is entitled to contractual holiday pay over and above the entitlements set out under the Working Time Regulations the case of **Morley v Heritage PLC** [1993] IRLR 400 will remain of relevance in deciding whether an employee is entitled to holiday pay that has been accrued on termination. The Court of Appeal held that there is no implied term that an employee will be entitled to accrued holiday pay and whether such a term exists depends on the nature of the contract and the status of the employee. In the particular case there was no need to imply such a term to give business efficacy to the contract.

Where a contract provides for a specified number of days holiday per year this will normally be calculated on the basis that five days equals one week (**Taylor v E Midlands Offender Employment** [2000] IRLR 760). It was stated in **Leisure Leagues UK Limited v Maconnachie** [2002] IRLR 600 that the daily rate of accrued holiday should be calculated by reference to 233 total working days in a year rather than 365.

The Directive

The Court of Appeal has held that the European Working Time Directive (93/104) is unconditional and not sufficiently precise to have direct effect so that it cannot be directly enforced against a State employer (**Gibson v East Riding of Yorkshire Council** [CA 21.6.2000]).

Working Time Regulations and Holidays Summarised **Entitlement to Leave: Regulation 13**	
Entitlement	Four weeks annual leave in each leave year (13(1)).
	In the first year, leave accrues at one twelfth of the amount of four weeks over the year, at the beginning of each month (15A). Where the amount of leave that has accrued includes a fraction other than a half day it shall be treated as a half day. Where it is more than a half day it shall be treated as a day (15A(3)).
	Where there is a Relevant Agreement and the employment begins after the date of the Agreement the employee shall be entitled to the proportion of the period of four weeks equal to the proportion of the leave year remaining (13(5))
Qualification	1. Leave year begins the anniversary of 1st October 1998 if employment had commenced before then or the date on which employment begins and each subsequent anniversary or 2. Date provided for in a Relevant Agreement (13(3))
Notice by Employee	Worker may take leave by giving notice, relating to all or part of leave, which shall: 1. specify the days on which leave is to be taken; 2. be given at least twice as many days in advance of the earliest date specified in the notice.
Notice by Employer	The employer may require the worker to take leave, by giving notice, which shall 1. specify the days on which leave is to be taken. 2. be given at least twice as many days in advance of the earliest date specified in the notice.

Notice by Employer *(continued)*	The employer may require the worker not to take leave by giving notice as many days in advance of the earliest date that leave is intended to be taken as the number of days to which the worker's notice related.

Payment and compensation relating to entitlement to leave — Regulations 16 and 14

Entitled to be paid in respect of any period of annual leave at the rate of a week's pay and ss 221–224 of the ERA apply. May be entitled to contractual sum.

Where employment is terminated during the leave year then payment will be for the proportion of leave that has not been taken. A Relevant Agreement may provide that the worker will pay back the employer where he had taken leave in excess of the proportion of the leave year to which he is entitled.

Variation of Contract

Holiday is a contractual (as well as a statutory) right. In some cases holidays may be traditionally taken at specific times and there is, in any event, an entitlement to statutory holiday unless there is an express provision to the contrary. An attempted unilateral variation is likely to be in breach of contract.

- **Tucker v British Leyland Motor Corporation** [1978] IRLR 493. British Leyland sought to move the August bank holiday and New Year's Day bank holiday to the week between Christmas and the New Year, which they agreed would be with the consent of all the unions. The TGWU did not consent and members alleged that they were entitled to be paid for 30th and 31st December. It was held that the claimants were entitled to take the stand they did unless their contracts of employment obliged them to accept transfer of statutory holidays without their consent. Since there was no express term or regular usage to this effect the claimants succeeded. The judge stated that the employer may insert in a contract of employment a term on the following lines:

    "You may be required to work on public holidays. If you are required to work on any public holiday you will be given another day's holiday on a day to be determined by the management.""

- **Evans v Gwent County Council** [Ch Division 5.7.1982].

   The Council designated half term as being from 26th May to 3rd June, during which nine days' paid holiday would be given. The claimant wished to take holiday from 24th May to 8th June and applied for unpaid leave from 24th/25th May and 4th/8th June. He was only permitted to take holiday on the basis that all the holiday was to be unpaid. Foster J held that the claimant was entitled to be paid for the half term as the claimant had not accepted this unilateral variation.

The Precedents

I1 Contains a precedent agreement that takes into account the Regulations.

I2 Is a precedent that may apply where the provisions of the Working Time Regulations have been excluded.

I3 Is a standard provision relating to public holidays.

I4 Relates to factory shutdowns and is dealt in Chapter 5 at 5.5.

I4 Is a standard document to claim holiday leave.

I5 Is a suggested 'rolled up' holiday precedent.

PART J: ABSENCES FROM WORK DUE TO SICKNESS AND THE PROVISION OF SICK PAY

Precedent J: **Absences from work due to sickness and the provision of Sick Pay**

J1: **Sickness or Injury Absence Policy**   679

Letters

1. **Letter expressing concern about persistent absence and giving informal warning**   685

2. **First written warning**   686

3. **Final written warning**   687

4. **Letter of dismissal**   688

J2: **Sick Pay**   688

J3: **Sickness and Unauthorised Absence**   689

J4: **Long Term and Persistent Sickness (Short Form)**   690

J5: **Return to Work**   691

J6: **Medical Suspension**   692

J7: **Non Payment whilst Absent due to Sickness**   692

J8:   **Contractual Payment whilst Absent due to Sickness**   692

J9:   **Contractual Payment whilst Absent due to Sickness dependant upon Length of Service**   692

J10:   **Statutory Sick Pay**   693

J11:   **Claims in Relation to Accidents outside Work**   693

J12:   **Permanent Health Disability Insurance**   694

J13:   **Medical Examination Procedures with Model Forms**   695

J14:   **Sickness Absence due to Disability**   700

Commentary: **Absence from Work due to Sickness**   701

Useful Websites

- STATUTORY SICK PAY

  Inland Revenue site

  http://www.inlandrevenue.gov.uk/employers/fgcat-ssp.shtml

- ACAS GUIDE TO ABSENCE

  http://www.acas.org.uk/publications/B04.html

Cross References

- Duggan *Unfair Dismissal*, Chapter 5 Capability And Qualifications (Contains A To Z of Different Illnesses)

- Duggan *Wrongful Dismissal*

  3.5.   Contractual Disability Benefits

  6.16. Sick Pay

Precedent J1:   Sickness or Injury Absence Policy

1   General

1.1   If for any reason you are unexpectedly unable to attend work for sickness reasons, you must inform your Manager as early as possible on the first day of absence. Whilst absent due to sickness you are to keep your Manager informed of the place where you are living and can be contacted.

1.2   If you are absent between one and _____ days (inclusive of Saturday, Sunday and Bank Holidays) you should complete a Company Self-Certification Form on your return to work. This form will be available from _____.

1.3   If you are absent for more than _____ days you must obtain a medical certificate from your doctor.

1.4   If you are absent again with a gap of 14 days or less between sicknesses, the two periods of illness may be linked. Therefore, even if you fall sick again on Saturday or Sunday, you should complete a Company self-certification form on your return.

1.5 After receiving 28 weeks of Statutory Sick Pay in any tax year, you will be transferred to State Sickness benefit.

1.6 The Company reserves the right to require any employee, who is absent due to sickness, to be examined by a medical practitioner appointed by the Company. If the Company wishes you to attend an examination it will nominate a medical practitioner and an appointment will be made that is convenient to you.

2 Long Term Sickness Absence

2.1 The efficient running of the Company depends upon employees regularly attending work. Long term or persistent short term absence jeopardises the ability of the Company to carry out its functions. In such circumstances your future employment with the Company may become an issue or the Company may have to consider altering your job functions or conditions or adjusting your working environment to accommodate your needs. In these circumstances the Company will first require you to be examined by a doctor appointed by the Company. They will nominate a medical practitioner and an appointment will be made that is convenient to you.

2.2 Upon receipt of a medical report, the Company may arrange an interview between yourself and the _____ to consider your future employment with the Company, which may lead to your employment being terminated on notice or the terms and conditions of your employment being altered if you will not be able to carry out your work for the long term future.

ANY STEPS THAT ARE TAKEN IN RELATION TO EMPLOYEES WHO ARE ABSENT ON LONG TERM SICKNESS WILL BE TAKEN IN CONJUNCTION WITH THE COMPANY'S DISABILITY POLICY WHICH WILL BE AUTOMATICALLY CONSIDERED IN RELATION TO SUCH ABSENCES.

2.3   Long term sickness absence is defined as _____ [set out periods].

3   Persistent absence

3.1   If your Manager, with the concurrence of _____, considers that you are persistently absent from work such that you are not properly performing your job functions or other employees have to cover for you, the procedure set out below may be implemented.

3.2   Short term persistent absence will normally be defined as [SET OUT THE NUMBER OF DAYS IN SET PERIODS WHICH WILL BE REGARDED AS SHORT TERM SICKNESS ABSENCE].

3.3   The Company recognises that employees will be sick from time to time and would not expect employees to attend work if they are unwell. However, short term persistent absence can cause serious problems for the Company because it leads to uncertainty as well as making it difficult for the Company to plan cover for employees who are sick on a persistent but unpredictable basis. Certain absences will be viewed differently, such as absence due to pregnancy (which will not be taken into account in calculating days under this procedure) and absences due to a disability (which will be considered under the Disability Policy). Where the Company considers that short term persistent absence is unsatisfactory or gives cause for concern, it will invoke the following policy.

(1)   You will first be interviewed by your line manager, who will explain the reasons for the Company's concerns and this may lead to you being given an informal oral warning.

(2)   If you are thereafter absent for [days] over a [period] you may be asked to attend a formal meeting by your line manager and may be issued with a first formal written warning. This warning will be placed on your file and will remain for [period] months.

(3) Following such warning, if you are absent from work at all during the following [period] months or on [number] separate occasions you will be interviewed by [set out whether more senior person] and you may be issued with a final written warning. This warning will be placed on your file and will remain for [period] months.

(4) Following a final written warning, if you are then absent for [days] over a [period] month period or on [number] separate occasions you will be asked to attend a meeting at which consideration may be given to your future employment with the Company.

3.4 At each stage of the above procedure you will be entitled to have a colleague present.

3.5 You will be given reasonable advance notice in writing of the request to attend at each stage and you will be provided with a copy of your attendance record and such personnel details as are relevant.

3.6 At each interview you will be entitled to give a full explanation of the reasons for your absences and you will be able to put forward any mitigating factors. The Company will give full consideration to your explanations and may adjourn any interview in order to obtain medical evidence or confirmation of the reason for your absences.

3.7 You will have a right of appeal at each stage. The person to whom you may appeal will be provided to you by [HR].

4   Unauthorised absence and Malingering

Where you have not followed the procedures for notification of sickness or facts or matters are drawn to the attention of the Company which could lead it to conclude that you are not in fact sick, the Company reserves the right to invoke its disciplinary procedures.

Prior to invoking such procedures the Company shall have the right to require that you be medically examined in accordance with its Company procedures.

5 Abuse of sickness absence

It is expected that employees who are absent because of sickness will act in such manner to facilitate their return to work as soon as possible whilst at the same time the Company recognises the need for employees to be fit and well and would not expect an employee to return before fully recovered. The fact that an employee is unable to work means that, normally, the employee would not be expected to take part in other activities. To that end:

- We would not expect you to take part in any sports, hobbies or social activities which are inconsistent with your illness and are not for recuperative purposes. In particular, activities which could prolong or aggravate any injury or could delay recovery should not be carried out.

- You must not carry out any other employment or work, whether it is paid or unpaid. It will be a serious disciplinary matter for you to engage in outside work whilst you allege that you are incapacitated from working for the Company.

- You must not engage in any activity that is inconsistent with the nature of your illness (such as shopping if you allege you are bedridden).

Any perceived abuse of the sickness absence policy is likely to be regarded as a disciplinary matter and result in disciplinary proceedings.

6 Sickness and holiday

6.1 Whilst you are absent due to sickness your entitlement to holiday will continue to accrue.

6.2 If you have already booked holiday but become sick before holiday is taken you must inform your manager as to whether you still wish to take such period as holiday. This may particularly apply where you have pre-booked, for example, a holiday abroad, and you will lose monies paid. In such circumstances the Company may treat the period as holiday but you will be expected not to do anything which may prolong or aggravate your illness.

6.3 If you fall sick once your holiday has commenced this period will remain as holiday, subject to the Company exercising its discretion in exceptional cases to treat it otherwise.

7   Absences outside work

Incorporate J11.

8   Suspension from work

Incorporate J6

9   Returning to work

Incorporate J5

DATED

Letters

Letter One

Dear   ,

I am writing to you to confirm the outcome of the interview which took place on [date] when we discussed the Company's concerns about your persistent absence over the last [number] months.

I confirm that you have been absent on the following dates:

We discussed at length the reasons for these absences and you advised me that [set out any explanation].

Unfortunately, the Company still views these absences as unsatisfactory given the significant disruption that they are causing to the Company. I must advise you that unless there is significant improvement this will lead to a more formal process whereby the Company may have to proceed to the first stage of the written warning procedure.

If you are absent due to sickness for [number] days over the next [number] months or on more than [number] occasions the Company will invoke the first stage of the warning procedure.

Yours etc

Second Letter

Dear   ,

I am writing to you to confirm the outcome of the meeting which took place on [date] at which your persistent absence record was further discussed.

You were invited to and had [name] present with you as a companion.

I explained to you that your absence record over the previous [number] months had been as follows and that this was in excess of the number of days/occasions which it was stated would not be acceptable to the Company.

I invited you to give an explanation and you [set out].

The explanation is not satisfactory to the Company. Therefore, should your attendance not improve over the next [period] months the Company may have to proceed to the next stage of its procedure.

If you are absent due to sickness for [number] days over the next [number] months or on more than [number] occasions the Company will invoke the second stage of the warning procedure.

You have a right to appeal against this written warning to [name].

This warning will remain on your file for [period].

Yours

Third Letter

Dear   ,

I am writing to you to confirm the outcome of the meeting which took place on [date] at which your persistent absence record was further discussed.

You were invited to and had [name] present with you as a companion

I explained to you that your absence record over the previous [number] months had been as follows and that this was in excess of the number of days/occasions which it was stated would not be acceptable to the Company.

I invited you to give an explanation and you [set out].

The explanation is not satisfactory to the Company. [You have not been able to provide any satisfactory explanation as to why your attendance has not improved despite having been warned both informally and formally about this]. Therefore, should your attendance not improve over the next [period] months the Company will proceed to the next stage of its procedure which may result in your dismissal.

If you are absent due to sickness for [number] days over the next [number] months or on more than [number] occasions the Company will invoke the final stage of its procedure. This is a final written warning.

You have a right to appeal against this written warning to [name].

This warning will remain on your file for [period].

Yours

Dismissal Letter

Dear   ,

Further to the hearing which took place on [date] at which your persistent absence record was discussed, I confirm that the decision has been taken to terminate your employment.

You were accompanied by [name] who acted as your companion.

At the meeting, your absence record was discussed in full and you were unable to provide any satisfactory explanation for the same.

You have a right to appeal against this decision within [number] days.

Yours

Precedent J2: Sick Pay

During periods of authorised absence due to your own sickness, it is the Company's policy to supplement Statutory Sick Pay (SSP) and State Sickness Benefits with additional benefits sufficient to maintain your income at approximately the same level as your normal salary. Details of your entitlement to sick pay if applicable will have been set out in your Letter of Appointment.

Precedent J3: Sickness Absence & Unauthorised Absence

It is a contractual requirement that you are available during your normal working hours or such other hours as have been agreed. You must attempt to attend work but if you are delayed you must inform your Manager by telephone as soon as possible and explain the reason for absence or delay. Failure to attend without justification may result in your pay being reduced and could also result in disciplinary action. **This will not occur until the Company has followed its disciplinary procedures**. When your absence is due to sickness you must:

1) Ensure that your manager has been notified on the first day of your absence and that your manager is told of the reason for absence. It is not acceptable to simply leave a message.

2) Complete a self certification form on your return.

3) Where the absence is for _____ days or more (including weekends) you must submit a doctor's certificate to _____ and further certificates must cover the total period of absence, at least once every seven days. You must keep the Company informed of your likely return date.

4) If you fall ill whilst you are on holiday this will not count as sick leave unless you have obtained a doctor's certificate and the Company agree, in their absolute discretion, to treat it as sick leave.

Abuse of sickness absence

It is expected that employees who are absent because of sickness will act in such manner to facilitate their return to work as soon as possible whilst at the same time the Company recognises the need for employees to be fit and well and would not expect an employee to return before fully recovered. The fact that an employee is unable to work means that, normally, the employee would not be expected to take part in other activities. To that end:

- We would not expect you to take part in any sports, hobbies or social activities which are inconsistent with your illness and are not for recuperative purposes. In particular, activities which could prolong or aggravate any injury or could delay recovery should not be carried out.

- You must not carry out any other employment or work, whether it is paid or unpaid. It will be a serious disciplinary matter for you to engage in outside work whilst you allege that you are incapacitated from working for the Company.

- You must not engage in any activity that is inconsistent with the nature of your illness (such as shopping if you allege you are bedridden).

Any perceived abuse of the sickness abuse policy is likely to be regarded as a disciplinary matter and will result in disciplinary proceedings.

Precedent J4: Long-term/Persistent Sickness Absence & Medical Reports (SHORT FORM)

1 The efficiency of the Company depends upon its employees attending work on a regular basis as agreed in their terms and conditions of employment. Long term or persistent absence can create difficulties for the Company.

2 Long term absence is defined as _____ days at any one time during the calendar year.

3 Persistent absence is defined as _____ days of absence which may be separate or at one time during the calendar year.

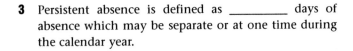

4 In such cases the Company may consider it necessary to take appropriate action **which could result in disciplinary sanctions such as warnings or could lead the Company to take the view that it has no choice other than to** terminate your employment or alter the terms and conditions on which you work. Before doing so:

- it will make full investigation;

- and you will have the right to attend a meeting to discuss the Company's concerns.

- You will have a right of appeal against any decision that the Company makes.

5 Should you be required to attend a meeting where some form of action may be taken then you will be entitled to bring along a companion.

6 The Company reserves the right to have a medical examination from a medical practitioner which it will nominate at the Company's expense.

7 In any event you are required at any time during the course of their employment at the request of the Company to a medical examination by a registered medical practitioner nominated by the Company for the purpose of considering whether you are fit to carry out your duties.

Precedent J5: Return to Work

You should not return to work until you have been certified as fit to return to work in cases where a premature return to work may affect your physical or mental well-being or create a risk to health and safety. In certain circumstances the Company may wish you, in the exercise of its discretion, to attend a medical examination, at the Company's expense, before it allows you to return to work.

Precedent J6: Suspension on Medical Grounds

The Company has the right to suspend you from work on medical grounds under section 64 of the ERA 1996. It will endeavour to find you suitable alternative work but if no such alternative work is available you will be paid during the period of suspension in accordance with the provisions of sections 64 and 65 of the ERA for a period of up to 26 weeks. If you are absent due to sickness you will be paid under the Company's sick pay scheme.

Precedent J7: No Payments while Absent due to Sickness

You are not entitled to sick pay but if you are unable to perform your duties due to illness or injury the Company may pay you in its absolute discretion.

Precedent J8: Payments while absent due to sickness

You may be paid sickness pay from your first day of absence if you comply with the rules as to notification of sickness and the Statutory Sick Pay Scheme. The Company may withhold any pay if you fail to adhere to the rules as to notification and such absence may be treated as unauthorised.

Precedent J9: Payments while absent due to sickness dependent upon length of service

1   You will be entitled to receive payment for periods of absence during any consecutive 12 month period through illness as follows:

1) Full salary for absences up to _____;

2) Half salary for absences between _____ and _____.

2 These payments are made entirely at the Company's discretion and may be withheld if it is considered that you should not be entitled to payment for any reason, including abuse of the sick pay entitlement.

3 The Company reserves the right to terminate your employment at any time during your absence from work even though at the time of giving notice you remain entitled to sick pay under the sick pay scheme.

4 Absence due to sickness has a significant cost implication for the Company's business. A high level of periodic absence for minor ill health causes will be of concern to the Company.

5 The Company maintains a permanent health insurance scheme to cover long term absence. The said scheme provides benefits for employees when the absence is longer than 26 weeks. Details of its scheme can be obtained from [the Human Resources Department.]

Precedent J10: Statutory Sick Pay

You will be paid statutory sick pay in accordance with the Statutory Sick Pay scheme that is in force from time to time. The relevant forms are available from _____

Precedent J11: Claims in Relation to Accidents Occurring Outside Work

Should you be absent from work due to the negligence or other actionable conduct of a third party all payments made to you during absence because of such injuries by the Company shall be regarded as loans and you agree that if you recover compensation for loss of earnings such sums will be repaid to the Company from the compensation that you have recovered. The Company shall also be entitled to recover from you any tax or national insurance monies that have been paid and you will include such sums in any claim that you may make against the third party.

Precedent J12: Permanent Health or Disability Insurance

See F12 for a Precedent and consider including:

The Company shall have no liability to the employee where:

- The insurer refuses to pay under the terms of the insurance policy in place from time to time.

- Until such monies as are due are advanced by the insurer.

Where the terms of the insurance policy in place from time to time means that the employee is not entitled to the benefit then the policy shall take precedence over the contract of employment, if and in so far as it leads the insurers to decline any application under the policy.

The Company shall have no duty other than to put forward to the insurer such evidence as the employee shall provide of his entitlement under the policy by way of ill health or disability and to request the insurer to consider the employee's entitlement under the policy. If and in so far as the employee requested the Company to take any further steps the employee shall provide a full indemnity for all costs and liabilities that may be incurred.

Or

The policy is held to the benefit of the employee under the Contracts (Rights of Third Parties) Act 1999 and the insurer has been informed of this.

Precedent J13: Medical Examination Procedure

Policy on obtaining Medical Reports

In certain circumstances, for insurance or employment reasons, the Company may wish to obtain a medical report from a medical practitioner who has responsibility for the clinical care of an employee. In such cases the following procedure will be followed.

1 The decision to request a medical report may be made for certain purposes relating to employment matters or if insurance issues (for example, permanent health insurance) arise. In such cases Personnel will ascertain whether the Access to Medical Records Act 1988 applies.

2 Where the Act applies the individual must be informed of rights under the Act and Form 1 provided for that purpose. It is the responsibility of the Manager/Personnel to ensure that the individual is so informed.

3 Individuals may have queries about the request which should be answered in conjunction with Personnel.

4 The individual is entitled to refuse to give consent to the provision of a report. However, where consent is withheld it will be necessary to ascertain the reasons and the individual must be informed that the lack of a report may affect decisions about the employment of the individual.

5 Where the individual consents it is necessary for Form 2 to be completed stating whether the individual has indicated if he or she wishes to see the report before it is provided to the Company. Personnel must be provided with a copy of the Form and will check that it has been correctly completed.

6 Upon application to the medical practitioner, the reasons for the application must be set out and the medical practitioner should be told that arrangements for access to the report through the medical practitioner should be made by the individual where the individual has so requested. The individual should be advised on Form 3 that a request has been made.

7 If arrangements are not made then the practitioner may supply the report to the Company without the individual's consent. The individual will then have six months to request access to the report from the medical practitioner not the Company.

8 The individual should consent to the Company seeing the report as soon as possible once he or she has seen the report. Where the individual, having seen the report, refuses consent, he or she should be told that any decision will have to be taken on such medical evidence as the Company has in its possession. The same procedure may apply where the individual unreasonably delays in giving consent.

9 All reports are confidential and the individual should be told that the report will be treated with the utmost confidence.

FORM ONE

TO _____

The Company wishes to obtain a report from your Doctor for the following purpose

SET OUT

_____ **SIGNED**

You have certain rights under the Access to Medical Records Act 1988, namely

1. You may refuse to give your consent.

2. You may ask to see the medical report before the Company receive it. You may advise the Company that you request access to the report in which case your medical practitioner will be advised at the time a request is made or you may ask your medical practitioner at a later time but before the report is supplied to the Company.

3. If you ask to see the report then you must contact your medical practitioner within 21 days of the Company applying for the report otherwise it may be given to the Company without your consent. You may ask your medical practitioner to amend the report if you think it is inaccurate or misleading and it may be amended. If the medical practitioner does not agree then a statement of your views will be attached to the report at your request.

4. Your medical practitioner may decide that you should not see the report or part of it if it is considered that it could seriously harm your physical or mental health or that it reveals information about others or the identity of a person who provided information unless that person consented or was a health professional involved in caring for you. You will be told why the part of the report has been withheld and can only amend what you are shown.

5. You may withdraw your consent to the Company seeing the report. The Company will then have to rely on such medical evidence as it has.

6. You can ask your medical practitioner to show you or provide a copy of the report up to six months after it has been provided.

I consent to the Company requesting a medical report from _____ of _____

SIGNED

I have been informed of my rights as set out above and I wish/do not wish to see the report before it is provided to the Company.

SIGNED

FORM TWO

TO _____ **OF** _____

ON BEHALF OF _____ **COMPANY**

The Company employs _____ I am writing to request a medical report from you as we have been informed that _____ is a patient of yours.

The report is subject to the provisions of the Access to Medical Records Act 1988. The employee has been informed of his/her rights and we enclose Form 1 in this respect. We would be grateful if you could provide your views on the following questions relating to the employee's state of health taking into account the employee's occupation which is _____

SET OUT QUESTIONS

The employee has asked to see a copy of the report. You therefore cannot supply it to the Company until the Employee has seen it and consents to its supply, or has asked for parts to be amended as being misleading or inaccurate and you have so amended, or you disagree and have attached a statement that the employee has objected **unless the employee has not contacted you within 21 days of this request in which case you may provide the report without the employee's consent.**

SIGNED

FORM THREE

TO _____

The Company requested a report from your Doctor on following permission being given by yourself. As you asked to see the report it will not be supplied to the Company unless you have seen it and, if you consider parts of it to be inaccurate or misleading, it has been amended or your Doctor has attached a statement that you consider parts to be inaccurate or misleading or **you have not contacted your Doctor within 21 days from the above date**.

_____ **SIGNED**

Precedent J14:   Disability Policy

For a full policy see Part T. Given the recent decision of the Court of Appeal (see text) it may be worth including a statement in sickness and absence procedures stating:

"Although contractual sick pay will only be paid for the periods of time set out in your contract/the Handbook and there are certain procedures in relation to long term or persistent absence or absences, if you believe that your absences are due to a disability within the meaning of the Disability Discrimination Act 1995, you should inform ...... and consideration will then be given as to whether a different procedure or a reasonable adjustment is appropriate in your case."

COMMENTARY: ABSENCE FROM WORK DUE TO SICKNESS

The CIPD survey for 2003 estimated that the annual cost per employee for sickness absence averages at about £567. The cost of such absences is huge and employers need to have a proper system in place for measuring levels of sickness absence, for carrying out the legal mechanisms to review the reasons, and for ensuring the application of appropriate sanctions where absence due to sickness has become unacceptable or excessive, or to deal with the malingerer. The employer may wish to have the employee medically examined. The impact of the Disability Discrimination Act must also be carefully considered.

This commentary will deal with the following issues:

(1) Measuring sickness absence.

(2) Medical examinations.

(3) Sickness absence as an employment issue.

(4) Handling long term or persistent sickness absence.

(5) Disability Discrimination.

(6) Unauthorised absence and Dealing with the malingerer.

(7) Suspension on medical grounds.

(8) Return to work.

(9) Sick pay.

(10) Accidents

(11) Insurance

(1) Measuring sickness absence

Absence measures may be used for a whole range of reasons (benchmark organisational levels; comparisons between departments; highlighting problem areas and health and safety and calculating attendance costs) as well as to monitor the employee to decide whether steps (attendance reviews, capability procedures etc.) need to be carried out by the employer. It is important that absences are accurately recorded and in some cases this may make the difference between a fair and unfair dismissal; for example, where the reason for the absence dictates who is selected for redundancy. It is therefore important, both that there is a record of the dates and reasons for absences and also that the employee has a means of analysing his absence records. In relation to the former the use of a certification process may assist, whilst in relation to the latter there are some relatively sophisticated methods whereby the employee may be measured against the statistical average in order to gauge whether his absence is above the norm.

Absence recording

The following considerations should be borne in mind:

- Most organisations have a self-certification process for the first few days of absence. The employee should be made aware of this process and, in particular of the time by which the employee should report in. Much inconvenience and disruption may be caused if the employee does not make the employer aware of his illness by a certain time and this may lead to employment sanctions.

- Doctor's certificates may have been provided but these are not conclusive.

- Return to work interviews and a record of the interview are to be encouraged as they give the employer the opportunity to gauge whether there is an underlying problem and also consider what steps may be taken to assist the employee.

Where a record is to be kept the requirements of the Data Protection Act 1998 must be satisfied and reference should be made to Chapter 2 for the general principles. The Information Commissioner has produced Part 4 of the Code in draft, entitled **Part 4: Information About Workers' Health**. Part 4 addresses the collection and subsequent use of information about a worker's physical or mental health or condition. Collection will often be done by some form of medical examination or test, but may involve other means such as health questionnaires. The Code is stated to apply to:

- a questionnaire completed by workers to detect problems with their health;

- information about a worker's disabilities or special needs;

- the results of an eye-test taken by a worker using a display screen;

- records of a worker's blood type kept in case the worker is involved in an accident;

- records of blood tests carried out to ensure the worker has not been exposed to hazardous substances;

- the results of a test carried out to check a worker's exposure to alcohol or drugs;

- the results of genetic tests carried out on workers.

The Code is stated as only applying to information which is or will be held electronically or recorded in a filing system. It will not be applied where no record is kept (the Code gives the example of someone being breath tested on the spot). The Sensitive Data Rules are likely to be engaged in this area (see Chapter 2 at page 114). Section 3 of the Code gives good practice recommendations, divided into:

1. Information about workers' health: general considerations;

2. Occupational health schemes;

3. Medical examinations and testing;

4. Drug & alcohol testing;

5. Genetic testing,

Reference should be made to the Code.

Measuring the absence rate

The *ACAS Advisory Booklet on Absence* sets out two methods of measuring the absence rate as follows:

See http://www.acas.org.uk/publications/B04.html.

The most common measure of absence is the lost time rate. This shows the percentage of the total time available which has been lost because of absence from all causes in a given period.

$$\frac{\text{Total absence (hours or days)}}{\text{Possible total (hours or days)}} \times 100 = \text{Lost time rate}$$

For example, if the total absence in the period is 124 hours, and the possible total is 1,550 hours, the lost time rate is:

$$\frac{124}{1,550} \times 100 = 8\%$$

The lost time rate can be regarded as an overall measure of the severity of the problem. If calculated separately by department or group of workers, it can show up particular problem areas.

Total time lost, however, may consist of a small number of people who are absent for long periods, or a large number absent for short spells. A measure of 'frequency' is needed to show how widespread the problem is, so that companies can formulate appropriate plans to reduce it.

The frequency rate shows the average number of spells of absence per worker (expressed as a percentage) irrespective of the length of each spell.

$$\frac{\text{No of spells of absence in the period}}{\text{No of workers in the period}} \times 100 = \text{Frequency rate}$$

organisation wishes to monitor the number of workers absent at all during the period the individual frequency rate can be used:

$$\frac{\text{No of workers having one or more spells of absence}}{\text{No of workers}} \times 100$$

= Individual Frequency rate

For example, in one month an organisation employed on average 80 workers. During this time 12 workers had periods of absence: one was away three times, two were away twice and nine were away once, a total number of 16 spells of absence. The frequency rate was therefore:

$$\frac{16}{80} \times 100$$

= 20%

The individual frequency rate was:

$$\frac{12}{80} \times 100$$

= 15%

Another individual index of absence, developed by Bradford University, highlights repeated short-term absence by giving extra weight to the number of absences. It is given by the formula:

Index $(I) = S \times S \times H$, where:

S = the number of absences; and

H = total hours absent in any given period

For example:

Worker with two periods of absence totalling 10 days (80 hours):

$I = 2 \times 2 \times 80 = 320$

Absentee with six periods of absence totalling 10 days (80 hours):

$I = 6 \times 6 \times 80 = 2880$

Organisations can use the indicator to provide a trigger point for action. It is important, however, to examine the particular circumstances leading to a high score before action is taken.

In measuring lost time in the above way, the employer can consider what is and what is not an acceptable level of absence and when this level is reached absence appraisal interviews may be triggered. In the first example a frequency rate of, say, over 15% may trigger the process, whilst in the second the absentee with six periods of absence may meet the benchmark and trigger the process. The employer simply decides what point score will have this effect.

(2) Medical examinations

The precedents at J13 set out the procedure that the Company may wish to follow in obtaining medical reports from a medical practitioner responsible for the clinical care of the individual. The precedent sets out a policy to be given to employees in relation to obtaining medical records as well the forms to be sent to the employee and GP.

The employer may wish to obtain from the employee's GP or some other doctor who is responsible for the clinical care of the employee an opinion as to the employee's medical condition and prognosis.

The procedure for obtaining a medical report is governed by the Access to Medical Records Act 1988. Under the provisions of that Act:

• An application cannot be made to a medical practitioner for a medical report for employment or insurance purposes unless the applicant (employer in this case) has notified the individual that he proposes to make the application and the individual has notified the applicant that he consents to the making of the application.

- The notification by the applicant must inform the individual that he has the following rights: (1) to withhold consent to the making of the application (2) to access to the report before or after it is supplied (3) to withhold consent once the he (the individual) has been given access to the report (4) to correct errors or to request amendments. He must also be informed that there are certain exemptions.

- For the purposes of the Act the medical practitioner in the case of an individual is the person registered under the Medical Act 1983 and the medical report means a report relating to the physical or mental health of the individual prepared by a medical practitioner who is or has been responsible for the clinical welfare of the individual.

The Individual's Rights

By section 4 these are:

The right, when giving consent to the making of an application, to state that he wishes to have access to the report before it is supplied. In this case the applicant must notify the medical practitioner of the individual's wish to access to the report, and at the same time the applicant must notify the individual of the making of the application.

The notification must contain a statement to the medical practitioner that the practitioner shall not supply the report unless he has given the individual access to it and that section 5 has been satisfied or that 21 days have elapsed beginning with the date of the application without his having received any communication from the individual concerning arrangements for the individual to have access.

If the medical practitioner is not given such notification but receives notification from the individual that he wishes to have access to it then he shall not supply the report unless he has given the individual access to it and section 5 has been satisfied or 21 days have lapsed without his having received any communication from the individual concerning arrangements for the individual to have access.

Access means making the report available for inspection or providing a copy of the report.

By section 5:

where the individual has been given access to the report it shall not be supplied unless the individual has notified the medical practitioner that he consents to it being supplied.

The individual shall be entitled to request the medical practitioner to amend any part or the report which he considers to be inaccurate and misleading and the medical practitioner shall so amend if he is prepared to accede to the request but if he is not so prepared he shall attach a statement of the individual's views in respect of the part which he declines to amend.

Retention of reports

The medical practitioner shall retain a copy of the report for six months from the date it was supplied and the individual is entitled to access to it during that period.

Exemptions

The medical practitioner is not obliged to give the individual access where he considers disclosure would cause serious harm to the physical or mental health of the individual or would indicate the intentions of the practitioner in respect of the individual or where it would reveal the identity of another person who has provided information unless that person has consented or has been provided by a health professional involved in the care of the individual. The individual may be notified in relation to the whole or part of a report.

Any applications should be made to the County Court.

(3) Sickness absence as an employment issue

A detailed sickness absence policy is set out at J1 together with sample letters that may be sent to an employee where there are concerns about persistent absence which may lead to a series of warnings and may eventually lead to dismissal.

It is important to note that where dismissal is being considered as one of the options the statutory Disciplinary and Dismissal procedures will become applicable.

Bearing in mind what is said above about the means of measuring sickness absence and taking into account the statutory procedures that are required in order to pursue a medical examination, the employer will need to have a clear scheme so that employees know what steps they should take in order to notify the employer of absence due to sickness and the potential repercussions should the employee be off sick for certain periods of time. The procedure should provide for the right on the part of the employer to insist that the employee is examined by a medical practitioner and there needs to be a procedure which will set out the likely consequences for certain types of sickness.

The new Disciplinary procedures and Grievance procedures are likely to apply to the case where an employer is considering dismissing the employee because of sickness absences. The Disciplinary procedures apply where the employer contemplates dismissing or taking "relevant disciplinary action". "Relevant disciplinary action" is action, short of dismissal, which the employer asserts to be based wholly or mainly on the employee's *conduct or capability*, other than suspension on full pay or the issuing of warnings (whether oral or written). Whilst some dismissals for absence may be based upon conduct (where it is believed that the employee is malingering) it is likely that cases will be based upon capability. The reason for the absence may raise questions as to whether the issue is one of conduct or capability; for example absence due to an alcohol or drug problem (see Part M and Precedent M3). It is not clear what would happen where there is a sickness dismissal for Some Other Substantial Reason as in **Wharfedale Loudspeakers v Poynton** [EAT 82/92]. The employee should be sure about the reason for dismissal as there is always the risk of falling into the type of trap that the employer fell into in the case of **Devonshire v Trico-Foklberth Limited** [1989] ICR 747. The employer changed the reason for dismissal from poor attendance to dismissal on medical grounds. The ET held that dismissal for the first reason would have been fair but the dismissal on medical grounds was procedurally unfair as there had been no medical report and no consultation. This was upheld by the Court of Appeal.

The ACAS Code of Practice on Disciplinary and Grievance procedures states:

"Dealing with absence from work

37 When dealing with absence from work, it is important to determine the reasons why the employee has not been at work. If there is no acceptable reason, the matter should be treated as a conduct issue and dealt with as a disciplinary matter.

38 If the absence is due to genuine (including medically certified) illness, the issue becomes one of capability, and the employer should take a sympathetic and considerate approach. When thinking about how to handle these cases, it is helpful to consider:

  • how soon the employee's health and attendance will improve;

  • whether alternative work is available;

  • the effect of the absence on the organisation;

  • how similar situations have been handled in the past; and

  • whether the illness is a result of disability in which case the provisions of the Disability Discrimination Act 1995 will apply.

39 The impact of long-term absences will nearly always be greater on small organisations, and they may be entitled to act at an earlier stage than large organisations.

40 In cases of extended sick leave both statutory and contractual issues will need to be addressed and specialist advice may be necessary."

The original draft of the Code stated that the law expected employers to be more tolerant of workers who are absent because they have a disability and recommended consideration of the DDA 1995 in any such case.

(See **British Coal Corporation v Bowers** [EAT 1021/93], however, from which it is clear from this case that the guidelines are not a checklist that must be followed.)

It is expected that, in addition to ensuring that the statutory procedures are complied with, the employee will at the least be expected to follow the approach set out in **International Sports Co Ltd v Thomson** [1980] IRLR 340 (see below under persistent absence).

Where it is apparent that the employee can no longer carry out the job the employer will wish to be in a position to terminate the contract after carrying out a proper procedure, which will involve warnings about the likely consequences of absence and a proper review of the employee's record (see **Lynock v Cereal Packaging Limited** [1988] ICR 670 and see Duggan, *Unfair Dismissal, Law and Practice*, at pages 139–144 for a full consideration of this topic).

As part of any sickness procedure it would be prudent for the employer to obtain a medical report. Indeed, a failure to do so may make any dismissal unfair (see **Parsons & Co Limited v Kidney** [EAT 788/87] and Duggan on *Unfair Dismissal* at page 134). The procedure should contain a right to request a medical report as there may be a constructive dismissal if a report is demanded without any express right (see **Bliss v South East Thames Regional Health Authority** [1987] ICR 700; [1983] IRLR 308).

Where the employee is persistently absent for short periods of time a medical report may not be quite as crucial: **Davis v Tibbett & Britten Group** [EAT 460/99] where Judge Collins stated:

> "An employer is perfectly entitled to dismiss an employee who has been frequently absent for medical reasons over a significant period of time, whether or not the employee is in any way at fault because of the absences, provided that the employer has carried out a proper procedure including warning and counselling.... This is not a case where it would have been helpful to seek medical evidence. The appellant had over the years a large number of unconnected ailments. The employers were entitled to look at the whole history, entitled to look at the warnings which had been given and decide whether or not they were prepared to continue to shoulder the burden of an employee who had been absent on so many occasions."

There is also no absolute requirement that the employee's GP be consulted (**London Borough of Tower Hamlets v Bull** [EAT 153/91]).

Where a report is sought from the employee's own GP or consultant then the procedures of the Access to Medical Reports Act 1988 set out above will apply.

(4) Disability Discrimination

In Chapter 1 the concepts relating to the definition of disability, less favourable treatment and reasonable adjustments were set out. In a case where the employee has been absent for long periods of time or has persistent absences this may be due to a disability which comes within the definition of the DDA.

From 1st October 2004 the DDA 1995 will apply to all employees (including previously excluded sectors such as the fire services, police and prison officers).

Given the fact that the effect of an impairment under the Act must last or be likely to last more than 12 months (Schedule 1 paragraph 2 DDA 1995) the Act will have particular repercussions in the case of long term absence. It is, however, likely to impact upon persistent short term absence as set out below, particularly where there is a recurring or progressive condition.

The reason for less favourable treatment must relate to the disability so that in **London Clubs Management v Hood** [2001] IRLR 719, where the employee was not paid sick pay because it was withdrawn from non-managerial employees, this did not relate to the disability. (Query where sick pay is only paid for a period of time and then withdrawn but the employee's disability means that he has higher levels than usual of sickness absence – it is now clear from *Meikle* (see page 727) that consideration will have to be given to altering the sick pay policy).

The employee may claim that the employer has failed, in breach of section 5(2), to make a reasonable adjustment under section 6. From 1st October 2004, where there has been such a failure the justification defence will not apply (see further discussion in Chapter 1) since this is removed by the Disability Discrimination Act 1995 (Amendment) Regulations 2003 SI 2003/1673. Section 6(3) gives some examples which are likely to apply in sickness cases:

(b) allocating some of the disabled person's duties to another person;

(c) transferring him to fill an existing vacancy;

(*d*) altering his working hours;

(*e*) assigning him to a different place of work;

(*f*) allowing him to be absent during working hours for rehabilitation, assessment or treatment;

where these adjustments would obviate the employee's illness and thus the reason for absence.

Where employees are dismissed they may bring a claim both under the DDA 1995 and for unfair dismissal if they have one year's service. It should, however, be noted that the statutory tests are different so that a case in which it is found that there has been disability discrimination will not automatically lead to a finding of unfair dismissal (**HJ Heinz Co Ltd v Kenrick** [2000] ICR 491).

The employer will not be able to justify direct discrimination based upon the failure to make a reasonable adjustment from 1st October 2004. It is apparent that there may be practical adjustments that can be made in respect of employees who are absent due to sickness that will get them back to work, as set out below.

Further examples of reasonable adjustments that could be made are given later in this chapter when considering the nature of the sickness in question.

(5) Handling long term or persistent sickness absence

As well as the main policy J1, reference may be made to a short form policy J4 in considering the nature of the policy that is appropriate for the employer.

Long-term/Persistent Sickness Absence and Medical Reports

Long term and persistent sickness absence raise specific issues if the employer considers that the business cannot continue to tolerate such absence on the part of the employee.

Frustration

It may be that long term absence has caused the contract to become frustrated (see **Marshall v Harland and Woolf Limited** [1972] ICR 101 for a consideration of the circumstances when this may be the case; and see Duggan, *Unfair Dismissal* at page 64–66).

Long term sickness

Where the employee is off sick long term the DDA 1995 may be particularly relevant. In considering whether there has been discrimination against the disabled employee, it was held by the Court of Appeal in **Clark v TDG Ltd t/a Novacold** [1999] IRLR 318 that the correct comparator in the case of long term dismissal of a disabled employee was someone to whom the employee's reasons for dismissal did not apply: that is an employee who had not been absent from work. The employee in *Clark* was discriminated against where she was dismissed because of over a year's absence from work due to a back injury (See also **Cosgrove v Caeser & Howie** [2001] IRLR 653 – absence from December 1997 to dismissal in a March 1999; **Allen v Hargrave & Co** [EAT 150/99]).

The employer will be under a duty to consider whether any reasonable adjustments can be made so that the employee's contract does not have to be terminated or in order to allow the employee to return to work. The dismissal does not in itself amount to a breach of the section 6 duty giving rise to a claim under section 5(2) of the DDA 1995. In **Fu v London Borough of Camden** [2001] IRLR 186 an employee suffered two accidents at work which caused her to be absent for a year and she needed a walking stick thereafter. In 1997, she had a further accident, injuring her right side and leg, and thereafter remained off work.

She repeatedly stated that she could return if adjustments were made but was offered ill health retirement or dismissal and opted for the former. The EAT held that the employer should have considered the extent to which the adjustments would have helped her return to work and overcome the medical problems. The adjustments that had been proposed included a voice-activated computer retrieval system, a hands-free telephone, and a specially adapted chair and shelves which rendered the files on which she had to work readily accessible.

The Code of Practice for the Elimination of Discrimination in the Field of Employment places the emphasis on consultation. It states at paragraph 6.20 that "the employer must first consider any reasonable adjustment that would resolve the difficulty. The employer may also need to consult the disabled person at appropriate stages about what his needs are and what effect the disability might have on future employment, for example, where the employee has a progressive condition. The nature of the reasonable adjustments which an employer may have to consider will depend on the circumstances of the case."

Section 6(3) of the DDA sets out examples of adjustments. There are a number of cases that have considered various adjustments that could be made in the context of long term sickness absence:

- Section 6(3)(c) refers to transferring an employee to another vacancy. In **Kent County Council v Mingo** [2000] IRLR 90 an employee who took extended leave after injuring his back was unable to return to his position and, although there was a redeployment category for staff who were disabled within the meaning of the DDA 1995, he was not moved into this category and was not offered jobs which were reserved for those at risk of redundancy. It was held that the Council could have made the reasonable adjustment of moving the employee into the category of those that were at risk of redundancy as he could then have been employed. In **London Borough of Hillingdon v Morgan** [EAT 1493/98] it was held that an employee should have been permitted to work from home to ease her back into full time employment. The employee had been treated as any other employee who returned and was to be re-deployed and the Council had failed to make a reasonable adjustment by providing her with small amounts of work at home.

- *Absence policies.* There are conflicting ET cases as to the question of whether the employer needs to modify its actual absence policies as a reasonable adjustment. In **Kerrigan v Rover Group Ltd** (ET Case No.1401406/97) it was held that the employer should have modified an absence improvement scheme whilst in **Bray v London Borough of Camden** (ET Case No.6000643/00) it was held that there was no duty to disregard the incapability procedure and to do otherwise would create ill feeling among staff. If a modification can be made it should be seriously considered as there is no guarantee that an ET will find there was no such duty.

- *Pay.* In **London Clubs Management Ltd v Hood** the EAT decided obiter that modifying company policy to provide for sick pay to be paid to a disabled person in excess of statutory sick pay requirements could be a reasonable adjustment. (Note that employees on long term sick pay will still accrue holiday: **Kigass Aero Components Ltd v Brown**)

The policy in relation to sick pay must now been seen in light of **Nottingham County Council v Meikle** (see page 727) which approved the statement in *Hood* that it may be a reasonable adjustment to extend payment of sick pay.

The employer is likely to want to investigate the reasons for long term or persistent sickness and, indeed, will be under a duty to carry out an investigation into the reasons for illness and inform itself of the true medical position (see **Spencer v Paragon Wallpapers Limited** [1976] IRLR 373 and Duggan, *Unfair Dismissal* at pages 131–137).

In the case of long term sickness, the employer's procedure should include:

• Discussion and consultation about the reason for absence which may bring to light facts and circumstances of which the employer was unaware and may assist in a return to work. See the classic statement in **East Lindsey District Council v Daubney** [1977] IRLR 181.

• Medical examination. See **Patterson v Messrs Brackets** [1977] IRLR 137.

• Consideration of alternative employment where it is the environment that causes the problem. See **Glitz v Watford Electric Co Limited** [1979] IRLR 89.

Persistent short term absences

In the case of persistent short term illness the employer will wish to have a definition of what is regarded as persistent short term illness that is not acceptable (see **International Sports Company Limited v Thomson** [1980] IRLR 340 and Duggan, *Unfair Dismissal* at pages 137–8). Persistent short term absence does not fit happily into the conduct or capability categories since there is unlikely to be a conduct issue where the sickness is genuine and the absences may not be of sufficient length to render the employee incapable of carrying out the job. The Court of Appeal confirmed in **Wilson v Post Office** [2000] IRLR 834 that such dismissals could be for SOSR. The employee had unacceptable levels of short term persistent absence. The ET did not consider that there was a conduct issue and decided that dismissal must therefore be for capability. It decided that the dismissal must be unfair since the employee had been declared fit by the company doctor, had worked out five weeks notice and there was no underlying medical condition. In the Court of Appeal it was considered that the real reason was failure to comply with the Post Office absence procedure.

In **International Sports Co Ltd v Thomson** [1980] IRLR 340 the employee was dismissed for persistent absenteeism. For the last 18 months of her employment she was absent on average for about 25% of the time. Most of these absences were covered by medical certificates which referred to conditions such as "dizzy spells, anxiety and nerves, bronchitis, virus infection, cystitis, althruigra of the left knee and dyspepsia and flatulence" It was said by the EAT that:

"Where an employee has an unacceptable level of intermittent absences due to minor ailments, what is required is, firstly, that there should be a fair review by the employer of the attendance record and the reasons for it; and, secondly, appropriate warnings after the employee has been given an opportunity to make representations. If there is then no adequate improvement in the attendance record, in most cases the employer will be justified in treating the persistent absences as a sufficient reason for dismissing the employee."

Cases that deal with long term sickness such as **Spencer v Paragon Wallpapers** [1976] IRLR 373 and **East Lindsey District Council v Daubney** [1977] IRLR 181 relating to dismissals on the ground of incapability are not applicable since it would be placing too heavy a burden on an employer to require him to carry out a formal medical investigation and, even if he did, such an investigation would rarely be fruitful because of the transient nature of the employee's symptoms and complaints.

The procedure for short-term persistent absence should therefore cover:

(1) A fair review by the employer of the attendance record and the reasons for it.

This will entail assessing the reasons for the absence and perhaps holding a return to work interview. The level of absence may have triggered such a review. The review may assist in bringing to light an underlying medical condition, at which stage medical evidence and the operation of the DDA 1995 may need to be considered, though it was held in **London Borough of Tower Hamlets v Bull** [EAT 153/91] that there is no duty to consult with the employee's GP in cases of persistent absenteeism.

Where the employer is made aware that the employee is disabled and the workplace is causing the short-term absences then the employee may have to consider whether a reasonable adjustment would remove the problem that is causing the absences.

(2) *Appropriate warnings after the employee has been given an opportunity to make representations.*

The giving of warnings will not bring the statutory procedure into play, though it would be prudent to adopt this as a minimum standard in any event. Indeed, the case law makes it clear that any dismissal is likely to be unfair if some form of warning procedure is not adopted and the employee is not given a chance to make representations/improve. The ability to make representations may give the employee the opportunity to explain what is causing the problems.

A warning system in the case of persistent absenteeism is not intended to be disciplinary but rather to advise the employee that, with the best will in the world, continued employment may not be possible if the attendance record does not improve (see **Lynock v Cereal Packaging Ltd** [1998] ICR 670).

The employer must make sure that absence triggers are applied consistently (though see **Wandsworth London Borough Council v D'Silva** [1998] IRLR 193 as to whether codes of practice on attendance are contractual and when they can be altered).

The employer may also have to consider an adjustment in such attendance schemes to cater for a disability such as asthma so, for example, an improvement scheme may have to take into account the disability.

Other matters that the employer should consider in deciding what to do about persistent short term absence include:

• Improvements in record and lapses over a period of time.

• Length of service and attendance record (But see **Regan v Magneti Marelli UK Limited** [EAT 577/99] where a dismissal was fair despite 30 years service.)

• Future service and likely improvement in absence record.

• Necessity for continuity in the job.

- Whether the job requires a high level of attendance or robust health (**Leonard v Fergus and Haynes Civil Engineering Ltd** [1979] IRLR 235; **Taylorplan Catering (Scotland) Limited v McInally** [1980] IRLR 53).

- In the case of a disabled employee it may be necessary to consider whether a transfer to another job would be appropriate, whether the employee should be able to work from home or whether the hours of work should be reduced with a gradual build up to a level where the disabled employee can cope.

The formal statutory procedure under the Employment Act 2002 will apply where dismissal or some other sanction such as alteration of terms and conditions (but not warnings) is being considered. Precedent J1 aims to cover this situation.

(6) Unauthorised absence and dealing with the malingerer

A precedent that deals with Unauthorised Absence is contained at J3. This may be incorporated into a more general precedent.

Where the employee does not comply with established procedures as to sickness absence or fails to advise the employer of the reason for absence then there should be provision that this will result in non-payment of salary and may amount to a disciplinary offence. However this will not negate the employer's duty to carry out an investigation into the reason for absence if disciplinary measures are being considered (as to this, see the detailed consideration in Duggan, *Unfair Dismissal*).

Where the employer has evidence that the employee who is purportedly absent because of sickness has been working elsewhere, a dismissal is likely to be for conduct and to be fair, as in **Nfengfack v London Borough of Southwark** [2002] EWCA 211 where a primary school teacher was dismissed when she was supposedly off ill and was seen working in a hairdressing salon. It must not, however, be assumed that because the employee is seen away from home he or she is guilty of misconduct. For example in **McMaster v Manchester Airport PLC** [EAT 149/97] the dismissal was unfair after an employee was dismissed for taking a day trip to France, as the tribunal found that the employee was off work suffering from stress and the trip may have improved his condition.

(7) Suspension on medical grounds

A precedent that deals with medical suspension is contained at J6 – again this may be incorporated into a more expansive precedent such as J1.

By section 64 of the ERA 1996 an employee who is suspended from work on medical grounds is entitled to be paid remuneration whilst he is suspended for a period of 26 weeks. The employee is regarded as being so suspended if he is suspended:

- in consequence of a requirement imposed by or under a provision of an enactment or an instrument made under an enactment;

- in consequence of a recommendation in a provision of a Code of Practice issued or approved under section 16 of the Health and Safety at Work etc. Act 1974; and

- the provision is specified in the Control of Lead at Work Regulations 1980, Regulation 24 of the Ionising Radiations Regulations 1999 or Regulation 11 of the Control of Substances Hazardous to Health Regulations 1988. At present these are the only enactments that will give rise to a claim in respect of suspension.

He will be regarded as suspended if he continues to be employed but is not provided with work or does not perform the work that he normally performed before the suspension.

There are exclusions from the right to claim in section 65 ERA 1996, namely:

- less than one month's employment;

- where the contract is for a fixed term of less than three months, unless three months has already elapsed;

- where the employee is incapable of being able to work by reason of disease or bodily or mental impairment;

- where suitable alternative employment has been offered or the employee does not comply with reasonable requirements imposed with a view to ensuring his services are available.

The employee will be entitled to a week' pay in respect of each week of suspension, as calculated in accordance with sections 220 to 229 of the ERA 1996. Any contractual payment will go towards discharging this liability.

(8) *Return to work*

Precedent J5 deals with return to work and can be incorporated into J1.

The prudent employer will ensure that the employee is not permitted to return to work until it is certain that he is fit to return. There is a danger that if the employee returns before he is fit he may bring claims in respect of any injuries he sustains or, alternatively, may be a danger to his co-workers. Precedent J5 is therefore intended to ensure that there are appropriate safeguards against an employee's return until the employer is satisfied that he is fit

(9) *Sick pay and statutory sick pay*

Different alternatives are covered by J2, 7, 8, 9 and 10.

It would normally be expected that there will be an express term relating to payment, along the lines of the Precedents in this book. Where there is no express term as to the payment of sick pay there is no presumption in common law that sick pay will be payable (**Mears v Safecar Security Limited** [1992] IRLR 183; ICR 626). The Tribunal is to approach the matter with an open mind and decide, on the facts and circumstances, what term would have been implied. Sick pay was never asked for in this case, no certificates were ever sent in and other employees were never paid sick pay. The Court refused to imply any term. This case reflects earlier authorities such as **Petrie v MacFisheries** [1939] 4 All ER 258 where the Court of Appeal stated that there was no general principle that employees were entitled to sick pay, and **Hancock v BSA Tools Limited** [1939] 4 All ER 538 where a term could not be implied when employees were only paid for work done. In **O'Grady v M Saper Limited** [1940] 2 KB 469 the employee had been absent for periods of weeks on several occasions without asking for sick pay. It was only when he read a reported case in the newspapers that he asked for sick pay. The Court of Appeal held that the evidence was clear that he was not entitled to sick pay.

In a case where sick pay is payable but the period for which it will be paid has not been expressed the court will imply a reasonable period during which it should be paid, which is applicable to the particular industry in which the employee is engaged (**Howman and Son v Blyth** [1983] ICR 416).

There may also be an implied term that the employer will not dismiss an employee whilst he is incapacitated, save for repudiatory conduct or some other terminating event specified in the contract (**Aspen v Webbs Poultry & Meat Group (Holdings) Limited** [1996] IRLR 521 – see Part J12). In **Hill v General Accident Fire & Life Assurance Corporation PLC** [1998] IRLR 641, Mr Hill was entitled to full salary for the first 104 weeks with the possibility of permanent accident insurance thereafter. He was absent from work from March 1994 and was dismissed for redundancy in November 1995. He alleged that the employer was in breach of the implied term of good faith and mutual trust as his dismissal frustrated his entitlement to long term sickness benefit. There was a genuine redundancy situation. The Court of Session held that the employer was not in breach of contract even if the practical effect of the dismissal brought an end to any entitlement. Insofar as *Aspen* laid down any principle that such a dismissal was in breach of the implied term of trust and confidence, this could not be accepted. The Court stated that:

> "...the employer cannot, solely with a view to relieving himself of the obligation to make such payment, by dismissal bring that sick employee's contract to an end. To do so would be, without reasonable and proper cause, to subvert the employee's entitlement to payment while sick. The same unwarranted subversion may occur if a sick employee were to be dismissed for a specious or arbitrary reason or for no cause at all."

It should be noted that dismissal during provision of sick pay will not necessarily be unfair and nor may it be fair to dismiss simply because sick pay entitlement has finished (c.f. **Coulson v Felixtowe Dock and Railway Co** [1975] IRLR 11 with **Hardwick v Leeds Area Health Authority** [1975] IRLR 319).

It should be noted that an employee on sickness absence who has exhausted his or her sick pay entitlement will be entitled to salary during notice period if the employer takes the decision to dismiss unless the employee was contractually entitled to one week more notice than the statutory minimum, in which case the employee remains disentitled to any pay during notice. This rather odd position is clear from the construction of the ERA 1996 and was confirmed as being correct in **Scotts Group (UK) Ltd v Budd** [2004] ICR 299; [2003] IRLR 145.

(10)Accidents outside work

An employer will be prudent to include a clause that it may recover the proceeds of damages from the employee, as in Precedent J11: Claims in relation to Accidents occurring outside Work.

Where the employee is unable to attend work due to an accident or other claim which gives him a right to claim damages against a third party and the employer has paid remuneration for a period where the employee is incapacitated as a result of the accident or other claim, then, in such circumstances, the employer will wish to include a provision whereby any payment will be regarded as a loan to be repaid if, and when, any claim for damages is satisfied (see **Dennis v London Passenger Transport Board** [1948] 1 All ER 779). The requirement to repay the debt should entitle the employee to recover damages, though some form of adjustment is likely to be necessary in terms of PAYE once the outcome of any claim is known.

Unless the agreement makes it clear, the employer will only be able to claim the net pay which was received by the employee and not tax or national insurance that has been paid (**Franklin v British Railways Board** [1993] IRLR 441).

(11)Insurance

Issues relating to permanent health insurance have already been considered at Manual Part F11. It is an important facet of permanent health insurance that, once granted, the employer should not act in a manner that effectively removes the benefit from the employee. Where there is a contractual disability benefit for the short or long term, it may be an express or an implied term that the employer will not do anything that will defeat the employee's entitlement under the scheme, including terminating the employee's employment.

Express terms

In **Adin v Sedco Forex International Resources Limited** [1997] IRLR 280, Mr Adin was entitled to long and short term disability benefits set out in the Group's employee guide. The short term scheme provided full pay for six months and 60% for a further six months, whilst the long term benefit covered the employee till death if disability continued. Where employment was terminated after total disability employees would continue to receive the long term benefits. Mr Adin was dismissed after receiving short term benefits for three months and it was asserted that he was not entitled to long term benefit as he had not received short term benefit for 12 months. His contract provided that he could be dismissed without cause at any time and would only be paid to that date. The Court of Session held that the express terms of the contract provided that the employer could not defeat his entitlement to short and long term benefits as the stated purpose was to provide income protection when the employee could not work. The disability plans would not give this protection if they could be taken away at the employer's discretion by dismissing without cause. The right to benefit was established by the combination of the contract terms and the unfitness of the employee and, once established, remained due.

Implied Terms

See **Aspen v Webbs Poultry and Meat Group (Holdings) Limited** [1996] IRLR 521 referred to at the commentary to F11.

The scope of Insurance Schemes

Where there is an insurance scheme between employer and employee any restrictions in the term of the scheme should be drawn to the attention of the employee. In **Villella v MFI Furniture Centres Limited** [1999] IRLR 468 it is was held that a former employee was entitled to receive payments under a Permanent Health Insurance scheme even though the insurance policy stated that it is would cease on the termination of employment. The restriction had never been drawn to the attention of the employee so that it was not incorporated into the employment contract. The restriction was merely contained in the policy between the employer and the insurer.

Where the terms of a permanent health plan are underwritten by an insurance scheme, no duty of care is owed by the insurer to the employee so that the only redress is by suing the employer for breach of contract. In **Briscoe v Lubrizol Limited & Anor** [Court of Appeal] [2000] ICR 694 it was alleged, *inter alia*, that the insurer was negligent in ascertaining the employee's entitlement under the health plan. The plan was in a common form and provided that:

- it had to be shown to the insurer's satisfaction that the employee had been totally unable to perform his occupation and had not engaged in any other gainful occupation or employment;

- the employer was under a duty to provide all particulars and information necessary to decide whether the employee fell within the definition.

When a claim was rejected the employee argued that the insurer was negligent in failing to take proper steps to commission the necessary medical evidence. The claim was struck out on the ground that there was no duty of care owed by the insurer. However, the Contracts (Rights of Third Parties) Act 1999 came into force in May 2000 and this may give an employee the right to claim against the insurer in such circumstances.

From the employer's perspective, it is important that liability to employees is linked to payment by the insurers so that if the insurer does not pay the employer is not liable. In **Jowitt v Pioneer Technology (UK) Limited** EWCA Civ 411 [2003] IRLR ICR 120, [2003] IRLR 365 the terms of the scheme between the insurers and employer (of which the employee was unaware) differed from the contract of employment. The insurers took the view that the employee was not entitled under the scheme and the employee claimed against his employer under his contract. The ET applied the insurance scheme and decided that since he was not disabled from following "any" occupation in terms of that policy, he was not entitled to benefit. The EAT and CA held that this was the wrong approach as the contract of employment referred to being 'unable to work'. The Court of Appeal held that an employee is unable to work "if there is no continuous remunerative full-time work which he can realistically be expected to do". (See also **Walton v Airtours plc** [2003] IRLR 161). The case was remitted to a tribunal. It is apparent from the decision that there may be liability on the part of the employer where the insurer is not liable to pay because the scheme requirements are not satisfied. The simple clause at J12 should therefore be included as it seeks to ensure the Company will not be under any duty other than to make an application under the policy. However, this may not work in the light of **Marlow v East Thames Housing Corp Limited** [2002] IRLR 798 where it was held that the employer owes a duty to take all reasonable steps to make sure the insurer pays on the policy if payment should properly be made. This may include suing the insurer but there is no reason why an indemnity should not be sought from the employee (other than the obvious issue of means to pay) before any action is commenced.

J14: Absence due to Disability

There may be an issue about entitlement under a sickness policy where the disabled person is absent for longer periods than an able bodied person due to the disability. It has been made clear by the Court of Appeal that the employer may be expected in such a case to make a reasonable adjustment to its sickness policy.

In **Nottingham County Council v Meikle** [2004] IRLR 703 (9 July 2004) the Court of Appeal considered whether a duty under section 6 potentially extended to making adjustments to a contractual sick pay policy. The employee suffered from a degenerative eye condition that led to her becoming sight-disabled. Her pay was halved following a period of absence due to her disability. The sick pay policy provided that employees were to be paid full pay for the first six months of sickness-related absence but that thereafter their pay would be reduced to half. The employee claimed she had been constructively dismissed because of her disability when the employer failed to agree her suggestions made over a period of time to deal with her disability. She further claimed that the reduction to half-pay was in breach of the DDA 1995 in that the employer had treated her less favourably on the ground of her disability and had failed to make reasonable adjustments to the pay policy in the light of her disability.

The employment tribunal rejected her claims. On the issue of the reduction in pay it ruled that, though putting M on half-pay constituted 'less favourable treatment', that treatment had been justified. The EAT and Court of Appeal reversed this decision. The employee had argued that (i) the reduction in sickness benefit to half-pay in view of her continued absence from work constituted less favourable treatment on the ground of her disability in contravention of section 5(1), and (ii) that the application of the sickness pay policy also breached the duty under sections 5(2) and 6 to make reasonable adjustments to her working arrangements.

The Court of Appeal focused on the general exclusion in section 6(11) of the duty to make reasonable adjustments and concluded that that exclusion applied only to occupational pension schemes and benefits provided under third-party insurance services. It did not extend to benefits such as contractual sick pay (approving **London Clubs Management Limited v Hood** [2001] IRLR 719).

The employer had a duty to make reasonable adjustments to its sick pay policy under section 6 and had breached that duty by failing to do so. A reasonable adjustment would have been to have placed the employee on full pay during the entire period of her disability-related absence.

Further since section 5(5) of the Act prevents an employer from justifying any less favourable treatment in circumstances where it has a duty under section 6 to make reasonable adjustments but has unjustifiably failed to comply with that duty, which was the case here, the only conclusion to be arrived at was that Ms Meikle had been discriminated against and that there was unlawful dismissal.

The case is of great significance for employers since it is likely to be a breach of the DDA 1995 not to extend full pay to employees who have a disability to the full period they are absent due to the disability, even if other employees receive half sick pay or no sick pay after a period of time.

PART K: PARENTS

Part One: Absences From Work Due To Maternity Or Paternity Leave, Parental Leave And Adoption Leave

Part Two: Flexible Working For Parents Of Young Children

PART ONE: MATERNITY OR PATERNITY LEAVE, PARENTAL LEAVE AND ADOPTION LEAVE

Precedent K: Parents

K1: Maternity Leave, Parental Leave and Paternity Leave Policy   **730**

K2: Letters   **748**

1. Letter notifying Employer of Pregnancy   **749**

2. Notification from Employer of maternity leave and date of return   **750**

3. Letter where maternity is triggered because employee is absent due to sickness in the four weeks before baby is due   **752**

4. Form requesting leave for adoption   **753**

5. **Notification from Employer of date of
    return from ordinary adoption leave**   **754**

6. **Letter stating why parental leave
    must be postponed and suggesting
    alternative date**   **756**

Commentary: **Ante-natal Care and Maternity, Paternity,
            Parental and Adoption Leave**   **756**

For useful websites: see commentary

•   The overall DTI website for working parents is:

    http://www.dti.gov.uk/er/workingparents.htm

•   THE TIGER inteactive website is at *http://www.tiger.gov.uk/*
    – timing of leave can be worked out by using this site.

Precedent K1: Maternity Leave, Parental Leave and Paternity Leave Policy

This Policy sets out the Company's position with regard
to the legislation that is currently in force relating to:

•   Maternity Leave

•   Parental Leave

•   Paternity Leave

This Policy also sets out what statutory pay you will be
entitled to claim, as a minimum, during leave.

The Company will at all times comply with the legislation that is in force from time to time. The Company values the work of its staff and will make such arrangements as it can to ensure that employees are able to combine their family commitments with gainful employment. This Policy sets out the Company's position so that there can be no misunderstandings on the part of employees about their rights and obligations.

The enclosed policies are intended to meet the requirements of the legislation whilst providing for the smoothest possible transition for the different kinds of leave and for return to work. This Policy should be read in conjunction with the Flexible Working and Equal Opportunity Policies.

Women who are pregnant are also entitled to take time off for ante natal care (such as attending your doctor or hospital and advice should be taken from [HR] as to how to go about doing this.)

Maternity Leave

You are entitled to Maternity Leave and Maternity Pay as set out below. It would be sensible to notify the Company as soon as possible that you are pregnant if you work in a post that may have an effect upon your pregnancy as the Company may have to find you an alternative job that is suitable or 'suspend' you on full pay (please note that such medical suspension does not have any adverse implications to your future employment).

You will be entitled to the following maternity leave under the provisions of the legislation:

1 Ordinary Maternity Leave

Entitlement

1.1 You will be entitled to maternity leave, known as Ordinary Maternity Leave (OML), for a period of 26 weeks, which cannot begin more than 11 weeks before the expected date of your confinement. You will be entitled to OML regardless of your length of service, whether you work full or part time or are employed on a temporary or permanent basis.

1.2   Your OML cannot commence before the 11th Week before your Expected Week of Confinement (the week when you are expecting to have your baby) unless the baby is born before then (See below).

Notification

1.3   No later than the 15th week before your expected week of confinement you should give the Company notice that you intend to take leave. You are required to give notice of:

- The fact that you are pregnant;

- Your Expected Week of Confinement; and

- The date on which you intend to commence your OML.

If you decide to change the date on which you wish to commence your OML you must give 28 days notice before your amended start date.

Proof

1.4   The Company may require you to provide confirmation of your pregnancy and it would be helpful if you could obtain your MATB1 form for presentation after you have been pregnant for 26 weeks.

Company Response

1.5   In each case the Company will respond in 28 days and set out the date you are expected to return to work. This will mean that you will not be entitled to return to work earlier than this date unless your have given 28 days notice or the Company gives you permission to do so.

Commencement

1.6 You are entitled to work right up to the date of the birth of your child provided that there is no health and safety reason to prevent this. You will, however, be required to take 2 weeks (Compulsory Maternity Leave) off work after the birth of your child which may mean that your OML period is extended.

1.7 You will start your OML on the date that you have notified to the Company unless:

- you have your baby earlier in which case you must take your Compulsory Maternity Leave from that date.

- you are absent due to a pregnancy related sickness between the 15th and 11th week before your Expected Week of Confinement as the Company may regard this as having 'triggered' your OML. In such case the Company will write to you if it takes the view that your OML has been triggered.

Your employment with the Company whilst on OML

1.8 Whilst you are absent from the Company on OML your contract of employment remains in place and your contractual rights will continue to accrue under the contract whether or not you have one's years service. Though you will not receive your normal remuneration (but may be entitled to Statutory Maternity Pay) your holiday entitlement and pension rights will continue to accrue.

1.9 If you have outstanding holiday you are encouraged to take such holiday before you commence your OML as holidays must be taken in the year that they accrued [under your contract/holiday policy].

Your return

1.10 The Company may permit you to return early from your OML but you must give 28 days notice of your intention to return.

   • You will be entitled to return to the job you held before your OML unless a redundancy position arises whilst you are absent in which case you will be notified in the same way as all other employees and will be offered suitable alternative employment on terms which are no less favourable if such a position is available.

   • If you have taken a period of parental leave of four weeks or less as well as OML you will be entitled to return to the job in which you were employed before absence.

   • If you take a period of parental leave of more than four weeks as well as OML you are entitled to return to the job in which you were employed unless it is not practicable in which case the Company will endeavour to ensure that you return to a job which is suitable and appropriate for you.

1.11 If opportunities for promotion arise whilst you are absent on Ordinary Maternity Leave you will be notified in the same way as all other eligible employees and will be given the same opportunities to apply for such a position.

Decision not to return during OML

1.13 If you decide that you do not wish to return to the Company you should give your normal notice to this effect to the Company.

2   Statutory Maternity Pay

2.1 If you will have worked for the Company for six months or have six months' continuous service by the 15th week before your Expected Week of Confinement you will be entitled to Statutory Maternity Pay whether or not you decide to return to work. You may claim Statutory Maternity Pay from the 11th week before the Expected Week of Confinement provided that you are on leave. You will receive 90% of your normal pay for six weeks and up to a further 20 weeks pay at the rate in force at the time, [which currently is [put in current figure]]. You should note that Statutory Maternity Pay is subject to tax and national insurance.

2.2 If you do not qualify for Statutory Maternity Pay you will qualify for Maternity Allowance.

2.3 If you do not work up until the 15th week before the Expected Week of Confinement you will lose your right to Statutory Maternity Pay unless the reason is that you are certified as incapable of work.

2.4 You will be required to give the proper notice (normally 28 day) to claim Statutory Maternity Pay but should consult [HR] about this.

3   Additional Maternity Leave

Entitlement

3.1 You will be entitled to Additional Maternity Leave (AML) if you have been continuously employed by the Company for at least six months (26 weeks) by the 15th week before your Expected Week of Confinement.

3.2 *You should note that Additional Maternity Leave is unpaid*

Notification

3.3 You do not have to inform the Company that you intend to take AML. However, it would be very helpful if you were able to inform the Company once you have made this decision so that it can arrange for the employee cover in relation to you position to be extended.

Commencement

3.4 When you advised the Company that you were pregnant you were given notification by the Company of your expected date of return after the expiration of your period of Ordinary Maternity Leave. This is the date from which your AML will commence. You are therefore entitled to a total of one year's leave.

Your employment with the Company whilst on AML

3.5 Your period of AML does not count for pension rights, seniority rights, and contractual service related rights and benefits such as salary rises do not continue to accrue.

3.6 Your contract continues in existence and both you and the Company will continue to owe certain rights and obligations to each other. The Company will continue to owe you a duty of trust and confidence and you are entitled to the benefit of terms and conditions in your contract of employment that relate to:

- Notice of termination of your contract.

- Compensation in the event that you are made redundant.

- The Company's Grievance procedure should you have a Grievance whilst you are on AML and the Disciplinary Procedure should any disciplinary matter parties.

Your duty of good faith to the Company continues and the obligations under the terms and conditions of your contract of employment continues in relation to:

- The notice of termination that you must give under your contract of employment.

- Disclosure of Confidential Information to any third parties. You may have signed a contract of employment which sets out in more detail the nature of this obligation and should refer to this for your duties. You should be aware that there will be implied terms that you may not disclose such information and you may wish to seek guidance from [HR].

- The Company's rules on accepting gifts or other benefits.

- Your obligations not to participate in any other business. You may have signed a contract of employment which sets out in more detail the nature of this obligation and should refer to this for your duties. You should be aware that there are implied terms about you participating or working elsewhere whilst in employment and you may wish to speak to [HR]. for guidance.

Your return

3.7 You will be entitled to return to the job you held before your AML unless a redundancy position arises whilst you are absent in which case you will be notified in the same way as all other employees and will be offered suitable alternative employment on terms which are no less favourable if such a position is available. If you have taken parental leave as well as AML you will be entitled to return to the same job unless this is not reasonably practicable in which case the Company will seek to find a similar job which is suitable for you and appropriate in the circumstances and which has the same or better status and terms and conditions.

3.8 You must give 28 days notice if you wish to return earlier than the final day of your AML. You will be entitled to return to the job that you held unless this is not reasonably practicable, in which case the Company will seek to offer you a job which is both suitable and appropriate in the circumstances.

In the case of employees who wish to return to work from OML or AML on different terms you should note the paragraphs set out in the policy below and the Company Policy on Flexible Working.

Parental Leave Policy
[*MAY BE USED AS A STAND ALONE POLICY*]

4 Parental leave

Entitlement

4.1 You will be entitled to take parental leave if:

(1) Your child is under a certain age, as follows

- You are the parent of a child who is under five years of age.

- You have formal parental responsibility for a child who is under five years of age.

- You adopted a child under the age of 18 in which case you are entitled to parental leave during a five year period from the date of adoption or the child's eighteenth birthday, whichever is the sooner.

- You were the parent of a child who was under the age of five on 15th December 1999 or who was placed with you for adoption between 15th December 1994 and 14th December 1999 (But note that you must take this leave by 31st March 2005 or you will lose your entitlement).

- You are the parent or adoptive parent of a child who has been awarded Disability Living Allowance and is under the age of 18 years.

(2) You have completed at least one year's continuous service with the Company or, where the child was under the age of five on 15th December 1999 or was placed for adoption in the five years before that date you had one year's continuous service with a previous employer between 15th December 1998 and 9th January 2002, in which case you will be deemed to have one years continuous service.

Overall Parental Leave period

4.2   In the case of parents or adoptive parents you will be entitled to take up to 18 week's leave.

4.3   Other qualifying employees will be entitled to take up to 13 week's leave.

Procedure for Parental Leave

4.4   The Company has adopted the 'default scheme' under Government Legislation [Note: this is contained in Schedule 2 of the Maternity and Parental Leave etc. Regulations 1999 – see Duggan *Family Friendly Policies* at page 358 for the SI.]

Proof of entitlement

4.5   You may not take parental leave unless you have first produced evidence of your entitlement to such leave. This means that you must produce evidence of:

- Your responsibility or expected responsibility for the child.

- The child's date or birth or the date on which the placement for adoption began.

- Where the child is disabled, proof that the child is entitled to a disability living allowance.

- Where applicable, proof that you worked for a previous employer for at least one year's continuous service between 15th December 1998 and 5th January 2002.

Notice to take leave

4.6   You must give at least 21 days notice that you wish to take parental leave and must specify the period for which you intend to take leave.

4.6   Where you are the father and the period of leave is to begin on the date when the child is born you should give notice of the Expected Week of Childbirth and the period for which you intend to take leave.

4.7   Where the child is to be placed with you for adoption and leave is to begin with the date of the placement you must specify the date in which placement is expected to occur and the period for which you intend to take leave. Notice must be given at least 21 days before the expected date of placement or, if that is not possible, as soon as reasonably practicable.

Postponement of leave

4.8   Unless parental leave is sought for the reasons set out in paragraphs 4.6 and 4.7 above, the Company may postpone leave if it considers that its business would be unduly disrupted were you to take the leave in the period set out in your notice. In this case the Company will agree to permit you to take a period of leave of the same duration beginning on a date which will be determined after consultation with yourself and which will be no later than six months after the commencement of that period.

4.9   You will be given notice in writing which sets out the reason for the postponement and which will specify the dates on which the Company agrees you may taken leave, stating the beginning and end date. This notice will be given to you no later than seven days after you gave your notice to the Company.

Periods of leave

4.10   You may not take leave in periods of less than one week, unless leave is sought in relation to a child who is disabled.

4.11   You may not take more than four week's leave in any particular year, which will commence with the period when you first became entitled to leave or, where employment has been interrupted, commence on the date when you mot recently became entitled to take leave.

4.12 Periods taken with previous employers count in calculating your total entitlement to paternity leave.

Your employment with the Company whilst on Parental Leave

4.13 During any period that you are on parental leave you remain employed by the Company. The Company will continue to owe you a duty of trust and confidence and you are entitled to the benefit of terms and conditions in your contract of employment that relate to:

- Notice of termination of your contract.

- Compensation in the event that you are made redundant.

- The Company's Grievance procedure should you have a Grievance whilst you are on AML and the Disciplinary Procedure should any disciplinary matter arise.

Your duty of good faith to the Company continues and the obligations under the terms and conditions of your contract of employment continues in relation to:

- The notice of termination that you must give under your contract of employment.

- Disclosure of Confidential Information to any third parties. You may have signed a contract of employment which sets out in more detail the nature of this obligation and should refer to this for your duties. You should be aware that there will be implied terms that you may not disclose such information and you may wish to seek guidance from [HR].

- The Company's rules on accepting gifts or other benefits.

- Your obligations not to participate in any other business. You may have signed a contract of employment which sets out in more detail the nature of this obligation and should refer to this for your duties. You should be aware that there are implied terms about you participating or working elsewhere whilst in employment and you may wish to speak to [HR]. for guidance

Your right to return

4.14 You are entitled to return to the same job if the period of parental leave was four weeks or less. If it was more than four weeks you will be entitled to return to the same job unless that is not practicable in which case you will be entitled to return to a similar job of the same status an terms and conditions. If no such job exists there may be a redundancy situation and there will be full consultation with you about the circumstances.

YOU SHOULD NOTE THAT THE LEGISLATION STATES THAT THE PURPOSE OF PARENTAL LEAVE IS TO TAKE TIME OFF TO CARE FOR THE CHILD. IF THIS IS NOT THE REASON THAT THE TIME HAS BEEN TAKEN OFF OR IF PARENTAL LEAVE IS BEING ABUSED BECAUSE IT IS BEING USED FOR OTHER PURPOSES THIS MAY BE A DISCIPLINARY MATTER AND LEAD TO THE COMPANY INVOKING ITS DISCIPLINARY PROCEDURES.

Paternity Leave

5 Paternity Leave Policy

5.1 You will be entitled to Paternity Leave when you have been employed for at least six months (26 weeks) by the 15th week before the Expected Week of Confinement.

5.2 Paternity Leave can commence after the birth of the child and must be taken in the two months after birth or after placement of an adopted child. If the child is born early then Paternity Leave must be taken within two months of the child's birth or the Expected Week of Confinement whichever is the later.

5.3 Paternity Leave consists of two weeks which you must take in one block.

Notification

5.4 You must give notice in the 15th week before the Expected Week of Confinement of the Expected Week of Confinement and the date on which you intend to commence leave. If you change your mind about the date on which you wish to commence leave you must give 28 days notice. You may state that you wish your leave to commence on the date of birth of your child.

5.5 You may take Parental Leave after you have taken Paternity Leave if you give proper notice.

Statutory Paternity Pay

5.6 Paternity Pay will be paid at the same rate as Statutory Maternity Pay. You will not be able to claim for any week during which you in fact work.

Adoption Leave

The Company welcomes the Government's initiative to give adoption leave rights to couples who have a child placed with them for adoption and, by this Policy, seek to implement the provisions of the legislation.

6 Ordinary Adoption Leave

Eligibility

6.1 You will be eligible for Ordinary Adoption Leave (OAL) if you have a child placed with you who is aged up to eighteen years of age. You must have worked for the Company for six months (26 weeks) prior to notification of being matched with a child for adoption. You will be entitled to OAL regardless of your length of service, whether you work full or part time or are employed on a temporary or permanent basis.

6.2 You or your partner may chose to opt for OAL. The other partner will be entitled take two weeks leave at the time of placement.

6.3 The adoption must be through an approved agency.

Commencement

6.4 OAL cannot commence more than 14 days before the Expected Week of Placement and the latest leave may begin is the date of placement.

Notification

6.5 You must give 28 days notice of when you intend to start leave, unless this was not reasonably practicable, in which case OAL will commence on the day that the child was placed with you for adoption.

6.6 You will receive a matching certification from your agency when an approved match has been made and must provide this within 7 days of receipt.

Duration of AOL

6.7 You are entitled to 26 weeks OAL. You do not need to give notice that you wish to return to work at the end of OAL but must give 28 days notice if you wish to return earlier. The Company will consider any requests to return with earlier than 28 days notice but the Company is entitled to require you to give the full 28 days notice.

Right to return after AOL

6.8 You have the right to return to work after OAL to the job you held before your absence on the same basis as with OML (see above).

7 Additional Adoption Leave

7.1 You will be eligible for Additional Adoption Leave (AAL) if you have been continuously employed for at least six months (26 weeks) before the week that you were notified of being matched with a child for adoption.

Duration

7.2 AAL will commence on the day after OAL and continue for six months (26 weeks).

Notification

7.3 It is not necessary to inform the Company that you intend to take AAL. It is hoped that you will in order that the Company can plan for your absence.

Right to return

7.4 You will be entitled to return to the job you held before your absence unless that is not reasonably practicable in which case the Company will endeavour to find another job which is both suitable and appropriate and which is of the same capacity, including status, seniority, pension rights that would have applied if you had returned after OAL on terms and conditions that are not less favourable than would have applied if you had returned after OAL.

7.5 AAL does not count for the purpose of accruing pension rights, Seniority rights and contractual rights such as salary increases.

8 Return from leave on different terms at the request of the Employee

The above sets out the Company policy in relation to return from leave. However, where you wish to return to work on a different basis than your original job the following may be considered:

a) opportunities for flexible or part time working which the Company will make every effort to accommodate;

b) the possibility of job sharing which will involve appropriately adjusted terms and conditions of employment;

c) where no such alternatives are available at the time of return to work you will be encouraged to work on a full time basis and we will continue to review the position to seek to accommodate your wishes.

Or: Alternatively:

The Company policy on return from work after leave is that it will, so far as it is able and in accordance with the requirements of the business, seek to accommodate employees who wish to return on different terms in order to balance work and childcare commitments. These guidelines are not intended to confer any contractual right. They should be read in conjunction with the Company policies on Part Time Work and Flexible Working.

i) Wherever possible the Company will seek to accommodate a request for part time working from an employee returning from leave. If such a request is made the Part Time policy and procedure will be invoked. There can be no guarantee of part time work as the needs of the business and the requirements of the particular job will need to be considered.

ii) Alternatively the employee may invoke the Flexible Working Policy where a change in hours or place of work is requested.

iii) It is important that the Company is informed as soon as possible by the employee of the request so that discussions can take place at the earliest opportunity as this will enable consideration to be given to the requests and arrangements that may be made at the earliest opportunity.

iv) If the request is granted this will entail a variation to the terms and conditions of employment and there will be no right to revert to previous terms without agreement from the Company.

v) Where a request for a variation is granted it will not take effect until the Company and employee have signed a written variation of the terms of the contract.

DATED

Precedent K2: Letters

1. Letter notifying Employer of Pregnancy   749

2. Notification from Employer of maternity
   leave and date of return   750

3. Letter where maternity is triggered
   because employee is absent due
   to sickness in the four weeks before
   baby is due   752

4. Form requesting leave for adoption   753

5. Notification from Employer of date
   of return from ordinary adoption leave   754

6. Letter stating why parental leave
   must be postponed and suggesting
   alternative date   756

Precedent K2: Letters

1 Letter One

Dear   ,

I am writing to confirm that I am pregnant and intend to take maternity leave. My medical advisers confirm that my baby is due on [   ].

I enclose a medical certificate which sets out my expected week of confinement from [my doctor/a registered midwife].

I wish to start my period of maternity on [   ].

It is my intention to return after maternity leave. [It is not my intention to return after maternity leave – NB this is not necessary].

Yours etc.

2 Letter Two

Model letter for employers to acknowledge notification of maternity leave. This letter should be used when only the statutory levels of leave and pay are provided. (Employer must respond within 28 days of receipt of employees notification.)

Date:

Dear [*name of employee*],

Congratulations and thank you for telling me about your pregnancy and the date that your baby is due. I am writing to you about your maternity leave and pay.

As we have discussed, you are eligible **for 26 weeks' ordinary maternity leave/52 weeks' maternity leave (26 weeks' ordinary maternity leave plus 26 weeks' additional maternity leave)** [*delete as appropriate*].

Given your chosen start date of [*insert date*], your maternity leave will end on [*insert date*].

If you want to change the date your leave starts you must, if at all possible, tell me at least 28 days before your proposed new start date or 28 days before [*insert date leave starts*] (your original start date), whichever is sooner.

If you decide to return to work before [*insert date leave ends*], you must give me at least 28 days notice.

As we discussed, you are eligible for **26 weeks' Statutory Maternity Pay/not eligible for Statutory Maternity Pay** [*delete as appropriate*].

Your maternity pay will be £[*insert amount*] from [*insert date*] to [*insert date*] and £[*insert amount*] from [*insert date*] to [*insert date*].

or

The form SMP1 (enclosed) explains why you do not qualify for Statutory Maternity Pay. You may however be entitled to Maternity Allowance. If you take this form to the Jobcentre Plus or Social Security Office at [*insert local details*], they will be able to tell you more.

As your employer I want to make sure that your health and safety as a pregnant mother are protected while you are working, and that you are not exposed to risk. I have already carried out an assessment to identify hazards in our workplace that could be a risk to any new, expectant, or breastfeeding mothers. Now you have told me you are pregnant I will arrange for a specific risk assessment of your job and we will discuss what actions to take if any problems are identified. If you have any further concerns, following this assessment and specifically in relation to your pregnancy, please let me know immediately.

If you decide not to return to work you must still give me proper notice. Your decision will not affect your entitlement to SMP.

If you have any questions about any aspect of your maternity entitlement please do not hesitate to get in touch with me. I wish you well.

Yours sincerely,

See *www.dti.gov.uk/er/individual/model.doc* from which this letter is taken.

3 Letter Three

Dear   ,

We are writing to you regarding the commencement of your maternity leave. As you know, you have written to state that you intend to commence your leave on [   ]. You are currently absent from work due to a pregnancy related illness.

Since your expected week of confinement is [   ] this illness has occurred within four weeks from the week in which your baby is due.

We therefore require you to commence your maternity leave with effect from the date of your absence due to illness. From that date you will no longer be entitled to normal remuneration or statutory sick pay but will receive Statutory Maternity Pay.

You anticipated date of return because the date of commencement of your maternity leave has changed is now [   ].

Please do not hesitate to contact [   ] if you wish to discuss this further.

[Express sentiments about recovery/baby etc. if appropriate].

Yours sincerely,

4 Form requesting leave for adoption

A similar document may be adopted in relation to fostering though there is no statutory entitlement in this case.

Form requesting leave	
Name of employee	
Date of commencement of employment	
Dates for which leave is requested	From _____ to _____
Date of placement	Adopted son/daughter due to be placed on _____ [who suffers from a recognised disability].
Previous leave	Previous periods of leave taken in relation to the above child: ____ weeks from ____ to ____
Signed Dated This form must be returned to [ ] at least 4 weeks prior to the date when your adoption leave is to commence	

5 Letter Five

Model letter for employers to acknowledge notification of adoption leave. This letter should be used when only the statutory levels of leave and pay are provided.

(Employer must respond within 28 days of receipt of employees' notification).

Date:

Dear [*name of employee*],

Congratulations and thank you for telling me that you will be adopting a child. I am writing to you about your adoption leave and pay.

As we have discussed, you are eligible for **52 weeks' adoption leave/you are not eligible for adoption leave** [*delete as appropriate*].

Given your chosen start date of [*insert date*], your adoption leave will end on [*insert date*]. If you want to change the date your leave starts you must give me the correct notice, if at all possible. Please contact me if you wish to discuss this.

If you decide to return to work before [*insert date leave ends*], you must give me at least 28 days' notice.

As we discussed you are eligible for **26 weeks' Statutory Adoption Pay/not eligible for Statutory Adoption Pay** [*delete as appropriate*].

Your adoption pay will be £[*insert amount*] from [*insert date*] to [*insert date*]

or

The SAP1 form (enclosed) explains why you do not qualify for Statutory Adoption Pay. You should contact your adoption agency to find out if you can get any other help.

If you decide not to return to work, you must still give me proper notice. Your decision will not affect your entitlement to SAP.

If you have any questions about any aspect of your adoption entitlements please do not hesitate to get in touch with me. I wish you well.

Yours sincerely,

(Taken from *http://www.dti.gov.uk/er/individual/ adoptmodel.doc*.)

6   Letter six

Dear   ,

I note that you have requested paternity leave to take place on [   ]

I regret to inform you that this is not possible as the disruption to the business will be too great This is because [SET OUT i.e. SEE THE EXAMPLES IN THE FLEXIBLE WORKING SECTION]

You are entitled to take your leave within six months of this letter. I suggest that you take it [dates] for the [   ] week block period you have requested. I would be pleased to discuss this at the earliest possible opportunity and suggest we have a meeting on [   ].

Yours etc.

COMMENTARY ON PART K: ANTE-NATAL CARE MATERNITY, PATERNITY, PARENTAL AND ADOPTION LEAVE

This part considered the right of employees to take maternity, paternity, parental and adoption leave, which have been greatly extended since 1999. The rights of the employee in relation to pay are briefly considered as are the relevant legislative provisions and recent cases on discrimination which may have a bearing on the way in which the employer conducts itself. A very full account of the law in this area is contained in Michael Duggan *Family Friendly Policies; A Handbook for Employer and Employee.*

Time Off for Ante-Natal Care

The right to take time off for ante natal care is contained in ss.55–57 of the Employment Rights Act 1996 ("the ERA 1996"). Under these sections the right may be exercised:

- where the employee will be entitled to avail herself of the right if she is pregnant;

- she has an appointment to receive ante natal care; and

- has produced a certificate for second or subsequent appointments.

Section 55(1) of the ERA provides that where an employee has "on the advice of a registered medical practitioner, registered midwife or registered health visitor, made an appointment to attend at any place for the purpose of receiving ante-natal care" she will be entitled to time off during the employer's working hours to keep the appointment.

The employee is entitled to time off where the employer requests her to produce (a) a certificate from a registered medical practitioner, registered midwife or registered health visitor stating that the employee is pregnant, and (b) an appointment card or some other document showing that the appointment has been made, and she has produced the documents, though this requirement does not apply to the first appointment for which she seeks permission to take time off.

The employee is entitled to take the time off in the employer's working hours even if she could arrange to attend at some other time and a complaint may be made under section 57 of the ERA 1996 if the employer unreasonably refuses to permit her to take time off. She may also make a claim to a tribunal if she is subjected to a detriment because she has taken time off, or for sex discrimination (including injury to feelings) and any dismissal will be automatically unfair. By section 56 she is entitled to be paid at the appropriate hourly rate calculated in accordance with that section.

Maternity Leave

The Government has amended the Regulations in recent years to increase the period of entitlement for ordinary maternity leave and additional maternity leave. Part VIII of the ERA 1996 contains the rights to maternity leave, which is considerably fleshed out by the Maternity and Parental Leave etc. Regulations 1999, SI 1999/3312, which came into force on 15 December

1999 (the Maternity Regulations) and which contain most of the provisions for maternity and parental leave. These regulations were amended by the Maternity and Parental Leave (Amendment) Regulations 2001, SI 2001/4010, with effect from 10 January 2001 and the Maternity and Parental Leave (Amendment) Regulations 2002 with effect from 24 November 2002. The latter Regulations provide that a number of rights come into play when the expected week of childbirth is on or after 6 April 2003 and consideration is here given to the legislation as amended.

The main reforms made are that the employee will be entitled to 26 weeks Ordinary Maternity Leave ("OML") regardless of length of service. An employee with 26 weeks service as at the 15th week before the Expected Week of Childbirth ("EWC") will be entitled to claim a further 26 weeks Additional Maternity Leave ("AML"). An employer will no longer be able to insist upon a date from the employee as to when she will return from AML but it will be assumed that the employee intends to return after the end of AML and no notification needs to be given by the employee. Maternity leave will be triggered when the employee is absent due to an illness related to pregnancy at any time during the four weeks before the EWC.

The DTI Publication, Maternity Rights Guide, Revision 8, contains a useful flow chart guide, which is reproduced below.

There are three stages of maternity leave that are applicable:

1. Compulsory Maternity Leave

By section 72 of the ERA 1996 and regulation 8 there is a prohibition against an employee working during compulsory maternity leave. This period is of two weeks from the date that childbirth occurs.

2. Ordinary Maternity Leave

By regulation 4 entitlement to Ordinary Maternity Leave is available to all employees whose babies were born after 30th April 2000 and commences on the day the date that the employee notifies her employer that she intends it to commence. By s.71(1) of the ERA 1996:

"An employee may, provided that she satisfies any conditions which may be prescribed, be absent from work at any time during an ordinary `maternity leave period."

The OML period is the period calculated in accordance with regulations (s.71(2)), which shall secure that no OML leave period is less than 26 weeks (regulation 7(1)).

The regulations are to allow the employee to choose the date on which the OML period starts (s.71(3)).

The date for commencement of OML is the earliest of:

- The first day after childbirth if OML has not already commenced, provided that notice is given in accordance with reg.4(4), that is, as soon as reasonably practicable by the woman after birth that she has given birth.

- The first day after absence due wholly or partly to pregnancy where this absence takes place in the four weeks (28 days) before the EWC even if a later date has been notified, provided that notice is given in accordance with reg.4(3).

- Otherwise the date of notification provided that 28 days' notice has been given in accordance with reg.4(1).

By regulation 4 an employee is entitled to OML if her expected week of confinement (EWC) is after 6 April 2003 and she has:

- No later than the *fifteenth week before her EWC* notified her employer of:

    1. her pregnancy;

    2. the EWC;

    3. the date on which she intends her OML to start; and

    4. if requested to do so, he must produce a certificate from a registered medical practitioner or registered midwife stating the EWC (4(9)(b)).

The employer must make it clear that a certificate is requested, though it is to be noted that it must be provided in any event if SMP is being claimed. Where it was not reasonably practicable to provide the above information before the fifteenth week before the EWC it must be provided as soon as reasonably practicable.

The employer may also require the date on which the employee intends to start Ordinary Maternity Leave to be in writing and such notification shall not specify a date earlier than the beginning of the eleventh week before the expected week of childbirth (reg. 4(2)).

However, maternity leave may be triggered earlier for a number of reasons.

- Where childbirth occurs before the maternity leave period would otherwise commence. Regulation 4(4) modifies the notification provision so that the employee must notify as soon as reasonably practicable after the birth that she has given birth and this must be in writing if so requested.

- Where the employee is absent from work wholly or partly because of pregnancy or childbirth after the beginning of the sixth week before the expected week of confinement. Regulation 4(3) modifies the position so that notification must be given as soon as reasonably practicable and be in writing if so requested.

Whilst the period of Ordinary Maternity Leave is 26 weeks this may be extended where any requirement imposed by or under any relevant statutory provision prohibits the employee from working for any period after the end of the ordinary maternity period (regulation 7(2)).

Where the employer has been notified of the date that OML will commence or has commenced the *employer* shall notify the employee of the date that the OML will end or that OML and AML will end. This notification must be given:

- within 28 days of the date of notification of OML (reg.4(1)(iii)); or

- within 28 days of the date of notification that OML has started within the four weeks before the EWC because of absence wholly or partly due to pregnancy (reg.4(3)(b)); or

- within 28 days of the date of notification due to childbirth (reg.4(4)(b)); or

- within 28 days of the date as varied under reg.4(1A).

This requirement is of some significance since the employer cannot refuse to permit the employee to return early if the notification has not been given.

Terms and conditions during OML

By ss.71(4)(a) and (b)) an employee who exercises her right under s 71(1) is:

- entitled, for such purposes and to such extent as may be prescribed, to the *benefit* of the terms and conditions of employment which would have applied if she had not been absent; and

- is bound by any *obligations* under those terms and conditions except in so far as they are inconsistent with s 71(1).

The employee will be entitled to the benefit of all the terms and conditions of employment which would have applied if she had not been absent save for terms relating to remuneration (regulation 9(1)(a)(2)). She will be subject to all the obligations save in so far as they are inconsistent to the right to leave (section 71(4)(b) ERA 1996 and regulation 9(1)(b)).

Remuneration is not included in the terms and conditions to which the employee is entitled during OML. Section 71(6) provides that regulations may specify what is or is not to be remuneration. By regulation 9(3) only sums payable to an employee by way of wages or salary are to be treated as remuneration. These are likely to include sums paid by way of life insurance, medical insurance or PHI, the private use of the company vehicle, loans and mortgage subsidies, share ownership participation subscriptions and use of other incidentals such as a mobile telephone. Bonuses and commission that have accrued before the OML period will be covered but those that would otherwise have to be earned during the OML are probably not covered. However, discretionary payments are likely to be covered as s 71(5) covers matters "whether or not they are under the contract of employment". Holiday pay will continue to accrue and sums normally paid by way of credits, where the employee has paid into a holiday fund, will be covered (see **Adcock v H Flude & Co (Hinckley) Limited** [EAT 521/97]).

3. Additional Maternity Leave

A new section 73 of the ERA 1996 was inserted by the Employment Relations Act 1999 with effect from 15 December 1999 and applies to employees whose EWC begins on or after 20 April 2000.

Regulation 5 provides that an employee is entitled to AML where:

- she has been entitled to ordinary maternity leave; and

- she has, at the beginning of the 14th week before the expected week of childbirth, been continuously employed for a period of not less than 26 weeks.

Additional maternity leave commences on the day after the last day of ordinary maternity leave. Additional maternity leave continues until the end of the period of 26 weeks beginning with the week of childbirth (regulation 7(4)).

Terms and conditions during AML

Section 73(4) of the ERA 1996 provides that an employee who exercises her right to AML, is entitled for such purposes and to such extent as may be prescribed, to the *benefit* of the terms and conditions of employment which would have applied if she had not been absent. The employee is bound by any *obligations* under those terms and conditions except in so far as they are inconsistent with the right to take leave. The regulations set out what rights and obligations will exist during AML.

By regulation 17(a) the employee is entitled to the benefit of the employer's implied obligations to her of trust and confidence and any terms and conditions of her employment relating to:

(i)   notice of the termination of the employment contract by her employer;

(ii) compensation in the event of redundancy; or

(iii) disciplinary or grievance procedures.

By regulation 17(b) the employee is bound by the implied obligation to the employer of good faith and any terms and conditions of her employment relating to:

(i)   notice of the termination of the employment contract by her;

(ii) the disclosure of confidential information;

(iii) the acceptance of gifts or other benefits, or

(iv) the employee's participation in any other business.

Terms and conditions relating to remuneration are not included.

Maternity Rights Flowchart

GP confirms employee is expecting a baby

Employee is entitled to paid time off for antenatal care. *See Section 2*

Employee is entitled to 26 weeks ordinary maternity leave (OML) regardless of length of service. *See Section 4*

And:
If they have completed 26 weeks continuous employment by the 15th week before EWC, they are also entitled to 26 weeks additional maternity (AML). This is usually unpaid and starts immediately after OML. *See Section 4*

And:
Average weekly earnings at or above Lower Earnings Limit. Entitled to 26 weeks Statutory Maternity Pay. *See Section 5*

No?

May be entitled to MA or other benifits. *See Section 5*

Pregnant employee must tell their employer of their intention to take maternity leave by the 15th week before EWC, unless this is not reasonably practical. She will need to tell employer:
- that she is pregnant
- the week her baby is expected to be born
- when she wants her maternity leave to start (in writing if employer requests it).

Employee qualifying for SMP must give her employer at least 28 days' notice of when she wants it to start and medical evidence of EWC (maternity certificate Mat B1 can be used for this purpose). *See Section 6*

continued on next page

Employee must give 28 days notice of any change of dates. *See Section 6*

Employer must respond to employees' notification within 28 days, setting out when they expect the employee to return to work if they take their full leave entitlement. *See Section 6*

Earliest start date for maternity leave is the beginning of the 11th week before EWC. *See Section 6*

If Employee is absent from work with a pregnancy related illness during the four weeks before the start of EWC, maternity leave starts automatically regardless of when she actually wants her maternity leave to start. *See Section 6*	If baby born before the date employee has notified for before any notification), maternity leave period starts automatically and employee must give employer notification as soon as is reasonably practicable. *See Section 6*

Employee continues to benefit from all terms and conditions during ordinary maternity leave except pay, and some of them during additional maternity leave. *See Section 4*

Employee returns to same job after OML as if she hadn't been away. *See Section 8*	Employee returns to same job after AML as if she hadn't been away, unless not reasonably practicable and then should be offered similar job on terms and conditions no less favourable than original job. *See Section 8*

Maternity Rights Guide Rev 8 – www.dti.gov.uk/er/individual/matrights-pl958.pdf

Return to work

At the end of the 26 week period of Ordinary Maternity Leave the employee merely has to present herself for work and is entitled to return. She may, however, wish to return earlier, in which case the provisions set out below apply. Section 71(4)(c) as substituted by the Employment Act 2002 (section 17) provides that the employee is entitled to return to a job of a prescribed kind. Regulations provide for the type of job to which the employee may return. By regulation 18 it is provided that, in relation to OML, AML or parental leave:

- By reg.18(1) an employee who returns to work after a period of ordinary maternity leave, or a period of parental leave of four weeks or less, which was:

  (a) an isolated period of leave, or

  (b) the last of two or more consecutive periods of statutory leave which did not include any period of additional maternity leave or additional adoption leave, or a period of parental leave of more than four weeks, is entitled to return to the job in which she was employed before her absence.

- By reg.18(2), an employee who returns to work after:

  (a) a period of additional maternity leave, or a period of parental leave of more than four weeks, whether or not preceded by another period of statutory leave, or

  (b) a period of ordinary maternity leave, or a period of parental leave of four weeks or less, not falling within the description in paragraph 18(1) is entitled to return from leave to the job in which she was employed before her absence or, if it is not reasonably practicable for the employer to permit her to return to that job, to another job which is both suitable for her and appropriate for her to do in the circumstances.

The effect of these provisions is that the employee is entitled to return to the same job but in the case of AML or parental leave of over four weeks where regulation 18(1) does not apply the employer may offer another job where it is not reasonably practicable to offer the old job back. The new job must be suitable and appropriate in the circumstances. The definition of "job" refers to the nature of the work which the employee is employed to do in accordance with her contract and the capacity and place in which she is so employed. Thus in the event of dispute the tribunal will take into account the job description, title and status so that the employee will be entitled to insist that her terms, including the place of work, remains the same. However, the employee cannot pick and choose, so she cannot, for example, request that she return part-time or with some different terms but insist that all other terms remain the same **(Bovey v Board of Governors of the Hospital for Sick Children** [1978] ICR 934).

By regulation 18(A)(1) seniority, pension rights and similar rights where the employee returns from AML, or consecutive periods of statutory leave or a period of additional adoption leave shall be as they would have been if the period or periods of employment prior to AML or additional adoption leave were continuous with the period of employment before it. This means that, whilst the employee is entitled to return, the period whilst she was absent is not counted in calculating certain rights. This provision is subject to the Social Security Act 1989 in so far as it applies to equal treatment under pension rights. In other cases seniority, pension rights and similar rights shall be as they would have been if she had not been absent (reg.18A(a)(ii)). Thus the period for OML will count as continuous employment.

Other terms and conditions shall be applicable as though the employee had not been absent (reg.18A(1)(b)). The provisions for an employee to be treated as if she had not been absent refer to her absence since the beginning of an isolated period of statutory leave or the first of any consecutive period of leave (reg.18A(3)). These provisions apply to OML, AML or additional adoption leave.

There are specific provisions where the employer asserts that there is a redundancy situation: see Michael Duggan, *Family-Friendly Policies, A Handbook for Employer and Employee* for the detail at pages 44–45 and regulation 10.

Notice to return

An employee who intends to return from maternity leave *earlier* than the end of OML or AML shall give not less than 28 days' notice of the date on which she intends to return (reg.11(1)). Otherwise it is simply a matter of the employee turning up at the end of OML or AML. Moreover, reg.11 will not apply if the *employer* did not notify the employee, in accordance with regs.7(6) or 7(7) of the date that the maternity leave period would end within the time limits set out in reg.7.

Where the employee attempts to return earlier than the end of the maternity leave period without giving 28 days' notice the employer may postpone the return for a period that will secure that the employer has 28 days' notice of her return (reg.10(2)). However, the employer is not entitled to postpone the return to the end of the maternity leave period so that the employee may give 28 days' notice at any time to return (reg.10(3)). Where the employee's return is postponed and the employee is notified that she is not to return to work before the date to which her return was postponed the employer has no contractual duty to pay remuneration until the date to which her return was postponed if she returns to work before that date (reg.10(4)).

See further:

- *Maternity Rights: A Guide For Employers And Employees* (PL958 REV 7)

  http://www.dti.gov.uk/er/individual/maternity.pdf

- Guidance giving information on the rights for women whose babies re due on or after 6 April 2003

- *Maternity Rights: A Guide For Employers And Employees* (PL958 REV 8)

  http://www.dti.gov.uk/er/individual/matrightspl958.pdf

- *Maternity Leave – Changes: A Basic Summary (Pl507) – A Short Guide For Employers And Employees*

  http://www2.dti.gov.uk/er/matleafr.htm

- *Maternity Rights: A Guide For Employers And Employees* (PL958 REV 8)

  http://www.dti.gov.uk/er/individual/matrightspl958.pdf

> • *Model Letter For Employers To Acknowledge Notification Of Maternity Leave*:
>
> *http://www.dti.gov.uk/er/individual/model.doc*

Statutory Maternity Pay and Maternity Allowance

Employees are entitled to the following SMP when on OML:

- 90 per cent of average weekly earnings earned during the eight weeks immediately before the qualifying week for the first six weeks of OML.

- As from 6 April 2004, the standard rate payable for the remaining 20 weeks being £102.80 per week (previously £75 per week), subject to a maximum of 90 per cent of previous earnings.

The provisions relating to the right to maternity pay are to be found in the Social Security Contributions and Benefits Act 1992 (SSCBA 1992) and the SMP (General) Regulations 1986 as amended. The General Regulations were amended by the Social Security, Maternity Pay and Statutory Sick Pay (Miscellaneous) Amendments Regulations 2002, SI 2002/2690.

Section 164(1) as amended by s.20 of the Employment Act 2002 provides that where a woman satisfies the conditions of s.164(2) she is entitled to SMP. The conditions are:

- the woman must have been in continuous employment for at least 26 weeks ending with the week preceding the 14th week before the EWC;

- Her normal earnings for the period of eight weeks ending with the week immediately preceding the 14th week before the EWC are not less than the lower earnings limit in force (currently £102.80); and

- she has become pregnant and reached or been confined before reaching the commencement of the 11th week before the expected week of confinement.

There is detailed provision for aggregating employment with different employers, in relation to continuous service and for calculating earnings and reference should be made to the legislation for the detail.

By s.165(1) SMP shall be payable in respect of each week during the maternity pay period of a duration not exceeding 26 weeks. Section 18 of the Employment Act 2002 substituted a period of 26 weeks for SMP into s.165 of the SSCBA 1992 and for maternity allowance in s.35(2) of the 1992 Act. Regulation 2(2) specifies that the maternity pay period shall be 26 consecutive weeks. By s.165(2)the first week of the maternity pay period is the 11th week before the expected week of confinement subject to the provisions of ss.165(3)–(7).

SMP is not payable where a woman works during any week (s 165(4)(6)).

The rate at which SMP is to be paid is specified as:

(a) at the earnings-related rate in respect of the first six weeks of which it is payable, and

(b) at whichever is the lowest of the earning-related rate and such weekly rates as may be prescribed in respect of the remaining portion of the maternity pay period.

By reg.6 the current rate of SMP under s.166(1)(b) is £102.80.

The earnings-related rate is a weekly rate equivalent to 90% of a woman's normal weekly earnings for the period of eight weeks immediately preceding the 14th week before the EWC (s.166(2)).

The weekly rate must be not less than the weekly rate of statutory pay for the time being prescribed in s.157 or, if two or more rates are specified, the highest of the rates (s.166(3)).

Maternity allowance is payable for women who do not qualify for SMP but who have satisfied requirements relating to NI contributions. The requirements are that:

• that the women is pregnant and has reached the start of the 11th week before the EWC or has recently given birth;

- she has been employed or self employed for at least 26 weeks in the 66 weeks preceding the EWC. It is not necessary that the 26 weeks be continuous or with the same employer;

- she is not entitled to SMP for the same week in respect of the same pregnancy;

- she is not working.

The woman may be disqualified from MA if she fails to look after her health without good reason or if she fails to submit to a medical examination without good reason before the birth of the baby (s.25(3) SSCBA 1992 and the regulations).

MA is not payable where the woman is in prison or legal custody or where the woman travels outside the European Economic Area.

Discrimination, Detriment and Dismissal

It will be unlawful discrimination to dismiss a woman or subject her to any other detriment because she is pregnant and a comparator will not be necessary (**Webb v EMO Air Cargo UK) Ltd** [1995] ICR 1021 HL). The Pregnant Workers Directive 92/85/EC makes dismissal unlawful if it takes place during the period from the beginning of the pregnancy to the end of the minimum fourteen weeks maternity leave provided for in the Directive at Articles 8 and 10. This is implemented in UK law by the Employment Rights Act 1996 section 99 and the Maternity and Parental Leave etc. Regulations 1999 regulation 20. Detailed consideration of these provisions is beyond the scope of this book (see Duggan on *Family Friendly Policies*) but the following recent developments should be noted:

- It will be discrimination to refuse to renew a contract if the reason is that the woman is pregnant, even if the woman would be unavailable for the work because of pregnancy (**Caruana v Manchester Airport PLC** [1996] IRLR 378).

- There will be an automatic unfair dismissal if the dismissal was for a reason connected with the pregnancy as in **O'Neill v Governors of St Thomas More RC School** [1997] ICR 33 where a teacher was dismissed when she became pregnant by a catholic priest because it was felt this did not set the appropriate moral standard for the pupils. Nevertheless, the dismissal was still due to the pregnancy and unfair.

- Dismissal of a woman who is absent due to a pregnancy related illness will be discrimination and will be unfair (**Brown v Rentokil Limited** [1998] IRLR 445).

- The fact that the woman has not informed the employer she is pregnant when engaged will not assist, as it will still be discrimination and automtically unfair dismissal if the woman is dismissed once the pregnancy is discovered ((**Tele Danmark A/S v Handels -og Kontorfunktionaernes Forbund i Danmark** (*ECJ 4th October 2001*).

- It was held in **Busch v Klinikum Neustadt** [2003] IRLR 625 that it would be discriminatory where a woman wishes to shorten her parental leave and return to work to first require her to state whether she is pregnant again, even if she will be unable to carry out all the functions of the job and even if the reason for returning is to obtain a maternity allowance that is greater than the parental leave allowance. The ECJ stated that to find otherwise would be contrary to the objectives of the Directive and would rob the protection of any practical effect.

- In an important case, the EAT held that a woman on maternity leave was entitled to be notified of a job vacancy and to fail to notify amounted to unfair constructive dismissal (**Visa International Service Association v Paul** [2004] IRLR 42). This was so even though the employee did not have the experience to be short listed for the post since she believed she was suitable for the post and the failure to notify fatally undermined her trust and confidence. *This case makes it clear that employers should ensure they have a system for notifying those on leave of vacancies or promotional opportunities.*

- In **Merino Gómez v Continental Industrias del Caucho** [2004] IRLR 407 the European Court of Justice has held that women on maternity leave must be able to take their holiday entitlement under the Working Time Directive *separate* during a period other than whilst on maternity leave. This will include annual holiday that is fixed in advance by a collective agreement. This has important practical implication for employers who will have to ensure that leave is taken beforehand or carried over, though the latter course is difficult because the WTR provides that holiday cannot be carried over to the next year. One possible way round this would be to give a woman notice under the Regulations that holiday must be taken though this may be discriminatory because the notice has been given due to the woman's pregnancy!

It should be noted that where an employer fails to notify a woman on maternity leave of the end date of the leave and she fails to return because she was not so notified, it will be an automatic unfair dismissal if she is dismissed in those circumstances (reg. 20(3(ee) of the Maternity and Parental Leave etc. Regulations). This provision was introduced with effect from 24th November 2002 and makes it all the more important for an employer to send the notification letter (see precedent).

Parental Leave

The Government has implemented Council Directive 96/34/EC on the framework agreement on parental leave concluded by UNICE, CEEP and the ETUC by enacting Schedule 4 Part II of the Employment Relations Act 1999, which in turn permits Regulations to be promulgated to cover the detail of parental leave (reversing the opt out in 1997 when Labour came to power). Those Regulations are now contained in Part III of the Maternity and Parental Leave etc. Regulations 1999, and came into force on 15th December 1999. In this section references to Act and Regulations are to the Employment Rights Act 1996 (the ERA) and to the Maternity and Parental Leave Etc. Regulations 1999 1999/3212.

DTI Guides

- *A Short Guide For Employers And Employees* (PL510)

  http://www.dti.gov.uk/er/parental.htm

- *Detailed Guidance For Employers And Employees* (PL509)

  http://www.dti.gov.uk/er/individual/parental.pdf

In order to be entitled to parental leave the employee must

- have been continuously employed for a period of not less than one year; and

- has or expect to have responsibility for a child.

The employee will be entitled to be absent from work on parental leave for the purpose of caring for the child (regulation 13(1)).

By regulation 13(2), the employee has responsibility for the child if

- the parent is named on the birth certificate of a child born after 15th December 1999 who is under five years old;

- the employee has parental responsibilities in relation to a child born on or a 14th December 1999 who is under five years old; or

- has adopted a child on or after 15th December 1999 who is under the age of eighteen.

Regulations 14 and 15 set out the extent of the entitlement on the part of an employee:

- an employee is entitled to thirteen weeks' leave in respect of any individual child;

- the number of hours for a week's leave is calculated by dividing the total of the periods for which the employee is normally required to work by 52 where there are some weeks that the employee would not otherwise be required to work;

- both parents are entitled to parental leave.

The entitlement lasts until the date of the child's fifth birthday unless the child is disabled, in which case it lasts until the 18th birthday, or where a child has been adopted, in which case it lasts for five years after placement up to the child being 18 years of age.

There is provision for the employer and employee to conclude their own agreement and the above provisions may be less favourable if concluded through a collective or workforce agreement. There are, however, irreducible standards as follows:

- The right to take parental leave for each child where there is one year's minimum service with the employer.

- The right to take up to 13 weeks' leave for each child and 18 weeks for each disabled child.

- The leave is to be taken for the purpose of caring for the child.

- The right applies where a child was born or adopted after 14 December 1999 until the child's fifth birthday or five years from the date of placement.

- The right applies for the parents of children born or adopted between 15 December 1994 to 15 December 1999 until 31 March 2005 or in the case of adoption until the child's eighteenth birthday if this is sooner

- Leave may be taken for the first five years of the child's life or until the child is eighteen in respect of disabled children.

- The employee remains in employment whilst on leave and there are minimum terms and conditions that continue to apply.

- The employee is entitled to return to the same job after leave of less than four weeks or to a job that is the same or suitable where leave is over four weeks and it is not practicable for the employee to return to the same job.

Nature of and entitlement to leave

In the absence of any agreement, employees can only take parental leave on the basis that:

- 21 days' notice is given to the employer;

- the leave can only be taken in blocks of one or more full weeks;

- four weeks leave can only be taken in any one year;

- the employer may postpone notice for up to six months where the business would be disrupted, save where leave is sought after a child is born or adopted. The Government Guide states that:

  "Employers may be justified in postponing leave when, for example, the work is at a seasonal peak, where a significant proportion of the workforce applies at the same time or when the employee's role is such that his or her absence at a particular time would unduly harm the business."

The employer must agree to permit the employee to take a period of leave of the same duration as identified in the notice beginning on a date determined by the employer after consulting the employee which is to take place no later than six months after the period mentioned in the notice and end before the child's 18th birthday.

The employer must give notice in writing of the reason for the postponement and specify the dates on which the leave will begin and end and be given no later than seven days after the employee gave his or her notice.

An employee may complain under s.80 that the employer has unreasonably postponed leave and the tribunal will then have to consider the reasonableness of postponement by balancing the needs of the employer against the wish of the employee to take leave. It was stated by the Minister of State at the DTI in Standing Committee that:

> "A parent who wants to be with a child recovering from an operation cannot postpone that need, but one who simply wants some time with a child might be asked not to take it during a rush period in the workplace."

Any agreement cannot reduce the minimum standards set out above but in the absence of agreement the default provisions or fall back provisions apply. The agreement may be with the individual, in a collective agreement or under a workforce agreement (which is similar to workforce agreements under the WTR 1998). The requirements are set out in Schedule 1 to the regulations.

Reasons for Absence

It is important to note that parental leave is intended to be taken for the purpose of caring for the child. If an employee takes time off under these provisions and it is not for such purpose this may be misconduct and the employee may be subjected to the employer's ordinary disciplinary process. The Act and regulations aim to achieve its purpose by providing for things which may be done for the purpose of caring for a child and by specifying how the contract may be modified in order to provide for parental leave. By s.76(5), regulations may:

- specify things which are, or are not, to be taken as done for the purpose of caring for a child;

- require parental leave to be taken as a single period of absence in all cases or in specified cases;

- require parental leave to be taken as a series of periods of absence in all cases or in specified cases;

- require all or specified parts of a period of parental leave to be taken at or by specified times and make provision about the postponement by an employer of a period of parental leave which an employee wishes to take;

- specify a minimum or maximum period of absence which may be taken as part of a period of parental leave;

- specify a maximum aggregate of periods of parental leave which may be taken during a specified period of time.

By s.78(3) regulations under s.76 may provide for an employee to be entitled to choose to exercise all or part of his entitlement to parental leave:

- by varying the terms of his contract of employment as to hours of work.

- by varying his normal working practice as to hours of work, in a way specified in or permitted by the regulations for a period specified in the regulations.

However, under s.78(4) the provision of the right in practice may restrict the employee's entitlement to specified circumstances; or may make an entitlement subject to specified conditions (which may include conditions relating to obtaining the employer's consent) and may include consequential and incidental provision. The provisions as to timing of leave are considered in the next two sections.

Regulation 13(1) confirms that leave is only for the purpose of caring for that child.

The Guide states that use of leave for some other purpose is dishonesty. The regulations do not contain an express definition of child care and, wisely, do not set out any criteria as would have been permitted under the Act. However, the Guide does contain some examples at p.9. It states:

"The purpose of parental leave is to care for the child. This means looking after the welfare of a child and can include making arrangements for the good of a child. Caring for a child does not necessarily mean being with the child 24 hours a day. The leave might be taken simply to enable the parents to spend more time with young children. Examples of the way leave might be used:

- to spend more time with the child in early years;

- to accompany a child during a stay in hospital;

- checking out new schools;

- settling a child into new child care arrangements;

- to enable a family to spend more time together, for example

- taking the child to stay with grandparents."

Terms and Conditions during Absence

By regulation 17, where additional maternity leave or parental leave is taken the employee is entitled to:

- the benefit of the employer's implied obligation of trust and confidence;

- any implied conditions relating to notice of the termination of the employment contract by the employer

- compensation in the event of redundancy;

- the benefit of any disciplinary or grievance procedure.

The employee is also bound by the implied obligation of good faith and any terms and conditions relating to:

- notice of termination of the employment contract by the employee;

- the disclosure of confidential information;

- the acceptance of gifts or other benefits;

- the employee's participation in any other business.

It can be seen that these provisions are similar to those relating to Maternity or Adoption leave.

Right to Return

There will be a right to return to work and the provisions are similar to that with OML or AML. There is also provision where redundancy occurs during leave for the employer to be required to offer alternative employment (see sections 76–78 of the ERA 1996).

Paternity Leave

A further aspect of the Government's 'family friendly' policies was to introduce a new right to paternity leave which, in distinction to parental leave, is paid. Employees are entitled to take up to two weeks' paternity leave and to be paid during such leave at the same rate as SMP. Employees on paternity leave will be entitled to the benefits of the terms and conditions of employment apart from remuneration and will be entitled to return to the same job in which they worked before taking paternity leave. The rights are contained in Sections 80A–80C of the ERA 1996, inserted by the EA 2002, contain and Part II of the Paternity and Adoption Leave Regulations 2002, SI 2002/2788,

The rights arise on the birth of a child or upon adoption.

Birth

By reg.4(1) an employee is entitled to be absent for the purpose of caring for a child or supporting the child's mother if he satisfied the conditions contained in para.4(2) and has complied with the notice requirements in reg.6 and the evidential requirements if applicable.

The conditions under reg.4(2) are:

- that the employee has been continuously employed for a period of not less than 26 weeks ending with the week immediately preceding the 14th week before the expected week of the child's birth.

The employee is treated as having satisfied this condition where he has not been continuously employed for 26 weeks but the date on which the child is born is earlier than the 14th week before the week in which the birth is expected and the employee would have been continuously employed for 26 weeks if the employment had continued until the 14th week (reg.4(3)).

- That the employee is either the father of the child or married to or the partner of the child's mother, but not the child's father. The employee will be treated as having satisfied the condition where he is not the child's father and the child's mother has died (reg.4(4)).

- that the employee has, or expects to have, if he is the child's father, responsibility for the upbringing of the child or, if he is the mother's husband or partner but not the child's father, the main responsibility (apart from any responsibility of the mother) for the upbringing of the child. The employee is treated as satisfying the condition if he would have satisfied it but for the fact that the child was stillborn after 24 weeks of pregnancy or has died (reg.4(5)).

By regulation 5 the employee may chose to take one week or two week's consecutive leave which must be taken within 56 days after the child is born. Under regulation 6 notice of intention must be given and the EWC must be specified. The employee must also provide a declaration if required by the employer (reg. 6(3)). There is provision for variation of the time at which the period of commencement will begin (reg. 6(5)).

Adoption

Regulation 8 contains similar provision in relation to adoption, whilst regulation 9 also gives the option for one or two week's leave, regulation 10 deals with notice and evidential requirements and there is provision for variation in regulation 10.

Rights during and after paternity leave

Section 80C contains provision for regulation to set out rights during and after paternity leave. The section follows very much the same format as the other sections which create rights during leave periods.

By s.80C(1), the employee is entitled to the *benefit* of the terms and conditions of employment which would have applied if he had not been absent and is bound, for such purposes and to such extent as may be prescribed, by *obligations* arising under those terms and conditions, except in so far as they are inconsistent with the right to leave.

Regulation 12 provides that the employee is entitled, during the period of leave to the benefit of all the terms and conditions of employment which would have applied if he had not been absent and is bound during the period by any obligations arising under those terms and conditions subject only to the exception in s.80C(1)(b) of the ERA 1996 relating to seniority, pension rights and similar rights and terms and conditions of employment on return (s.80C(7)).

Regulation 13(1) provides that an employee who returns from a period of paternity leave which was an isolated period of leave or the last of two or more consecutive periods of statutory leave (*not including* AML or AAL or parental leave of more than four weeks) is entitled to return from leave to the job in which he was employed before his absence. If the employee returns from paternity leave which does not fall into the former, then the employee is entitled to return from leave to the job in which he was employed before his absence, or if that is not reasonably practicable, to another job which is both suitable and appropriate for him to do in the circumstances (reg.13(2)).

By reg.14 the employee's right to return is a right to return with his seniority, pension rights and similar rights where the employee is returning from consecutive periods of statutory leave which included a period of AAL or AML if the period or periods of his employment prior to the AAL or were continuous with the period of employment following it or in any other case, as they would have been if he had not been absent, and on terms and conditions not less favourable that those which would have applied if he had not been absent.

The provisions concerning the treatment periods of additional maternity leave or additional adoption leave are subject to the requirements of paras.5 and 6 or Schedule 5 to the Social Security Act 1989. It is to be noted that these provisions are very similar to those that apply for parental leave. The employee is treated as if he or she has not been absent, but where the leave is taken after AML or AAL, the period of absence is ignored in calculating service.

By s.80C(5) that terms and conditions of employment under s.80C(1)(c) includes matters connected with an employee's employment whether or not they arise under the contract of employment but do not include terms and conditions about remuneration. Paternity pay may be payable.

There is specific provision regarding redundancy and the right to return in section 80D(1).

Paternity pay

In conjunction with the right to paternity leave the 2002 reforms give a right to be paid. Section 2 of the Employment Act 2002 inserts a Part 12ZA into the SSCBA 1992. The Statutory Paternity Pay and Statutory Adoption Pay (General) Regulations 2002, SI 2002/2822, flesh out the provisions.

The DTI Guides

- *Working Fathers: Rights To Paternity Leave And Pay* (PL517)

  http://www.dti.gov.uk/er/individual/patrightspl517.htm

- *Paternity Leave And Pay: A Basic Summary* (PL514)

  http://www.dti.gov.uk/er/individual/paternitypl514.htm

An employee may become eligible for paternity pay in the following circumstances:

Adoption Leave

The right to adoption leave was added by s.3 of the Employment Act 2002 which added a new Chapter 1A, ss.75A–75D to the Employment Rights Act 1996. The detail is contained in the Paternity and Adoption Leave Regulations 2002, SI 2002/2788. Reference in this section are to the provisions of this Act and regulations.

DTI Guides

- *Adoptive Parents: Rights To Leave And Pay When A Child Is Placed For Adoption Within The Uk* (PL518)

  http://www.dti.gov.uk/er/individual/adoptionpl518.pdf

- *Adoptive Parents: Rights To Leave And Pay – A Basic Summary* (PL515)

  http://www.dti.gov.uk/er/individual/adoptpl515.htm

There is a useful flowchart in the DTI Guide which is set out below.

The right to take time off in relation to adoption is a fairly new right introduced in the round of 'family friendly' legislation in 2002. It follows a similar pattern to maternity leave The adoption rights are available to an individual employee who is adopting a child or to a couple adopting jointly.

Where a couple are adopting, one person may take the adoption rights whilst the other may take the benefit of paternity rights. In order to be eligible for adoption the employee must have 26 weeks' continuous service at the start of the week in which the employee is notified of being matched with a child for adoption. The employee will be entitled to 26 weeks' paid leave for ordinary adoption and to a further 26 weeks' additional adoption which is unpaid.

The employee is not required to give notice of intention to return at the end of the full adoption period and it will be assumed that the employee will return.

If the employee stops working for the employer after the child is placed the employee will be entitled to Statutory Adoption Pay (SAP) or Statutory Paternity Pay (SPP) except for time spent working for another employer. The rate of SAP is currently £102.80 and is recoverable in the same way as SMP.

Advance funding may be sought by the employer from the Inland Revenue. Where the employer does not believe that the employee is entitled to SAP it must provide the employee with a written statement to that effect. The employee must notify the employer within seven days of being notified by an adoption agency that a match had been made for adoption and that the employee intends to take adoption leave. The employee must provide a matching certificate and declare that he or she has chosen to receive SAP instead of SPP.

Adoption Rights Chart from DTI Guide PL518

Adoption Rights Flowchart

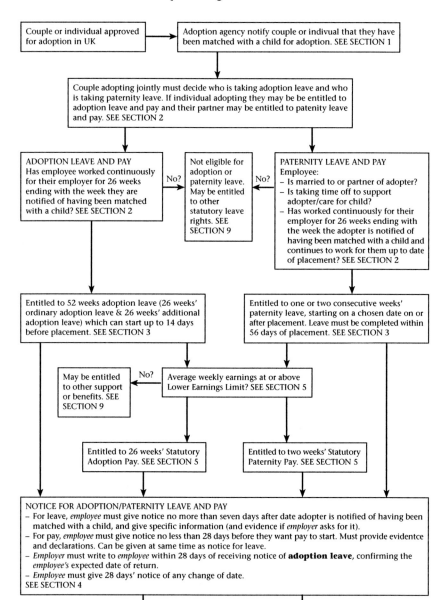

Couple or individual approved for adoption in UK

Adoption agency notify couple or indivual that they have been matched with a child for adoption. SEE SECTION 1

Couple adopting jointly must decide who is taking adoption leave and who is taking paternity leave. If individual adopting they may be be entitled to adoption leave and pay and their partner may be entitled to patenity leave and pay. SEE SECTION 2

ADOPTION LEAVE AND PAY
Has employee worked continuously for their employer for 26 weeks ending with the week they are notified of having been matched with a child? SEE SECTION 2

No?

Not eligible for adoption or paternity leave. May be entitled to other statutory leave rights. SEE SECTION 9

No?

PATERNITY LEAVE AND PAY
Employee:
– Is married to or partner of adopter?
– Is taking time off to support adopter/care for child?
– Has worked continuously for their employer for 26 weeks ending with the week the adopter is notified of having been matched with a child and continues to work for them up to date of placement? SEE SECTION 2

Entitled to 52 weeks adoption leave (26 weeks' ordinary adoption leave & 26 weeks' additional adoption leave) which can start up to 14 days before placement. SEE SECTION 3

Entitled to one or two consecutive weeks' paternity leave, starting on a chosen date on or after placement. Leave must be completed within 56 days of placement. SEE SECTION 3

May be entitled to other support or benefits. SEE SECTION 9

No?

Average weekly earnings at or above Lower Earnings Limit? SEE SECTION 5

Entitled to 26 weeks' Statutory Adoption Pay. SEE SECTION 5

Entitled to two weeks' Statutory Paternity Pay. SEE SECTION 5

NOTICE FOR ADOPTION/PATERNITY LEAVE AND PAY
– For leave, *employee* must give notice no more than seven days after date adopter is notified of having been matched with a child, and give specific information (and evidence if *employer* asks for it).
– For pay, *employee* must give notice no less than 28 days before they want pay to start. Must provide evidentce and declarations. Can be given at same time as notice for leave.
– *Employer* must write to *employee* within 28 days of receiving notice of **adoption leave**, confirming the *employee's* expected date of return.
– *Employee* must give 28 days' notice of any change of date.
SEE SECTION 4

Placement delayed or early

Continued on page 276

Placement on expected date

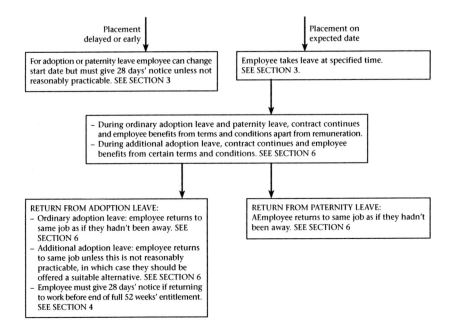

For a very detailed consideration of these rights see Michael Duggan, *Family-Friendly Policies, A Handbook for Employer and Employee.*

Statutory Adoption Pay

Statutory adoption pay was also introduced by the Employment Act 2002. It is now governed by Part 12ZB of the Social Security Contributions and Benefits Act (SSCBA) 1992 and the Statutory Paternity and Statutory Adoption Pay (General) Regulations 2002. The provisions follow a similar schematic format to SMP.

By s.171ZL(1) a person is entitled to SAP where the conditions set out in s.71ZL(2) are satisfied. There are five conditions set out in the section:

(1) that he is a person with whom a child is, or is expected to be placed for adoption under the law of any part of the United Kingdom;

(2) that he has been in employed earner's employment with an employer for a continuous period of at least 26 weeks ending with the relevant week;

(3) that he has ceased to work for the employer;

(4) that his normal weekly earnings for the period of eight weeks ending with the relevant week are not less than the lower earnings limit in force under s.5(1)(a) at the end of the relevant week; and

(5) that he has elected to receive SAP.

Reference should be made to Michael Duggan, *Family-Friendly Policies, A Handbook for Employer and Employee* for the detail.

PART TWO: FLEXIBLE WORKING

[The DTI has issued a number of Forms which set out the requirements of the procedure and these are referred to in the pages that follow.] In addition, the DTI site contains a number of examples that are useful guides as precedents. These are set out in the text. The timelines from the Working Committee Report are produced as well as the timeline from the Guidance. It is hoped that, by collating all this information in one place, a complete picture is provided as to the way in which the Government expects the flexible working procedures to be applied in practice. As forms may change, the site references are provided. Many are reproduced in full in Duggan *Family Friendly Policies*.

COMMENTARY ON FLEXIBLE WORKING

As part of its family friendly policies, the Government has introduced a right for parents to request flexible working where he or she has young children. The procedure largely follows the recommendations of the Work and Parents Taskforce and reference is made in this part to this report. The history of the legislation is considered in detail in Michael Duggan, *Family Friendly-Policies, Handbook for Employer and Employee* and reference should be made to that work for the detail. This section will consider:

(1) The nature of flexible working as defined in the Regulations.

(2) Entitlement to make a request for flexible working.

(3) Contractual issues.

(4) The nature of the application.

(5) The meeting to discuss the application and the right to be represented.

(6) Notification of decision and reason to refuse the application.

(7) Grounds for Refusal.

(8) Appeals.

(9) Extensions of time and disposal by agreement.

(10)Remedies.

The rights and procedures are contained in the Employment Rights Act 1996, Part 8A , sections 80F to 80I, which were added by the Employment Act 2002 and apply from 6th April 2003. Regulations have been promulgated to set out the rights and procedures:

- The Flexible Working (Eligibility, Complaints and Remedies) Regulations 2002, SI 2002/3236: "The Eligibility Regulations".

- The Flexible Working (Procedural Requirements) Regulations 2002, SI 2000/3207: "The Procedural Regulations".

See the DTI Guidance at: *http://www.dti.gov.uk/er/individual/flexwork-pl520.pdf.*

(1) The nature of flexible working

By section 80F(1) of the ERA a qualifying employee may apply for a change in the terms and conditions of employment if:

- the change relates to—

    (i) the hours he is required to work,

    (ii) the times when he is required to work,

    (iii) where, as between his home and a place of business of his employer, he is required to work, or

    (iv) such other aspect of his terms and conditions of employment as the Secretary of State may specify by regulations, and

- his purpose in applying for the change is to enable him to care for someone who, at the time of application, is a child in respect of whom he satisfies such conditions as to relationship as the Secretary of State may specify by regulations.

(2) Entitlement to make a request for flexible working

To be a qualifying employee conditions as to duration of employment as provided for in regulations must be satisfied and the application must be made when the child is under a certain age, as set out below:

An agency worker cannot qualify (s.80F(8)(a)). By section 80F(8)(b) as person is an agency worker if he is supplied by a person ("the agent") to do work for another ("the principal") under a contract or other arrangement made between the agent and the principal.

By reg.3 of the Eligibility Regulations an employee is entitled to make an application for a contractual variation if he:

•   has been continuously employed for a period of not less than 26 weeks.

The Taskforce considered that the period of six months was consistent with the maternity and paternity rights. Continuous employment is calculated in accordance with the provisions of Chapter 1, Part 14 of the Employment Rights Act 1996 (ERA).

The employee must be either the mother, father, adopter, guardian or foster parent of the child, or married to or the partner of the child's mother, father or adopter, guardian or foster parent.

•   An *adopter* is a person who has been matched with a child for adoption.

•   A *foster parent* means a foster parent within the meaning of reg.2 of the Fostering Service Regulations 2002 or a foster carer within the meaning of reg.2 of the Fostering of Children (Scotland) Regulations 1996.

•   A *guardian* means a person appointed as a guardian under s.5 of the Children Act 1989 or s.7 or s.11 of the Children (Scotland) Act 1995.

•   A *partner* is, in relation to a child's mother, father, adopter, guardian or foster parent a person (whether of the same or a different sex) who lives with the child and the mother, father, adopter, guardian or foster parent but is not a relative of the mother, father, adopter, guardian or foster parent.

- By reg.2(2) of the Eligibility Regulations the relatives are the mother's, father's adopters', guardian's, or foster parent's parent, grandparent, sister, brother, aunt or uncle, whilst by reg.2(3) references to these relationships are to relationships of the full blood or half blood or such as those relationships that would exist but for adoption and include the relationship of a child with his adoptive or former adoptive parents.

It is unnecessary that the employee has or expects to have responsibility for the upbringing of the child.

Latest age of child for application

An application for flexible working must be made before the 14th day before the day on which the child reaches the age of six or, if disabled, eighteen (s.80F(1)(3)) though these ages may be amended by regulation (s.80F(6)).

A disabled child is a child who is entitled to a disability living allowance within section 71 of the Social Security Contributions and Benefits Act 1992.

No more than one application may be made in any twelve months (s.80F(4)). The Report considered at what stage in a child's life employers should no longer have a duty to seriously consider parents' requests. It stated that the age should be six and considered that there should be no exemptions for small business though they may need additional support.

At para.3.14 of the Report, the Taskforce recognised that there was a considerable level of demand from parents of all ages and that the greatest levels are associated with birth, around the age of five when a child starts school and when they change school at 11. It stated (para.3.19) that it was aware that the majority of parents and some employers would like the age to be higher than six but considered that the prudent way forward was to recommend that the employer's duty to consider a request should cover two of the three key points of demand and end when the parent's child reaches its sixth birthday.

(3) *Contractual issues*

The legislation gives the employee the ability to request a change in hours, times and the place of work, whether it be the employer's workplace or home. However, it is silent as to what happens when the employer accedes to the request and there may be an issue as to whether the contract of employment has been varied so that the employee can continue to work on such terms when the child has reached school age; i.e. does the change become incorporated as a term so that it cannot be varied back to the old term without agreement. The Taskforce stated at paragraph 3.21:

> "We do not believe that once a child reaches the cut-off age the employer should have the right to insist that parents revert back to their original working pattern. Nor do we believe that parents should have a right to return to their original working pattern. Employers and parents will have invested time in making the necessary changes to their organisation and family life to accommodate the working pattern. They are unlikely to have either the will or the time to unpick the arrangement, particularly if the employer has hired another person to help implement the original request."

(4) *The nature of the application*

The Regulations set out a procedure from application to appeal to be followed in relation to any applications that are made. There is a very useful chart in the DTI Guide and time charts at appendix 2 of the Taskforce Report which are reproduced below.

- The Government has produced a form FW(A) on which an application may be made. It is available on the DTI website as are the other forms referred to in this chapter at

  http://www.dti.gov.uk/er/individual/flexforms.htm.

- For The Application See Form A:

  http://www.dti.gov.uk/er/individual/flexA.pdf

The application

The Taskforce stated that the procedure was intended to be light touch sensitive and to encourage dialogue in the workplace in order to promote the adoption of flexible working between employer and employee.

The application for flexible working must:

- state that it is such an application.

- specify the change applied for and the date on which it is proposed the change should become effective.

- explain what effect, if any, the employee thinks making the change applied for would have on his employer and how, in his opinion, any such effect might be dealt with; and

- explain how the employee meets, in respect of the child concerned, the conditions as to relationship with the child.

The Government has produced a form FW(A) on which an application may be made. It is available on the DTI website as are the other forms referred to in this chapter see above for full references.

The Eligibility Regulations (Reg. 4) provides that an application shall be in writing, state whether a previous application has been made by the employer to the employee and, if so when and be dated. The application will be taken to have been made on the day that the application is received unless the contrary is proven (Eligibility Regulations 5(1)). The reference to the day on which the application is received will be the day it is transmitted by electronic communication or the day on which the application would be delivered in the ordinary course of post if posted (Eligibility regs.5(2)).

A useful timeline is provided at:

www.dti.gov.uk/er/individual/flexwork-pl520.pdf

Acceptance by the employer of the application for flexible working

If the employer is prepared to accede to the request then it will be a simple matter to notify the employee that this is the position. The employer may wish to give consideration to the following (which are not covered by the Regulations):

- To stating that the employer will accede to the application for a trial period and it will be decided whether the request is feasible at the end of the trial period. It is important to note that the Regulations do not force the employer to accept a request for flexible working but merely to follow the procedure and to provide proper detail as to why the request has been rejected. The reasons for rejection cannot be challenged. It would seem to be sensible to agree a trial period to see if the request will work and this would be a sensible approach in any event in order to lessen the risk of a discrimination claim.

- Where the employee wishes to work from home it is important to note that there are various requirements for home working that may need to be satisfied and due consideration should be given to these matters.

- The employer may wish to expressly specify that the request is only accepted on the express basis that it applies until the child is six, and that the original contract terms will continue to be the overriding terms.

- For a Form Accepting The Request See Form Fw(B) Flexible Working Application Acceptance Form

  http://www.dti.gov.uk/er/individual/flexB.pdf

(5) *The meeting to discuss the application and the right to be represented*

By section 80G(1) the employer is under a duty to deal with the application in accordance with the regulations. Section 80G(2)(a) provides that a meeting should be held within 28 days after the date the application was made. Regulation 3 of the Procedural Regulations provides that an employer shall hold the meeting within 28 days and reg. 11 provides that it will be at a place convenient to employer and employee.

The employee has the right to be accompanied at the meeting and there is provision for postponement where the companion is not able to attend. Regulation 14 of the Procedural Regulations corresponds to the provisions for the attendance of a companion in relation to disciplinary or grievance hearings.

By Regulation 14 of the Procedural Regulations where a first or appeal meeting is held and the employee reasonably requests to be accompanied at the meeting the employee is entitled to representation. The employee must permit the employee to be accompanied by a single companion who is chosen by the employee and is a worker employed by the same employer as the employee and the companion must be permitted to address the meeting, but not answer questions on behalf of the employee, and to confer with the employed during the meeting (reg.14(2)(3) of the Procedural Regulations).

If the employee has a right to be accompanied and his chosen companion will not be available at the time proposed for the meeting by the employee, the employer must postpone the meeting to the time proposed by the employee if an alternative is proposed which is convenient for employer, employee and companion and falls before the end of the period of seven days beginning with the first day after the day proposed by the employer(reg.14(4)(5) of the Procedural Regulations).

The employer shall permit a worker to take time off during working hours for the purpose of accompanying an employee (reg.15(6) of the Procedural Regulations). A complaint may be presented by reg.15 of the Procedural Regulations where the employer has failed or threatened to fail to comply with reg.14(2) and compensation may be awarded not exceeding two weeks pay. By reg.16 of the Procedural Regulations complaints may be presented of unfair dismissal and detriment where he is subjected to a detriment or dismissed because he has sought to exercise rights under reg.16.

(6) Notification of decision and reason to refuse the application

The employer has to notify the employee of the decision within 14 days of the meeting (section 80G(2)(b)). This should set out the grounds for the decision where there has been a refusal. It is also necessary for there to be a sufficient explanation of the grounds for refusal (section 80G(2)(j)). The notification must contain information about the right to appeal.

Regulations 4 and 5 of the Procedural Rules provides that an employee shall give the employee notice of his decision on the application within 14 days of the meeting. If the employer agrees to the application the employer must specify the variation agreed to and state the date on which the variation is to take effect. Where the decision is to refuse the application the employer must state which of the grounds of refusal are considered by the employer to apply, contain a sufficient explanation as to why those grounds apply in relation to the application, set out the appeal procedure and be dated.

- For A Form Where The Request Is Refused See Form Fw(C) Flexible Working Application Rejection Form

  http://www.dti.gov.uk/er/individual/flexC.pdf

---

(7) The Grounds for Refusing

Section 80G(b) contains eight grounds for refusing the request by the employee with provision for the Secretary of State to specify further grounds The grounds are:

(i)   the burden of additional costs,

(ii)   detrimental effect on ability to meet customer demand,

(iii)   inability to re-organise work among existing staff,

(iv)   inability to recruit additional staff,

(v)   detrimental impact on quality,

(vi)   detrimental impact on performance,

(vii) insufficiency of work during the periods the employee proposes to work,

(viii) planned structural changes, and

(ix)   such other grounds as the Secretary of State may specify by regulations.

The Taskforce Report commented about the approach that may be taken in relation to the grounds at paragraph 4.2.1 of its report:

> "The employment tribunal will not be able to ask an employer to provide additional explanation over and above the level defined but they will be able to verify any disputed facts. They will not have the power to question the employer's actual reasons for declining a request. For example, if a parent who has responsibility for opening a small shop asks to start work at 9.30 am it would not be sufficient for the employer to say, without explanation, that this would mean that the store could not open at its usual time. They would need to explain why. For example, the employer might explain in the letter that for security reasons staff who are key holders must have worked for the company for more than a year. They might add that of the four staff, the two longest-serving members of staff had repeatedly made it clear that they did not want the responsibility of being a key holder and the other member of staff had been working for the company for only four months. Parents would have the power to raise matters of fact not of judgments; for example, they might dispute how long people had worked at the shop or that the policy is that they have to work for that length of time to be key holders. The employment tribunal will look to satisfy itself of these points of fact. Although other issues quite rightly may be raised at the appeal hearing, these should not be re-opened at the tribunal."

Examples of the detail that one would expect to be contained in Requests by Employees and Rejections by Employers are contained in Annexe A, pages 42–43 of the Taskforce report *http://www.dti.gov.uk/er/individual/ flexwork-pl520.pdf*); the Guidance notes to the Employment Act 2002 and the TIGER (Tailored Interactive Guidance on Employment Rights). These examples provide useful Precedents and are set out below.

Precedent examples of requests and rejections contained in the TIGER site and under the Guidance notes to the Employment Act 2002

Section 80G(b)(i) the burden of additional costs

The TIGER website states that:

> "This business reason can be used where the requested working pattern will result in one or more costs, which clearly outweigh the gains, and overall are detrimental to the business."

The following example is given:

> Sasha, a systems administrator for a small IT company, applies to change from working weekends to her existing days off in the week. Sasha has recently participated in an extensive training programme to undertake the role. The systems administrator role includes undertaking maintenance of the computer system to ensure that all IT equipment is working fully during trading hours.

Her manager discusses the request with Sasha but is unable to agree to a change to the days when Sasha is required to work. When stating the business grounds she includes *inability to recruit additional staff* and the *burden of additional costs* within the explanation about why the grounds apply in the circumstances.

> "The role of the weekend administrator is vital to the running of the company. It is essential that the IT equipment is operational from the moment staff arrive on a Monday morning and maintenance occurs out of our core hours. You are aware of the difficulties that we have had during the past year of filling the Systems Administrator posts. The vacancy was advertised twice (at the job centre and in trade press) and on both occasions no suitable applicant was found. You subsequently expressed an interest and agreed to receive the necessary training. We discussed at the time that a necessary part of the job was to fulfil the weekend systems administrator's duties. It was on this basis that I made the case to our board to invest substantially more on training this year than was planned and, specifically, to fund your course. The training programme was extensive and completed only last month. As such, we do not presently have the budget or resources to train anyone else. When we met to discuss your application I agreed to also speak to John, our other administrator, to explore whether he can change his hours but he is unable to help. I am therefore afraid on this

occasion I am unable to amend your working hours. I have attached details
of the appeal procedure should you wish to appeal."

Section 80G(b)(ii) detrimental effect on ability to meet customer demand

The TIGER website states that:

"This business ground can be used where the change in working pattern would have a detrimental effect on the businesses ability to meet customer demand. For example, inability to serve customers during a busy lunch period."

The following example is given:

Marie, an experienced hair stylist working in a small hairdressers, applies to reduce her full-time hours to working between 10.00 am and 3.00pm. In the letter refusing the request the manager gives the business reason of detrimental effect on ability to meet customer demand as the basis of refusal and explains that the salon does not have the spare capacity to manage the parent's customers in her absence.

> *"For the last six months all stylists have been fully booked up in advance on almost every day of the week, with the beginning and end of each day being particularly busy. As you are aware, you are highly regarded by our customers and the majority ask for you by name and would not accept a trainee stylist in your absence.*
>
> *I regret therefore that I am unable to cover your absence at present Your absence would mean that we are unable to serve our usual number of customers. I would, however, be happy to revisit your request in a year's time when Sally, our trainee stylist, will have completed her training."*

The Guidance Notes to the Employment Act 2002 provide an example, as follows:

Where an employer rejects an application the intention is that the employer should set out their business reasons (which will have to be from the list shown above) backed up with an explanation of the reason why, in their opinion, it applies. This is to help the employee understand why the employer has arrived at his decision and to help demonstrate that the request has been considered seriously. It is envisaged that a couple of paragraphs will usually be sufficient. The intention is that the guidance to accompany the right will include a variety of differing examples for each of the business reasons. One illustrative explanation might be:

> *"I am sorry that I cannot grant your request to leave at 3:30pm each day as this will severely effect our ability to meet customer demand and I am unable to cover your absence. You are currently the only certified forklift truck driver that works at the end of the day and it is essential that we are able to load the lorries for overnight delivery. Due to the fact that we supply perishable goods it is not possible to load the delivery lorries any earlier in the day. I have spoken with our other two forklift truck drivers, and they are presently unable to change their hours. I also advertised in the local paper when Sam left and notified the Job Centre of the vacancy but could not find anyone to cover his job. As that was only two months ago it is not appropriate to go through the process again now."*

Section 80G(b)(iii) inability to re-organise work among existing staff

The TIGER Website states that:

> "This business ground can be used where the inability to re-organise work among other staff prevents you from accepting the request."

The following example is given:

Colin a pharmacist makes an application to the owner of a chemist if he can amend his hours so that he can drop off and collect his child from school. At the meeting to discuss the request the owner explains that it is a legal requirement for a pharmacist to be on duty at all times. In his written decision the employer states that due to the business ground of an *inability to re-organise work* amongst existing staff he is unable to accept the request.

> *"Because we handle prescriptions we are contracted by the NHS to provide a dispensing service between 8:30 and 5:30 each day. Despite both dispensers being prepared to cover your absence, by law I must have a qualified pharmacist on duty between these times. The only other weekday pharmacist is Sam who works part-time over the busy lunch period and does not want to change his hours of work. You suggested during our discussion that I could make use of locum pharmacists to cover the periods when you would be absent, in the same way that I use*

locum pharmacists during periods of leave. I explored this with the locum agency and, as I speculated during our discussion, they confirmed that it is unlikely that a locum pharmacist would be willing to work for an hour in the morning and at the end of the day. As such, the agency said that they could not guarantee cover. I regret therefore that I cannot agree to the work pattern set out in your application. You do have a right to appeal this decision" which is set out below.

Section 80G(b)(iv)inability to recruit additional staff

The TIGER website states:

"This business ground can be used where you have tried and been unable to recruit a new member of staff."

The following example is given:

"... that I cannot grant your request to leave at 3:30pm each day. You are currently the only certified forklift truck driver that works at the end of day and due to the perishable nature of our products it is essential that we are able to load the lorries for over-night delivery. I have spoken with our other two forklift truck drivers and they are unable to change their hours. I also spoke to Job Centre Plus when George left and advertised in the local paper but got no suitable applicants. As that was only a month ago it is not yet appropriate to repeat the process. Should the circumstances change I will be happy to reconsider your application."

Details about how to appeal against this decision are detailed below.

Section) 80G(b)(v) detrimental impact on quality

The TIGER website states:

"This business ground can be used where the change in your employee's working pattern would result in a detrimental impact on the quality of service or product that you provide."

The following example is given:

A skilled furniture finisher applies to not work on a Friday.

"... but I am afraid it would have a detrimental impact on our ability to quality check our furniture before it was dispatched to stores for the

weekend. You are the only skilled furnisher who works at the end of the week to provide pieces with a final polish and check and remedy any marks that may have appeared on the furniture during the final stages of manufacture. This is not uncommon and your role is vital to ensure that we dispatch quality pieces.

Without your quality check we could not ensure the quality finish that store owners and our eventual customers expect. This would eventually damage our reputation for high quality furniture which we have established over the last ten years and that our products have become known for ..."

Section) 80G(b)(vi)detrimental impact on performance

The TIGER website states:

"This business ground can be used where the change in your employee's working pattern would result in a detrimental impact on the performance of your business."

The following example is given:

"I am sorry that I cannot grant your request to change the days that you work, but to allow you to not work on a Thursday would have a detrimental effect on the performance of the business. Thursday is our busiest day of the week when all staff are required to ensure that the machinists can continue making curtains while stock is received, and finished curtains are packaged ready to be dispatched the following morning. You are aware that on a Thursday morning we receive our weekly delivery of fabric. This requires the involvement of all staff to help move the material from the delivery bay into the storeroom, before the newly made curtains can be prepared for dispatch the following morning. As I indicated when we met to discuss the application, if you decide to change the day you would prefer not to work to one earlier in the week, then I would be happy to reconsider your application."

Section) 80G(b)vii) insufficiency of work during the periods the employee proposes to work

The TIGER website states:

"This business ground can be used where the change in your employee's working pattern would mean that there was insufficient work at the times proposed by your employee."

The following example is given:

Emma an employee at a fish and chip shop applies to work on a Monday and Tuesday instead of Thursday and Friday. The employer provides insufficiency of work during the period the employee proposes to work as a business ground for not being able to agree to the request.

> *"As you know Thursday and Friday are two of our busiest days of the week. Only Saturdays are busier. It is during this busy time when I need extra people to help out in the shop. However, at the beginning of the week, the shop is relatively quiet and as such, I do not need extra staff at this time. I am therefore afraid that I am unable to agree to your request. You do have a right to appeal this decision and details are attached."*

Section 80G(b)(viii) planned structural changes

The TIGER website states:

"This business ground can be used where the change in your employee's working pattern would be incompatible with planned structural changes."

The following example is given:

John who works in a pub in the business district of a city applies to the bar manager to work on a Sunday instead of a Monday. The manager is unable to accept the request because the owner has established that it is not profitable to open the bar at weekends when there are very few customers and has decided that it will no longer open for weekends.

> "...unfortunately from next month we will no longer be opening at the weekend. As you may know the vast majority of our customers are from other businesses in our immediate vicinity and who operate Monday to Friday only. We have not had many customers at the weekend for quite some time and it is no longer profitable for us to open then. The landlord has therefore decided to close the bar at weekends. I am sorry that I cannot be any more helpful in the circumstances. Details of the appeal procedure are attached."

(8) Appeals

Provision should be made for the employer to appeal within 14 days after the date when the employer notifies the employee that the request has been rejected (section 80(G)(2)(b); Regulation 6 of the Procedural Regulations). The contents of the appeal notice shall be in writing, set out the grounds of appeal and be dated.

- *For The Appeal Precedent See Form Fw(D) Flexible Working Form*

  http://www.dti.gov.uk/er/individual/flexD.pdf

There is no need to hold an appeal if the employer upholds the appeal within 14 days after the notice of appeal is given. The employer must notify the employee in writing, specifying the contractual variation that has been agreed and stating the date from which the contractual variation is to take effect (reg. 8 of the Procedural Regs).

There must be provision to hold an appeal meeting within 14 days after the date when the notice of appeal has been given and the time and place is to be convenient for the parties (regs. 8 and 11 of the Procedural Regs).

The employee has the right to be accompanied at the appeal.

Notice of the decision is to be given within 14 days after the holding of the meeting (regulation 9 of the Procedural Regs). The notice should state the grounds for the decision to dismiss and provision shall be made for a statement of the decision to dismiss to contain a sufficient explanation of the grounds for the decision. Regulation 10 of the Procedural Regulations provides that notification of the decision shall be in writing and be dated. If the appeal is upheld that notification shall specify the contract variation agreed and the date from which the variation is to take effect.

- *For A Form Of Decision See Form Fw(E) Flexible Working Appeal Reply Form*

  http://www.dti.gov.uk/er/individual/flexE.pdf

---

(9) *Extensions of time and disposal by agreement*

Regulation 12 of the Procedural Regulations provides for extensions of time in relation to any of those parts of the regulations where there is a time period and an extension is agreed. The extension shall be in writing and the employer's record must specify the period the extension relates to, the date the extension is to end, be dated and sent to the employee. If the individual who would normally consider the application is absent on annual leave or because of sickness on the day on which the application is made the period of 28 days commences on the day the individual returns to work or 28 days after which the application is made, whichever is sooner (reg.13 of the Procedural Regulations).

- *For A Form Relating To Extensions Of Time See Form Fw(F) Flexible Working Extension Of Time*

  FORM *http://www.dti.gov.uk/er/individual/flexF.pdf*

Regulation 17 of the Procedural Regulations provides the employer shall treat the application as withdrawn where the employee has notified to him whether orally or in writing:

- that he is withdrawing the application,

- where without reasonable cause he has failed to attend a meeting more than once or

- where without reasonable cause he has refused to provide the employer with information the employer requires in order to assess whether the contact variation should be agreed to.

> - For a form giving notice of withdrawal *see Fw(G) Flexible Working Notice Of Withdrawal Form*
>
>   *http://www.dti.gov.uk/er/individual/flexG.pdf*

(10) Remedies

The employee may complain to an employment tribunal that the employer has failed to comply with the procedure contained in section 80H(1) or that the decision to reject the request was based upon incorrect facts. The tribunal may make a declaration that the complaint is well founded and make an order for reconsideration or an award of compensation. See Duggan, *Family Friendly Policies* for further consideration.

PART L: ABSENCE FOR OTHER REASONS

Precedent L: Absences for other reasons

L1:	Dependants	806
L2:	Other special leave arrangements	807
L3:	Marriage	807
L4:	Public duties	807
	Form in relation to public duties	808
L5:	Jury service	809
	Form in relation to jury service	809
L6:	Religious holidays	809
L7:	Other absences	810
L8:	Letter agreeing to unpaid absence	810
L9:	Sabbatical leave policy	811
Commentary:	Absence for other reasons	813

Precedent L1: Dependants

Under the Employment Rights Act 1996 you are entitled to time off to care for dependants and the Company will comply with the provisions of the legislation. The following provisions are applicable in relation to such time off.

1   A dependant will be your spouse, child or parent or someone who lives in the same household as yourself otherwise than by being lodger, boarder or tenant, or who you can show is a person who reasonably relies on your assistance to make arrangements for the provision of care when that person falls ill or is injured or assaulted.

2   You will be entitled to a reasonable amount of time off in order to take action that is necessary:

a)   to provide assistance when your dependant is ill, injured or assaulted;

b)   to make arrangements for the provision of care when your dependant is ill, injured or assaulted;

c)   in consequence of the death of a dependant;

d)   because of the unexpected disruption or termination of arrangements for the care of a dependant;

e)   to deal with any incident that involves your child and has occurred unexpectedly in a period when he is in an educational establishment that is responsible for him or her.

3   You must tell the Company of the reason for your absence as soon as reasonably possible including how long you think you will be absent.

Precedent L2: Other Special Leave Arrangements

The Company is always prepared to consider requests for leave because of special circumstances. You should make any request to your manager who will consider whether it should be granted and whether it should be paid or unpaid.

Precedent L3: Marriage

You are entitled to _____ days paid leave in addition to your holiday entitlement from the date when you marry.

Precedent L4: Public Duties

Term for Contract/manual

If you are carrying out public duties you will have a statutory right to reasonable time off in order to fulfil these duties. You must first notify the Company who will then consider whether you are entitled to time off for such duties and whether your time off should be paid or unpaid. If the Company decides that you will be paid during time off for public duties you must still claim such payment as you are entitled from the public body and inform the Company of the amount that you are paid. The Company will be entitled to offset these amounts from your salary and you agree to the Company deducting such sums from your wages.

Request for time off to perform public duties and agreement to deduction of sums from salary

I _____ request time of work on the following dates:

_____

in order to serve on [SET OUT BODY]

I expect to be paid for the duties that I perform and will inform the Company of the amounts that are paid to me. I expressly agree that these amounts may be offset against the salary which the Company pays me during the period I am off work and I agree to the sums being deducted at source from my wages.

SIGNED   DATED

APPROVAL

I confirm that the above request for time off work has been approved on the express basis that the employee is to perform the duties set out above.

SIGNED   DATED

For record purposes

Length of time off:

Sums paid by Company during absence:

Sums received by employee from public body:

Offet from Salary: Yes/no   DATE OFFSET

Precedent L5: Jury Service

You are entitled to time off from the Company for jury service. You will be paid for such time off. You must produce the Summons to the Company to confirm that you have been called for jury service. At the discretion of the Company you may be paid your normal rate of pay whilst on Jury Service subject to deduction of any monies received from the court relating to loss of earnings. In order to be paid at the normal rate of pay you must signify your consent in writing to the sums that you will receive by way of Financial Loss Allowance being deducted from your salary.

I HEREBY AUTHORISE THE COMPANY TO DEDUCT FROM MY SALARY THE SUMS SET OUT BELOW IN RESPECT OF WHICH I RECEIVE A FINANCIAL LOSS ALLOWANCE FROM THE COURT WHILST ON JURY SERVICE

£ _____ for _____ full days

£ _____ for _____ half days

I hereby consent to the above deductions

SIGNED

DATE

Precedent L6: Religious Holidays

The Company recognises that religious beliefs may mean that you need to take time off at certain times and it will seek to allow time off to observe religious holidays. These holidays will form part of your holiday entitlement.

Alternative clause

The Company will grant reasonable time off for religious observance. You are entitled to take [...] days off to observe religious festivals. The time off will be unpaid and must be authorised in advance.

Precedent L7:   Other Absences

Any absences for domestic reasons such as house moving, deliveries of furniture or such similar reason must be taken as part of your holiday entitlement.

Precedent L8:   Draft letter confirming an agreed period of unpaid absence

[THIS LETTER MAY BE WRITTEN FURTHER TO L2 ABOVE]

Dear [name],

Further to our recent meeting and discussions, I wish to confirm the following agreement in relation to your request to take a period of leave.

It has been agreed between the Company and yourself that you will take a period of unpaid leave commencing on [date] and to last until [date].

Your employment with the Company will therefore terminate on [date]. You will be paid all outstanding remuneration, holiday pay and other benefits upon termination. The full details will be notified [in your last pay slip].

You will return your company car, mobile telephone and all other property belonging to the Company by the termination date.

It has also been agreed that the Company will re-employ you after the above period of leave. Your employment will re-commence on [date] but in any event must re-commence no later than [date]. If you do not present yourself for full time employment by the latter date then this offer to re-employ you will lapse.

You are not entitled to any salary whilst you are absent on leave or to any other benefit from the Company.

The Company will, however, pay for [set out if i.e. Study leave and expenses are to be paid].

There is no guarantee that your re-employment will be on the same terms and conditions of employment but we will seek to employ you in a suitable position taking into account your skills and experience and your level or seniority. You must contact [name] at least [number of] weeks prior to the re-commencement date when your terms and conditions, [which will be not less favourable than your current terms], can be agreed.

Would you please sign and return a copy of this letter as your agreement to its terms.

Yours sincerely,

Precedent L9: Sabbatical Leave Policy

It is the policy of the Company to offer sabbatical leave/short career breaks for a period up to [set out] months to employees who have a minimum period of [set out] years' continuous service with the Company. No more than one period of such leave will be granted to an employee during any period of [set out] years.

Full and part time employees may apply for sabbatical leave. Part time employees are entitled to sabbatical leave on a pro-rata basis but this may be extended at the Company's discretion.

The grant of sabbatical leave, its timing and the period for which it is granted are entirely within the discretion of the Company and are not a contractual right.

Sabbatical leave is unpaid. The Company may, at its complete discretion, pay some or all of the employee's salary if it considers that the reason for the leave and the activities that will be carried out on sabbatical may benefit the Company. This may include:

- Leave where the employee intends to carry out research that may be of benefit or relevant to the Company's activities. The Company may consider leave on a paid basis at its discretion.

- Leave to follow a course of study that is relevant to and may benefit the Company. The Company may consider leave on a paid basis and/or payment of fees (in accordance with its policy on this matter) in such circumstances.

- Leave intended to undertake specific activities, which may broaden the employee's skills.

- Leave for the purpose of travelling, in particular where the employee intends to visit relations who are resident overseas.

- Leave to carry out voluntary work.

- Leave where the period of absence will be used constructively.

It is the intention of the parties that the employee will remain in employment during Sabbatical leave so that although the leave may be unpaid, the employee will continue to accrue continuous service and will not be able to undertake other employment unless agreed in writing by the Company.

The employee must provide a written statement of activities [at least once a month] in a form agreed between the parties. [e.g. E-Mail if Abroad].

The employee must return from leave on the date agreed or by giving the agreed notice to the Company if the employee wishes to return at an earlier date.

Where the employee has been paid during sabbatical leave he will be required to work an agreed period of [weeks] for each week of leave taken and may be required to repay, on a pro rata basis, sums of money, fees and expenses paid to him during the period of leave.

Although the Company will endeavour to place the employee in the same job in which the employee worked before taking leave, there can be no guarantee that employment on return from sabbatical leave will be on the same terms and conditions of employment. If the Company cannot employ the employee in the same job it will seek to employ the employee in suitable alternative employment on terms and conditions which are no less favourable than the employment that was carried out immediately before taking sabbatical leave.

Your continuity of employment is/is not preserved whilst you are on sabbatical leave so that if you return to the Company continuity of employment for all contractual and statutory purposes will be broken/preserved.

COMMENTARY: ABSENCE FOR OTHER REASONS

At common law there is generally no implied term that an employee would be allowed reasonable time off in an emergency. Though it may be implied into contracts of employment for employees working for very large organisations this is unlikely to be the case with a small employer (**Warner v Barbers Stores** [1978] IRLR 109). In the Warner case a small employer had refused an employee time off to look after her son who was a diabetic. The EAT stated:

"It seems to us that whereas it is true that these days there is either an express or implied term in many contracts of employment that there should be reasonable time off in an emergency, there is certainly no authority, nor do we think it would be right, nor do we think it would be common sense, to extend such an implied term over the whole realm of employer/employee relationship. It seems to us that this is the sort of situation in which every case has to be looked at on its own and quite separately from any general principle. On the facts of this case we could not persuade ourselves that such an implied term ought to be read into this contract. That means that, as the Industrial Tribunal found in this very sad case (and one has a great deal of sympathy with this lady) she has no implied term in her contract on which to rely. The employer was entitled to say 'You must come in'. That was a matter which might perhaps have been more closely and helpfully discussed. It may well be that somehow or other they would have managed on the Saturday; perhaps they did. But unfortunately the lady damaged irreparably and permanently her case by not turning up for work on the Monday."

However, there are a number of areas where by statute an employee is entitled to time off or where discrimination law may have some impact. Precedents L1 to L7 cover the most common areas where an employer may seek to take time off work.

Precedent L1: Dependants

The Employment Relations Act 1999 introduced a new right for employees to take time off to look after dependants. Council Directive 96/34/EC requires member states to make provision for unpaid leave on grounds of: *force majeure*; urgent family reasons in cases of sickness; or accident making the immediate presence of the worker indispensable (clause 3.1). The 1999 Act has inserted sections 57A and 57B into the Employment Rights Act 1996 to cover the situation. By section 57A(1) an employee is entitled to be permitted to take a reasonable time off during the employee's working hours in order to take action which is necessary:

(a) to provide assistance on an occasion when a dependant falls ill, gives birth or is injured or assaulted;

(b) to make arrangements for the provision of care for a dependant who is ill or injured;

(c) in consequence of the death of a dependant;

(d) because of the unexpected disruption or termination of arrangements for the care of a dependant;

(e) to deal with an incident which involves a child of the employee and which occurs unexpectedly in a period during which an educational establishment which the child attends is responsible for him.

The section only applies where the employee tells the employer as soon as reasonably practicable of the reason for absence and how long the employee expects to be absent (section 57A(2)). There is no express limit on the amount of time off that may be taken.

For the purposes of (a) to (e), a dependant means:

• a spouse;

• a child;

- a parent;

- a person who lives in the same household as the employee otherwise than by reason of being his employee, tenant, lodger or boarder.

For the purposes of (a) and (b), a dependant also includes any person who reasonably relies on the employee:

- for assistance on an occasion when the person falls ill or is injured or assaulted; or

- to make arrangements for the provision of care in the event of illness or injury.

For the purposes of (d), dependant also includes any person who reasonably relies on the employee to make arrangements for the provision of care.

By section 57B the employee may make a complaint to a Tribunal that the employer has unreasonably refused time off under section 57A.

Precedent L1 is intended to implement the provisions of section 57A.

The EAT considered the operation of the section in **Qua v John Ford Morrison Solicitors** [2003] IRLR 184. The employee was absent from work for 17 days as a result of her young son's medical problems from when she started work in January 2000 until her dismissal on 27 October. The Employment Tribunal dismissed her complaint on grounds that she had failed to comply with her obligation under section 57A(2) to tell her employer, "as soon as reasonably practicable", "for how long she expected to be absent". The EAT allowed the appeal and remitted the case. It emphasised that the statutory right is to take a reasonable amount of time off work during working hours in order to deal with a variety of unexpected or sudden events affecting dependants and in order to make any necessary longer-term arrangements for their care. It is not a right for employees to take time off in order themselves to provide care for a sick child, beyond the reasonable amount necessary to enable them to deal with the immediate crisis. Once it is known that a child is suffering from an underlying medical condition, which is likely to cause the child to suffer regular relapses, such a situation no longer falls within the scope of s.57A at all. The EAT stated that the key is "foreseeability and it will inevitably be a question of fact and degree in each situation."

In determining what is a "reasonable" amount of time off, a tribunal should not take into account the disruption or inconvenience caused to the employer's business by the employee's absence. The EAT stated that:

> "The operational needs of the employer cannot be relevant to a consideration of the amount of time an employee reasonably needs to deal with emergency circumstances of the kind specified. Taking into account the employer's needs as relevant to the overall reasonableness of the amount of time taken off would, in our view, frustrate the clear purpose of the legislation which is to ensure that employees are permitted time off to deal with such an event, whenever it occurs, without fear of reprisals, so long as they comply with the requirements of s.57A(2)."

The EAT also held that section 57A(2) does not require daily updates by the employee. The duty on an employee is to tell her employer about the reason for her absence and, save where she is unable to do so before she returns to work, how long she expects to be absent.

Precedent L2: Other Special Leave Arrangements & Precedents L8, L9 relating to 'sabbatical leave'

Although there is no express or implied right to have time off for compassionate or other leave arrangements, the reasonable employer may wish to include a clause which states that it will consider time off, whilst reserving the discretion to actually grant time off.

Whilst young employees may be entitled to time off for study or training under the ERA 1996 and the Right to Time Off for Study or Training Regulations 2001, SI 2001/2801, there is no right to a career break, although many employers now permit a career break or sabbatical after a period of employment or in order to carry out study or research. The period of service should be the same for full time employees and part timers otherwise discrimination may be alleged (see Chapter 5.11).

Where it is agreed that a career break will take place and that the job will be kept open for the employee, continuity of employment will be preserved as the absence will have been by way of arrangement under section 212(3)(c) of the Employment Rights Act 1996.

In **Curr v Marks & Spencer plc** [2003] IRLR it was held by the EAT that the employer's four-year child break scheme which required the employee to resign from employment, nevertheless entailed a continuing relationship as it was an "arrangement" by which she was "absent from work in circumstances such that ... [she was] regarded as continuing in the employment of [her] employer" within the meaning of s.212(3)(c) of the ERA 1996. Continuity of employment was preserved during this period. The Court of Appeal has now reversed that decision on grounds that in order for s.212(3)(c) to apply, to preserve continuity during a week when there is no contract of employment, the ex-employee must be "regarded" as continuing in the employment for some purpose by each of the parties. Notwithstanding that the child break scheme contained a number of conditions and provided for regular contact between the employer and the former employee, and despite what the ex-employee thought about her position, there was not the requisite mutual recognition that her employment was continuing for any purpose during the child break. The editors of the IRLR note that the main lesson to be learnt from the case is that Schemes should make it clear what happens to continuity when a break is taken.

Precedent L3: Marriage

It is also quite common for there to be a provision that the employee may be granted additional time off upon marriage, in order to take a honeymoon. Such provision can only be conducive to good relations with the workforce!

Precedent L4: Public Duties

Section 50 of the Employment Rights Act 1996 gives employees the right to take time off work to perform public duties where the employee is:

- a justice of the peace;

- a member of a local authority, a statutory tribunal, a police authority, the Service Authority of the National Crime Intelligence Service or the Service Authority for the National Crime Squad, a board of prison visitors or a prison visiting committee, a relevant health body, a relevant education authority or the Environmental Agency or the Scottish Environmental Protection Agency. In these cases the employee can take time off work to attend at meetings of the body or any of its committee or sub-committees and for the doing of anything approved by the body or anything of a class so approved for the purposes of the discharge of the functions of the body or committee or sub-committees.

Sections 50(5) to 50(9) contain further elaboration of the definitions of the relevant bodies and reference should be made to these subsections.

By section 50(4) the amount of time off which an employee is to be permitted to take and the occasions on which, and any conditions subject to which, time off may be taken are those that are reasonable to the circumstances having regard to:

- how much time off is required for the performance of the duties of the office or as a member of the body in question, and how much time off is required for the performance of the particular duty;

- how much time off the employee has already been permitted time off under sections 168 or 170 of the Trade Union and Labour Relations (Consolidation) Act 1992 for trade union duties and activities;

- the circumstances of the employer's business and the effect of the employee's absence on the running of the businesses.

It is clear that the circumstances of the employer must be taken into account. As was stated in **Borders Regional Council v Maule** [1993] IRLR 199:

"It would normally be expected that, where an employee is undertaking duties of the kind to which s50 applies, there would be discussion between employer and employee in order to establish, by agreement, a pattern for the absences from work required by the duties; indeed, it does appear that attempts were made in the present case to agree such a pattern, although they may not have been wholly successful. It is also, we think, legitimate to observe that an employee who is undertaking a variety of public and other duties may have some responsibility to plan the absences from work, and to scale the level of commitment which such public duties involve so as to produce a pattern which can be regarded as reasonable in all the circumstances. The statute requires the Industrial Tribunal to consider the whole circumstances, and those circumstances must include the number and frequency of similar absences which have been permitted by the employer. In order to show that they have performed their statutory function, it is, in our view, necessary for the Industrial Tribunal to explain what considerations have been taken into account, and make some attempt to explain how those considerations have been balanced, before reaching the conclusion that the employer has acted unreasonably. That is perhaps particularly important in a case such as this, where the Industrial Tribunal is considering a single refusal of time off in the context of a previous history which is said to have been reasonable. In the present case, the Industrial Tribunal have, in our opinion, failed to make clear that they did take all relevant considerations into account or to explain how the various considerations were balanced. The reasons, so far as they go, indicate that they concentrated on one consideration, to the exclusion of others, when they came to their actual decision."

The draft precedent is deliberately open ended so that the employer can consider what is reasonable in the circumstances.

Other areas where there is a statutory right to time off cover:

- Time off for trade union activities (section 170 TULRCA 1992);

- Time off for trade union officials (section 178 TULRCA 1992);

- Time off to look for work on notification of redundancy (section 52 ERA 1996);

- Time off for safety representatives. Safety representatives will be entitled to time off to perform their functions and for training and are entitled to be paid. The decision to grant time off should be based upon what is reasonable rather than what the employer may think is necessary (See **Duthie v Bath and North East Somerset Council** [EAT/561/02; 29.4.2003)

- Time off for ante-natal care

- Time off for Occupational Pension Trustees (sections 58–60 ERA 1996);

- Time off for employee representatives (section 61 ERA 1996).

- Time off for study or training. (section 63A ERA 1996; section 63B ERA 1996 and The Right to Time Off for Study or Training Regulations 2001 SI 2001/2801).

- Time off to accompany a worker at a disciplinary or grievance hearing (Employment Relations Act 1999 sections 10 and 12).

Precedent L5: Jury Service

Whilst there is no express provision that permits time off for jury service, the employer who refused permission will probably be in contempt of court. Precedent L5 adopts the pragmatic and sensible approach that time off will be given.

Precedent L6: Religious Holidays

There is no statutory entitlement to time off for religious holidays. However, there may be two grounds on which it is sensible for the employer to permit time off but to make it clear that this forms part of holiday entitlement. The Religion or Belief Regulations should also be considered.

Discrimination

A refusal to allow an employee time off for religious observance may possibly amount to indirect racial discrimination where it can be argued that the requirement or condition to attend work has a disproportionate effect upon the racial group of the employee and cannot be justified. However, it must be related to race and not to religion for the Race Relations Act 1976 to apply (for the distinction; see **Seide v Gillette Industries** [1980] IRLR 427). It may thus be difficult to argue that there is actionable discrimination under the terms of the Act.

However, in **Hussain v J H Walker** [1996] ICR 291 a claim for race discrimination succeeded where Asian employees were disciplined because they took unauthorised time off to celebrate the festival of EID. There was indirect discrimination because the requirement for all employees to work over the festival was one which a significantly lower proportion of Asian Workers could comply with, compared with non Asian workers.

The current CRE Code of Practice (it is in the process of being revised) gives "Observance of prayer times and religious holidays" as an example of a matter the employer needs to consider in the context of the RRA 1976 as "although the Act does not specifically cover religious discrimination, work requirements would generally be unlawful if they have a disproportionately adverse effect on particular racial groups and cannot be shown to be justifiable."

The Employment Equality (Religion or Belief) Regulations 2003 will be relevant as a refusal to allow an employee off for the purpose of religious observance could be direct or indirect discrimination unless the refusal can be justified. Where there is a factory shut down there may be no other time when holidays can be taken and, provided, the employer can show sound reasons for the holiday being required at this then discrimination is unlikely to be made out. The ACAS Guidance gives specific examples on this point:

Example

A small toy shop employing four staff may be unable to release an individual for a religious festival in the busy pre-Christmas period. It may be justifiable to refuse a request for such absence.

A large department store employing 250 staff would probably be unable to justify refusing the same absence for one person because it would not substantially impact on the business as other staff would be able to cover for the absence.

The Human Rights Act

The Human Rights Act 1998, which came into force on 2 October 2000, incorporates the European Convention for the Protection of Human Rights and Fundamental Freedoms. Under Article 9 of the Act individuals have the right to hold religious beliefs, to change their religious beliefs and to "freedom to manifest his religion or belief, in worship, teaching, practice and observance." By Article 9.2, this is subject to

> "such limitations as are prescribed by law and necessary in a democratic society in the interests of public safety, for the protection of public order, health or morals, or for the protection of the rights and freedoms of others."

However, the European Court of Human Rights has tended to apply this Article restrictively. In **Ahmad v UK** [1982] 4 EHRR 126 an employee resigned from a teaching post because he was refused permission to attend worship at his mosque each Friday. The European Commission on Human Rights decided that the terms of his contract had been clearly known to him at the time that he started employment. A claim was rejected in **Stedman v UK** [1997] 23 EHRR 23 where the employee refused to work on Sundays because of her religious beliefs. It was held that she had been dismissed because she had refused to respect working hours and not because of her religious beliefs. It thus remains to be seen what impact the Convention will have upon this area.

Precedent L7: Other Absences

This precedent makes it clear that time off for certain domestic matters will not entail a right to time off but must be taken as holiday. During the debates on the dependency provisions it was questioned whether a right to time off would arise in a domestic emergency such as when a washing machine needed repairing! As we have seen, the provisions of section 57A are severely curtailed and employees will have to rely upon their holiday entitlement for such matters.

PART M: CONDUCT AND STANDARD OF BEHAVIOUR AT WORK

Precedent M: **Conduct and Standard of Behaviour at Work**

M1:	Standard of work	824
M2:	Non smoking policy	824
M3:	Alcohol and drugs	824
M4:	Personal telephone calls from work	827
M5:	E-mail policy	827
M6:	Computers and data protection	828
M7:	Personal relationships	829
M8:	Clothing and appearance	829
M9:	Entertaining Clients/Office Social Functions	830
M10:	Mobile telephones	831
Commentary:	Conduct and Standard of Behaviour at Work	831

Precedent M1: Standard of Work

You must at all times carry out your duties to the best of your ability and you shall obey all lawful and reasonable orders given to you. You must keep the Company informed of your conduct in relation to the Company's business and provide explanations for any conduct, as your Manager considers appropriate.

Precedent M2: Non-Smoking Policy

It is the Company policy that smoking will not be allowed in the workplace. Smoking poses risks to health both in relation to the smoker and others who are otherwise forced to passively smoke. The Company has therefore imposed a ban on smoking in the Company premises [other than in designated areas]. Smoking on the premises or in an area that is not designated for smoking is a disciplinary offence under the Company's disciplinary procedure.

The Company will have regard to complaints by any member of staff that this policy is being ignored and will ensure that any person making such a complaint does not suffer any detriment by reason of such complaint. It will be a disciplinary offence to abuse or otherwise maltreat any person who has made a complaint.

Precedent M3: Alcohol and Drugs

Policy

It is the policy of the Company to offer support and assistance to any employee who has a problem, which is related to drugs or alcohol. The Company priority is to maintain a working environment which is safe for all and, within this environment to assist in the identification of alcohol or drug related problems and to encourage and assist employees to seek help with these problems.

Disciplinary matters

The Company distinguishes between the use of alcohol and drugs in the workplace which will be regarded as a disciplinary offence and treated appropriately and sickness arising out of alcohol or drug problems. However, you should be aware that abuse of alcohol or drugs in the workplace is likely to lead to dismissal. The following rules apply:

1. If you are found consuming alcohol or taking drugs on the Company's premises or are under the influence of alcohol or drugs in the workplace then this will be treated as gross misconduct under the Company's disciplinary procedure. The possession of drugs for any reason other than medical is forbidden. You must inform your Manager if you are taking drugs for medical reasons and in particular if they are likely to affect your ability to work.

2. You may be required to undergo a medical examination in order to ascertain whether there is a problem in relation to drink or drugs which is affecting your ability to work. You may be suspended from work until the problem has been resolved. The Company will decide whether to require you to undergo a programme of rehabilitation or whether abuse of alcohol or drugs should be treated as a disciplinary matter.

3. The following may be treated as disciplinary matters:

    •   If you are offered a programme of rehabilitation and do not comply with the programme.

    •   If you refuse to accept that you have a drug or alcohol related problem and are guilty of poor attendance, poor or impaired performance or conduct which is inconsistent with your position or which affects the work environment, well-being or health and safety of co-employees.

    •   Where you have completed a course of treatment but lapse back into alcohol or drug related problems which leads to poor attendance, poor or impaired performance or conduct which is inconsistent with your position or which affects the work environment, well being or health and safety of co-employees

4. You should be aware that the Company would not hesitate to inform the police if it believes that there has been an abuse of controlled drugs for which criminal sanctions are appropriate. However, where the employee recognises that he or she has a problem and seeks support the Company may, in its discretion, not inform the police if the employee has volunteered information about the use of illegal substances.

Employee support

5. If an employee considers that he or she may have an alcohol or drug related problem then the employee is encouraged to discuss these problems with [Human Resources/their line manager]. Any discussions will be in complete confidence and the Company will offer support by way of medical treatment, counselling or leave for the purpose of rehabilitation.

6. Co-employees who notice signs of alcohol of drug abuse in a work colleague should report their suspicions and the reason for them to [   ]. This will be treated in total confidence.

7. A manager who believes that an employee has a drug related problem or who has received information about suspected abuse from a work colleague will take the appropriate action to discuss the matter with the employee concerned. This will not be regarded as a disciplinary matter at this stage but the employee may be required to stop work where it poses a risk to health or safety. Depending on the circumstances the conduct of the employee may be treated as a disciplinary matter under 1 to 4 above.

8. The Company offers the following support:

    • Confidential Counselling or referral to an appropriate agency [The Company has access to expert Counselling services for this purpose].

    • The use of the Company's medical doctor.

    • Time off work or a variation in the employee's duties during any period of treatment.

    • Payment of sick pay under the Company's sickness absence policy.

9. Where its medical doctor advises the Company that the abuse of alcohol or drugs is sickness then it may suspend disciplinary procedures during any period of rehabilitation provided that the employee co-operates with such treatment. This does not, however, negate the fact that the use of alcohol or drugs during Company time is prima facie a disciplinary matter especially if it involves a risk to health and safety or where 3 above applies.

Precedent M4: Personal Telephone Calls from Work

It is the Company policy that you may not generally use the Company telephones to make personal calls from work. The Company recognises that there may be an occasional necessity to make such a call from work and permission should first be sought from your manager. Similar considerations apply in relation to other office equipment such as photocopying and stationery.

Mobile or car telephones must be used for business telephone calls only and you will be required to reimburse any private calls. You must immediately report the loss or theft of your mobile phone so that steps can be taken to disconnect it. **Mobile telephones must not, under any circumstances be used whilst you are driving and it will be regarded as a serious disciplinary offence if you caught using a mobile phone in such circumstances (whether by the police or by the Company). The Company will invoke its disciplinary procedures in such circumstances.**

Precedent M5: E-Mail Policy

The Company has an e-mail system which is intended to promote the Company's business by making communication more effective. The Company may be liable if the system is misused by, for example, defamatory messages being sent to third parties through the e-mail system. The e-mail system is not meant for personal messages and they should be avoided so far as is possible. The following rules are applicable:

1. The language and content of any messages must be of an appropriate standard and should be succinct and to the point.

2. Inappropriate language which may include malicious gossip or messages that may amount to a breach of the Company's equal opportunity policies or be otherwise inappropriate will be treated as a disciplinary offence.

3. Confidential information must not be sent by e-mail.

4. E-mail sent through the Company shall remain the property of the Company and the Company shall have the right to retrieve all e-mails for such reasons as it considers appropriate.

5. If you receive an e-mail for which you were not the intended recipient you should immediately notify the sender. If you, yourself, receive an e-mail that is considered to contain inappropriate matter you should notify your Manager.

6. Deliberate or knowing misuse of the e-mail system may constitute gross misconduct and the Company will not tolerate the sending of e-mails that are malicious, untrue, obscene or defamatory. The Company will operate its disciplinary procedures in respect of any such misuse.

7. You should not open unsolicited e-mail if you do not know its source because it may contain a virus. You must immediately report receipt of such e-mail to [. . . . . . .].

Precedent M6:   Computers and Data Protection

The Company will comply with all laws that regulate the use of computers, data protection and confidentiality and you are expected to assist in ensuring that the law is complied with. The following rules are applicable.

1. You are not permitted to use the Company's computer for personal use unless you have been given express permission.

2. You should only use your computer for the purpose of your job and should not use the computer system or information for any other purpose.

3. You are responsible for maintaining your computer equipment and software and where you have access to confidential information you must ensure that it remains secure.

4. If you have a password you must make sure that it is kept confidential and you must not give any other person access to your password.

5. You are not permitted to make copies of any software where this will amount to a breach of copyright or in any way make or distribute copies of software.

6. Breach of the above may result in disciplinary action.

Precedent M7:   Personal relationships

The nature of the Company's business may mean that you or other employees have access to confidential information or have authority to make decisions, which involve other members of staff, budgets or customers. It is not therefore acceptable to the Company that you should form romantic or sexual relationships with other members of staff who work in the same department as you or who may be your subordinates or superior. Such relationships can be disruptive and can also cause ill feeling amongst other members of staff who may feel that a co-worker is being treated differently because of the relationship. The Company therefore has a policy that members of staff [who are in the same department] who have formed close personal relationship should not work together. If this should occur you should report to [   ] in confidence and consideration will be given to whether one or other of the parties can be redeployed. If this should not prove to be possible the Company may terminate the contracts of employment of one or both of the parties and make payment in lieu of notice.

The Company will treat any failure to report such relationship as an act of gross misconduct and may institute its disciplinary procedures should the parties fail to report such relationship. In these circumstances the Company shall be entitled to suspend one or both employees on salary during any investigation and disciplinary procedure.

Precedent M8:   Clothing and appearance

The Company expects you at all times whilst working for the Company to maintain a well groomed appearance. In particular:

*   Hair must be neat and tidy.

*   Employees who do not wear uniforms are required to wear smart business suits or dress and smart shoes in accordance with the image that the Company would expect. Jeans, leggings, shorts and training shoes are not permitted.

*   Employees who wear uniform are expected to keep it clean and laundered [for which an allowance is given each month]. New uniforms will be provided depending on wear and tear and request should be made to [   ] if one is required.

- Where the nature of your job entails the wearing of safety equipment you must strictly comply with these rules for health and safety reasons and it will be your responsibility to ensure that the equipment is kept in a proper condition.

Breach of the above rules may be a disciplinary matter and may amount to gross misconduct (particularly in relation to wearing of safety equipment).

Where you are unable to comply with the rules as to dress and appearance for any reason (in particular on religious grounds) you should inform [HR] who will discuss the position with you and an exception may be made depending upon the nature of the inability to comply with the rules and the reason for such non-compliance.

Precedent M9:   Entertaining Clients/Office Social Functions

It is a strict rule of the Company that no alcohol shall be brought onto or consumed on the Company Premises and a breach of this rule will be regarded as gross misconduct. In relation to entertaining clients and attending social functions (including office parties) you must adhere to the following rules:

1. You should not drink alcohol at lunchtime. Where this is unavoidable because you are entertaining clients you will be limited to [SET OUT e.g. one glass of wine].

2. When you entertain clients at other times you will be expected to drink in moderation and to conduct yourself in a sensible and dignified manner at all times.

3. You are expected to conduct yourself sensibly and with moderation at any social functions, in particular where clients are present, including at any office party. If you are driving you must abstain from drinking alcohol. You may be required to leave if your conduct is unacceptable and such conduct will be regarded as a serious disciplinary matter.

Precedent M10: Mobile telephones

It is now a criminal offence to use a mobile telephone in a vehicle whilst driving. Since during the course of your employment, you drive a Company Car [Drive during working hours] whilst on Company business, you are reminded that you are **absolutely forbidden** to use your mobile telephone whilst driving. Such use is gross misconduct and will warrant summary dismissal.

You may only use your mobile phone for Company business [or must pay for private use]. The mobile telephone remains the property of the Company who may demand its return at any time and you must forthwith deliver it up.

The Company may monitor the numbers and contents of the mobile telephone to ensure that the use of it is not being abused.

COMMENTARY TO M: CONDUCT AND STANDARD OF BEHAVIOUR AT WORK

This section covers various miscellaneous matters where the employee may feel it is important to have a specific policy. Indeed, in relation to telephone calls, e-mail and data protection, the Data Protection Act 1998, the Regulation of Investigatory Powers Act 2000 and the Telecommunications (Lawful Business Practice) (Interception of Communications) Regulations 2000 [SI 2000 No 2699] have a fundamental impact upon employer's rights and powers. (See Chapter 2 for detailed consideration.)

M1: Conduct and Standard of behaviour at work

It is sensible to include in a manual a statement that employees must obey all lawful instructions, though the reality is that this is likely to be implied by law. However, in **Diggle v Ogston Motor Company** [84 LJKB 2165; 112 LR 1029] there was a provision that an employer could terminate the contract in the event of the employee not performing to the satisfaction of the employer. It was held that such provision meant it was for the employer to judge the quality of the employee's work provided it did not act dishonestly or capriciously. The case was of course, long before the right to claim unfair dismissal came about. However, where a skilled worker is taken on there will be a warranty that he can carry out the work to be undertaken with reasonable competence (**Harmer v Cornelious** [1858] 5 CB 236).

M2: Non Smoking Policy

Of increasing concern over recent years have been health issues relating to smoking at work which has lead to many employees imposing smoke free environments. Particular issues may arise in relation to passive smoking with employees arguing that there health is being affected, and this has been addressed in case law and in legislation. Under regulation 25 of the Workplace (Health, Safety and Welfare) Regulations 1992 an employer is obliged to make arrangements so that employees are protected from discomfort caused by tobacco smoke.

Implied terms

It is was held in **Dryden v Greater Glasgow Health Board** [1992] IRLR 469 by the Court of Session that, although it could not be said that it was impossible to have an implied term based on custom and practice that allowed smoking, in a case where there had been full consultation about a non smoking policy, the employer was entitled to replace this policy with a permission to smoke in various areas that had hitherto existed. The employee left twelve days after a total smoking ban was introduced because of the discomfort she suffered. The Court of Session rejected the argument that the ban was in breach of an implied term that the employer must not do anything that frustrates the employee's ability to carry out the contract and damaged the duty of mutual trust and confidence. Lord Coulsfield said:

> "There can, in our view, be no doubt that an employer is entitled to make rules for the conduct of employees in their place of work, as he is entitled to give lawful orders, within the scope of the contract; nor can there be any doubt, in our view, that once it is has been held that there is no implied term in the contract which entitled the employee to facilities for smoking, a rule against smoking is, in itself a lawful rule."

The opposite side of the coin was considered in **Waltons & Morse v Dorrington** [1997] IRLR 488, in which an employee claimed that the smoking of fellow employees was adversely affecting her health. The EAT held that it is was an implied term that employers will, so far as is reasonably practicable, provide and monitor a working environment that is not injurious for their health and the starting point is section 2(2)(e) of the

Health and Safety at Work Act 1974 which requires a working environment that is reasonably safe.

> "In one sense, the right of an employee not to be required to sit in a smoke-filled atmosphere affects the welfare of employees at work, even if it is not something which directly is concerned with their health or can be proved to be a risk to health."

The employer did have steps it could take in that it could indicate to smokers that, as there were no adequate ventilation facilities within the building, they would not be allowed to smoke.

Precedent M2 sets out a clear policy that smoking will not be allowed in the workplace.

M3: Alcohol and Drugs

In certain circumstances the use of alcohol and drugs may be treated as a disciplinary issue. However, it is apparent from the case law that the abuse of alcohol and drugs may be a sickness or capability issue and be approached in this way by the employer. The cases on this area are considered in detail in Duggan on *Unfair Dismissal*, at pages 145 and 193 to 197). In summary:

* the employer will need to consider whether the use of alcohol or drugs is a sickness or a conduct matter. If there are clear disciplinary rules that relate to the consumption of alcohol then it may be treated as a disciplinary matter (**Strathclyde Regional Council v Syme** [EAT 223/79] see also **Evans v Bass North** [715/86]).

* Where performance or safety is affected or the consumption of alcohol results in unacceptable behaviour then this may justify treating the matter as a disciplinary one (**Weir v Stephen Allen Jewellers** [EAT 550/97]).

* A full and proper investigation should be carried out (see the cases cited at page 194 of Unfair Dismissal and factors such as consistency, the content of any rules and the gravity of the offence, taking into account and mitigation be considered. (See **Chaimberlain Vinyl Products Limited v Patel** [EAT 796/94] where the employee suffered from recurrent depression and no investigation was carried out).

In **Angus Council v Edgley** [IDS Brief 647; EAT 289/99] a failure to apply a policy on alcohol abuse where the employee had a long standing problem was held to make a dismissal unfair. The employee had been employed for 28 years and had been subject to a final warning in 1991. He denied that he had an alcohol problem for which the employer could have offered assistance under its policy. He was given a final warning in 1995 in relation to travel and subsistence claims and this warning was to remain permanently on his file and further warning in 1997 relating to abuse of the flexible working hours scheme. A further disciplinary hearing was held on 4th June 1998 relating to him clocking out and visiting a public house. The employer took the view that this was a one off occasion to which the policy did not apply and he was dismissed in accordance with the disciplinary procedure. This was despite the fact that he produced a letter from his G.P. stating that he had been treated for an alcohol problem for years. The tribunal and EAT took the view that this was clearly a case where the employee had an alcohol problem so that the disciplinary procedure on misuse of alcohol should not have been applied. The alcohol policy stated that the employee would be given an opportunity to seek diagnosis and specialist help where the employee had an alcohol problem. The policy should have been applied as it was clear that the employee had a long standing problem.

- Where there are serious safety issues the employer may be justified in dismissing even where there was no specific rule (**Connor v George Wimpey ME & C Ltd** [EAT 387/82]).

- It would appear from **O'Flynn v Airlinks the Airport Coach Co Ltd** [EAT 0269/01] that testing for drink or drugs will not contravene the Human Rights Act 1998 (but query whether random drug testing where there is no effect on performance of the job will be in breach).

Policy

The policy should make it clear that:

- The use of prescribed or illegal drugs is banned and will normally be regarded as a disciplinary offence;

- Employees may not drink at work or be under the influence of alcohol whilst at work. This is particularly important where there are safety issues.

Precedent M4 seeks to implement such a policy.

M4: Telephone Calls

There is nothing unlawful in a provision that an employee may not make personal telephone calls from work or that they may be on a limited basis.

However, in order to supervise the use of telephones the employer may wish to monitor telephone calls. This may be to ensure that they are not abused or to monitor performance or transactions. However, monitoring calls may give rise to a number of difficulties (See IDS Brief 645 page 15 'Telephone Monitoring at Work' and Brief 672 'Monitoring e-mails and telephone calls'). Such monitoring is now subject to the specific provisions of the Data Protection Act 1998, the Regulation of Investigatory Powers Act 2000 and the Telecommunications (Lawful Business Practice) (Interception of Communications) Regulations 2000 [SI 2000 No 2699]. The following points should be noted.

- Where there is a licence arrangement for a private telephone system (Self Provision Licences or Telecommunications Service Licences) it may be a provision of the licence that the licensee informs parties to telephone conversations that the call is being monitored.

- The right to privacy under Article 8 of the European Convention on Human Rights may make it illegal to intercept calls unless the defence under Article 8(2) that the interference takes place in accordance with the law and is:

   "necessary in a democratic society in the interests of national security, public safety or the economic well being of the country, for the prevention of disorder or crime, for the protection of health or morals, or for the protection of the rights and freedom of others".

It was held in **Halford v United Kingdom** [1997] IRLR 471 that the Article had been infringed where the Merseyside police had monitored Mrs Halford's internal calls without her knowledge in circumstances where she had a reasonable expectation of privacy since there was a phone for private use in her office. Since there was no legal regulation of private telephone calls the Article 8(2) defence could not be applicable. The use of the Convention is also limited to employees of the State or to a claim that the United Kingdom is in breach by not providing any effective remedy and necessitates a petition to Strasbourg.

- The Human Rights Act 1998, however, will provide a more effective remedy since it is incorporates Article 8 and the courts and tribunals are to act in a manner that is compatible with the Convention or to make a declaration of incompatibility.

- In the light of the Halford case the Government issued Circular HOC 15/1999 which notes that a legitimate expectation of privacy may not exist where the employee has been warned that telephone calls may be monitored though this may not, in itself be sufficient, since:

> "It is not reasonable to expect that employees will never be contacted on a domestic matter in work time, or that the employee will never have reason to make personal calls from the office."

OFTEL has also issued Guidance which makes it clear that warnings in themselves may not be sufficient and that employees should have access to a private telephone to make personal calls. The Guidance also states that employers should have a clear policy in relation to private telephone calls.

- The Government Consultation Paper (Cm 4368) proposes a system whereby employers will be required to notify that calls will be monitored and there will then be no reasonable expectation of privacy.

- Article 5 of the EU telecommunications Data Protection Directive (97/66) provides that the interception or monitoring of communication on public or non public networks may only take place if legally authorised. The Government was under a duty to implement this by October 2000 and has done so in the Regulations set out below.

- The Data Protection Act 1998 came into force on 1st March 2000. (See Bainbridge, *Data Protection*, XPL and Chapter 2.)

See also below under M6.

- The Regulation of Investigatory Powers Act 2000 provided a framework to ensure that any investigatory powers are used in accordance with human rights. Section 1 provides that it is unlawful for a person, without lawful authority, to intercept a communication in the course of its transmission by way of a public or private telecommunications system. Section 4(2) provides that the Secretary of State has the power to issue regulations to authorise any such conduct described in the relations as appear to constitute a legitimate practice reasonably required for the purpose, in connection with the carrying on of any business, of monitoring or keeping a record of:

  (a) communications by means of which transactions are entered into in the course of that business; or

  (b) other communications relating to that business or taking place in the course of its being carried on.

Section 4(3) makes it clear that only communications using apparatus or services provided by or to the person carrying on the business for use wholly or partly in connection with that business will be authorised.

- The Lawful Business Practice Regulations, by regulation 3, authorise businesses to monitor or record communications without consent where the purpose is:

  - to establish the existence of facts relevant to the business i.e. records of transactions where it is necessary to know the contents of conversations;

  - to ascertain compliance with regulatory or self regulatory practices or procedures;

  - to ascertain or demonstrate standards that ought to be achieved by the person using the system;

  - to prevent or detect crime;

  - to investigate or detect the authorised use of telecommunications systems, i.e. abuse of e-mail or the Internet;

  - to ensure the effective operation of the system.

- In addition it is possible to monitor, but not record, for the purpose of determining whether or not the communications are relevant to the business and for the purpose of monitoring calls to a confidential anonymous counselling or support helpline.

- The employer may also be in breach of the implied term of trust and confidence where calls are monitored without informing the employee.

Policy

The policy should make it clear which calls are permitted, in particular where the calls are made from the employer's own telephones. It should state when calls may be made (e.g. premium rates may be regarded as unacceptable because of cost and there may be times when it is essential that the telephone lines are clear for business calls). It is may be that the employer wishes to stipulate that the employee bears the cost of certain calls. In addition, it is important that any disciplinary sanctions for abuse of telephones are made clear.

M5: E-Mail Policy

There are two issues in relation to e-mail policy:

- the monitoring of e-mails by employers for the purpose of the business, as to which see the commentary on telephone calls and Chapter 2.

- the sanctions that may be applicable in cases of abuse of the e-mail system or the Internet. Precedent M5 makes it clear that deliberate abuse of the e-mail system is a disciplinary matter. There are three particular areas of concern:

  1. Matters posted through the Internet may be defamatory and in **Godfrey v Demon Internet Limited** (26.3.1999) the High Court held that an Internet service provider was liable for a defamatory e-mail even though it was not the publisher of the statement. Employers may therefore be at risk if employees post defamatory e-mails.

  2. Downloading of pornography may lead to complaints of sexual harassment by women staff (see **Morse v Future Reality Limited** [London North ET] cited at IDS Brief 637 and the other cases there cited about when dismissal will be appropriate.

  3. Unauthorised access may in itself be a disciplinary matter (but see **British Telecommunications Plc v Rodrigues** [EAT 854/92]).

Any policy should therefore set out very clearly what will amount to a disciplinary matter and the possible sanctions.

M6: Computers and Data Protection

The Data Protection Act 1998 came into force on 1st March 2000. It contains detailed provision for the regulation and management of data (see Chapter 2). The Data Protection Commissioner has issued a detailed Code for consideration entitled The Use of Personal Data in Employer/Employee Relationships which covers every stage of the employment relationship from recruitment, employee records, monitoring, medical testing to discipline and dismissal and reference should be made to that Code for the principles which are wide ranging and considered in Chapter 2. Precedent M6 is intended to set out in general terms what computer misuse will not be tolerated.

(See Chapter 2 for more detail)

M7: Personal relationships

The employer may have strict rules against personal relationships at work (office romances) on the ground that they may be disruptive or create difficulties of confidentiality; for example the secretary to the MD has a romance with one of the mangers or the atmosphere is soured when a relationship breaks down.

In such cases there is a risk of discrimination if females are treated differently from their male colleagues. In **Brooks Explosives v Montgomery** [EAT 141/91] a male and female colleague went on holiday together and were dismissed (without any discussion or consultation with the female employee) on their return, following an anonymous 'tip-off'. The female did not have sufficient service to claim unfair dismissal but succeeded in her discrimination claims as the EAT held that two men would not have been dismissed if they had gone on holiday together. Similarly, in **JS McClean v Patis Travel Services Limited** [1976] IRLR 202 a female employee succeeded in her claim of sex discrimination after she was dismissed when she announced that she was going to marry the assistant manager since the tribunal was satisfied that a man would not have been dismissed if he had announced that he was going to marry another employee.

M8: Clothing and Appearance

Employers may wish to impose clothing and appearance rule to project the image that they consider is appropriate for their company. Alternatively, the Company rules may require the wearing of a uniform and employers will wish to ensure that standards are maintained. There are a number of pitfalls relating to rules on clothing and appearance and there has been quite a lot of case law that considers the topic, not always in a consistent manner. The recent case of **Department for Work and Pensions v Thompson** [2004] IRLR 348 illustrates the problems. The Employment Tribunal was of the view that it was sex discrimination against men for an employer to adopt a dress code whereby all staff are required to dress "in a professional and businesslike way", but men are required to wear a collar and tie, whereas women are required merely "to dress appropriately and to a similar standard" on the ground that that it meant that women working in Jobcentre Plus had greater choice in what they could wear than men. The EAT allowed the appeal and remitted the case back to another tribunal for a rehearing. It took the view that the employment tribunal erred in law in finding that the appellant employers discriminated against the applicant on grounds of sex by requiring him to wear a collar and tie at work. The tribunal had wrongly taken the view that if members of one sex are required to wear clothing of a particular kind, and members of the other sex are not, the former are necessarily treated less favourably than the latter. Mr Justice Keith, stated that the question is whether, in the context of an overarching requirement for staff to dress in a professional and businesslike way, "applying contemporary standards of conventional dress wear, the level of smartness which Jobcentre Plus required of all its staff could only be achieved for men by requiring them to wear a collar and tie." Keith J stated:

> "If, for example, a level of smartness for men which equates to dressing in a professional and businesslike way which is appropriate for an undertaking like Jobcentre Plus can be achieved by men dressing otherwise than in a collar and tie, then the lack of flexibility in the dress code introduced by Jobcentre Plus would suggest that male members of staff are being treated less favourably than female members of staff because it would not have been necessary to restrict men's choice of what to wear in order to achieve the standard of smartness required. The issue is not resolved by asking whether the requirement on men to wear a collar and tie meant that a higher level of smartness was being required of men rather than women. It is resolved by asking whether an equivalent level of smartness to that required of the female members of staff could only be achieved, in the case of men, by requiring them to wear a collar and tie."

There are several issues that are likely to arise in relation to clothing and appearance standards:

(1) Whether an employee can be fairly dismissed for failing to adhere to the standards imposed by the employer.

Where the employer has sound reasons for imposing a particular dress code and an employee refuses to comply then the employer may be justified in dismissing the employee, as in **Boychuck v HJ Symons Holdings Limited** [1997] IRLR 395 where the employee insisted on wearing badges proclaiming her lesbian tendencies. The EAT held that it was within the employer's discretion to forbid badges that may cause offence to employees and clients.

It may be fair to dismiss employees who cannot wear safety equipment but an investigation should first be carried out (**British Aircraft Corporation Ltd v Austin** [1978] IRLR 332).

It was held in **Singh v RHM Bakeries (Southern) Ltd** [EAT 818/77] that a dismissal for hygiene reasons was fair when the employee, who handled food, refused to shave off his beard. However, there may be a claim for race or religions discrimination in such circumstances.

If the employee objects to the rule because it causes discomfort or ill health, then dismissal may be unfair unless the rule can be justified. Dismissal for breach of a rule that men had to be clean shaven was held to be unfair in **FME Ltd v Henry** [EAT 874/86] where the applicant suffered from a rash if he shaved everyday.

It will be necessary to go through the proper disciplinary procedures if the rule is to be enforced.

(2) Whether the employer is liable for sex discrimination by imposing different requirements between men and women.

The courts have tended to adopt the approach that if rules are enforced even-handedly, discrimination is not made out, so in **Schmidt v Austicks Bookshops Ltd** [1978] ICR 85 the EAT held that where, on a consideration of the rules as a whole, it was not possible to say that they were enforced more restrictively against one sex, discrimination was not made out. In this case, female shop assistants could not wear trousers but men could not wear T shirts so that a female employee could not show less favourable treatment. (see also **James v Bank of England** [EAT 226/94], **Rewcastle v Safeway PLC** [ET 22482/89), **Cootes v John Lewis PLC** [EAT 1414/00] and **Smith v Safeway PLC** [1996] ICR 868). In the latter case the Court of Appeal held that the tribunal was entitled to find that prohibiting pony tails for men was not less favourable treatment because the same standard of conventional appearance at work was applied.

(3) Whether there has been race discrimination.

Certain ethnic groups may have religions or cultural requirements for clothing or appearance so that dress rules which disallow such clothing or appearance may lead to less favourable treatment under the Race Relations Act 1976. It may be that the requirement can be justified on, for example health and safety grounds (see **Panesar v Nestle Co Limited** [1980] IRLR 64; **Singh v Rowntree MacIntosh Limited** [1979] ICR 554). The employee will have to show a good reason why it is imposing a rule if it serves to exclude certain minorities from employment.

(4) Whether there is a breach of the Employment Equality (Religion or Belief) Regulations 2003.

The ACAS Guidance notes refer to the fact that certain clothing or appearance requirements may have been adopted for religious reasons and an employer who insists that clothing rules be followed may be in breach of the Regulations if there is no sound reason for the rule (and see regulation 26 in relation to Sikhs on constructions sites). It may be that the employer can justify the rules on grounds such as health and safety but clearly employers cannot simply impose a blanket rule without sound reasons.

M9: Entertaining Clients/Office Social Functions

Employers should have strict rules in relation to conduct at staff functions and entertaining as tolerating certain conduct will then make it more difficult to dismiss employees who behave in similar fashion; see **Williams & Ors v Whitbread Beer Company** [Court of Appeal 19.6.1996] where three employees were unfairly dismissed despite drunken, rowdy and abusive behaviour because the heavy drinking session had been paid for by the employer and had been tolerated in the past. However, if health and safety is a relevant factor then the employer may be less tolerant of such behaviour (**McGrath v Third Generation Nursing Home** [EAT 791/93]). A one off breach may attract the sanction of dismissal, even where some latitude has been tolerated in the past, if the conduct is aggressive or has grave consequences, as in **Paul v East Surrey District Health Authority** [1995] IRLR 305 where an employee abused patients whilst he was drunk.

It may be that the employer would wish to put a limit on the amount of alcohol that may be consumed, the amount of the employer's expenses that may be spent or the nature of the venue to which the employee may take clients.

Precedent M10: Mobile telephones

The use of mobile telephones whilst driving is an offence.

The Road Vehicles (Construction and Use) (Amendment) (No. 4) Regulations 2003 SI2003/2695 adds a new regulation to the Road Vehicles (Construction and Use) Regulations 1986, as follows:

" Mobile telephones

110.–(1) No person shall drive a motor vehicle on a road if he is using –

    (a) a hand-held mobile telephone; or

    (b) a hand-held device of a kind specified in paragraph (4)"

It is further provided by Regulation 110(2) that no person shall *cause or permit* any other person to drive a motor vehicle on a road while that other person is using a hand-held mobile telephone; or a hand-held device of a kind specified in paragraph (4).

The devices referred to in paragraph 110(4) is a device, other than a two-way radio, which performs an interactive communication function by transmitting and receiving data.

There are exceptions in regulation 110(5) in that an employee does not contravene regulation 110 if:–

(a) he is using the telephone or other device to call the police, fire, ambulance or other emergency service on 112 or 999;

(b) he is acting in response to a genuine emergency; and

(c) it is unsafe or impracticable for him to cease driving in order to make the call (or, in the case of an alleged contravention of paragraph (3)(b), for the provisional licence holder to cease driving while the call was being made).

It is vitally important that employers prohibit the use of mobile telephones whilst driving as they otherwise may be liable for *causing or permitting* such use and liable to conviction. Precedent M10 aims to achieve this.

PART N: STAFF DEVELOPMENT AND APPRAISAL

Precedent N: **Staff Development and Appraisal**

N1: **Provision of staff training and development** 844

Commentary: **Staff Development and Appraisal** 845

Precedent N1: Provision of Staff Training and Development

The Company believes that the skills and expertise of its workforce are of paramount importance in ensuring that it can provide the best possible service and product to its customers. A well motivated and highly trained workforce can only improve the business of the Company. The Company has therefore devised a policy of staff development and appraisal. The general terms of the policy are set out below and you will have received further details in your Letter of Appointment or at your interview for your post.

1 **Induction training** You will have received induction training at the outset of your employment in order that you are made fully aware of the needs of the job and Company procedures. If you have any queries you should raise them with your Manager.

2 **Appraisals** You will be subject to an annual appraisal at which your performance will be discussed and any ongoing training to assist you in your job will be considered. The purpose of the appraisal is to assist you in your job rather than because of any disciplinary reason. The Company will also make available to you a programme of in house training as it considers appropriate which will be discussed with you.

3 **Leave** You may be given paid leave in order to attend classes and to sit examinations. You may also be given leave to revise at the discretion of the Company. However, it is expected that your studies will take place in your own time.

4 **Fees** The Company may pay tuition fees and other costs related to your studies or agree to reimburse the same to you if it considers appropriate.

5 **Professional subscriptions** The Company will reimburse annual subscriptions to the appropriate professional bodies as it considers appropriate.

6 **Repayment of subscriptions** If you do not complete your course of study or leave the employment of the Company before you have completed your studies the Company reserves the right to require that the monies be reimbursed.

COMMENTARY TO N: STAFF DEVELOPMENT AND APPRAISAL

There will be an implied term in the contracts of employment of probationary employees that the employer takes reasonable steps to appraise and to give instruction, guidance and warning during the period of probation. In **White v London Transport Executive** [1981] IRLR 261 a number of complaints were made about Ms White after she had been promoted to manager on a probationary basis so that she was transferred back to her previous job at another site. She claimed constructive dismissal. The claim was rejected on the facts. The EAT stated:

> "For ourselves we consider that in relation to probation the law would be ill-advised to imply detailed contractual rights relating to the rights of a probationer. We think that the right term to imply is that which the industrial tribunal took in this case, namely an obligation on the employer to take reasonable steps to maintain an appraisal of a probationer during a trial period, giving guidance by advice or warning where necessary."

The precedent contained in the manual is deliberately written in general terms so as to give employers a general discretion as to the training that it will provide. One point that an employer will wish to consider is the issue of repayment of subscriptions or training costs should the employee leave prematurely.

ACAS has produced a detailed Guide on Staff Development and Appraisals and reference should be made to the booklet for guidance: see *http://www.acas. org.uk/publications/B07.html* The following are particularly useful:

Introducing appraisals – a checklist

Why? What are the objectives?

☐ Assessment of past performance and the improvement of future performance

☐ Assessment of future potential/promotability

☐ Assessment of training and development needs

☐ To assist reward review

Who is to be appraised?

☐ Managers

☐ Supervisors

☐ Scientists, technologists and technicians

☐ Sales and marketing

☐ Clerical

☐ Skilled

☐ Semi-skilled

☐ Unskilled

☐ Any other

How often?

☐ Annually

☐ Bi-annually

☐ Quarterly

☐ Other

Who should carry out the appraisals?

☐ Immediate supervisor

☐ More senior manager

☐ Self assessment

☐ Personnel manager

☐ Any other

What methods?

☐ Rating scales

☐ Comparisons with objectives

☐ Critical incidents

☐ Ranking

☐ Narrative report

☐ Behaviourally Anchored Rating Scales

☐ Other/a mixture of the above methods

Should appraisals be 'open' or 'closed'?

☐ 'Open'

☐ 'Closed'

☐ Partially open (that is: certain parts of the report not disclosed to the lemployee)

Example of an appraisal scheme for manual employees

Name _____

Job title _____

Department _____

Length of time in post _____ Date of appraisal _____

1 Job description (to be agreed with the employee)

_____

_____

_____

2 Assessment of performance (tick as appropriate)

	Supervisor's Comments	A Well ahead of standard	B More than satisfactory – slightly above job requirements	C Less than satisfactory – needs slight improvement	D Unsatisfactory – below the standard reasonably expected
Volume of work How does the amount of work done compare with the job requirements?		☐ Exceptionally high output	☐ Output is usually above average	☐ Output is occasionally unsatisfactory	☐ Insufficient – improvement needed
Job knowledge Does the employee have the knowledge to do the job properly?		☐ Exceptionally thorough knowledge of own and related work	☐ Good knowledge of own job and related work aspect	☐ Lack of job knowledge sometimes hinders progress	☐ Inadequate knowledge of own work
Safety awareness Consider in regard to safe working practices		☐ Highly motivated towards safety. Always insists on safe working practices	☐ A good attitude to safety and encourages others likewise	☐ Sometimes has to be reminded of safety precautions at work	☐ Disregards basic safety precautions

	Supervisor's Comments	A Well ahead of standard	B More than satisfactory – slightly above job requirements	C Less than satisfactory – needs slight improvement	D Unsatisfactory – below the standard reasonably expected
Dependability How well does the employee follow procedures?		☐ Always thoroughly reliable	☐ Little supervision required	☐ Requires more frequent checks than normal	☐ Requires constant supervision
Teamwork How well does the employee work with others to accomplish the goals of the job and work group?		☐ Works extremely well with others and responds enthusiastic-ally to new challenges	☐ Co-operative and flexible	☐ Usually gets along reasonably well but occasionally unhelpful	☐ Unco-operative, resists change
Attendance & punctuality What is the employee's pattern of absence and punctuality?		☐ Exceptionally punctual. Rarely absent	☐ Attendance levels are acceptable and is rarely late	☐ Absence and/or lateness levels are higher than average	☐ Frequently late and/or absent
Work planning Consider employee's success in planning own work		☐ Displays excellent planning ability	☐ Organises work well	☐ Needs to improve some aspects of work planning	☐ Does not plan effectively
Communic-ation How effective is the employee at verbal and written comm-unication?		☐ Exceptionally effective in all written and verbal communic-ation	☐ Usually a good communicator	☐ Some difficulties with written and/or verbal communic-ation	☐ Does not communicate effectively
Overall marking		☐ Well ahead of standard performance	☐ More than satisfactory – slightly above job requirements	☐ Less than satisfactory – needs slight improvement	☐ Unsatisfactory – below the standard reasonably expected

General comments by supervisor on this assessment

_____

_____

_____   Signed _____

General comments by supervisor manager

_____

_____

_____   Signed _____

Comments by employee

_____

_____

_____   Signed _____

Action plan agreed to develop employee and/or the job
Include any training or counselling requirements

_____

_____

_____

Career development – possible steps in career development

_____

_____

_____

Agreed action plan – job and development objectives – time scale

_____

_____

_____

PART 0: EMPLOYEE REPRESENTATION

Precedent 0: **Employee Representation**

01: **Trade union representation** **851**

02: **Staff Association representation** **852**

Commentary: **Staff Association representation** **852**

Precedent 01: Trade Union Representation

1 The Company recognises the _____ union for the purpose of collective bargaining and the terms of any collective agreement with the union are incorporated into your contract of employment.

2 You have the right to belong to an independent trade union. You are entitled to participate in the activities of the union and to become an officer, official or steward of the union.

3 You have the right to decide not to join a trade union and the Company will respect your wishes if you elect not to be a trade union member.

4 You are entitled to time off in order to carry out trade union activities if you are a trade union representative and you may be entitled to paid time off as agreed in order to carry out official duties as a trade union official.

Precedent 02: Staff Association Representation

There is a staff association which the Company communicates with for the purpose of dealing with matters that are of mutual interest and importance to the Company and employees. Staff representatives are elected onto a committee on an annual basis. You are entitled to stand for election to the committee as and when there are vacancies or when the posts come up for election. All staff may vote in any election. The matters which the staff association and the Company discuss include:

1   Company activities including sales, business plans, productivity of the Company and proposals to improve the profitability of the Company.

2   The terms and conditions of employment of staff including salary reviews and other benefits to which staff may be entitled.

3   Health and safety matters.

4   Recreational and social activities.

5   Any other matters as may be agreed between the Company and the Staff Association from time to time as being relevant.

COMMENTARY TO O: STAFF ASSOCIATION REPRESENTATION

The Employment Relations Act 1999 has introduced significant new rights to recognition by trade unions and the relationship between the employer and trade union representatives or employee representatives are likely to be covered by detailed provisions of a collective or other agreement. Precedents O1 and O2 are merely meant to be general statements of the existence of a trade union or staff representation and should be included in the Manual to make it clear that these rights exist.

The right to trade union recognition is considered in Bowers, Duggan and Reade, *The Law of Industrial Action and Trade Union Recognition* (OUP 2004).

There are a number of situations where employers must consult with employees of their representatives, namely:

- In Unfair Dismissal or redundancy cases.

- When there are Business transfers under the Transfer of Undertakings (Protection fo Employment) Regulation 1981.

- For the purpose of collective bargaining.

- In relation to Occupational pension scheme arrangements.

- In relation to health and safety matters with health and safety representatives (see the Safety Representatives and Safety Committees Regulations 1977, SI 1977/500, as amended by SI 1992/2051 and the Health and Safety (Consultation with Employees) Regulations 1996, SI 1996/1513).

- In cases where Works Councils are required under the Transnational Information and Consultation of Employees Regulations 1999, SI 1999/3323.

New provisions are to come into force from 6 April 2005 to give effect to the National Information and Consultation Directive 2002/14/EC.

Consultation is to take place by 22 October 2004 in relation to the draft Information and Consultation of Employees Regulations 2004. These Regulations will provide for consultation with employers' representative from 6 April 2005 where they have at least 150 employers, from 6 April 2007 where they have 100 and from 6 April 2008 where they have at least 50 employees.

The Regulations are very detailed and beyond the scope of this book: See the DTI Draft Guidance at *http://www.dti.gov.uk/er/consultation/draftguidance.doc.*

PART P: PUBLIC INTEREST DISCLOSURE

Precedent P: Public Interest Disclosure

P1: Public Interest Disclosure Policy   856

P2: Public concern at Work's Checklist for
Small Employers who do not wish to set
up a Full Whistleblowing Policy   858

Commentary: Conduct of Employee/other Employees
& Public Interest Disclosure   860

Useful Websites

- Public Concern At Work

  http://www.pcaw.co.uk/

  http://www.pcaw.co.uk/policy_pub/case_summaries.html – which provides a summary of cases in the Employment Tribunal.

- DTI Guide

  http://www.dti.gov.uk/er/individual/pidguide-pl502.htm

- Public Interest Disclosure (Prescribed Persons) Amendment Order 2002 [2003/1993]

  http://www.legislation.hmso.gov.uk/si/si2003/20031993.htm

Precedent P1: Public Interest Disclosure Policy

The Company operates a strict policy in relation to wrongdoing (which will be regarded as a disciplinary offence) and will not tolerate actions which may amount to a criminal offence or breaches of legal obligations, a miscarriage of justice, danger to health or safety, or which may damage the environment ('wrongdoing'). All employees are expected to maintain the highest of standards of integrity and good faith. Under Part 1VA of the Employment Rights Act 1996 employees who report wrongdoing to certain parties are protected. However, it is the policy of the Company that any wrong doing that has occurred should be reported to the Company. Accordingly, the Company has devised the following policy in order to encourage you to report any matters that you believe are of concern to the Company and to reassure you that you will be protected in respect of any such disclosures.

1 You may be concerned about the repercussions to you in reporting matters that are of concern. The Company assures you that you will be protected and will not be subjected to any detriment because you have reported a matter that you believe in good faith to amount to wrongdoing or potential wrongdoing.

2 However, you must note that if you make any allegation which you do not believe or which is made maliciously or for some ulterior motive (i.e. a grudge against a fellow worker) then this may be treated as a disciplinary matter and the Company may invoke the disciplinary procedure.

Reporting wrongdoing

3 In the first instance you may wish to raise the matter with your Manager on an informal basis and discuss with him what steps should be taken to report the matter to more senior management.

4 You may at any time raise the matter formally with your Manager, whether orally or in writing and he pass on the matter to the appropriate level of management.

5 If your concern is about your Manager or someone at a higher level of management then you should feel free to raise the matter with whichever level of management you consider to be appropriate.

6 At all stages all statements that you make will remain confidential unless you express a contrary wish or it becomes necessary to divulge such statements during the course of an investigation.

Investigations

7 You must recognise that a complaint about wrongdoing may lead to the Company wishing to carry out an investigation into the allegations of wrongdoing. In these circumstances you will be informed before any of the matters that you have raised are put to the alleged wrongdoer and you will be protected by the Company who will ensure that your work environment is not affected because you disclosed the matter to the Company.

8 You will be informed of the outcome of any investigation and what action has been taken.

9 If you have any concern or complaint about the manner in which you feel you are being treated because you made the disclosure, whether by the alleged wrongdoer or any co-employees, you should raise this with whatever level of management you consider to be appropriate and this may be dealt with as a disciplinary matter in relation to such individuals.

10 If you are unhappy about the manner in which your disclosure was treated by the person to whom it was reported or you consider that it is not being properly investigated then you should report the matter to whatever level of management you consider appropriate which may include a Director of the Board of Directors. You will not suffer any detriment by making such a report unless point 2 above applies.

At all times the intention of the Company will be to resolve the allegations that have been made and to ensure that wrongdoing has not occurred or, if it has occurred, it is dealt with appropriately. However, the Company will not hesitate to report wrongdoing to the appropriate body if it considers that this is the correct approach to adopt in the circumstances.

There are no third parties that have the authority of the Company to be treated as your employer for the purpose of making disclosures. To the extent that the Company provides third party Counselling or other services these bodies are not to be regarded as having the authority of the Company for the purpose of making disclosures and will not be regarded as your Employer.

[The Company considers that you should always first express your concerns to a person in the Company but if you wish to make a disclosure to an external body the Company suggests that you take advice from your Trade Union of Public Concern at Work.]

Precedent P2: Public concern at Work's Checklist for Small Employers who do not wish to set up a Full Whistleblowing Policy

See *http://www.pcaw.co.uk/policy_pub/checklist.html*

Making whistleblowing work

Practical hints for small organisations

Organisations with a small number of employees may think it is not necessary to set up a full whistleblowing policy. The practical tips set out below may be useful in these circumstances.

Explain the issue

- Involve your employees and listen to their sense of right and wrong. Explain how wrongdoing affects your organisation: the effect on jobs, morale and everyone you work with and for. Discuss with them any particular risks your organisation may face.

- Encourage your employees to keep their eyes open and keep you informed of their concerns. Explain that this is a key way you can ensure management's accountability and your own commitment to good practice across the organisation. This message will help deter anyone tempted to take advantage of their position and your trust. If there is a staff association or union, get them to back this approach.

- Explain that a whistleblower is a witness, not a complainant. This will help you, employees and managers separate the message from the messenger.

- Stress that you want employees to raise the matter when it is just a concern, rather than have them wait for proof or investigate the matter themselves.

Practise what you preach

- Employees need to know what conduct is unacceptable. If in doubt, they should be encouraged to ask management if something is appropriate before – not after – the event.

- When you find serious wrongdoing (whether by employees or managers), deal with it seriously. Remember you cannot expect your employees to practise higher standards than those you apply.

Be open to concerns

- Remember it can be awkward and embarrassing to raise a concern, particularly one which may have an impact on friends, colleagues or managers.

- Try to ensure that all managers are open to any such concern before it becomes part of a grievance. If it is uncomfortable for the employee or manager to deal with a particular matter, tell them they can and should raise it at a senior level.

- Make it clear that you will support concerned employees and protect them from reprisals. This will ensure that most employees will raise concerns openly.

- Aside from line management, make sure employees have another route to raise a concern. This should be to a senior officer such as the Chief Executive or a Board member. Tell employees how they can contact that person in confidence in case they do not want their identity to be disclosed without their prior consent.

- Promote relevant external routes such as a regulator, as this will reassure employees and others that you want to deal with concerns properly.

- Reassure them that if they are unsure whether or how to raise a concern they can get free confidential independent advice from Public Concern at Work (**020 7404 6609**).

Responding to a concern

- Remember there are two sides to every story.

- Thank the employee for raising the matter, even if the concern proves to be mistaken.

- Respect and heed legitimate employee concerns about their own position or career.

- Report back to the employee about the outcome of any enquiry and any remedial action you propose to take.

- Always remember you may have to explain how you handled the concern.

Loose ends

- Emphasise to managers and employees that victimising people who raise genuine concerns is a disciplinary offence.

- Make it clear that raising an untrue allegation maliciously is a disciplinary offence.

COMMENTARY TO P: CONDUCT OF EMPLOYEE/OTHER EMPLOYEES & PUBLIC INTEREST DISCLOSURE

It is necessary to consider, briefly, the common law position and then to consider the protection afforded by the Public Interest Disclosure Act 1998, which incorporates Part 1VA of the Employment Rights Act 1996, to employees who choose to 'whistleblow'.

Implied Terms: parties' duty to inform the other of breaches

There is no general duty on the part of an employer to inform its employees that it has committed a breach of contract so that a compromise agreement will remain binding even if the employer has been guilty of fraud (**Bank of Credit and Commerce International SA (in liquidation) v Ali** [1999] IRLR 226:

> "The current law as generally understood may be stated as follows that (1) (subject to one exception) neither party to a contract is obliged to disclose facts material to the decision of the other party whether to enter into that contract; (2) the exception is limited to contracts which are uberrimae fidei; (3) neither contracts of employment or contracts of compromise (unless by way of family arrangement) fall within this exceptional category; and (4) neither the employer nor the employee, once in contractual relations, are under a duty as such to disclose to each other their own breaches of contract."

It was held in **Macmillan Inc v Bishopgate Investment Trust PLC** [1993] ICR 385; IRLR 393 that there is no general duty on the part of an employee to disclose information which it is in the employer's interests to know, regardless of how it is has been obtained. The information must have been obtained "in the course of employment" so that where an employee gave evidence to a liquidator about the insolvency of a third party company it could not be said that the employer had any power over the transcripts of the interview which the employee held.

It has been clear ever since **Bell v Lever Bros Limited** [1932] AC 161 that an employee is under no duty to disclose his own misconduct. As Lord Atkin said in his speech:

> "I agree that the duty in the servant to protect his master's property may involve the duty to report a fellow servant whom he knows to be wrongfully dealing with that property. The servant owes a duty not to steal, but having stolen, is there superadded a duty to confess that he has stolen? I am satisfied that to imply such a duty would be a departure from the well established usage of mankind and would be to create obligations entirely outside the normal contemplation of the parties concerned."

(See also **Fletcher v Krell** [1873] 28 LT 105; **Healey v Societe Anonyme Francaise Rubastic** [1917] 1 KB 946; **Hands v Simpson Fawcett & Co** [1928] 44 TLR 295).

There is also no general duty to report the wrongdoing of fellow employees by way of an implied term. In **Sybron Corporation v Rochem Limited** [1983] IRLR 253; ICR 801 a Mr Roques, European Zone Manager for a subsidiary of Sybron, was involved in setting up rival companies in competition, together with subordinates, and he concealed this from his employer. After retirement the matters came to light and the company sought to recover a lump sum it had paid under his pension scheme. The Court of Appeal dismissed an appeal that he must repay such monies. He had been in a senior executive position and there was a continuing fraud of which he was well aware. Fox LJ cited the dicta of Greene LJ in **Swain v West (Butchers) Limited** [1936] 3 All ER 261 that:

> "The plaintiff was responsible for the management of the business and was responsible for seeing that the business was conducted honestly and efficiently by all who came under its control. If the dishonesty of a fellow servant came to his notice, he should tell the board."

This was so, notwithstanding that it would reveal his own dishonesty. Thus, it depends upon the status of the employee as to whether or not there will be such an implied term. If there is an express term on the contract this difficulty will, of course, not arise. Very senior employees and executives may be under a duty to disclose wrongdoing: see **Industrial Development Consultants Ltd v Cooley** [1972] 1 WLR 443 and see **RGB Resources PLC v Rastogi** [2002] EWHC 2728. In the latter case Laddie J accepted that a senior employee may owe a duty to whistleblow in relation to a major fraud carried out by directors. He considered that, in certain circumstances, a director may be under a duty to carry out investigations where there is suspicious conduct and to disclose the same to co directors and eternally to auditors.

> For a full consideration of the above issues see Duggan, *Wrongful Dismissal and Breach of Contract* at 223 and 255.

Public Interest Disclosure

The Public Interest Disclosure Act 1998 came into force on 2nd July 1999 and added 11 new sections to the ERA 1996. It was passed in response to a number of disasters and scandals after it became known through official inquiries that workers had been aware of dangers but had been too scared to whistleblow. The provisions protect workers against dismissals and detrimental treatment arising out of them disclosing any of the six matters set out in section 43B of the ERA 1996. There is no requirement for a qualifying period of employment or statutory ceiling on compensation (in a case in 2000 an accountant who was dismissed for blowing the whistle on his managing director was awarded £293,441 by a Tribunal and the Public Concern at Work Website refers to one case where the Applicant received £805,000).

In order for there to be a detriment within the meaning of the Act the disclosure must be the real cause of the detriment in the sense of being the real reason or motive for the detrimental treatment. In **Aspinall v MSI Mechforge Limited** (EAT/891/01) the EAT stated that for there to be detriment under section 47B "on the ground that the worker has made a protected disclosure" the protected disclosure has to be causative in the sense of being "the real reason, the core reason, the *causa causans*, the motive for the treatment complained of". In relation to a dismissal, the making of the protected disclosure has to be the reason or principal reason for the dismissal.

In **Aspinall** the steps that the employer took were solely because of the perceived breach of the confidentiality of MSI's manufacturing process.

The European Commission has set up its own internal whistleblowing arrangements (EC Press Notice IP/00/1380 29th November 2000 – *http://europa.eu.int/rapid/pressReleasesAction.do?reference=IP/00/1380&format= HTML&aged=0&language=EN&guiLanguage=en*).

Part IVA of the ERA 1996 contains a number of provisions whereby the employee will be protected if he makes a disclosure for one of several reasons. Any dismissal because the employer made such a disclosure will be automatically unfair and the employer may not subject the employee to a detriment because he has made such a disclosure.

It is necessary to consider:

- The definition of a qualifying disclosure. There are six categories of subject matter ('the relevant failures')

- Those circumstances where a disclosure will be protected (see further Duggan, *Unfair Dismissal* Chapter 19).

Section 43A of the Employment Rights Act 1996 provides that a 'protected disclosure' means a qualifying disclosure (as defined by section 43B) which is made by a worker in accordance with any of sections 43C to 43H. It is necessary for an Applicant to sufficiently particularise the allegations in the Originating Application so that a tribunal can ascertain whether the disclosure provided information about one of the six relevant failures (**Sim v Manchester Action on Street Health** [EAT 0085/01]).

Disclosure

Section 43B refers to 'any disclosure of information' relating to one of the six categories. The word disclosure is not defined but it is apparent that the worker only need communicate the information by effective means in order for there to be a disclosure of information. There may be a disclosure of information even though the information is already known to the recipient (section 43L(3)).

A verbal communication will be sufficient but informal or general conversations may not be sufficient to amount to a disclosure as in **Douglas v Birmingham City Council** [EAT 0518/02] where a governor verbally conveyed concerns about the school's equal opportunities policy to another governor in a confidential conversation. HHJ McMullen QC stated that: there was no protected disclosure

> " ... because Mrs Canning was being consulted for the purposes only of advice and the Applicant indicated that she would herself pursue the matter and did not want the matter to be handled on her behalf by Mrs Canning. The relationship was one of confidentiality and thus, at first sight and on close analysis thereafter, a statute which is designed in the public interest to protect disclosures ought not to apply to a private conversation between these two governors of the school."

However, a letter which expressed the concerns did amount to a protected disclosure. The same result was reached in **de Haney v Brent Mind** [EAT 0054/03] where an oral conversation did not amount to a protected disclosure but two letters that were written and which asserted the Respondent to be in breach of its equal opportunities policies did amount to a disclosure. (See also **Kraus v Penna PLC** [2004] IRLR 260 where a disclosure to the client company was held to be sufficient as the statutory scheme did not require disclosure to other persons including the employer.)

Qualifying Disclosure

By section 43B a qualifying disclosure means any disclosure of information which, in the 'reasonable belief' of the worker making the disclosure, tends to show one of the six relevant failures. It is necessary that the employee has a 'reasonable belief'. It was held in **Darnton v University of Surrey** [2003] IRLR 133 that the reasonableness of the belief will depend in each case upon the volume and quality of information available to the worker at the time the decision to disclose is made. There must be some information which tends to show that the specified malpractice occurred. The test is whether the employee has a reasonable belief; not whether the belief is true or accurate so that it does not matter that the allegations are not factually correct, as in *Darnton* where a criminal offence had in fact not been committed. So either there is a belief:

1. that a criminal offence has been committed, is being committed or is likely to be committed. Where the employee believes that a criminal offence has been committed but, as a matter of law, this is not the position, the logic of the *Kraus* case (see below) would appear to be that the employee may be mistaken about the facts but if there is no offence as a matter of law, the employee's genuine belief that a criminal offence has been committed is not enough. Thus, in two employment tribunal cases it was found that there was no protected disclosure where no

criminal offence had been committed (**Coke v Moss Side and Hulme Community Development Trust** [EAT no 240227/01] and **Williamson v Karl Suss (GB) Ltd** [ET No 2702198/00]; or

2. that a person has failed, is failing or is likely to fail to comply with any legal obligation to which he is subject. This head will cover a failure to comply with a contractual obligation under the contract of employment as in **Parkins v Sodexho Ltd** [2002] IRLR 109, where the dismissal was alleged to have been instigated because of a complaint about on-site supervision breaching the implied term of health and safety. It would seem that this claim could have been brought under 43B(1)(d) – see head 4 below. The breach of the employee's own contract (*Parkins*) or another workers contract (**Odong v Chubb Security Personnel** [EAT 0819/02]) may amount to a breach of a legal obligation.

It is necessary to show that the law actually imposes the obligation to which the breach relates. It was stated in **Kraus v Penna PLC** [2004] IRLR 260 that information disclosed should, in the reasonable belief of the worker at the time it is disclosed, tend to show that it is probable or more probable than not that the employer will fail to comply with the relevant legal obligation. Mr Kraus was engaged to provide services as a human resources professional in connection with that company's reorganisation and redundancy programme. Within a very short time, he was informed that his services were no longer required and his consultancy agreement was terminated. The company contended that they had decided to dispense with his services because of his appearance and demeanor and lack of enthusiasm for the project. Mr Kraus brought proceedings in the employment tribunal claiming that he had been subjected to a detriment, i.e. the termination of his consultancy agreement, for making a protected disclosure. He alleged that his services had been dispensed with because he had advised one of the Company's directors that the redundancies proposed could breach employment legislation and make the company vulnerable to claims for unfair dismissal.

It was held that the applicant's advice to one of the directors that the company "could" breach employment legislation could not be a qualifying disclosure within s.43B(1)(b). At its highest, the applicant's belief was limited to the possibility or the risk of a breach of employment legislation, depending on what eventually took place. This did not meet the statutory test of "likely to fail to comply". The Employment Tribunal was also entitled to find that the applicant had failed to demonstrate that the employers were under any specific legal obligation with respect to the proposed redundancies which they were likely to breach. Mrs Justice Cox stated that:

> "The information disclosed should, in the reasonable belief of the worker at the time it is disclosed, tend to show that it is probable or more probable than not that the employer will fail to comply with the relevant legal obligation."

The issue for any tribunal will be whether the statutory criteria have been fulfilled. In **ALM Medical Services Ltd v Bladon** [2002] EWCA Civ 1085; [2002] IRLR 807 the Court of Appeal stated that in cases where it is alleged that dismissal is due to a protected disclosure the critical issue, where the employee has not served the qualifying period needed to acquire the general right not to be unfairly dismissed, is whether the requirements of the protected disclosure provisions have been satisfied on the evidence. It is not substantive or procedural unfairness, which would be central to a claim for "ordinary" unfair dismissal; or

3. that a miscarriage of justice has occurred, is occurring or is likely to occur. Query whether this would include engineering the dismissal of an employee (see *Coke* referred to above); or

4. that the health or safety of any individual has been, is being or is likely to be endangered. It will be necessary to provide sufficient details in the disclosure of the threat to health and safety. In **Fincham v HM Prison Service** [EAT 0925/01] where there was an allegation of racial harassment, the words 'I feel under constant pressure and stress awaiting the next incident' were held by the ET not to be sufficient to be a disclosure but the EAT took the view that the words 'under pressure and stress' were a statement that health and safety was being or likely to be endangered; or

5. that the environment has been, is being or is likely to be damaged; or

6. that information tending to show any of the five matters set out before has been or is likely to be deliberately concealed.

A disclosure of such information will not be a qualifying disclosure if a criminal offence is committed by disclosing such information (43B(3)) or if it relates to information that was disclosed in the course of taking legal advice (43B(4)).

The formulation refers to the 'reasonable belief of the worker'. This means that that there can still be a qualifying disclosure if the worker is later shown to have made a reasonable mistake as in **Darnton v University of Surrey** [2003] IRLR 133. Judge Serota QC stated:

> "In our opinion, the determination of the factual accuracy of the disclosure by the Tribunal will, in many cases, be an important tool in determining whether the worker held the reasonable belief that the disclosure tended to show a relevant failure. Thus if an Employment Tribunal finds that an employee's factual allegation of something he claims to have seen himself is false, that will be highly relevant to the question of the worker's reasonable belief. It is extremely difficult to see how a worker can reasonably believe that an allegation tends to show that there has been a relevant failure if he knew or believed that the factual basis was false, unless there may somehow have been an honest mistake on his part. The relevance and extent of the Employment Tribunal's enquiry into the factual accuracy of the disclosure will, therefore, necessarily depend on the circumstances of each case. In many cases, it will be an important tool to decide whether the worker held the reasonable belief that is required by s.43B(1). ...We consider that as a matter of both law and common sense all circumstances must be considered together in determining whether the worker holds the reasonable belief. The circumstances will include his belief in the factual basis of the information disclosed as well as what those facts tend to show. The more the worker claims to have direct knowledge of the matters which are the subject of the disclosure, the more relevant will be his belief in the truth of what he says in determining whether he holds that reasonable belief."

Exclusions

Disclosures will not be qualified disclosures if the employee commits a criminal offence by making it (section 43B(3)) or where the disclosure is one in relation to which legal professional privilege could be claimed in legal proceedings and is made by the person to whom the information was disclosed (section 43B(4)).

Good Faith

In **Street v Derbyshire Unemployed Workers' Centre** [2004] EWCA Civ 964 (21 July 2004); [2004] IRLR 687 the Court of Appeal considered the issue of good faith under the whistleblowing provisions. Mrs Street, who had worked as an administrator for the Derbyshire Unemployed Workers Centre ("the Centre") from 1989, was dismissed by the Centre in January 2001 after making a series of allegations against the manager of the Centre. She made a claim to an employment tribunal maintaining that she was entitled to be regarded as unlawfully dismissed under section 103A. The tribunal dismissed her claim, holding that, in making the disclosure, she had lacked the good faith required under section 43C(1) or 43G(1)(a). The Employment Appeal Tribunal upheld that ruling and remitted the case back to the Tribunal to decide unfair dismissal on ordinary grounds. In the Court of Appeal, Auld LJ stated:

> "In considering good faith as distinct from reasonable belief in the truth of the disclosure, it is clearly open to an Employment Tribunal, where satisfied as to the latter, to consider nevertheless whether the disclosure was not made in good faith because of some ulterior motive, which may or may not have involved a motivation of personal gain, and/or which, in all the circumstances of the case, may or may not have made the disclosure unreasonable. Whether the nature or degree of any ulterior motive found amounts to bad faith, or whether the motive of personal gain was of such a nature or strength as to "make the disclosure for purposes of personal gain" or "in all the circumstances of the case" not reasonable, is equally a matter for its assessment on a broad basis."

His Lordship considered that the Tribunal:

> "should only find that a disclosure was not made in good faith when they are of the view that the dominant or predominant purpose of making it was for some ulterior motive, not that purpose."

(See also paragraphs 71 and 75 of Wall LJ's judgment.)

There are six sections, which set out the circumstances in which qualifying disclosures may take place and the requirements as follows:

1. Disclosure to employer or other responsible person

By section 43C a qualifying disclosure is made where:

- the worker makes the disclosure in good faith;

- to his employer; or

- to another person where he believes that the failure relates solely or mainly to the conduct of a person other than the employer or a matter for which a person other than the employer has legal responsibility.

By section 43C(2) a worker who, in accordance with a procedure whose use by him is authorised by his employer, makes a qualifying disclosure to a person other than his employer, is to be treated as making the qualifying disclosure to his employer. It is important that the employer has a whistleblowing procedure that makes it clear that a person other than the employer is *not authorised*. In the absence of such a clause there is a risk that protected disclosures will be made to parties which had not been anticipated by the employer. In **The Brothers of Charity Services Merseyside v G Eleady-Cole** [EAT/0661/00] the employee was employed for a period of under three months between 1 May and 29 July 1999 as a full time support worker in a hostel for disadvantaged persons which the employer operated in Liverpool. The applicant alleged that his employment was not continued at the end of his probationary period because of protected disclosures that he had made to a third party. The respondent provided an Employee Assistance Programme whereby it had a commercial contract with a company called PPC Ltd. All employees had access to the service, which consisted of a confidential telephone report service that enabled an employee to seek assistance on any matter of concern. The applicant made use of this facility to voice certain concerns. The tribunal stated that it

"was the accepted practice under the arrangements between the employer and PPC Ltd that in the event of a disclosure being made to PPC Ltd of the fact of criminal activities within the employer's homes or organisation, then a disclosure *would* be made by PPC to the employer of that fact, though subject to preserving the anonymity and confidentiality of the informant. If, for example, with a procedure in place of that nature, an employee made a confidential disclosure of the fact that criminal activity or suspected criminal activity was going on in the workplace and this was then reported by the advisory service to the employer, in confidence, and then despite the attempts to maintain confidentiality, the employer subsequently became aware which employee had been responsible for the matters coming to light and that employee was then immediately dismissed by the employer for that reason, we have little doubt that such a dismissal is contrary to Section 103A."

2. Disclosure to legal adviser

By section 43D a disclosure qualifies if it is made in the course of taking legal advice. There is no requirement in this section that the disclosure be made in good faith. However, 'legal adviser' is not defined so that it is a moot point whether taking advice from a non-legally qualified adviser (i.e. a CAB volunteer) would be covered.

3. Disclosure to Minister of the Crown

A disclosure will qualify if made to a Minister of the Crown in circumstances where the employer is an individual or a body appointed by a Minister of the Crown. It is necessary that the disclosure be made in good faith.

4. Disclosure to a prescribed person

The requirements of this section are:

- the disclosure must be made in good faith;

- the disclosure must be made to a person prescribed by an order made by the Secretary of State for the purposes of the section;

- the worker must reasonably believe that the failure falls within any description of matters in relation to which the person is so prescribed;

- the worker must believe that the information disclosed and any allegation are substantially true.

The Public Interest Disclosure (Prescribed Persons) Order 1999 (SI 1999/1549), amended by SI 2003/1993, sets out in detail the prescribed persons to whom complaints should be made (see list at end of this commentary).

5. Disclosure in other cases

A qualifying disclosure is made in accordance with section 43G where:

- the worker makes the disclosure in good faith;

- the worker reasonably believes that the information disclosed and any allegation are substantially true;

- the worker does not make the disclosure for personal gain;

- it is reasonable for him to make the disclosure, taking into account those matters set out in section 43F(3), being:

  (a) the identify of the person to whom the disclosure is made;

  (b) the seriousness of the relevant failure;

  (c) whether the failure is continuing or likely to continue in the future;

  (d) whether the disclosure is made in breach of a duty of confidentiality;

  (e) what action was taken or could reasonably be expected to have been taken in relation to previous disclosures;

  (f) whether the worker complied with procedure in relation to previous disclosures made to the employer;

  and one of the following conditions is met:

  1. at the time that the disclosure is made the worker believes that he will be subjected to a detriment by his employer if he makes the disclosure to the employer or to a prescribed person in accordance with section 43F;

  2. where no person is prescribed under section 43F the worker reasonably believes that it is likely that the evidence relating to the relevant failure will be concealed or destroyed if he makes disclosure to the employer;

  3. that the worker has previously made a disclosure of substantially the same information to his employer or a prescribed person under section 43F (which may include information about action taken or not taken by any person as a result of the previous disclosure (43G(4)).

6. Disclosure of exceptionally serious failure

A qualifying disclosure is made in accordance with section 43H where:

- the worker makes the disclosure in good faith;

- the worker reasonably believes that the information disclosed and any allegation are substantially true;

- the worker does not make the disclosure for personal gain;

- the relevant failure is of an exceptionally serious nature;

- it was reasonable in all the circumstances for him to make the disclosure and, in this respect, regard is to be had to the identity of the person to whom the disclosure was made (43H(2)).

Clauses that prohibit making protected disclosures

Section 43J(1) provides that any provision in an agreement to which this section applies is void in so far as it purports to preclude the worker from making a protected disclosure. By 43J(2) the section applies to any agreement between a worker and his employer, whether a worker's contract or not, including an agreement to refrain from instituting or continuing any proceedings under this Act or any proceedings for breach of contract.

Definition of worker

By section 43K there is an extended meaning of 'worker' for Part IVA of the ERA 1996. Under section 43K(1) 'worker' includes an individual who is not a worker as defined by section 230(3) but who—

(a) works or worked for a person in circumstances in which—

(i) he is or was introduced or supplied to do that work by a third person; and

(ii) the terms on which he is or was engaged to do the work are or were in practice substantially determined not by him but by the person for whom he works or worked, by the third person or by both of them.

By section 43K(2) 'employer', in relation to a worker falling within paragraph (a), includes the person who substantially determines or determined the terms on which he is or was engaged.

(b) contracts or contracted with a person, for the purposes of that person's business, for the execution of work to be done in a place not under the control or management of that person and would fall within section 230(3)(b) if for 'personally' in that provision there were substituted '(whether personally or otherwise)'.

(c) works or worked as a person providing general medical services, general dental services, general ophthalmic services or pharmaceutical services in accordance with arrangements made (i) by a [Primary Care Trust or] Health Authority under section 29, 35, 38 or 41 of the National Health Service Act 1977, or (ii) by a Health Board under section 19, 25, 26 or 27 of the National Health Service (Scotland) Act 1978.

By section 43K(2) 'employer', in relation to a worker falling within paragraph (c) means the authority or board referred to in that paragraph.

(d) is or was provided with work experience provided pursuant to a training course or programme or with training for employment (or with both) otherwise than under a contract of employment, or by an educational establishment on a course run by that establishment;

By section 43K(2) 'employer', in relation to a worker falling within paragraph (d) means the person providing the work experience or training whilst by 43K(3) 'educational establishment' includes any university, college, school or other educational establishment.

Section 43KA was added by the Police Reform Act 2002 to include the police who have protection from 1 April 2004.

The Precedent seeks to set out policy that is both fair to the employee making the complaint but also protects the rights of others should the complaint be malicious or untrue. It makes it clear that the employee will not be victimised but will be given a fair opportunity to state his case and will be protected. Note that the policy cannot prevent a complaint being made to an outside body where that is appropriate and any attempt to stop the worker is likely to amount to a detriment under the Act or a potentially automatically unfair dismissal if the worker resigns or is dismissed.

It should be noted that the guidelines for assessing compensation are the same as in discrimination cases (**Virgo Fideis Junior School v Boyle** [2004] IRLR 268).

Schedule to the Prescribed Persons Order

First Column	Second Column
Persons and descriptions of people	**Descriptions of matters**
Accounts Commission for Scotland and auditors appointed by the Commission to audit the accounts of local government bodies.	The proper conduct of public business, value for money, fraud and corruption in local government bodies.
Audit Commission for England and Wales and auditors appointed by the Commission to audit the accounts of local government, and health service, bodies.	The proper conduct of public business, value for money, fraud and corruption in local government, and health service bodies.
Certification Officer.	Fraud, and other irregularities, relating to the financial affairs of trade unions and employers' associations.
Charity Commissioners for England and Wales.	The proper administration of charities and of funds given or held for charitable purposes.
The Scottish Ministers.	The proper administration of charities and of funds given or held for charitable purposes.
Chief Executive of the Criminal Cases Review Commission.	Actual or potential miscarriages of justice.
Chief Executive of the Scottish Criminal Cases Review Commission.	Actual or potential miscarriages of justice.
Civil Aviation Authority.	Compliance with the requirements of civil aviation legislation, including aviation safety.

First Column	Second Column
Persons and descriptions of people	**Descriptions of matters**
The competent authority under Part IV of the Financial Services and Markets Act 2000.	The listing of securities on a stock exchange; prospectuses on offers of transferable securities to the public.
Commissioners of Customs and Excise.	Value added tax, insurance premium tax, excise duties and landfill tax. The import and export of prohibited or restricted goods.
Commissioners of the Inland Revenue.	Income tax, corporation tax, capital gains tax, petroleum revenue tax, inheritance tax, stamp duties, national insurance contributions, statutory maternity pay, statutory sick pay, tax credits, child benefits, collection of student loans and the enforcement of the national minimum wage.
Comptroller and Auditor General of the National Audit Office.	The proper conduct of public business, value for money, fraud and corruption in relation to the provision of centrally-funded public services.
Auditor General for Wales.	The proper conduct of public business, value for money, fraud and corruption in relation to the provision of public services.
Auditor General for Scotland and persons appointed by or on his behalf under the Public Finance and Accountability (Scotland) Act 2000 to act as auditors or examiners for the purposes of sections 21 to 24 of that Act.	The proper conduct of public business, value for money, fraud and corruption in relation to the provision of public services.
Audit Scotland.	The proper conduct of public business, value for money, fraud and corruption in public bodies.

First Column	Second Column
Persons and descriptions of people	**Descriptions of matters**
Director General of Electricity Supply.	The generation, transmission, distribution and supply of electricity, and activities ancillary to these matters.
Director General of Gas Supply.	The transportation, shipping and supply of gas through pipes, and activities ancillary to these matters.
Director General of Telecommunications.	The provision and use of telecommunications systems, services and apparatus.
Director General of Water Services.	The supply of water and the provision of sewerage services.
Water Industry Commissioner for Scotland.	The supply of water and the provision of sewerage services.
Director of the Serious Fraud Office.	Serious or complex fraud.
Lord Advocate, Scotland.	Serious or complex fraud.
Environment Agency.	Acts or omissions which have an actual or potential effect on the environment or the management or regulation of the environment, including those relating to pollution, abstraction of water, flooding, the flow in rivers, inland fisheries and migratory salmon or trout.
Scottish Environment Protection Agency.	Acts or omissions which have an actual or potential effect on the environment or the management or regulation of the environment, including those relating to flood warning systems and pollution.

First Column	Second Column
Persons and descriptions of people	**Descriptions of matters**
Food Standards Agency.	Matters which may affect the health of any member of the public in relation to the consumption of food and other matters concerning the protection of the interests of consumers in relation to food.
Financial Services Authority.	The carrying on of investment business or of insurance business; the operation of banks and building societies, deposit-taking businesses and wholesale money market regimes; the operation of friendly societies, benevolent societies, working men's clubs, specially authorised societies, and industrial and provident societies; the functioning of financial markets, investment exchanges and clearing houses; money laundering, financial crime, and other serious financial misconduct, in connection with activities regulated by the Financial Services Authority.
General Social Care Council.	Matters relating to the registration of social care workers under the Care Standards Act 2000.
Care Council for Wales.	Matters relating to the registration of social care workers under the Care Standards Act 2000.
Scottish Social Services Council.	Matters relating to the registration of the social services workforce by the Scottish Social Services Council.
Children's Commissioner for Wales.	Matters relating to the rights and welfare of children.

First Column	Second Column
Persons and descriptions of people	**Descriptions of matters**
Health and Safety Executive.	Matters which may affect the health or safety of any individual at work; matters, which may affect the health and safety of any member of the public, arising out of or in connection with the activities of persons at work.
Housing Corporation.	The registration and operation of registered social landlords, including their administration of public and private funds and management of their housing stock.
Local authorities which are responsible for the enforcement of health and safety legislation.	Matters which may affect the health or safety of any individual at work; matters, which may affect the health and safety of any member of the public, arising out of or in connection with the activities of persons at work.
Information Commissioner.	Compliance with the requirements of legislation relating to data protection and to freedom of information.
Scottish Information Commissioner.	Compliance with the requirements of legislation relating to freedom of information.
National Care Standards Commission.	Matters relating to the provision of regulated care services, as defined in the Care Standards Act 2000.
National Assembly for Wales.	Matters relating to the provision of social care services liable to be registered or inspected under the Care Standards Act 2000 or the Children Act 1989.

First Column	Second Column
Persons and descriptions of people	**Descriptions of matters**
National Assembly for Wales. (*continued*)	The registration and operation of registered social landlords, including their administration of public and private funds and management of their housing stock.
Scottish Commission for the Regulation of Care.	Matters relating to the provision of care services, as defined in the Regulation of Care (Scotland) Act 2001.
Occupational Pensions Regulatory Authority.	Matters relating to occupational pension schemes and other private pension arrangements.
Office of Fair Trading.	Matters concerning the sale of goods or the supply of services, which adversely affect the interests of consumers. Competition affecting markets in the United Kingdom.
Rail Regulator.	The provision and supply of railway services.
Standards Board for England.	Breaches by a member or co-opted member of a relevant authority (as defined in section 49(6) of the Local Government Act 2000) of that authority's code of conduct.
Local Commissioner in Wales.	Breaches by a member or co-opted member of a relevant authority (as defined in section 49(6) of the Local Government Act 2000) of that authority's code of conduct.

First Column	Second Column
Persons and descriptions of people	**Descriptions of matters**
Standards Commission for Scotland and the Chief Investigating Officer.	Breaches by a councillor or a member of a devolved public body (as defined in section 28 of the Ethical Standards in Public Life etc. (Scotland) Act 2000) of the code of conduct applicable to that councillor or member under that Act.
Treasury.	The carrying on of insurance business.
Secretary of State for Trade and Industry.	Fraud, and other misconduct, in relation to companies, investment business, insurance business, or multi-level marketing schemes (and similar trading schemes); insider dealing. Consumer safety.
Secretary of State for Transport.	Compliance with merchant shipping law, including maritime safety.
Local authorities which are responsible for the enforcement of consumer protection legislation.	Compliance with the requirements of consumer protection legislation.
Local authorities which are responsible for the enforcement of food standards.	Compliance with the requirements of food safety legislation.
A person ("person A") carrying out functions, by virtue of legislation, relating to relevant failures falling within one or more matters within a description of matters in respect of which another person ("person B") is prescribed by this Order, where person B was previously responsible for carrying out the same or substantially similar functions and has ceased to be so responsible.	Matters falling within the description of matters in respect of which person B is prescribed by this Order, to the extent that those matters relate to functions currently carried out by person A.

PART Q: RESTRICTIONS DURING AND AFTER EMPLOYMENT

Precedent Q: Restrictions during and after employment

Q1:	Employment that conflicts with your duties	881
Q2:	Confidential information	882
Q3:	Intellectual Property	883
Q4:	Intellectual Property Agreement	883
Q5:	Model restrictive covenants	884
Commentary:	Restrictions during and after Employment	888

Precedent Q1: Employment that Conflicts with your Duties

It is the Company's policy that you will work exclusively upon the Company's business. You are not allowed to undertake any other paid employment during the time that you are employed by the Company without the express agreement in writing of the Company. If you wish to take up any outside appointment you must have the express written permission of _____ in the Company. You will not, in any event, be able to take up any employment that may amount to a conflict of interest between your work with the Company and you should not have any interest, whether directly or indirectly, in a business that may place you in conflict of interest. You must inform the Company if you are involved or become involved in such a businesses.

Precedent Q2:   Confidential Information

The Company operates a very strict policy with regard to confidential information. You will appreciate that the nature of the business of the Company is such that its continued success is dependant upon information remaining confidential and any disclosure of such information may be harmful to the Company's business. This information includes, but is not limited to:

[SET OUT LIST OF INFORMATION THAT IS TO BE REGARDED AS CONFIDENTIAL SUCH AS:

• Marketing and sales policies;

• Pricing information;

• Customer information and details.]

By the same token the affairs of the Company's clients are private and any information that you obtain about clients or customers during the period that you are employed must be regarded as confidential. The Company will regard any breach of confidentiality as a disciplinary offence and any breaches may lead to dismissal.

Accordingly, you agree that during and after your employment you will not disclose any confidential information that has come to your attention during the course of your employment. You will at all times protect and maintain the confidentiality of the Company's information and that of its clients and may only disclose such information as required by law or as is necessary during the course of your duties with the Company. You understand that this obligation will continue at all times both during and after the termination of your employment unless and until the information has come into the public domain.

You may have been required to sign a confidentiality undertaking when you signed your letter of appointment. You must abide by the terms of that confidentiality undertaking at all times and it will be regarded as an act of gross misconduct if you breach the terms of that undertaking, which may lead to disciplinary proceedings and possible dismissal.

Precedent Q3:   Intellectual Property

If you were employed by the Company to carry out any functions that involve making new inventions or improving original inventions or that relate to the use of confidential information or creating material that it subject to copyright or in applying designs, manufacturing methods, plans, processes or techniques that are new or have been improved then you must have signed an agreement that relates to the protection of all such material ("the Intellectual Property"). You agree that you will keep confidential all such information and will promptly disclose to the Company all such Intellectual Property whether made by yourself or in conjunction with others during the course of, or arising out of, your employment. You will hold in trust for the Company all such Intellectual Property and will take whatever lawful steps the Company requires to assign the Intellectual Property to the Company and ensure that it is lawfully vested in the Company. Where it is necessary to secure a patent to protect the Intellectual Property or to take any other steps you will render all assistance and do everything that is necessary to assist the Company in obtaining such protection. The use of the Intellectual Property is at the absolute discretion of the Company.

In any event by signing your Statement of Written Terms and Conditions you agree to be bound by the terms of the Agreement, which is described as the "Intellectual Property Agreement". For the avoidance of doubt about its contents the terms of that Agreement are set out hereafter.

Precedent Q4:   Intellectual Property Agreement

You agree that during the course of your employment your job functions may require you to assist, participate or otherwise be involved in the creation or improvement of designs, plans, manufacturing methods, processes or techniques in relation to new or improved inventions relating to the Company's business. For the purposes of this Agreement the term "Intellectual Property" shall mean every design, development, discovery, formula, improvement or process ("the inventions") and every work or design in which copyright may exist, including moral rights as defined in the Copyright Designs and Patents Act 1988.

Should you make an invention in the course of the normal duties of your employment or in relation to duties that have been specifically assigned to you but would not otherwise have been your normal duties or where the invention was made in the furtherance of the Company's undertaking then all such inventions will belong to the Company and all Intellectual Property made during the course of your duties will so vest in the Company to the absolute extent that is permitted by law.

You agree that you will forthwith notify to the Company all Intellectual Property which you may make during your employment, whether made by yourself or with other persons and you will keep the Company appraised at all times of the stage that has been reached in relation to any improvement or creation of such Intellectual Property.

You agree that you will take all steps and carry out all acts that may be necessary to ensure that the Intellectual Property is lawfully vested in the Company, including signing all applications and any other documents that may be necessary to apply for any Patent rights or any other form of application in the United Kingdom and Worldwide and to transfer the entire rights and interests in the Intellectual Property to the Company and you will carry out such acts and steps with expedition on the instructions of the Company, in particular, where the filing of any claim to such Intellectual Property right may give the Company priority.

You will not be entitled to payment in respect of any Intellectual Property other than your normal provisions for remuneration. However, if you are entitled to additional compensation by section 40 of the Patents Act 1977 the Company will pay this to you and your rights under sections 39 to 43 of the Patents Act 1977 are recognised. The Company will incur any expenses to enable you to comply with the provisions of clause 4 herein.

These provisions remain in force with regard to Intellectual Property notwithstanding the termination of your employment.

Precedent Q5: Model Restrictive Covenants

Acknowledgements

1   In entering into employment with the Company the Employee recognises and acknowledges that:

(1) The Company [and each Company in the Group] possesses Confidential Information that is important to the business of the Company [Group].

(2) The Company will give the Employee access to such Confidential Information in order that he may carry out his duties.

(3) The Employee has a duty to act at all times in the best interest of the Company and owes duties of fidelity and trust and confidence to the Company.

(4) The Employee will directly benefit from access to the Confidential Information as it will enable him to carry out his duties or to make sales and to earn commissions thereon.

(5) Other employees are required to accept restrictions which are similar to those set out herein or are appropriate to the employees and which are for the mutual protection of the Company and of the Employee's position.

(6) Disclosure of Confidential information to any Customer, Supplier or actual or potential competitor is likely to place the Company or Group at a competitive disadvantage or otherwise cause immeasurable financial or other harm to the business of the Company or Group.

(7) That if the Employee were to take up or hold a position with any Competitor of the Company or Group this would be likely to likely to place the Company or Group at a competitive disadvantage or otherwise cause immeasurable financial or other harm to the business of the Company or Group.

Confidentiality

Precedents Q1 and Q2 should be incorporated.

Non Poaching of Employees

The Employee will not at any time during his employment and for a period of [...] months after the termination of his employment seek to entice, persuade, solicit or employ, or provide any work, whether directly or indirectly, through any company firm, person or other entity, or for the benefit thereof, or agree to provide any such work to any person who was for the period of [...] months employed or engaged by the Company and who by reason of his employment is likely to be a position to solicit or deal with Customers or Suppliers of the Company or to cause harm to the Company or

Group if he should accept work from any business which is in competition with the Company or Group.

Post Termination Restrictions

The Employee shall not, whether directly or indirectly, and whether through any company, firm, person or other entity, and whether as Employee, servant or agent or otherwise, howsoever:

1   For a period of [...] months after the termination of his employment, in relation to any business which is or is likely to be wholly or partly in competition with the business of the Employer [or Group]:

   1.1.   the Employee shall not hold any position as director, officer, employee, consultant, partner, principal or agent, which is the same as or similar to the position that he held when he was an employee of the Company [or Group], or which will or may involve him using Confidential Information in order to fulfil the duties of that position;

   1.2.   the Employee shall not have any direct or indirect control or ownership of any shares or debentures, whether jointly or alone in any such business, save for investment purpose or not more than [...]% of the issued ordinary shares of any Company;

   1.3.   the Employee shall not give financial assistance whether directly or indirectly to any such business.

2   For a period of [...] months after the termination of his employment, in relation to any business that which is or is likely to be wholly or partly in competition with the business of the Employer [or Group] the Employee shall not hold any position as director, officer, employee, consultant, partner, principal or agent, which is the same as or similar to the position that he held when he was an employee of the Company [or Group] where that position requires or might be reasonably thought by the Employer to require him to disclose or make use of any Confidential Information belonging to the Employer in order to carry out his duties or to promote or further such business. For this purpose Confidential Information shall mean [LIST].

3 For a period of [...] months after the termination of his employment the Employee shall not, whether directly or indirectly, or as servant, agent or otherwise howsoever:

3.1. Solicit, canvass, procure orders from or otherwise seek to obtain business from customers or clients who were customers or clients of the Employer at any time during the period of [...] months prior to the termination of the Employee's employment and with whom the Employee dealt or had contact during that period.

3.2. Solicit from or place orders with or otherwise seek to obtain business from suppliers who were suppliers of the Employer at any time during the period of [...] months prior to the termination of the Employee's employment and with whom the Employee dealt or had contact during that period.

3.3. Seek any business, orders or custom in relation to any products or services provided by the Employer with which the Employee was concerned during the time he was employed by the Employer.

3.4. Deal with or otherwise accept business from customers or clients who were customers or clients of the Employer at any time during the period of [...] months prior to the termination of the Employee's employment and with whom the Employee dealt or had contact during that period.

3.5. Deal with, or otherwise have contact with, suppliers who were suppliers of the Employer, in relation to products supplied or to be supplied to the Employer, at any time during the period of [...] months prior to the termination of the Employee's employment and with whom the Employee dealt or had contact during that period.

3.6. Accept business from customers or clients who were customers or clients of the Employer at any time during the period of [...] months prior to the termination of the Employee's employment and with whom the Employee dealt or had contact during that period.

3.7. Induce or attempt to persuade, procure or otherwise facilitate employees of the Employer to leave their employment or to accept employment with any business that is wholly or partly in competition with the Employer.

4   The Employee shall not:

4.1.   At any time after the termination of his employment represent or hold himself out as being in any way connected with the Employer or any Group Company.

4.2.   At any time after the termination of his employment disclose to any person, firm, or company or otherwise howsoever any Confidential Information belonging to the Employer or any Group Company.

5   For the purpose of the above covenants Confidential Information shall mean [list] ... provided that the Employee is able to use his own personal expertise and information that has come into the public domain.

6   Each of the above clauses is independent and severable and shall be regarded as separately enforceable. If any provisions are unenforceable but would be enforceable if any parts were deleted then the parties agree that such words must be deleted in order to make them enforceable.

COMMENTARY TO Q: RESTRICTIONS DURING AND AFTER EMPLOYMENT

The employer will want to protect his business during the period that the employee is employed and, so far as he can, for some time after the termination of the employment of the individual employee. It is vital that the employer has in place covenants that are clearly enforceable by the courts. Where the covenants are dubious at first instance then interim relief may be refused and the employer limited to his remedy in damages (see **Wincanton Limited v Cranny** [2000] IRLR 716). The nature of the interest to be protected must be sufficiently clearly defined. Where it is alleged that the employee has access to Confidential Information then such information needs to be specified in the covenant.

The Precedents in Q cover each stage of the employment relations and thereafter, as well as taking into account matters such as Confidential Information and Intellectual Property Rights. These comprise:

Q1:   Working exclusively for the Employer whilst the employment relationship is ongoing;

Q2:   Protection of Confidential Information;

Q3:   Intellectual Property;

Q4:   Intellectual Property Agreement;

Q5:   A detailed restrictive covenant relating to non-poaching, confidentially and non-competition after employment has terminated.

Precedent Q1: Employment that conflicts with your duties

There will be an implied term between the employer and employee whereby the employee owes a duty of fidelity. This will mean that competing with an employer whilst the employment relationship subsists will be a breach of duty (**Thomas Marshall (Exports) Limited v Guinle** [1978] ICR 905) and this will be so even if the activities are carried out in the employee's spare time where they affect the business of the employer (**Beloff v Pressdram Limited** [1973] 1 All ER 241; **Hivac Limited v Park Royal Scientific Instruments Limited** [1946] Ch 169; **Lancashire Fires Limited v S A Lyons & Co Limited** [1996] FSR 629). Precedent Q1 makes it clear that the employee will not be permitted to act in any way that does create a conflict but must devote his whole duties to the employer.

Where the nature of the work is such that the employee could not assist a competitor it is unlikely that the employee will breach the implied duty of fidelity by working for another company in the employee's spare time (**Nova Plastics Limited v Froggatt** [1992] IRLR 146 where the employee was an odd job man).

Precedent Q2: Confidential Information

An employer is entitled to protect information that is confidential to itself. It is a matter of law as to whether the information is in truth confidential. A mere assertion that it is confidential may not make it so. The leading case is **Faccenda Chicken Limited v Fowler** [1986] ICR 297. In that case the test was laid down as follows:

"The relevant principles of law to be applied to the use by an employee of information acquired during his employment can be stated as follows:

(1) Where the parties are, or have been, linked by a contract of employment, the obligations of the employee are to be determined by the contract between him and his employer.

(2) In the absence of any express term, the obligations of the employee in respect of the use and disclosure of information are the subject of implied terms.

(3) While the employee remains in the employment of the employer the obligations are included in the implied term which imposes a duty of good faith or fidelity on the employee.

(4) The implied term which imposes an obligation on the employee as to his conduct after the determination of the employment is more restricted in its scope than that which imposes a general duty of good faith. The obligation not to use or disclose information may cover secret processes or manufacture such as chemical formulae, or designs or special methods of construction, and other information which is of a sufficiently high degree of confidentiality as to amount to a trade secret. The obligation does not extend, however, to cover all information which is given to or acquired by the employee while in his employment, and in particular may not cover information which is only "confidential" in the sense that an unauthorised disclosure of such information to a third party while the employment subsisted would be a clear breach of the duty of good faith.

(5) In order to determine whether any particular item of information falls within the implied term so as to prevent its use or disclosure by an employee after his employment has ceased, it is necessary to consider all the circumstances of the case. The following matters are among those to which attention must be paid:

(a) The nature of the employment. Thus employment in a capacity where "confidential" material is habitually handled may impose a high obligation of confidentiality because the employee can be expected to realise its sensitive nature to a greater extent than if he were employed in a capacity where such material reaches him only occasionally or incidentally.

(b) The nature of the information itself. Information will only be protected if it can properly be classed as a trade secret or as material which, while not properly to be described as a trade secret, is in all the circumstances of such a highly confidential nature as to require the same protection as a trade secret *eo nomine*. Therefore, the court could not accept the suggestion by the judge below that an employer can protect, by means of a restrictive covenant, the use of confidential information which has become part of the employee's own skill and knowledge, even though it does not include either a trade secret or its equivalent. Restrictive covenant cases demonstrate that a covenant will not be upheld on the basis of the status of the information which might be disclosed by the former employee if he is not restricted, unless it can be regarded as a trade secret or the equivalent of a trade secret. It is impossible to provide a list of matters which will qualify as trade secrets or their equivalent. Secret processes of manufacture provide obvious examples, but innumerable other pieces of information are capable of being trade secrets, though the secrecy of some information may be only short-lived. In addition, the fact that the circulation of certain information is restricted to a limited number of individuals may throw light on the status of the information and its degree of confidentiality.

(c) Whether the employer impressed on the employee the confidentiality of the information. Thus, though an employer cannot prevent the use or disclosure merely by telling the employee that certain information is confidential, the attitude of the employer towards the information provides evidence which may assist in determining whether or not the information can properly be regarded as a trade secret.

(d) Whether the relevant information can be easily isolated from other information which the employee is free to use or disclose. The separability of the information in question is not conclusive, but the fact that the alleged "confidential" information is part of a package and that the remainder of the package is not confidential is likely to throw light on whether the information in question is really a trade secret.

In the present case, neither the sales information as a whole which the Defendants had acquired while in the employ of the Claimants (the names and addresses of customers, the most convenient routes to be taken to reach individual customers, the usual requirements of individual customers, the days of the week and times of day when deliveries were made to individual customers, and the prices charged to individual customers) nor their knowledge of the prices charged to individual customers looked at by itself, fell within the class of confidential information which an employee is bound by an implied term of his contract of employment or otherwise not to use or disclose after his employment has come to an end. The argument on behalf of the Claimants that any information about the prices charged to individual customers was confidential, and that, as this information formed part of the package of sales information, the package taken as a whole was confidential too, could not be accepted. Although in certain circumstances information about prices can be invested with a sufficient degree of confidentiality to render that information a trade secret or its equivalent, in the present case the following factors led to the conclusion that neither the information about prices nor the sales information as a whole had the degree of confidentiality necessary to support the Claimants' case: the sales information contained some material which the Claimants conceded was not confidential if looked at in isolation; the information about the prices was not clearly severable from the rest of the sales information; neither the sales information in general, nor the information about prices in particular, though of some value to a competitor, could reasonably be regarded as plainly secret or sensitive; the sales information, including the information about prices, was necessarily acquired by the defendants in order that they could do their work and each salesman could quickly commit the whole of the sales information relating to his own area to memory; the sales information was generally known among the van drivers who were employees, as were the secretaries, at quite a junior level, so that this was not a case where the relevant information was restricted to senior management or to confidential staff; there is no evidence that the Claimants had ever given any express instructions that the sales information or the information about prices was to be treated as confidential."

The above passage is worth citing in full, since it contains a clear and comprehensive statement of the law in this area (see also **Lock International PLC v Beswick** [1989] 1 IRLR 1268; **Wallace Bogan v Cove** [1997] IRLR 453 and **Brooks v Oyslager OMS (UK) Limited** [1998] IRLR 590 in each case where the information was found not to be really confidential).

Some doubts have been expressed over whether a clause can protect information which is merely confidential (See **Balston Headline Filters Limited** [1987] FSR 330 and **Systems Reliability v Smith** [1990] IRLR 377). However, the *Faccenda* decision has been extended to include confidential information of a non-technical or non-scientific nature: **Lansing Linde v Kerr** [1991] IRLR 80). In *Linde* a trade secret was described by Staughton LJ:

"A "trade secret" is information used in a trade or business which, if disclosed to a competitor, would be liable to cause real or significant damage to the owner of the secret. In addition, the owner must limit the dissemination of it or at least not encourage or permit widespread publication. Trade secrets can thus include not only secret formulae for the manufacture of products but also the names of customers and the goods they buy."

Butler-Sloss LJ stated:

"In the age of multinational businesses and worldwide business interests, information may be held by very senior executives which, in the hands of competitors, might cause considerable harm to the companies employing them. "Trade secrets" has to be interpreted in the wider context of highly confidential information of a non-technical or non-scientific nature, which may come within the ambit of information the employer is entitled to have protected, albeit for a limited period."

In **AT Poeton (Gloucester Plating) Limited v Horton** [2000] ICR 1208 information relating to a technological process was not so confidential as to amount to a trade secret.

The precedent aims to set out clearly what the employer may or may not do.

Even if there is a confidentiality clause the employee cannot be restrained from using his or her skill or knowledge acquired during employment as the Court will only restrain the employee where the information "can fairly be regarded as a separate part of the employee's stock of knowledge which a man of ordinary honesty and intelligence would recognise to be the property of his old employer and not his own to do as he likes with: **Printers and Finishers Ltd v Holloway** [1965]1 WLR 1 at 5A–C. See also **FSS Travel and Leisure Systems Limited v Johnson** [1998] IRLR 382 from which it is apparent that intricate knowledge of computer systems gained whilst in employment can nevertheless be regarded as part of skill and knowledge.(*C.f.* **Norbrook Laboratories Ltd v Smyth** (unreported 30.9.1986, High Court NI)). The fact that the employee may be able to retain knowledge in his head does not prevent it from being the property of the employer, as in **SJB Stephenson Limited v Mandy** [2000] IRLR 233 where information relating to the affairs of the company or a client could be protected. (*C.f.* **Lancashire Fires Limited v SA Lyons Limited** [1997] IRLR 113).

Business plans may not be confidential so that an express term should be included if they are to be protected (see **Berkeley Administration Inc v McClelland** [1990] FSR 505).

It is necessary to list the confidential information. It was stated in **Malden Timber Ltd v Leitch** (Unreported 6.8.1999 Court of Session) that one cannot stipulate for the protection of confidential information and then leave it to the court to find content for that expression. The court is likely to find the restrain to be too wide if there is wide and unqualified terminology (See also **Hinton & Higgs (UK) Limited v Murphy and Valentine** [1989] IRLR 519).

Precedents Q3/4: Protection of Intellectual Property

It is outside the scope of this book to consider the law relating to intellectual property rights but, in order to explain why Precedent Q4 is necessary it is worth considering section 39 of the Patents Act 1977 and a case arising therefrom which is a good illustration.

Under section 39 of the Patents Act 1977 an invention will be taken as belonging to the employer where:

- it is made in the course of the employee's normal duties or of duties specially assigned to him, in circumstances such that the invention might reasonably be expected to result from the carrying out of those duties; or

- it was made in the course of the employee's duties and, at the time, (because of the nature of his duties and the particular responsibilities arising out of them) there was a special obligation to further the employer's undertaking.

The employee may, in certain circumstances, be awarded compensation where the invention was of outstanding benefit to the employer (sections 40 and 41).

In **Reiss Engineering Co Limited v Harris** [1985] IRLR 232 the employee was taken on as a fitter by a company that sold valves and was eventually promoted to sales manager. It had no research and design facilities and had never designed, modified or improved any valve. If there were problems it would refer to its supplier. Mr Harris was given notice of redundancy and during this period he invented and designed a new kind of valve that was an improvement on the valves sold by the employer. The employer claimed that the invention belonged to them under section 39 of the Patents Act 1997. Falconer J rejected the claim. He held that the invention was not made in the course of the employee's normal duties such that an invention might reasonably be expected to result from the carrying out of the duties (section 39(1)(a)) and that there was no special obligation to further the employer's interests within the meaning of section 39(1)(b). Mr Harris had never been employed to design or invent and his duty was to sell valves and to deal with after sales service. He had no special duty beyond this to further the interests of the employer.

Precedent Q4 sets out clearly when the employee is to be under the duties contained in section 39 and seeks to protect the employer's position.

Precedent Q5: Model Restrictive Covenants

Precedent Q5 is intended to be a model restrictive covenant that provides for all eventualities upon termination of employment, and as such it contains restrictions relating to:

- Confidentiality;

- Non poaching of employees;

- Non competition by having an interest in a competing business;

- Non solicitation;

- Non dealing.

Each of these will be considered in turn. However, it must be noted that the starting point is that such covenants are prima facie in restraint of trade and will only be enforced if they are regarded as reasonable. There is a vast amount of case law on this area and a summary can only be provided in the space of this book (see Brearly and Block QC, *Employment Covenants and Confidential Information* [2nd Edition] which runs to some 378 pages). The restriction must be no wider than that needed to protect the employer (**Office Angels Limited v Rainer-Thomas** [1991] IRLR 214).

The covenant must be carefully tailor-made to the employee's position and there are a number of general factors which will be taken into account in considering this:

- The subject matter of the restraint. There must be a legitimate business interest to protect (See **Cantor Fitzgerald (UK) Limited v Wallace** [1992] IRLR 215).

- The nature of the employee's work and whether it gives him access to confidential information or contact with customers.

- The class of customers: if customers include those who have not dealt with the employer for some time or with whom the employee has no contact this may be unreasonable (**Marley Tile Co Limited v Johnson** [1982] IRLR 75 and see **International Consulting Services UK Limited v Hart** [2000] IRLR 227);

- The period of restriction. Each case will turn on its own facts as to whether the period of restraint is reasonable (**D v M** [1996] IRLR 192 – three years too long).

- Which activities are covered: if the employee worked in one particular area he should not be prevented from working across the whole spectrum of the employer's business (see *Wincanton*). In **A Mont (UK) Limited v Mills** [1993] a restriction against working in any sector of the tissue industry was too wide as it prevented the employee from working in any capacity whatsoever. Where the employer seeks to restrain the employee from working in areas in which the employer does not have a business interest this will almost certainly be too wide (**Scully UK Limited v Lee** [1998] IRLR 259).

- Where it will be difficult for an employee not to pass on information (whether knowingly or otherwise) a restriction may be regarded as reasonable (**Polylina Limited v Finch** [1995] FSR 751) not least because of the difficulty of policing the employee.

- Where business is at an advanced state of preparation (maturing business opportunity) a clause may be upheld (**Dawnay Day & Co Limited v De Braconier D'Alphen** [1997] IRLR 442).

Acknowledgements

It is sensible to contain an acknowledgement as to the fact that confidential information is bring provided as this brings the situation clearly to the attention of the employee.

Confidentiality

See Q2.

Non-Poaching of employees

Although a covenant of this nature was struck down in **Hanover Insurance Brokers Limited v Shapiro** [1994] IRLR 82 another division of the Court of Appeal upheld the covenant in **Ingham v ABC Contract Services Limited** [12.11.1993] and such a clause is likely to be upheld provided that it is not too generalised. It appears to be now settled by **Dawnay Day & Co v de Braconier d'Alphen** [1997] IRLR 442 that this is an interest that can be protected.

Non-Competition

Clauses 1 and 2 of the Post Termination Restrictions seek to prevent the employee from holding an interest in a competing business and, in the case of clause 2, where he may use confidential information. The former is a dubious clause as it may go to pure competition but where there is a risk of confidential information being used or where customers are not readily identifiable so that it is difficult to police a non-dealing or solicitation clause then such a clause may be valid (see **Lansing Linde Limited v Kerr** [1991] ICR 428; **Dawnay Day & Co Limited v de Braconier d'Alphen** [1997] IRLR 442).

A non competition covenant or a covenant restraining the employee from working for a competitor may be too wide if other covenants will suffice (**Firepond (UK) Limited v Stubbs** (unreported 15 August 2002).

Non-solicitation

Clauses 3.1. to 3.3. are aimed at preventing non-solicitation of customers and suppliers. These covenants are more likely to be upheld where they relate to those with whom the employee had dealings for a limited time before termination of employment (see **G W Plowman & Son v Ash** [1964] 1

WLR 568; **Dentmaster (UK) Limited v Kent** [1997] IRLR 636 and **International Consulting Services (UK) Limited v Hart** [2000] IRLR 227 for examples). The aim of the covenant will be to prevent the employee from using his personal influence over the employer's customers (**Stenhouse Australia Ltd v Phillips** [1974] 1 All ER 117). The restraint should relate to those clients with whom the employee dealt (Office Angels).

It is necessary that there be a solicitation so that a letter which does no more than inform clients that an employee has left his employer may not be a breach (**Taylor Stuart v Croft** (*Law Society Gazette* 22nd October 1997 at page 56). See also **Ward-Evans Financial Services Limited v Fox** [2002] IRLR 120 – no solicitation where the client merely took the business away and gave it to the former employee.

The covenant must be sufficiently clear. In **International Consulting Services (UK) Limited v Hart** [2000] IRLR 227 a covenant which prohibited an IT specialist from soliciting any person with whom the employer had had negotiations or which whom he had contact was held to be sufficiently precise and was not too wide given the employee's central and influential position in the Company.

Non-dealing

Clauses 3.4. to 3.6. contain non-dealing covenants. Non-dealing covenants are likely to be upheld where it is difficult to police a non-solicitation covenant (see **John Michael Design PLC v Cooke** [1987] 21 All ER 332; **Marley Tile Co Limited v Johnson** [1982] IRLR 75).

Area Covenants

Where a non-compete covenant is not limited by area it will be regarded as worldwide and this is likely to make it unenforceable (**Commercial Plastics Limited v Vincent** [1965] 1 QB 623 see also **Scully UK Ltd v Lee** [1998] IRLR 259). An area covenant is not likely to be upheld where there are other means of protection (**Office Angels Limited v Rainer-Thomas** [1991] IRLR 214;). If the covenant is expressed to cover an area that is too wide, it will likewise not be upheld (**Greer v Sketchley Limited** [1979] IRLR 445 – covenant which covered the UK too wide where the business interest was in the Midlands; **Spencer v Marchington** [1988] IRLR 392 – 25 mile radius too wide where customers were all in 20 mile radius). A ten mile covenant was upheld in **Hollis & Co v Stocks** [2000] IRLR 712.

Severing the clause

Note that there is a clause at the end of the precedent whereby the covenants can be severed if any part is too wide. The courts will be prepared to blue pencil or sever covenants provided that the independent part left still has meaning, hence the reason that the clauses are broken down in the way they have been drafted (see **Rex Stewart Jeffries Parker Ginsberg Limited v Parker** [1988] IRLR 483; **Hanover Insurance Brokers Limited v Shapiro** [1994] IRLR 82; **Sadler v Imperial Life Assurance Co of Canada** [1988] IRLR 388) but setting out too many overlapping covenants may make the covenant too uncertain to be enforceable (**Linhoff v Petela** 10 February 1997, unreported).

Breach by the employer

Where a party is in breach of contract the other party may treat the contract as repudiated and the obligations under the contract as at an end (**General Billposting Co Limited v Atkinson** [1909] AC 118). In the employment context the employee may assert that the restrictive covenants are no longer binding because of the employer's breach. However, it was stated in **Rock Refrigeration Limited v Jones** [1996] IRLR 675) that the covenants do not necessarily become invalid. In **Campbell v Frisbee** [2002] EWHC 328 (ChD) the Court drew a distinction between restrictive covenants and confidentiality covenants and held that a post termination confidentiality covenant is likely to remain valid (see also the case judgment at [2003] ICR 141).

The breach must go to the root of the contract if it is to render the covenant unenforceable (**CRS Computers v Mackenzie** [EAT 1259/01]).

Since the duty of confidentiality goes to the heart of the contract, a diary for work purposes that is kept by an employee will be the property of the employer (**Lady Archer v Williams** (3 July 2003).

PART R: DISCIPLINARY PROCEDURES

Precedent R: Disciplinary Procedures

R1:	**Short Form Disciplinary Procedure**	**901**
R2:	**Alternative Disciplinary Procedure**	**906**
R3:	**Sample Letters produced by the DTI**	**915**
Commentary:	**Dismissal and Disciplinary Procedures and Grievance Procedures**	**921**

Useful Websites

- ACAS Disciplinary and Grievance Code of Practice

   http://www.acas.org.uk/publications/pdf/CP01.2.pdf

- The DTI Guidance

   http://www.dti.gov.uk/er/resolvingdisputes.htm

Cross References

- Duggan, *Wrongful Dismissal and Breach of Contract*:

  3.6. Express terms of Contractual Disciplinary Procedures and

  6.7. Implied terms of Contractual Disciplinary Procedures.

- Duggan, *Unfair Dismissal*

  Chapter 2: Reasonableness of Dismissal

  Conduct at chapter 6, which considers conduct issues on an A–Z basis.

Precedent R1: Short Form Disciplinary Procedure

1 The following procedure is designed to be fair to all and to ensure that everyone has a chance to put her/his side of the case where a disciplinary matter arises. Its intention is to resolve problems as far as possible without resort to formal sanctions. It applies to all employees.

The procedure is intended to comply with minimum statutory requirements but goes beyond what is required by statute and gives you as an employee additional safeguards in your employment. For example there is no statutory right to a hearing when a written warning is contemplated, but this procedure will permit a hearing in such circumstances. Save that the Company will maintain the irreducible standards provided by statute the Company does reserve the right to modify these procedures in appropriate circumstances.

2 Any breach of the duties set out herein, of the Company's Terms and Conditions, Rules, Policies or Procedures or any other serious breach of contract, misconduct, inefficiency or neglect by you whilst carrying out your duties may be treated as a disciplinary matter. Conduct outside working hours which, in the opinion of the Company, affects the performance of your duties or may bring the Company into disrepute or adversely affect it may also be considered a reason for implementing the procedure set out herein.

Informal stage

3   If your work or conduct is considered unsatisfactory, at the discretion of your Manager an informal meeting may be arranged to explain any short comings and suggest ways of correcting them in the future. This is not part of the formal procedure set out hereafter but ensures that, normally, matters are not raised through the procedure unless they have first of all been discussed informally. If any conduct or breach is considered sufficiently serious the Company in its absolute discretion may move on to the formal procedure set out below.

4   When your Manager raises something with you which she/he feels may lead to the formal procedure being implemented, she/he will write to you confirming the nature of the problem, agreed objectives to remedy it and the time scale within which any breaches must be rectified. These informal warnings may be kept on your file as a record for a period of six months and any further breaches may lead to the formal procedure being implemented.

Formal procedure

5   This will be initiated by the Company if the informal stage fails to result in the desired improvement or in the case of any matter that is considered sufficiently serious. Your Manager will produce a formal written statement setting out the nature of the complaint or breach. This statement will be forwarded to a Director of the Company for his/her consideration. A copy will be given to you in good time for you to consider the contents prior to the meeting referred to below. This statement will set out the reason that the Company is contemplating taking disciplinary action and the nature of the action that is being contemplated.

6   Following production of such a statement the Director [or set out relevant person] will, as soon as reasonably practicable, arrange a meeting with you and with such other persons as he/she may consider necessary. If you do not consider that you have been given reasonable time to prepare for this hearing you should advise [   ] and consideration will be given to allowing you further time. You are entitled as a matter of law to be accompanied by a fellow employee. If the date or time arranged for the meeting is unsuitable you may suggest another date or time within five working days from the hearing date that has been proposed. You may be entitled to call witnesses at such meeting but must first give the Director reasonable notice of the witnesses that you intend to call as it may be necessary to make arrangements to cover the duties of witnesses if they are employed by the Company.

7 After investigating the complaint and taking submissions and evidence from you, any witnesses that you have called and from any other source as necessary, the Director shall decide what action should be taken, and may:

- decide that you are not in breach of your contract of employment;

- consider that there has been a breach which warrants giving you an oral warning that such a breach must not recur;

- in more serious cases issue a formal written warning that any repetition of the breach may result in your employment being terminated;

- terminate the employment on notice (but only where you have been advised that this is a possible sanction that the Company is considering).

- terminate the employment without notice where your breach of contract is considered sufficiently serious to warrant summary dismissal (but only where you have been advised that this is a possible sanction that the Company is considering otherwise the Company may adjourn the procedure in order to provide you with further information as to why it is considering such action and arrange for another hearing to take place).

8 The decision will be communicated to you and confirmed in writing. Any warning will indicate the breaches of your employment contract and what steps you must take to prevent a repetition of such breach. If you are dissatisfied with that decision you may appeal against it to the [Managing Director]. Such appeal must be made in writing to the [Managing Director] within a reasonable period which shall be regarded as [ ] days of receiving written confirmation of the decision. You should set out your reasons or other submissions you may wish to make in the appeal.

- Where the disciplinary sanction involved warnings the Managing Director may require such submissions to be supplemented orally or in writing as he considers appropriate.

- Where the sanction was dismissal, suspension without pay, demotion or some other similar sanction, an appeal hearing shall be arranged as soon as is reasonable and normally within [   ] days. You will be entitled to be accompanied at the appeal and make such representations as you consider appropriate [CONSIDER IF APPEAL IS A REHEARING].

9 On receipt of notice of your appeal the [Managing Director] shall be entitled to seek such other submissions, orally or in writing, from you or such other persons as he may think fit. You shall be entitled to make representations in relation to any further submissions. The [Managing Director] shall then either confirm the decision or substitute it by such decision that is considered appropriate within a reasonable period.

10 In considering whether termination of your contract of employment is appropriate the following matters will be taken into account:

You will not normally be dismissed for breach unless it is of a serious nature. Examples of serious misconduct which is likely to lead to your contract being terminated are:

- violence or verbal abuse towards fellow employees;

- giving information about the Company to third parties without permission or otherwise disclosing or assisting in the disclosure of information gained or overheard in the course of your employment where the information is likely to harm the interests of the Company;

- serious insubordination;

- sexual, racial, religious, harassment based on sexual orientation or other harassment;

- deliberate damage to the Company's property;

- inability or physical incapability of carrying out your duties due to the influence of drugs or alcohol;

- criminal conduct in relation to the Company, including driving Company vehicles whilst using a mobile telephone;

- conduct likely to bring the Company into disrepute (either inside or outside working hours);

- dishonesty.

It must be stressed that this is not an exhaustive list and summary dismissal may follow where the gravity of the offence is considered to warrant this sanction.

11 The following are examples of misconduct that may lead to a warning and, unless rectified, could lead to dismissal:

- unauthorised absence from work;

- lateness;

- inappropriate standard of dress;

- smoking on the Company's premises otherwise than in accordance with this manual;

- time wasting;

- use of the Company's telephones or photocopiers other than in accordance with this manual.

If your performance remains unsatisfactory after written notice of breach and of the improvements required and the period of time within which it is expected that they should be achieved, or if further breaches occur, you may be dismissed. You will be entitled to the benefit of the procedures set out above if further disciplinary sanctions are invoked.

The Company reserves the right, however, to dismiss without warning where the breaches of your contract of employment are considered sufficiently grave or irredeemable but will not do so until you have had an opportunity to make representations as set out in this procedure document.

Precedent R2: Alternative Disciplinary Procedure

1   You recognise that it is necessary for the Company to maintain a standard
of discipline conversant with good industrial relations practice and that
the appropriate standard of work is maintained in relation to your
employment. The Company has separate disciplinary policies in relation
to alcohol and drug abuse, equal opportunities, sexual harassment and
public interest disclosure but the procedures set out in this section may be
implemented should it be considered that you may be guilty of any act of
misconduct (including matters relating to the other procedures) or your
standard of work or attendance become unacceptable.

**The procedure is intended to comply with minimum statutory
requirements but goes beyond what is required by statute and
gives you, as an employee additional safeguards in your
employment. For example there is no statutory right to a
hearing when a written warning is contemplated but this
procedure will permit a hearing in such circumstances. Save
that the Company will maintain the irreducible standards
provided by statute the Company does reserve the right to
modify these procedures in appropriate circumstances.**

2   The primary objective of the procedures contained herein is to correct
rather than to punish you and to encourage you to maintain the standards
of attendance, behaviour and performance that are commensurate with
your position. The Company is always there to assist you in your job
should you have any difficulties and you should refer to _____ who will
discuss any problems and counsel you in respect of any assistance that
may be appropriate. The Company regards it of importance that the
procedures contained herein are applied fairly and consistently in
accordance with good industrial relations practice. It must however, be
noted by you that in certain cases your conduct may warrant disciplinary
action in which case the Company will follow the enclosed procedures
wherever possible.

Misconduct

3   If your performance falls below standard or your attendance or behaviour
becomes unacceptable, then, after receiving warnings as set out in this
procedure you may be liable to dismissal. The decision as to whether or
not your performance, attendance or behaviour is unacceptable will be

made by the Company acting as a reasonable employer and no action will be taken until, as a minimum:

- A full investigation has been undertaken.

- You have been advised in writing of the causes for concern and the sanctions that are being considered.

4   The following is a non-exhaustive list of examples of offences which amount to misconduct falling short of gross misconduct:

a)   Absence from work that is unauthorised. For this purpose absence from work will be regarded as unauthorised if you have not complied with the Company absence policy;

b)   Behaviour that is disruptive or which amounts to time wasting or may cause minor loss to the Company;

c)   Breach of safety regulations that is minor;

d)   Lateness for work without good excuse. For this purpose persistent lateness which is minor may amount to misconduct;

e)   Standard of work performance that falls below the expected standard of your post;

f)   Standard or appearance or dress that is not appropriate to the workplace;

g)   Smoking on company premises or in zones where smoking is prohibited. Smoking may in certain circumstances however be regarded as gross misconduct if it brings the Company into disrepute or if you have already been warned about smoking on the Company's premises and the procedure in relation to gross misconduct may then be operated.

Gross Misconduct

5   If the Company reasonably forms the view that you are guilty of gross misconduct you may be summarily dismissed. The Company will not normally dismiss until it has followed the procedures contained in this procedure unless it takes the view that the conduct was so serious that the only course was to dismiss with immediate effect. In such case you will be provided with written reasons for the dismissal and will be entitled to attend a hearing to appeal against the dismissal in accordance with the appeal stage of this procedure.

6 The following is a non-exhaustive list of examples of offences which the Company will regard as amounting to gross misconduct:

a) Accepting any bribes or any gifts which could be construed as bribes. In the case of any gifts from clients or customers that are of a minor or inconsequential nature this must nevertheless still be cleared with your Manager before you may accept such a gift;

b) Attendance at work whilst intoxicated or influenced by drugs that have not been prescribed to you by a medical practitioner. You must be aware of the Company's policy in relation to alcohol or drug abuse;

c) Being abusive or rude to clients or customers;

d) Breach of rules and regulations relating to health and safety matters that may constitute a danger to the health and safety of yourself, your fellow workers or anyone visiting the premises on Company business;

e) Bringing the Company into disrepute by conduct whether at work or outside;

f) Conviction for any offence that is incompatible with your employment, which may bring the Company in to disrepute or which causes the Company to lose trust and confidence in you;

g) Damaging Company property or the property of any employee with deliberate intent;

h) Discrimination against any fellow workers or clients or customers on the grounds of sex, race, sexual orientation or disability. You must be aware of the Company's policy on discrimination;

i) Dishonesty at work whether or not it will cause the Company loss;

j) Dishonesty outside work that may bring the Company into disrepute or is incompatible with your employment;

l) Failing to adhere to any statutory or regulatory requirements where such failure is wilful or amounts to gross negligence or incapability;

m) Failing to correctly fill out your application or any documents relating to your employment which may affect your qualifications for the job, your ability to carry out the job or may affect the Company's trust and confidence in you;

n) Falling asleep whilst on duty;

o) Falsification of any Company documents whether or not they give you a pecuniary advantage or whether it is likely to cause the Company loss;

p) Harassment on the grounds of sex, race, sexual orientation, disability or for any other reason. You must be aware of the Company's policy on harassment and comply with it at all times;

q) Insubordination to your superiors which is incompatible with your position. Insubordination will be regarded as incompatible if it occurs in front of fellow workers and you must follow the grievance or public interest disclosure procedure if you have a complaint;

r) Misuse of your Company vehicle. It will be a dismissible offence if you drive your vehicle whilst intoxicated. It may be a dismissible offence if damage is caused to your vehicle by reckless or negligent conduct on your part;

s) Negligent behaviour which may be gross or which may affect the Company's trust and confidence in your ability to carry on your job;

t) Use of any confidential information belonging to the Company or of information which the Company considers may cause the Company harm or bring it into disrepute. The Company has a policy on public interest disclosure and encourages its workers to disclose wrongdoing under the terms of its policy. However, use or disclosure of any commercial or other information belonging to the Company is prohibited unless if comes within the Company's Public Interest Disclosure Policy;

u) Use of a mobile telephone whilst you are driving a Company vehicle.

v) Violent behaviour towards fellow workers or clients or customers. This will include physical or verbal behaviour or conduct or words that may be regarded as intimidating.

Right to be Accompanied at a Disciplinary Hearing

7   You have the right to be accompanied at a disciplinary hearing where you have been required or invited by the Company to attend a disciplinary hearing and you reasonably request to be accompanied to the hearing. A hearing will be regarded as a disciplinary hearing if it could result in a formal warning or some other action on the part of the Company or confirmation of a warning or other action.

8   If you make such a request the Company will permit you to have a single companion at the hearing who is employed as a trade union official and is an official who has reasonably been certified as having experience of training in acting as a companion at disciplinary proceedings or who is another worker of the Company.

9   Your companion may be permitted to address the disciplinary panel and make submissions on your behalf and will be permitted to confer with you during the hearing.

10   If your companion is not available at the time that the Company has proposed for the disciplinary hearing you may propose an alternative time for the hearing provided it is a reasonable time and is no further away than five working days after the day that the Company had proposed for the disciplinary hearing, excluding Saturdays, Sundays, Christmas Day, Good Friday or Bank Holidays.

11   If your Companion is a Company worker he may have time off to accompany you to the hearing.

Investigation

12   If there is a concern about your conduct the Company will investigate and for this purpose may, at its discretion, nominate an investigating officer who was not involved in the allegations relating to the disciplinary matters. Where the Company considers it appropriate because of the nature of the offence it may, at its absolute discretion, suspend you from work in which case you will be paid your basic remuneration. This suspension may last as long as any investigation and disciplinary process is continuing.

13 The nature and scope of the investigation will be appropriate to the allegation that is being investigated and the Company, in its discretion may:

1. Require you to attend investigatory hearings for the purpose of being questioned about the allegation(s). Refusal to answer appropriate questions may in itself be regarded as a disciplinary matter.

2. Take witness statements from other individuals that were involved in relation to the allegations or who may assist.

3. Take time to collate documentary or other evidence that may be relevant to the allegations.

14 The Company will ensure that the investigation is carried out as quickly as possible but you will in any event be kept informed of the stage that the investigation has reached and if you have any queries you should address them to [YOUR MANAGER/THE INVESTIGATING OFFICER].

15 Once the investigation has been carried out a decision will be made and you will be informed in writing of the results of the investigation as soon as possible. There are however no time limits relating to the length of the investigation or the time in which you will be so informed.

16 The above procedure is not contractual and may be amended by the Company in its absolute discretion.

Disciplinary concerns

17 If the Company considers that you may have committed a disciplinary offence you will be informed in writing of the allegations against you. [You may be sent witness statements if they have been produced depending on the nature of the allegations.] [You will be given an opportunity to see any witness statements prior to the disciplinary hearing.] [You will be given details of the evidence against you.]

18 You will be given a reasonable opportunity to consider the charges against you before any disciplinary hearing takes place and the date of any hearing will be confirmed to you in writing.

The Disciplinary Hearing

19 The nature and format of the disciplinary hearing will be dependant upon the charges that have been made and are subject to the absolute discretion of the disciplinary panel. However, the following procedures may be adopted:

1. At the outset of the hearing the charges will be read to you and it will be confirmed whether or not you wish to have a companion present. If you wish to have a companion present then he or she will be entitled to address the disciplinary panel and to represent you.

2. You will be informed of the gist of the evidence against you which you will have already received a reasonable period before the hearing. If there is an investigating officer then he may outline the allegations that have been made against you.

3. You or your companion will be permitted to make whatever representations you wish in relation to the allegations.

4. Where witnesses are called you, or your companion, may be allowed to ask questions that are appropriate.

5. Your attention will be drawn to relevant documentary evidence.

6. Where there is an investigating officer he will normally make closing submissions.

7. You or your companion may be permitted to make closing submissions to the panel.

8. The panel will then retire to see if it can reach a decision immediately. However, where the allegations are such that the panel considers it to be appropriate to take further time the hearing may be adjourned pending the decision of the panel.

20 You will be informed as soon as possible of the decision of the panel and in any event within [...] days.

The Disciplinary Sanctions

21 Where the panel decides that your conduct did not amount to gross misconduct you may be subject to the following sanctions:

1. Where the disciplinary offence is minor or your conduct amounts to a failure to attain satisfactory standards you may be issued with a formal verbal warning. This will be administered to you by [your Manager].

2. Where the disciplinary offence or failure to perform satisfactorily is regarded as serious or there have been persistent minor disciplinary breaches a warning in writing may be given to you. This will be administered by [your Manager/Head of Department].

3. Further repetition of disciplinary offences or continued failure to perform satisfactorily may result in a further warning or, if sufficiently serious, a final written warning. You may receive a final written warning before any other warnings if the disciplinary offence is sufficiently serious. The warning will be issued by [your Manager].

4. The warnings will remain on your personnel file as follows:

    •   verbal warning: six months in the absence of any other disciplinary offence

    •   first or second (if it is considered appropriated to issue a second warning that is not final) written warning: 12 months in the absence of any other disciplinary offence

    •   Final written warning: 12 months.

5. These warnings will not be taken into account once they have expired unless they relate to a disciplinary matter that has become repetitive (i.e. alcohol or drug abuse or rudeness to customers or clients).

22 Where you are guilty of gross misconduct or have committed a further disciplinary offence after receiving a final written warning you are liable to be dismissed without notice. In the event of such dismissal you will not receive any pay in lieu of notice and will not be paid any accrued holiday pay.

Appeals

23 If you do not agree with the result of any disciplinary decision you will have the right of appeal provided it is made in writing within [...] days of you being notified. You must set out in full the grounds on which you are appealing the decision, stating whether it is because you disagree with the findings of misconduct or the sanction that was imposed.

24 The appeal will be to [...]. [It will be by way of review of the decision and not a full rehearing.] [The appeal will consist of a full rehearing.]

25 In the case of warnings you only have the right to appeal in writing and there will not be a hearing. You have the right to a hearing before [...] in relation to any other disciplinary sanction and have the right to have a companion present at the hearing as you did with the disciplinary hearing.

26 Where you have been dismissed the date of your dismissal will stand if the appeal is rejected and the date of the termination of your employment will not be the date that your appeal was rejected.

These procedures may be varied, departed from or be regarded as having brought to a conclusion at any stage if you engage in behaviour which is threatening to any person involved in the procedure or to any Company property or which consists of harassment by you of others or the Company has reasonable grounds for believing that the same may occur or reoccur.

MANAGERIAL LEVELS IN DISCIPLINARY PROCEDURE

[It may be sensible to set out the different level at which matters will be heard.]

27 The following levels of management will deal with disciplinary matters:

- Misconduct/Verbal warnings: Manager

- Misconduct/Written or final written warnings: Manager

- Misconduct: Appeal panel consisting of Appeals: [Director, etc.]

Dated

Precedent R3:   Sample letters produced by the DTI

Sample letters for employees

Letter 1: to be set by the employer, setting out the reasons for the proposed disciplinary action or dismissal and arranging the hearing.

Dear ....   Date ....

I am writing to tell you that .... [insert organisation name] is considering dismissing OR taking disciplinary action [insert proposed action] against you.

This action is being considered with regard to the following circumstances: ....
....
....

You are invited to attend a disciplinary hearing on .... at .... am/pm which is to be held in .... where this will be discussed.

You are entitled, if you wish, to be accompanied by another work colleague or a trade union representative.

Yours sincerely

Signed .... Manager

Letter 2: to be sent by the employer after the hearing

Dear ....   Date ....

On .... you were informed that .... [insert organisation name] was considering dismissing OR taking disciplinary action [insert proposed action] against you.

This was discussed in a meeting on .... Following that meeting, it was decided that: [delete as applicable]

> Your conduct/performance/ etc was still unsatisfactory and that you be dismissed

> Your conduct/performance/ etc was still unsatisfactory and that the following disciplinary action would be taken against you ....

> No further action would be taken against you.

I am therefore writing to you to confirm the decision that you be dismissed and that your last day of service with the Company will be .... The reasons for your dismissal are

....
....
....

I am there writing to you to confirm the decision that disciplinary action will be taken against you. The action will be .... The reasons for the disciplinary action are:

....
....
....

You have the right of appeal against this decision. Please [write] to .... within .... days of receiving this disciplinary decision.

Yours sincerely

Signed .... Manager

Letter 3: Notice of appeal hearing

Dear ....   Date ....

You have appealed against your dismissal on ....
confirmed to you in writing on .... Your appeal will be
heard by .... in .... on .... at ....

You are entitled, if you wish, to be accompanied by another work
colleague or a trade union representative.

The decision of this appeal hearing is final and there is no further
right of review.

Yours sincerely

Signed .... Manager

Letter 4: Notice of result of appeal hearing

Dear ....   Date ....

You appealed against the decision of the disciplinary hearing that you be dismissed/subject to disciplinary action [delete as appropriate]. The appeal hearing was held on ....

I am now writing to confirm the decision taken by .... [insert name of the manager] who conducted the appeal hearing, namely that the decision to .... stands/the decision to .... be revoked (specify if no disciplinary action is being taken or what the new disciplinary action is).

You have now exercised your right of appeal under the Company Disciplinary Procedure and this decision is final.

Yours sincerely

Signed .... Manager

Example letters for employees

- Letter 1 – Raising a grievance

- Letter 2 – Request for appeal hearing (grievance procedures)

- Letter 3 – Request for appeal hearing (dismissal or disciplinary action procedures)

Letter 1 – Raising a grievance

Dear ....   Date ....

I am writing to tell you that I wish to raise a grievance.

This action is being considered with regard to the following circumstances:

....

....

....

I am entitled to a hearing to discuss this matter. I am entitled, if I wish, to be accompanied by another work colleague or my trade union representative. Please reply within (not more than 28) days of the date of this letter.

Yours sincerely

Signed .... Manager

Letter 2 – Request for appeal hearing (grievance procedures)

Dear ....   Date ....

On .... I was informed that the Company had decided to
.... based on my grievance of ....
raised on ....

I would like to appeal against this decision. I wish the following
information to be taken into account:
....
....
....

Please reply within x days from the date of this letter.

Yours sincerely

Signed .... Manager

Letter 3 – Request for appeal hearing (dismissal or disciplinary action procedures)

Dear ....   Date ....

On .... I was informed that .... [insert organisation name] was considering dismissing OR taking disciplinary action [insert proposed action] against me.

I would like to appeal against this decision. I wish the following information to be taken into account.

....
....
....

Yours sincerely

Signed .... Manager

COMMENTARY TO R: DISMISSAL AND DISCIPLINARY PROCEDURES AND GRIEVANCE PROCEDURES

The above two precedents set out disciplinary procedures in short and long form. Both sets of procedures are intended to comply with the provisions of the Employment Act 2002 which provides for statutory disciplinary procedures. These provisions come into force on 1 October 2004. The procedures set out above go far beyond the fairly basic requirements of the statutory provisions and a simple procedure can be adopted from the tables in the commentary. However, whilst these basic procedures may be sufficient to satisfy the statute, they are unlikely to be sufficient for an employer who is facing a claim of unfair dismissal. The principles built up in case law over many years remain extant and a reasonable employer must have these in mind in considering the question of reasonableness under section 98 of the Employment Rights Act 1996. The precedents are therefore intended to set out the procedure that the reasonable employer would be expected to follow. This commentary considers the new legislation in some depth with a footnote concerning the steps that a reasonable employer would be expected to take. A full exposition of the topic is way beyond the scope of this book and is found in *Unfair Dismissal* (the conduct chapter alone runs to some 80 pages).

The following commentary is adopted from the very useful Guidance Notes provided by the DTI and the ACAS Code of Practice.

Part 3 and Schedule 2 of the Employment Act 2002 and the Employment Act (Dispute Resolution) Regulations 2004 [SI 2004/752] come into effect on 1st October 2004 and will have a significant impact upon the ability of employees to bring tribunal proceedings as well as the approach that tribunals will take in deciding whether certain dismissals are automatically unfair as well as assessing compensation. Broadly speaking:

- Dismissals will be automatically unfair where employers have failed to follow the statutory dismissal and disciplinary procedures (**DDPs**).

- Employees will be precluded from commencing tribunal proceedings where they have failed to follow the statutory grievance procedures.

- Time limits will be extended where the statutory procedures have been commenced or are ongoing.

- Tribunals will be able to adjust compensation up or down by 10 to 50% where the procedures have not been complied with by employer or employee.

The dramatic effect of the DDPs is somewhat subverted by the fact that they do not apply to oral or written warnings or to suspension on full pay or to constructive dismissals. Since warnings are likely to make up the bulk of disciplinary sanctions short of dismissal, such non-inclusion significantly reduces the scope of application of the new rules. However, if an employer does not follow even the minimal procedures that are set out in the legislation it is easy to conceive that a tribunal will take the view that, for example, a final written warning imposed without any fair procedure which leads to a constructive dismissal is an unfair dismissal on the merits under section 98 of the Employment Rights Act 1996. It is more likely that the provisions which preclude an employee from commencing proceedings before he has utilised the statutory grievance procedures (**GPs**) will have an impact upon the number of tribunal cases that are commenced; indeed that is the hope of the Government as it estimates that the new procedures should entail an annual reduction in tribunal cases of at least 34–37,000 fewer claims (See Government Response to Public Consultation January 2004).

Jurisdiction

Section 29 of the EA 2002 provides that Schedule 2 (which sets out the statutory dispute resolution procedures) shall have effect. It is further provided by section 29(2) that the Secretary of State may by order amend Schedule 2; make provision for the Schedule to apply, with or without modifications, as if any individual of a description specified in the order who would not otherwise be an employee for the purposes of the Schedule were an employee for those purposes; and a person of a description specified in the order were, in the case of any such individual, the individual's employer for those purposes. Before making any such order the Secretary of State must consult with ACAS. The Employment Act 2002 (Dispute Resolution) Regulations 2004 (the Regulations) flesh out the Act by stating when the DDP's and GPs are to be used, the exemptions and exceptions that apply and the consequences of non compliance. The structure of the Regulations is as follows:

- Regulation 2 contains the definitions that are applicable.

- Regulation 3 provides for the application of DDPs.

- Regulation 4 specifies when DDPs are not to apply.

- Regulation 5 sets out when the parties will be treated as having complied with the DDPs.

- Regulation 6 provides for the application of GPs.

- Regulations 7 to 10 sets out when the parties will be treated as complying with the GPs.

- Regulation 11 sets out general circumstances in which both statutory procedures will not apply or will be treated as having been complied with because of the conduct of one of the parties.

- Regulation 12 sets out the consequences of failing to comply with the statutory procedures.

- Regulation 13 sets out the consequences of failing to attend a meeting.

- Regulation 14 confirms that certain questions to obtain information will not be regarded as constituting a statement of grievance.

- Regulation 15 deals with extension of time limits to commence employment tribunal proceedings where either of the procedures is applicable.

- Regulation 16 provides for an exemption from the procedures where there are national security issues.

- Regulation 17 contains consequential amendments to other legislation whilst regulation 18 contains transitional provisions.

ACAS has produced a new Code of Practice on Disciplinary and Grievance Procedures laid before Parliament on 17 June 2004, and formally published on 15th September 2004, whilst the DTI has produced 'Guidance on the Employment Act 2002 (Dispute Resolution) Regulations 2004 and associated provisions in the Employment Act 2002'. The latter publication, in particular, contains clear explanation about the scope and effect of DDPS and GPs.

Statutory Terms

Section 30(1) provides that every contract of employment shall have effect to require the employer and employee to comply, in relation to any matter to which a statutory procedure applies, with the requirements of the procedure. This provision will have effect notwithstanding any agreement to the contrary but will not affect an agreement, which is additional to, and not inconsistent with, the requirements of the statutory procedure (30(2)).

Section 30 provides for statutory terms to be incorporated into contracts of employment. It should be noted, however, that this provision will not be commenced in October 2004. The Government has decided to consider the need to commence this provision in light of the evidence it received evaluating the impact of the Regulations. The review will take place in 2006. (See: *http://www.dti.gov.uk/er/individual/disputeregs_govresp.pdf*)

Dismissal and Disciplinary Procedures

The EA 2002 and the Regulations contain minimum procedural standards where the employer is contemplating dismissal or certain disciplinary action. The procedures:

- Do not come into play until dismissal or relevant disciplinary action is contemplated so that they do not apply during an investigatory process or where the sanction is not a relevant sanction under the legislation.

- Do not negate the employer's duty to act reasonably if the dismissal is to be fair under section 98 of the ERA 1996 so that a dismissal can be unfair even if the statutory DDPs are complied with.

Scope of Disciplinary Procedures

The procedure applies where the employer is contemplating dismissal or action within the meaning of the Regulations. By Regulation 2:

"relevant disciplinary action" means action, short of dismissal, which the employer asserts to be based wholly or mainly on the employee's conduct or capability, other than suspension on full pay or the issuing of warnings (whether oral or written).

It is important to note that the definition does not include warnings, whether oral or written. Strictly speaking, this means that the employer could carry out a disciplinary process that did not go so far as meeting the requirements of advising the employee in writing of the nature of the complaint and/or holding a meeting without being in breach of the legislation. However, it is difficult to conceive of a case where a formal warning would be given without some level or formality, particularly where such warnings may lead to dismissal and it may be dangerous not to adopt a proper process where matters may emerge that are more serious than was at first thought. Whilst it may be explicable that the Government has excluded warnings so that employers do not get bogged down with formality every time a warning is given, for example oral warnings where there are no serious employment consequences, it must not be thought that such exclusion will lead to a relaxation of attitude or expectation from Tribunals about what they will expect during the normal disciplinary process which includes warnings and suspension on pay.

Other sanctions such as demotion, transfer, loss of promotion prospects or suspension without pay will bring the Regulations into play.

Application of dismissal and disciplinary procedures

Regulation 3(1) provides that the standard dismissal and disciplinary procedure applies when an employer contemplates dismissing or taking relevant disciplinary action against an employee. This is subject to a number of exceptions set out in the regulations and to circumstances where the modified procedure will apply. By regulation 3(2) the modified dismissal procedure applies in relation to a dismissal where –

- the employer dismissed the employee by reason of his conduct without notice;

- the dismissal occurred at the time the employer became aware of the conduct or immediately thereafter;

- the employer was entitled, in the circumstances, to dismiss the employee by reason of his conduct without notice or any payment in lieu of notice; and

- it was reasonable for the employer, in the circumstances, to dismiss the employee before enquiring into the circumstances in which the conduct took place.

Thus, where an employee has been summarily dismissed in circumstances where the employer was entitled to summarily dismiss and it was reasonable to dismiss without further inquiry the shorter modified procedure will nevertheless apply. It will be quite rare that the employer will have behaved reasonably and the dismissal be fair where the employee has been summarily dismissed without any form of investigation. However, the DTI Guidance states:

> "15. It is almost always unfair to dismiss an employee instantly, without first going through some form of procedure or carrying out some form of investigation, even in a case of apparently obvious gross misconduct. However, tribunals have occasionally found such dismissals to be fair. The Regulations will allow this possibility to continue for a small minority of gross misconduct dismissals, but even in these cases the employer will be required to use the modified (two-step) dismissal procedure after dismissing."

Neither of the dismissal and disciplinary procedures applies in relation to such a summary dismissal where the employee presents a complaint relating to the dismissal to an employment tribunal at a time when the employer has not complied with paragraph 4 of Schedule 2; that is, has not set out the position in writing. The logic of this is that, the employee, having been summarily dismissed without any form of process, should not be forced to wait to see if the employer intends to comply with the modified procedure but should be entitled to issue tribunal proceedings in relation to his summary dismissal without more.

The Standard Dismissal Procedure

Schedule 2 Part 1 of the Act sets out three steps that the employer must comply with as follows:

Step 1: statement of grounds for action and invitation to meeting

By paragraph 1(1) the employer must set out in writing the employee's alleged conduct or characteristics, or other circumstances, which lead him to contemplate dismissing or taking disciplinary action against the employee. By paragraph 1(2) the employer must send the statement or a copy of it to the employee and invite the employee to attend a meeting to discuss the matter.

Step 2: The meeting

By paragraph 2(1) the meeting must take place before action is taken, except in the case where the disciplinary action consists of suspension. Paragraph 2(2) provides that the meeting must not take place unless—

- the employer has informed the employee what the basis was for including in the statement under paragraph 1(1) the ground or grounds given in it, and

- the employee has had a reasonable opportunity to consider his response to that information.

The employee must take all reasonable steps to attend the meeting. After the meeting, the employer must inform the employee of his decision and notify him of the right to appeal against the decision if he is not satisfied with it (paragraphs 2(3)(4)).

Step 3: The appeal

By paragraph 3(1) if the employee does wish to appeal, he must inform the employer and the employer must invite him to attend a further meeting (3(2)). The employee must take all reasonable steps to attend the meeting (3(3)) though the appeal meeting need not take place before the dismissal or disciplinary action takes effect (3(4)). After the appeal meeting, the employer must inform the employee of his final decision.

The DTI Guidance sets out the above procedure in a useful chart, as follows:

Standard (three-step) dismissal and disciplinary procedure	
Step One	The employer must set down in writing the nature of the employee's conduct, capability or other circumstances that may result in dismissal or disciplinary action, and sends a copy of this statement to the employee. The employer must inform the employee of the basis for his/her complaint.
Step Two	The employer must invite the employee to a hearing at a reasonable time and place where the issue can be discussed. The employee must take all reasonable steps to attend. After the meeting, the employer must inform the employee about any decision, and offer the employee the right of appeal.
Step Three	If the employee wishes to appeal, he/she must inform the employer. The employer must invite the employee to attend a further hearing to appeal against the employer's decision, and the final decision must be communicated to the employee. Where possible, a more senior manager should attend the appeal hearing.

The above standard dismissal and disciplinary procedure will apply when the employer is *contemplating* dismissal which will include dismissal on grounds of capability, conduct, redundancy, non-renewal of a fixed term contract and retirement. Failure to follow the procedure when it applies will make any dismissal automatically unfair.

The procedure will also apply when the employer is contemplating any disciplinary actions short of dismissal in relation to an employee, wholly or mainly by reason of the employee's conduct or capability. However, as noted, it will *not* apply to actions which the DTI Guidance describes as "part of a workplace procedure, i.e. warnings (oral or written) and suspension on full pay. "

Disciplinary suspension, where the employee is suspended without pay or on reduced pay, *will* attract the application of the standard dismissal and disciplinary procedure since the withholding or reduction of pay is a conduct- or capability-related action additional to the suspension itself.

Investigatory suspension on full pay will not trigger the application of this procedure. However, the DTI Guidance notes that if the employee is dissatisfied with this, he/she can initiate the standard grievance procedure.

The following dismissals are covered:

- **Retirement dismissals**

  The three step procedure will apply to compulsory retirement so that where an employer seeks to compulsory retire the employee because of age in circumstances where the employee is entitled to claim unfair dismissal (before the normal retirement age for the job, or before age 65 where there is no such normal retirement age) the three steps must be followed. If retirement is by mutual consent, there is no need to follow the procedures and where the employee cannot claim unfair dismissal (because he is over normal retirement age or 65) then no legal consequences flow from failing to follow the procedure.

- **Fixed term contract dismissals**

  The three-step procedure must be used when dismissal consists of the non-renewal of a fixed term contract. It should be noted that Fixed-term and permanent employees must be treated equally, as required by the Fixed Term Employees (Prevention of Less Favourable Treatment) Regulations 2002, unless differences in treatment can be objectively justified (see Chapter 5). The statutory procedures will apply to both fixed term and permanent employees though in the case of fixed-term contracts of less than one year's duration there will obviously be no right to claim unfair dismissal.

The Modified Dismissal Procedure

The modified dismissal procedure is set out in Schedule 2, Part 1, Chapter 2, as follows:

Step 1: statement of grounds for action

By paragraph 4 the employer must set out in writing:

- the employee's alleged misconduct which has led to the dismissal;

- what the basis was for thinking at the time of the dismissal that the employee was guilty of the alleged misconduct; and

• the employee's right to appeal against dismissal; and

the statement or a copy of it must be sent to the employee.

Step 2: The appeal

By paragraph 5(1) if the employee does wish to appeal, he must inform the employer. If the employee informs the employer of his wish to appeal, the employer must invite him to attend a meeting (5(2)). The employee must take all reasonable steps to attend the meeting (5(3)).

After the appeal meeting, the employer must inform the employee of his final decision (5(4)).

The DTI Guidance sets out the above procedure in a useful chart, as follows:

Modified (two-step) dismissal procedure	
Step One	The employer must set down in writing the nature of the alleged misconduct that has led to the dismissal, the evidence for this decision, and the right to appeal against the decision, and send a copy of this to the employee.
Step Two	If the employee wishes to appeal, he/she must inform the employer. The employer must invite the employee to attend a hearing to appeal against the employer's decision, and the final decision must be communicated to the employee.

The modified dismissal procedure is only to be used only when:

• The employer dismissed the employee without notice based on his or her conduct. Thus, the procedure will only apply to summary dismissals.

• The dismissal took place at the time the employer became aware of the gross misconduct (or immediately after). The clear intention of this rule is that if the employee has known about the conduct for some time and has contemplated dismissal it should have followed the standard procedure.

• The employer was entitled to dismiss for gross misconduct without notice or payment in lieu of notice. In order for the modified procedure to be invoked it is necessary that the employee was guilty of gross misconduct which would have permitted the employer to dismiss.

- It was reasonable for the employer to dismiss without investigating the circumstances.

The modified dismissal procedure must be completed in full if the above criteria are satisfied. Since the employer will take the view that it was reasonable to dismiss, as that is what it has done, the procedure is likely to be applicable in all cases where the employer dismissed for gross misconduct (subject to the exceptions in the regulations, especially regulation 4).

Failure to follow the modified procedure will normally result in any dismissal being automatically unfair.

The modified procedure does not apply if the employee presents his complaint to an employment tribunal before the employer has written to the employee setting out the employee's alleged misconduct that gave rise to the dismissal (see further below).

Requirements common to both DDPS and GPS

The general requirements for the procedures are set out in Parts 3 and 4 of Schedule 2 which apply to both standard and modified procedures in relation to both Dismissal and Disciplinary Procedures and in relation to Grievance Procedures (paragraph 11). It should be noted that when a disabled employee is involved in a statutory dispute resolution procedure, the employer might be required to make "reasonable adjustments" to the process so that the employee is not disadvantaged in any way.

Timetable

By Schedule 2 paragraph 12, each step and action under the procedure must be taken without unreasonable delay. There is no definition of reasonable or unreasonable in the legislation and it will be a matter for the employment tribunal to decide what is reasonable.

Meetings

By Schedule 2 paragraph 13(1), timing and location of meetings must be reasonable. Paragraph 13(2) provides that meetings must be conducted in a manner that enables both employer and employee to explain their cases and, under 13(3), in the case of appeal meetings which are not the first meeting, the employer should, as far as is reasonably practicable, be represented by a more senior manager than attended the first meeting (unless the most senior manager attended that meeting).

Paragraph 15(1), entitled Scope of Grievance Procedures, confirms that the procedures set out in Part 2 are only applicable to matters raised by an employee with his employer as a grievance so that the procedures are only applicable to the kind of disclosure dealt with in Part 4A of the Employment Rights Act 1996 (c 18) (protected disclosures of information) if information is disclosed by an employee to his employer in circumstances where—

- the information relates to a matter which the employee could raise as a grievance with his employer; and

- it is the intention of the employee that the disclosure should constitute the raising of the matter with his employer as a grievance.

The legislation thus seeks to draw a distinction between 'whistleblowing' and complaints where it is intended to bring a grievance.

If the procedures are not started or completed satisfactorily, this will have an impact on the outcome of any subsequent tribunal cases as set out below.

Right to a companion

By Schedule 2, Paragraph 14, status of meetings, it is confirmed that a meeting held for the purposes of Schedule 2 is a hearing for the purposes of section 13(4) and (5) of the Employment Relations Act 1999 (c 26) (definition of 'disciplinary hearing' and 'grievance hearing' in relation to the right to be accompanied under section 10 of that Act). (See below as to definition.)

By section 10 of the Employment Relations Act 1999 where a worker is required or invited by his employer to attend a disciplinary or grievance hearing, and reasonably requests to be accompanied at the hearing, the employer must permit the worker to be accompanied at the hearing by a single companion who is chosen by the worker and

- is employed by a trade union of which he is an official within the meaning of sections 1 and 119 of the Trade Union and Labour Relations (Consolidation) Act 1992;

- an official of a trade union (within that meaning) whom the union has reasonably certified in writing as having experience of, or as having received training in, acting as a worker's companion at disciplinary or grievance hearings; or

• another of the employer's workers.

The ACAS Code at paragraph 103 notes that "it would not be reasonable to insist on being accompanied by a colleague whose presence would prejudice the hearing or who might have a conflict of interest. Nor would it be reasonable for a worker to ask to be accompanied by a colleague from a geographically remote location when someone suitably qualified was available on site. The request to be accompanied does not have to be in writing."

Under the Employment Relations Act 2004 the companion is now permitted to address the hearing in order to do any or all of the following—

(i)   put the worker's case;

(ii) sum up that case;

(iii) respond on the worker's behalf to any view expressed at the hearing;

and to confer with the worker during the hearing.

However, the employer is not required to permit the worker's companion to—

(a) answer questions on behalf of the worker;

(b) address the hearing if the worker indicates at it that he does not wish his companion to do so; or

(c) use his powers in a way that prevents the employer from explaining his case or prevents any other person at the hearing from making his contribution to it.

Where the worker has a right to be accompanied at a hearing but his chosen companion will not be available at the time proposed for the hearing by the employer, and the worker proposes an alternative time which is reasonable, and falls before the end of the period of five working days beginning with the first working day after the day proposed by the employer the employer must postpone the hearing to the time proposed by the worker (sections 10(4)(5) ERA 1999). The ACAS Code states that where possible, employers should allow a companion to have a say in the date and time of a hearing. If the companion can't attend on a proposed date, the worker can suggest another date that must suit everybody involved and must not be more than five working days after the original date. The ACAS Code further states that in the same way that employers should cater for a worker's disability at a disciplinary or grievance hearing, they should also cater for a companion's disability.

The employer must permit a worker to take time off during working hours for the purpose of accompanying another of the employer's workers in accordance with a request under section 10(1).

By section 13(4) and (5) of the Employment Relations Act 1999 for the purposes of section 10:

•   a disciplinary hearing is a hearing which could result in—

    (a) the administration of a formal warning to a worker by his employer,

    (b) the taking of some other action in respect of a worker by his employer, or

    (c) the confirmation of a warning issued or some other action taken.

•   a grievance hearing is a hearing which concerns the performance of a duty by an employer in relation to a worker.

In **Heathmill Multimedia Asp Limited v Jones** [2003] IRLR 856 a meeting to inform an employee that he was to be dismissed for redundancy was held not to come within the meaning of 'some other action'. This may be at odds with the new DDPs which appear wide enough to cover such a situation.

On the other hand, the definition is wider than DPPs in that there is a right to bring a companion when a warning is contemplated.

Rearranging meetings

If the employer, the employee or the employee's companion cannot reasonably attend a Step Two or Step Three meeting for a reason that was not reasonably foreseeable, for example, where one of the parties falls ill, or his/her car breaks down on the way to the meeting, the meeting must be rearranged. If either party did not attend the meeting and the failure could be reasonably foreseen, then neither party will be under any further obligation under the statutory procedures. The tribunal may in those circumstances choose to attribute responsibility for failure, with the commensurate impact on award adjustment.

The employer is obliged to rearrange the meeting once so that if the meeting falls through a second time for unforeseeable reasons, neither party will be under any further obligation under the statutory procedures. In these circumstances, neither party will be held at fault for failure to complete the procedure; therefore award adjustment will not apply. Furthermore, both parties will be treated as having complied with the relevant statutory procedures so, if applicable, the normal time limit for making a tribunal application may be extended. This is made clear by regulation 13, which provides that if it is not reasonably practicable for the employee, or, if he is exercising his right under section 10 of the 1999 Act (right to be accompanied), his companion; or the employer, to attend a meeting organised in accordance with the applicable statutory procedure for a reason which was not foreseeable when the meeting was arranged, the employee or, as the case may be, employer shall not be treated as having failed to comply with that requirement of the procedure (reg. 13(1). Under reg. 13(2), the employer shall continue to be under the duty in the applicable statutory procedure to invite the employee to attend a meeting and, where the employee is exercising his rights under section 10 of the 1999 Act and the employee proposes an alternative time the employer shall be under a duty to invite the employee to attend a meeting at that time.

By Regulation 13(3) the duty to invite the employee to attend a meeting shall cease if the employer has invited the employee to attend two meetings and reg. 13(1) applied in relation to each of them. Where the duty in reg. 13(2) has ceased as a result of reg. 13(3), the parties shall be treated as having complied with the applicable statutory procedure.

Dismissals to which the dismissal and disciplinary procedures do not apply

Regulation 4(1) contains a list of dismissals where the standard and modified dismissal and disciplinary procedures will not apply. According to the DTI Guidance the rationale is that these are dismissals in which the individual characteristics of the employee will play no or no real role in the decision to dismiss and they are often collective dismissals. In those circumstances, accordingly to the DTI, it would not be right, in the context of setting a minimum legal standard, to require the parties to go through the procedures (notwithstanding that the DTI states it will often be good practice for the employer to discuss such dismissals with the employees at an individual level as well as a collective one, and failure to do so may render the dismissal unfair). It would be a foolish employer who departs from the jurisprudence built up over many years as to what a reasonable employer should do if a dismissal is to be fair under section 98 of the ERA 1996. All that regulation 4 does is provide that the DDPs do not apply; it does not mean that other law on unfair dismissal can be ignored.

As the procedures do not apply, any subsequent tribunal claim must be made within the normal time limit for that jurisdiction, since the time limit will not be extended as it would if the procedures applied.

The areas where the DDPs do not apply are as follows:

Dismissal then re-engagement

The DDPs do not apply where all the employees of a description or in a category to which the employee belongs are dismissed, and the employer offers to re-engage all the employees so dismissed either before or upon the termination of their contracts. Regulation 4(2) provides that an employer shall be regarded as offering to re-engage an employee if that employer, a successor of that employer or an associated employer of that employer offers to re-engage the employee, either in the job which he held immediately before the date of dismissal or in a different job which would be suitable in his case.

The DTI Guidance notes that:

> "Dismissal and re-engagement is a widely used mechanism for reissuing contracts or changing terms and conditions of employment. It will not be necessary to go through the statutory procedures before the employer seeks to dismiss all the employees of a description or a category, provided that re-engagement is offered before or on termination of the existing contract. However, the dismissals may still be unfair under the normal unfair dismissal rules, if there was no fair reason for them or the employer acted unreasonably."

Collective redundancies

The DDPs do not apply where the dismissal is one of a number of dismissals in respect of which the duty in section 188 of the Trade Union and Labour Relations (Consolidation) Act 1992 (duty of employer to consult representatives when proposing to dismiss as redundant a certain number of employees) applies. Under the 1992 Act where an employer wishes to make 20 or more employees at the same establishment redundant within a 90-day period, there is a statutory obligation to consult representatives of the affected employees. This particular obligation will not be affected by the statutory dispute resolution procedures as there is no requirement to follow the statutory procedures as well (though the courts have long recognised the need for individual and collective consultation). Where there are redundancies which affect fewer than 20 employees, or where the redundancies will take effect in a period longer than 90 days so that the requirements of TULR(C)A are not applicable, the statutory procedures will apply as usual.

Industrial action dismissals

The DDPs do not apply where at the time of the employee's dismissal he is taking part in –

(i)   an unofficial strike or other unofficial industrial action, or

(ii) a strike or other industrial action (being neither unofficial industrial action nor protected industrial action), unless the circumstances of the dismissal are such that, by virtue of section 238(2) of the 1992 Act, an Employment Tribunal is entitled to determine whether the dismissal was fair or unfair.

By Regulation 4(2) "unofficial" shall be construed in accordance with subsections (2) to (4) of section 237 of the 1992 Act; "strike" has the meaning given to it by section 246 of the 1992 Act; and "protected industrial action" shall be construed in accordance with section 238A(1) of the 1992 Act;

(See further Bowers, Duggan, Read, *The Law of Industrial Action and Trade Union Recognition* [2004] OUP).

The DDPs do not apply where the reason (or, if more than one, the principal reason) for the dismissal is that the employee took protected industrial action and the dismissal would be regarded, by virtue of section 238A(2) of the 1992 Act, as unfair for the purposes of Part 10 of the 1996 Act.

Where an employer seeks to dismiss employees engaged in *lawfully organised* industrial action, the statutory procedures do not apply. Instead, the employer should follow the different statutory requirements set out in the Employment Relations Act 1999. The 1999 Act provides that the employer should take reasonable steps to promote the settlement of the dispute before the employer can fairly dismiss strikers taking lawfully organised industrial action.

See also now the Employment Relations Act 2004. The Government took the view that it would be confusing and inappropriate for the statutory dispute resolution procedures to cut across the operation of the other legislative requirements. The exception to the rule is where the employer makes selective dismissals amongst the strikers, in circumstances where those dismissed could bring an unfair dismissal claim. In these exceptional circumstances, the statutory procedures would apply. In the case of other *unofficial or non-protected* strikes or other industrial action, the employer is not required to follow either the statutory dispute resolution procedures or any other statutory requirements before dismissing or taking other disciplinary action.

The employer's business suddenly and unexpected ceases to function

The DDPs do not apply where the employer's business suddenly ceases to function, because of an event unforeseen by the employer, with the result that it is impractical for him to employ any employees. The example given by the DTI Guidance is that of the business burning down.

Contravening a duty or restriction

The DDPs do not apply where the reason (or, if more than one, the principal reason) for the dismissal is that the employee could not continue to work in the position which he held without contravention (either on his part or on that of his employer) of a duty or restriction imposed by or under any enactment. The DTI Guidance gives the example, of it being unlawful to employ someone with certain medical conditions in a number of industries; or a valid driving licence being necessary where a statutory ban applies. The procedures will not apply but a dismissal could still be unfair where, for example, there was alternative employment available. (But note that there are cases where the EAT has found dismissal to be unfair in the example given; see Duggan on *Unfair Dismissal*.)

Dismissal procedures agreement

The DDPs do not apply where the employee is one to whom a dismissal procedures agreement designated by an order under section 110 of the 1996 Act applies at the date of dismissal. If the employee is covered by such an agreement, the statutory disciplinary procedures will not apply.

Constructive dismissal

Under Regulation 2, 'dismissed' has the meaning given to it in section 95(1)(a) and (b) of the ERA 1996 so that constructive dismissal is not included. Instead, the employee will need to follow either the standard or modified grievance procedure if the individual wishes to make a tribunal claim relating to the constructive dismissal or to take proceedings before the employer has provided the letter setting out the reason for dismissal (see next paragraph).

Exemption for modified dismissal procedure only

Where the employee has been summarily dismissed and presents a complaint to a tribunal before the modified procedure Step One letter is sent the issue of proceedings will effectively forestall the carrying out of the procedure. The Government has taken this approach because it took the view that it would be unfair to leave open the possibility that the employee might be held at fault for failure to complete the statutory procedure if he presented a tribunal complaint before the employer had written, given that the employer might delay writing for some considerable time, or might ultimately fail to write at all. If, however, the employer sends the Step One letter to the employee *before* the employee has presented a tribunal complaint, the procedure must be gone through, and the exemption will not apply. If the employee in those circumstances subsequently presents a complaint before the procedure has been completed, either party may be subject to award adjustment.

Exemptions which apply to both dismissal and disciplinary procedures, and to grievance procedures: threats or harassment

By regulation 11(1) where the circumstances specified in 11(3) apply and in consequence, the employer or employee does not commence the procedure that would otherwise be the applicable statutory procedure, the procedure does not apply. If the relevant procedure has not been started for reasons of significant threat, harassment or not being practical within a reasonable period, then the procedure will not apply. Therefore, in any subsequent tribunal applications, the normal time limits will apply, and, in the case of grievance claims, the admissibility requirements will not apply. The employee may submit a tribunal claim within the normal time limit and is not required to write a Step One grievance letter then allow 28 days.

By regulation 11(2) where the applicable statutory procedure has been commenced, but the circumstances specified in 11(3) apply and in consequence a party does not comply with a subsequent requirement of the procedure, the parties shall be treated as having complied with the procedure. If the relevant procedure has been started but not subsequently completed for reasons of significant threat, harassment or not being practical within a reasonable period, the procedure will apply but the parties are treated as having complied with that procedure *without having to go through the remaining stages*. For example, if during a Step Two meeting, one party becomes violent, there will be no requirement to continue either the meeting or the rest of the procedures. In any subsequent tribunal applications, the time limit for making an application may be extended. In the case of grievances, the employee will have already sent the Step One letter so, provided he or she has then allowed 28 days before submitting a tribunal claim, the admissibility requirements will have been met.

Whether there is a complete exemption from the procedures, or the procedures apply but are regarded as having been complied with will depend on the circumstances. As set out above the significance of this is that where the procedures apply but are regarded as having been complied with, there are time limit extensions for Tribunal claims and, if a grievance is involved, the statutory admissibility conditions must be met.

The circumstances specified in regulation 11(3) are that

- the party has reasonable grounds to believe that commencing the procedure or complying with the subsequent requirement would result in a significant threat to himself, his property, any other person or the property of any other person.

- the party has been subjected to harassment and has reasonable grounds to believe that commencing the procedure or complying with the subsequent requirement would result in his being subjected to further harassment;

   "Harassment" means conduct which has the purpose or effect of –

   (a) violating the person's dignity, or

   (b) creating an intimidating, hostile, degrading, humiliating or offensive environment for him.

Conduct shall only be regarded as having that purpose or effect if, having regard to all the circumstances, including in particular the perception of the person who was the subject of the conduct, it should reasonably be considered as having that purpose or effect.

- it is not practicable for the party to commence the procedure or comply with the subsequent requirement within a reasonable period. This provision will be used in circumstances where there are long-term barriers to either starting or completing the procedures. These issues might include illness, incapacity, and cessation of the employer's business. If it was not practical to either start or complete the procedures within a reasonable period, then neither party will be held at fault for the procedure's failure, and so award adjustment will not apply. However, if any subsequent dismissal has failed to follow the basic principles of reasonableness, then a Tribunal may still find this dismissal to be unfair on ordinary principles.

National security

By regulation 16 where it would not be possible to comply with an applicable statutory procedure without disclosing information the disclosure of which would be contrary to the interests of national security, nothing in the regulations requires either party to comply with that procedure. The provision may impact upon time limits and admissibility since, in relation to a grievance, the employee will normally have sent his Step One letter before the national security issue arises and so admissibility will have been secured and the time limit will be extended. However, if national security issues arise earlier (i.e. before the grievance is raised), then the procedure might never start and there would, therefore, be no need for Step One letter or time limit extension.

Where the parties are treated as complying with dismissal and disciplinary procedures

By regulation 5(1) where either of the dismissal and disciplinary procedures is the applicable statutory procedure in relation to a dismissal, but the employee presents an application for interim relief to an employment tribunal pursuant to section 128 of the 1996 Act (interim relief pending determination of complaint) in relation to his dismissal, and at the time the application is presented:

- the requirements of paragraphs 1 and 2 or, as the case may be, paragraph 4 of Schedule 2 have been complied with (i.e. the letter has been sent and a meeting held in the case of the standard procedure and the letter sent in the case of the modified procedure); but

- the requirements of paragraph 3 or 5 of Schedule 2 have not (i.e. the appeal has not taken place) the parties shall be treated as having complied with the requirements of paragraph 3 or 5 of Schedule 2 (i.e. treated as though an appeal has taken place). This provision is necessary since in relation to dismissals arising out of trade union membership or activities; health and safety; occupation pension trustee; business transfer or redundancy representation; working time; protected disclosure; or right to be accompanied, the employee can make a claim for interim relief. If the tribunal considers it likely that at the full hearing it will uphold the complaint for any of those reasons, the tribunal will either order reinstatement, re-engagement or will make an order for the temporary continuation of the contract of employment. Since an application for interim relief has to be made within 7 days of dismissal, both parties are treated as having complied with the appeal stage of the standard or modified dismissal and disciplinary procedure, if such an application has been made.

By Regulation 5(2) where:

- either of the dismissal and disciplinary procedures is the applicable statutory procedure in relation to the dismissal of an employee or to relevant disciplinary action taken against an employee; but

- at the time of the dismissal or the taking of the action an *appropriate procedure* exists

the employee is entitled to appeal under *that procedure* against his dismissal or the relevant disciplinary action taken against him instead of appealing to his employer, and the employee has appealed under that procedure, the parties shall be treated as having complied with the requirements of paragraph 3 or 5 of Schedule 2 (the appeal paragraphs).

By regulation 5(3) for the purposes of 5(2) a procedure is appropriate if it gives the employee an effective right of appeal against dismissal or disciplinary action taken against him, and operates by virtue of a collective agreement made between two or more employers or an employer's association and one or more independent trade unions. In some industries, employers and trade unions have jointly developed sophisticated dispute resolution procedures which may allow the appeal stage in dismissal cases to be heard by a panel of employer and union representatives. If the procedure has been agreed by two or more employers or an employers' association and at least one independent trade union, and this kind of external appeals panel exists, and if an employee appeals to this body against a dismissal, then the parties will be treated as having complied with the appeal stage in the statutory disciplinary procedure. This exemption applies *only* to the appeal stage of the statutory dismissal and disciplinary procedures so that it will be necessary to follow the earlier steps in full.

As the procedures apply, any subsequent tribunal application may benefit from extended time limits. If the applicant has reasonable grounds for believing a statutory or workplace disciplinary procedure in relation to a particular issue is still ongoing at the point where the normal time limit expires, then the time limit for making a tribunal claim about that matter will be extended by three months.

The effect of the statutory procedures

DPPs and GPs will have a fundamental impact upon the way in which Employment Tribunals will have to approach claims that are made to it under the jurisdictions set out in Schedules 3 and 4. In the case of Grievances, Tribunal proceedings cannot even be commenced, in certain circumstances, unless and until the GP has been instigated. This is considered further below in the section on Grievances. It is necessary to consider:

(1) The effect of failure to comply with a procedure and when this failure will be attributed to one of the parties.

(2) The effect of non-commencement of Grievance procedures (this is considered in the section on Grievances).

(3) The effect of non-commencement or failure to carry through the procedures where one of the exemptions applies.

(4) The relationship between the procedures and other procedures, in particular discrimination questionnaires.

(5) Additional awards that may be made where procedures have not been complied with and other compensation that may be paid.

(6) Extension of time limits in order for procedures to be carried out.

(7) The requirement for Written Particulars.

(8) Overlapping procedures i.e. where disciplinary procedures and grievances procedures have been commenced.

(9) The reversal of the 'Polkey' principle.

Failure of either party to comply with the statutory procedures

By regulation 12(1) if either party fails to comply with a requirement of an applicable statutory procedure, including a general requirement contained in Part 3 of Schedule 2, which sets out the general requirements as to timetabling and meetings, the non-completion of the procedure shall be attributable to that party and neither party shall be under any obligation to comply with any further requirement of the procedure.

This is subject to the provision in regulation 12(2) that where the parties are to be treated as complying with the applicable statutory procedure or any requirement of it, there is no failure to comply with the procedure or requirement.

However, where regulation 11(1) applies so that the procedure that would otherwise be the applicable statutory procedure does not apply, because the circumstances in sub-paragraph (a) or (b) of regulation 11(3) apply (i.e. threats or harassment) and it was the behaviour of one of the parties that resulted in those circumstances applying, that party shall be treated as if the procedure had applied, and there had been a failure to comply with a requirement of the procedure that was attributable to him (regulation 12(3)).

Similarly, by regulation 12(4) in a case where regulation 11(2) applies so that procedures have been commenced but the circumstances in regulation 11(3)(a) or (b) apply (threats or harassment), and it was the behaviour of one of the parties that resulted in those circumstances applying, the fact that the requirement was not complied with shall be treated as being a failure, attributable to that party, to comply with a requirement of the procedure.

The effect of non commencement or failure to carry through the procedures where one of the exemptions apply

Where the parties are not required to go through the relevant statutory procedure the following conditions will apply:

- In relation to a grievance, the employee does *not* have to meet the admissibility conditions set out in section 32 of the Act; and

- The employee must submit a tribunal application *within the normal time limit* for doing so as the time limit extension will not apply.

The DTI Guidance gives the example, of an employee who has a grievance but illness prevents the employee from sending a Step One grievance letter. In this case it is noted that a complete exemption will apply so that any tribunal claim would not be subject to either the admissibility conditions or the time limit extensions.

Where the parties are *treated* as having complied with the statutory procedures (or, where procedures have already been commenced but not completed, with the remaining stages of them), the following conditions will apply:

- In relation to a grievance, the employee *must* meet the admissibility conditions set out in section 32 of the Act; and

- Time limit extensions may also be invoked, if the necessary conditions have been met.

Award adjustments will not generally apply in cases where the parties are not required to follow or are treated as having complied with the statutory procedures. However, if the exemptions apply because one party has subjected the other party to either significant threat or harassment, the Tribunal may find that one party is responsible as provided for in Regulation 12, set out above, and so would be liable to an adverse adjustment of any award made. In a dismissal case where the employer was at fault in this way, the tribunal will also find such a dismissal to be automatically unfair.

The relationship between the procedures and other procedures, in particular discrimination questionnaires

Discrimination legislation provides for the use of questionnaires by employees to gather evidence from their employers about potential discrimination claims. The proposed changes to time limits for submitting tribunal claims will also affect these questionnaires, whose validity is time-limited. Regulation 17 therefore ensures that the time limits for submitting both tribunal claims and discrimination questionnaires remain consistent, and that the information in these questionnaires will be admissible evidence in tribunals where time limit extensions apply.

Adjustment of awards and other compensation that may be paid

Section 31 of the Act provides that failure to complete the statutory dispute resolution procedures will affect subsequent employment tribunal cases under the jurisdictions specified in schedule 3 to the Act, unless either party was otherwise exempt. Section 31(1) (which relates to employee failures) and (2) (which relates to employer failures) requires employment tribunals to increase or decrease compensation by 10 per cent and allows them to do so by up to 50 per cent where the statutory procedures have not been completed and that failure is attributable to one of the parties.

By section 31(4) the duty to adjust the award does not apply where there are exceptional circumstances that would make such an adjustment unjust or inequitable; in those circumstances the tribunal can adjust by a lesser amount or make no adjustment at all.

Regulation 12, considered above, sets out how a tribunal will attribute any failure to complete a procedure.

The DTI Guidance contains the following chart, which illustrates how compensation is to be assessed:

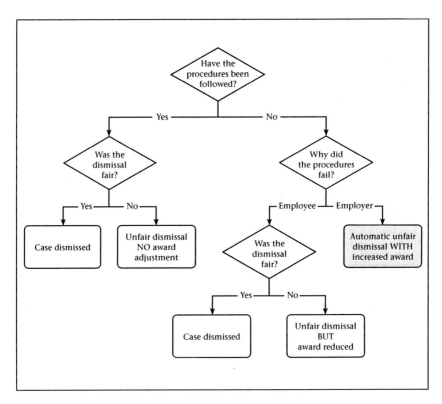

The Guidance sets out the following as 'key' points:

- "If an employer dismisses an employee without completing the statutory dismissal and disciplinary procedure, and if the failure was wholly or mainly attributable to him or her, that dismissal is automatically unfair (subject to any qualifying conditions e.g. the 12 month qualifying period). The dismissed employee will in these circumstances receive at least four weeks' pay in compensation. The tribunal will only specifically award four weeks' pay if it orders reinstatement or re-engagement. If it awards compensation and the basic award is less than four weeks' pay it must increase it to four weeks. If the award is already greater than four weeks' pay, no additional payment will be made for automatically unfair dismissal. Note that any additional compensation for the employee should be increased by 10 per cent and can be increased by up to 50 per cent. In exceptional circumstances compensation may be adjusted by less than 10 per cent.

- However, if an employment tribunal finds a dismissal to be unfair on its substantive merits, but the statutory procedures were completed satisfactorily, there will be no adjustment of awards.

- If the procedure is not completed, because the employee did not meet his/her obligations, any ensuing award will be *reduced* by between 10 per cent and 50 per cent. In exceptional circumstances compensation may be adjusted by less than 10 per cent."

The current limit for a compensatory award for ordinary unfair dismissal is £55,000 (as provided for in section 124(1) of the Employment Rights Act 1996). The new regulations will **not** affect this limit, and any adjustments cannot be made above the limit.

Extension of time limits in order for procedures to be carried out

The DTI Guidance contains the following chart to illustrate the way in which time limits may be extended:

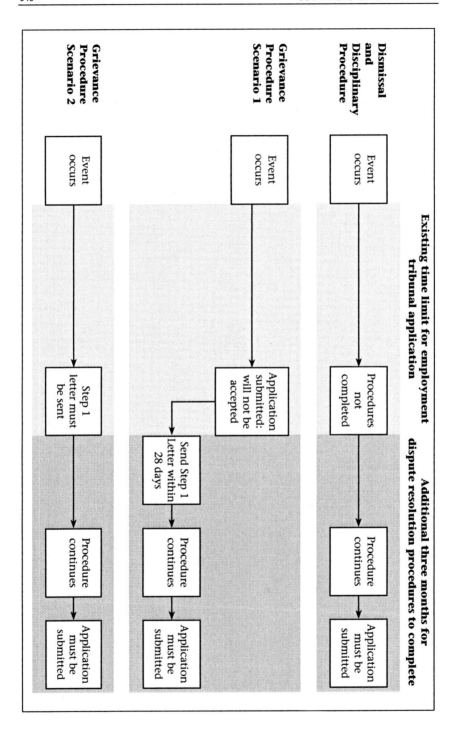

Section 33 of the Act permitted the Secretary of State to make regulations to adjust time limits. By regulation 15(1) where a complaint is presented to an employment tribunal under a jurisdiction listed in Schedule 3 or 4 and either of the dismissal and disciplinary procedures is the applicable statutory procedure and the circumstances specified in regulation 15(2) apply; or either of the grievance procedures is the applicable statutory procedure and the circumstances specified in regulation 15(3) apply, then the normal time limit for presenting the complaint is extended for a period of three months beginning with the day after the day on which it would otherwise have expired.

Regulation 15(2) provides that time is extended in circumstances where the employee presents a complaint to the tribunal after the expiry of the normal time limit for presenting the complaint but had reasonable grounds for believing, when that time limit expired, that a dismissal or disciplinary procedure, whether statutory or otherwise, including an appropriate procedure for the purposes of regulation 5(2), was being followed in respect of matters that consisted of or included the substance of the tribunal complaint. This extension only applies where the employee had reasonable grounds for believing that the procedures were ongoing.

Regulation 15(3) provides that time is extended in circumstances where the employee presents a complaint to the tribunal within the normal time limit for presenting the complaint but in circumstances in which section 32(2) or (3) of the 2002 Act does not permit him to do so because he must comply with the grievance procedure or a complaint is presented after the expiry of the normal time limit for presenting the complaint, having complied with paragraph 6 or 9 of Schedule 2 (i.e. sending the letter) in relation to his grievance within that normal time limit.

This Regulation will apply where the employee has not written the Step One letter under the procedure and allowed twenty-eight days. In such a case the tribunal will decline to register the application as the relevant admissibility conditions will not have been met. This will however trigger an automatic three-month extension of the time limit from the date when it would otherwise have expired. In this event, the claimant must send the Step One letter by no later than 28 days after the date when the normal time limit would have expired. If he does so, there will still be an opportunity to present a valid tribunal claim under the jurisdiction in question, within the extended time limit. If not, however, he will be barred from doing so, subject to the normal discretion of the tribunal to extend a time limit where it was not reasonably practicable for it to be met or where such an extension is just and equitable.

Where the employee has sent the Step One letter to the employer under the grievance procedure, within the normal time limit for presenting a Tribunal claim under a jurisdiction relevant to that grievance, this will trigger an automatic three month extension of the time limit from the date when it would otherwise have expired. It will not be necessary for either party to have contacted a tribunal in any way for this automatic extension to be triggered. Where the employee has written to the employer setting out a grievance that relevant disciplinary action is unlawfully discriminatory, or a collective grievance has been raised in writing by an appropriate representative, then this time limit extension will also apply.

Regulation 15(4) sets out a number of acts that, for the purposes of Regulation 15(3) and section 32 of the 2002 Act shall be treated, in a case to which the specified regulation applies, as constituting compliance with paragraphs 6 or 9 of Schedule 2 (which require the grievance to be stated in writing):

- in a case to which regulation 7(1) applies, compliance by the employee with the requirement in regulation 7(2) (see Part S – circumstances where deemed compliance with GP);

- in a case to which regulation 9(1) applies, compliance by the appropriate representative with the requirement in sub-paragraph (a) or (b) of that regulation, whichever is the later (see Part S – collective grievance);

- in a case to which regulation 10 applies, the raising of his grievance by the employee in accordance with the procedure referred to in that regulation (see Part S – alternative collectively agreed dispute resolution procedure).

The normal time limit under Regulation 15 means –

- subject to the provision with regard to the Equal Pay Act, the period within which a complaint under the relevant jurisdiction must be presented if there is to be no need for the tribunal, in order to be entitled to consider it to exercise any discretion, or make any determination as to whether it is required to consider the complaint, that the tribunal would have to exercise or make in order to consider a complaint presented outside that period; and

- in relation to claims brought under the Equal Pay Act 1970, the period ending on the date on or before which proceedings must be instituted in accordance with section 2(4) of that Act.

The existing discretion of the tribunal to extend a time limit where it was not reasonably practicable for it to be met.

The requirement for Written Particulars of Employment

Sections 35 to 37 of the Act sets out the particulars that now need to be given of disciplinary and grievance procedures (see Chapter 4). If an employee brings a tribunal claim under the jurisdictions set out in Schedule 5 of the Act, the tribunal may consider the nature of the employee's written statement. By section 38 of the Act, if there is no statement, or it is found to be incomplete or inaccurate, the tribunal is required to give compensation. If an award is made under the jurisdiction of the complaint, then that award can be increased by 2 or 4 weeks' pay. If compensation is not a remedy for the particular complaint, or it is not the remedy that the tribunal chooses, it can make an award of 2 or 4 weeks' pay. It is a matter for the tribunal's discretion as to whether the award should be two or four weeks. No award need be made or increased if the tribunal considers that to do so would be unjust or inequitable.

All employers, regardless of the number of staff they employ, must mention their disciplinary rules and the new minimum procedures in the written statement.

Overlapping Disputes

The Act deals separately with disciplinary and grievance procedures but it may be the case that there is an overlap or the distinctions are blurred in certain circumstances. The regulations seek to establish what is required to deal with such situations by setting out what is required and by seeking to avoid obliging the parties to go through any unnecessary repetition of procedures. The DTI Guidance gives examples of some 'typical' areas where there may be an overlap:

- "Where an employer takes disciplinary action against an employee, this may prompt the employee to raise a grievance, either about that action or about something else, or to resign and complain of constructive dismissal;

- An employer may have multiple disciplinary issues to address with an employee;

- An employee may have multiple grievances to raise with an employer".

As noted in the DTI Guidance, the position under the regulations in relation to the different procedures and where there is an overlap, is that:

• Where the employer is contemplating dismissal (other than constructive dismissal), the circumstances do not fall under the statutory grievance procedure. The onus is on the employer to 'initiate workplace dialogue' under the applicable dismissal and disciplinary procedure. The employer will still need to ensure that the dismissal is for a fair reason, and free of any taint of unlawful discrimination.

• If action taken by the employer is *not* taken on the grounds of conduct or capability, then there is no need for the employer to initiate the dismissal and disciplinary procedures. Thus, if an employee is dissatisfied, he should start the grievance procedure.

• If the disciplinary action taken by the employer is asserted to be on the basis of conduct or capability, then the standard (three-step) dismissal and disciplinary procedure must be followed, and the statutory grievance procedures will not normally apply.

• The grievance procedures will apply if the employer has taken or contemplates taking conduct or capability related disciplinary action, and *either* the employee feels it is unlawfully discriminatory *or* the action is really being taken for reasons other than conduct or capability. For example, the employee might feel the disciplinary action is being taken because of a personality clash with the line manager, rather than his or her ability to do the job.

If the employee raises this grievance in writing at any stage before the appeal stage of the dismissal and disciplinary procedure, he or she will be treated as having complied with the grievance procedure. The DTI Guidance states that in this way, the aims of the statutory procedures are fulfilled, as the problems will have been discussed in the workplace, and the risk of unnecessary duplication of procedures is avoided.

If both statutory procedures apply, but the employee raises the grievance only *after* the disciplinary procedure has finished, then it will be necessary for the grievance procedure to be completed in full.

The DTI Guidance states that whilst many employers choose to disentangle related disciplinary and grievance matters in separate procedures, this will not be required for the statutory procedures as the regulations explicitly set out that both letters and meetings under the statutory procedures can be multi-purpose. For example, an employer writing to invite an employee to a Step Two meeting in relation to one disciplinary matter could use the same letter as the Step One letter in relation to another disciplinary matter

Changes in the way that unfair dismissal cases are judged: reversal of the rule in "Polkey"

The position with regard to fairness of a dismissal since **Polkey v A E Dayton Services** [1988] was that an employer could not justify a dismissal as being fair where procedures had not been followed (subject to the limited exception where such consultation would have been futile). Section 34 of the 2002 Act changes this position by inserting a new section 98A into the Employment Rights Act 1996. The position after 1 October 2004 will be that:

- Where the employer dismisses without following the relevant DDP the dismissal will be automatically unfair. If the relevant procedure has not been followed the employee will receive a minimum of four weeks' pay as compensation where he or she was found to have been unfairly dismissed (34(3) inserting a new section 112(5) in the ERA 1996) Thus if the employee is not allowed to appeal there will be an automatic unfair dismissal.

- Even if the employer strictly follows either dismissal procedure, the dismissal may still be found to be unfair if, for example, the reason for dismissal is not potentially fair or the employer acted unreasonably in some other way or following the additional procedural actions would have affected the decision to dismiss.

- Section 98A(2) of the ERA 1996 as inserted by section 34(1) of the EA 2002, provides that a failure by an employer to follow a procedure (other than a DDP) shall not be regarded as itself making the employer's action unreasonable if he shows that he would have decided to dismiss the employee if he had followed the procedure. This limited reversal of *Polkey* means that where the employer has followed the DDP but has not otherwise complied with a reasonable procedure it will be possible to argue that such procedure would have made no difference and that other than this breach of procedure the dismissal was substantively fair.

The provision may become particularly relevant in a case where the Regulations provide that no DDP is applicable or the DDP is treated as having been completed. In such case, even though there was no meaningful procedure it may be possible to argue that it would have made no difference. For example:

- In cases where the employer must undertake collective redundancy consultation there is no obligation to follow a DDP (regulation 4(1)(b)).

- In a case where it would be illegal for an employee to work (i.e. a driver how loses his licence) (regulation 4(1)(f)) no DDP may be applicable.

In both these cases the employer may argue that the employer would have dismissed if a correct procedure had been followed.

Fairness in general – the requirement to act reasonably

Following the new statutory procedures will not inevitably make any dismissal fair. It is still possible for a tribunal to find that the dismissal is unfair even if the employer has stuck to the letter of the procedures. The tribunal will look at whether or not the employer had a fair reason for dismissal and behaved reasonably in the way he or she went about the dismissal.

There is a vast amount of case law relating to disciplinary offences and these are fully considered in Duggan *Unfair Dismissal: Law Practice and Guidance* at Chapter 6 pages 149 to 230. This section will summarise the procedures that should be followed in order for there to be a fair and reasonable disciplinary process. The two precedents that have been provided are intended to provide comprehensive procedures in this respect. The precedents should be considered along with the new ACAS Code on Disciplinary and Grievance Procedures published on 15th September 2004. A fair procedure will encompass the following:

The tribunal may refer to the ACAS Code of Practice on Disciplinary and Grievance Procedures to determine if the employer behaved in a reasonable manner. Indeed the ACAS Code sets out in some detail what would be expected on the part of the employer over and above the statutory procedures.

The employer will need to show an admissible reason for dismissal under section 98 of the ERA 1998, being:

- Capability or qualifications of the employee

- Conduct of the employee

- Redundancy

- Contravention of a duty or restriction or

- Some other substantial reason

It will then need to demonstrate that it has acted fairly. These principles are considered in detail in Duggan: *Unfair Dismissal* to which reference should be made.

Paragraphs 59–60 of the new ACAS Code sets out the requirements of a fair procedure as does the DTI Guidance and this is referred to below together with some case law examples.

The Code states that

> " ...employees should be given the opportunity of a meeting with someone who has not been involved in the matter. They should be informed of the allegations against them, together with the supporting evidence, in advance of the meeting. Employees should be given the opportunity to challenge the allegations before decisions are reached and should be provided with a right of appeal."

Paragraph 60 states that:

"Good disciplinary procedures should:

- be put in writing;

- say to whom they apply;

- be non-discriminatory;

- allow for matters to be dealt without undue delay;

- allow for information to be kept confidential;

- tell employees what disciplinary action might be taken;

- say what levels of management have the authority to take disciplinary action;

- require employees to be informed of the complaints against them and supporting evidence, before a meeting;

- give employees a chance to have their say before management reaches a decision;

- provide employees with the right to be accompanied;

- provide that no employee is dismissed for a first breach of discipline, except in cases of gross misconduct;

- require management to investigate fully before any disciplinary action is taken;

- ensure that employees are given an explanation for any sanction; and

- allow employees to appeal against a decision."

The DTI Guidelines (at paragraph 25) set out the following eight points in relation to a fair dismissal procedure to which the following considerations may be added:

1) Procedures should be used to encourage employees to improve, where possible, rather than just as a way of imposing a punishment.

2) The employer should carry out a full investigation into the matters that may amount to misconduct. The procedure that will be followed if an investigation is to be carried out before any 'charges' are laid The following should be borne in mind in considering the nature of any investigation to be carried out:

   - Any breach of discipline should be dealt with speedily but no disciplinary action should be taken until the case has been fully investigated (see **RSPCA v Cruden** [1986] ICR 205; Duggan, *Unfair Dismissal* at page 162–3);

   - Where police investigations are being carried out there is no absolute rule that an investigation cannot take place but the employee may feel inhibited. He may be given an opportunity to state whether he wishes to make any comment (*Unfair Dismissal* at 197–199);

   - Where evidence from informants is to be relied upon the safeguards set out in **Linford Cash & Carry Limited v Thomson** [1989] ICR 518 should be followed (see *Unfair Dismissal* at pages 164–165);

- Any investigating officer should be independent and the manner in which the investigation is to be carried out be made clear to the employee;

- Consider whether witness statements will be taken and provided to the employee;

- Is the investigating officer to provide a report with recommendations?

The employer must inform the employee about the complaint against him or her; the employee should be given an opportunity to state his or her case before decisions are reached. Once the investigation has been carried out and a decision is made to conduct a disciplinary hearing, the employee should be made aware of the charges with sufficient certainty that he knows the allegations he has to meet and be informed in good time (*Unfair Dismissal* at pages 167–169 and the cases there cited).

3) The employee is entitled to be accompanied at disciplinary and grievance meetings

- There will not necessarily be a right to cross examine witnesses at a disciplinary hearing (**Santamera v Express Cargo Forwarding t/a IEC Ltd** [2003] IRLR 273).

4) The employer should not take disciplinary action until the facts of the case have been established (see **A v B** [2003] IRLR 405 as to what investigation is needed where there are serious allegations).

5) The employer should never dismiss an employee for a first disciplinary offence, unless it is a case of gross misconduct. The employee should know what sanctions certain breaches of discipline will attract so that he is aware of circumstances in which he may be dismissed for gross misconduct. Figure to specify that a matter amounts to gross misconduct may make any dismissal unfair; see **Aberdein v Robert L Fleming** [EAT 1277/97] and Duggan on *Unfair Dismissal* at page 159. The two precedents contain lists of offences that may attract different sanctions.

The panel must avoid any appearance of bias (*Unfair Dismissal* at page 174);

The panel should consider how it will come to and deliver its decision.

Once the panel has decided that there has been a breach on the part of the employee they will consider the sanction to be imposed. There are a wide range of factors that can be taken into account, which are considered exhaustively in *Unfair Dismissal* at pages 177 to 182 and in relation to specific areas of misconduct at pages 187–230.

6) The employer should always give the employee an explanation for any disciplinary action taken and make sure the employee knows what improvement is expected. However, it should be noted that the unjustified imposition of a disciplinary sanction may be grounds for constructive dismissal (as in **Stanley Cole (Wainfleet) Ltd v Sheridan** [2003] IRLR 52; **Thackeray v Acequip Limited** [EAT/0396/03/MAA]

7) The employer must give the employee an opportunity to appeal. The Disciplinary procedure will provide for a right of appeal and consideration must be made as to whether this is a complete rehearing or a review. Again this is covered exhaustively in *Unfair Dismissal* at pages 183–187 and in relation to the specific misconduct at 187–230.

8) The employer should act consistently (see **Hadjiionnou v Coral Casinos Limited** [1981] IRLR 352).

THE SCHEDULE TO THE EMPLOYMENT ACT 2002
CASES WHERE NON COMPLETION OF THE STATUTORY
PROCEDURE WILL LEAD TO AN ADJUSTMENT OF AWARD
UNDER SECTION 31

SCHEDULE 3:
TRIBUNAL JURISDICTIONS TO WHICH SECTION 31 APPLIES

Section 2 of the Equal Pay Act 1970 (c 41) (equality clauses)

Section 63 of the Sex Discrimination Act 1975 (c 65) (discrimination in the employment field)

Section 54 of the Race Relations Act 1976 (c 74) (discrimination in the employment field)

Section 146 of the Trade Union and Labour Relations (Consolidation) Act 1992 (c 52) (detriment in relation to trade union membership and activities)

Paragraph 156 of Schedule A1 to that Act (detriment in relation to union recognition rights)

Section 8 of the Disability Discrimination Act 1995 (c 50) (discrimination in the employment field)

Section 23 of the Employment Rights Act 1996 (c 18) (unauthorised deductions and payments)

Section 48 of that Act (detriment in employment)

Section 111 of that Act (unfair dismissal)

Section 163 of that Act (redundancy payments)

Section 24 of the National Minimum Wage Act 1998 (c 39) (detriment in relation to national minimum wage)

...

The Employment Tribunal Extension of Jurisdiction (England and Wales) Order 1994 (SI 1994/1623) (breach of employment contract and termination)

The Employment Tribunal Extension of Jurisdiction (Scotland) Order 1994 (SI 1994/1624) (corresponding provision for Scotland)

Regulation 30 of the Working Time Regulations 1998 (SI 1998/1833) (breach of regulations)

Regulation 32 of the Transnational Information and Consultation of Employees Regulations 1999 (SI 1999/3323) (detriment relating to European Works Councils)

[Regulation 28 of the Employment Equality (Sexual Orientation) Regulations 2003 (discrimination in the employment field)]

[Regulation 28 of the Employment Equality (Religion or Belief) Regulations 2003 (discrimination in the employment field).]

SCHEDULE 4:
TRIBUNAL JURISDICTIONS TO WHICH SECTION 32 APPLIES SO THAT THE GRIEVANCE PROCEDURE MUST FIRST BE

FOLLOWED BEFORE ANY TRIBUNAL PROCEEDINGS ARE BROUGHT

Section 2 of the Equal Pay Act 1970 (c 41) (equality clauses)

Section 63 of the Sex Discrimination Act 1975 (c 65) (discrimination in the employment field)

Section 54 of the Race Relations Act 1976 (c 74) (discrimination in the employment field)

Section 146 of the Trade Union and Labour Relations (Consolidation) Act 1992 (c 52) (detriment in relation to trade union membership and activities)

Paragraph 156 of Schedule A1 to that Act (detriment in relation to union recognition rights)

Section 8 of the Disability Discrimination Act 1995 (c 50) (discrimination in the employment field)

Section 23 of the Employment Rights Act 1996 (c 18) (unauthorised deductions and payments)

Section 48 of that Act (detriment in employment)

Section 111 of that Act (unfair dismissal)

Section 163 of that Act (redundancy payments)

Section 24 of the National Minimum Wage Act 1998 (c 39) (detriment in relation to national minimum wage)

...

Regulation 30 of the Working Time Regulations 1998 (SI 1998/1833) (breach of regulations)

Regulation 32 of the Transnational Information and Consultation of Employees Regulations 1999 (SI 1999/3323) (detriment relating to European Works Councils)

[Regulation 28 of the Employment Equality (Sexual Orientation) Regulations 2003 (discrimination in the employment field)]

[Regulation 28 of the Employment Equality (Religion or Belief) Regulations 2003 (discrimination in the employment field).]

PART S: GRIEVANCE PROCEDURES

Precedent S: Grievance Procedures

    S1:   **Grievance Procedure**   **963**

    S2:   **Grievance Procedure Form intended to comply
with Standard Statutory Requirements**   **967**

Commentary: Grievance Procedures   **971**

Useful Websites

- ACAS Disciplinary and Grievance Code of Practice

  http://www.acas.org.uk/publications/pdf/CP01.2.pdf

- The DTI Guidance

  http://www.dti.gov.uk/er/resolvingdisputes.htmhttp:

Cross References

- Duggan, *Wrongful Dismissal and Breach of Contract*, Chapter 6.7.

Precedent S1: Grievance Procedure

1 This Grievance Procedure is designed to ensure that you are able to raise any grievance that you have about your employment or your working environment. You should read this grievance procedure in conjunction with the Company's procedures and policies relating to discipline, public interest disclosure, the equal opportunity policy and the policy on sexual harassment.

There is a distinction between grievances that you may have about actions which you may consider the Company is taking against you and complaints you may have about your work environment. In the case of the former the Company has certain statutory obligations with which it will comply in full. In the case of grievances which do not entail statutory obligations the Company will apply the Grievance Procedure at its absolute discretion and may depart from it should the Company consider it appropriate to do so.

2 The Company regards it as important that you are able to air any grievances that you have about your employment or working environment without feeling worried about making a grievance. You will not be prejudiced by making a grievance and any grievance will be dealt with as soon as possible. You will not be penalised in any way for making a grievance unless the grievance is untrue and brought for malicious purposes in which case the Disciplinary Procedure may be invoked.

3 In the first instance any grievance should be communicated to your immediate supervisor or manager. If the complaint is about your immediate supervisor or manager then you should communicate the grievance to the next level of management. Where the grievance is of a serious nature then you should communicate the grievance to senior management or director level as is appropriate. You may in any event at all times bring your grievance to the attention of the Human Resources Department.

4 Any grievance you have will be dealt with in the following stages, at the Company's absolute discretion:

1) Your grievance may be raised on an informal basis at the first stage, which will normally entail a verbal discussion with your manager or supervisor. You may, however, submit a grievance in writing on an informal basis if you so wish.

2) You may submit a formal grievance after stage one, or move straight on to submitting a formal grievance without passing through stage one. This should be in writing. You must be aware that once you have submitted a formal grievance the Company may wish to investigate it even if you decide that you do not want to pursue it, depending on the nature of the grievance. Submission of a grievance in writing will form STEP ONE of the Grievance Procedure where the complaint is about something which you allege the Company has done to you or which you allege may place the Company in breach of employment legislation [CONSIDER WHETHER TO APPEND THE LIST OF STATUTES REFERRED TO IN THE ACT AS BEING THOSE WHERE THE GRIEVANCE PROCESS IS RELEVANT]

3) Your formal grievance will be considered once it has been submitted in writing. Once the Company has had the opportunity to consider your written grievance it will arrange for a meeting to take place between yourself and the manager responsible for hearing the grievance. This meeting will be STEP TWO of the formal Grievance Procedure. You will:

• Be entitled to bring a companion to the meeting.

• Be entitled to make such representations as you consider to be appropriate.

The Manager may request further information in order to assist him to resolve the grievance. The meeting will be arranged at a time and date which is convenient for all parties. You are expected to co-operate in relation to the timing of the meeting. The Company reserves its right to treat the Grievance Procedure as having been complied with if you unreasonably refuse to attend a meeting at a time that is regarded as reasonable for all parties or you fail to attend a meeting that has been arranged.

• If your companion is not available at the time that the Company has proposed for the meeting you may propose an alternative time for the hearing provided it is a reasonable time and is no further away than five working days after the day that the Company had proposed for the meeting, excluding Saturdays, Sundays, Christmas Day, Good Friday or Bank Holidays. If your Companion is a Company worker he may have time off to accompany you to the hearing.

The Company will make all reasonable efforts to ensure that the meeting takes place at time that is suitable for all parties.

4) You will be informed of the decision in respect of your formal grievance as soon as possible which will normally be within [. . .] days but may be sooner if the grievance is urgent or take longer if the grievance is complicated.

5) If you are not satisfied with the result of your grievance or consider that it is taking too long to resolve you may refer it to the next level of management. In the case of being dissatisfied with the result of your grievance you have [. . .] days to refer it to the next level. This will be treated as an appeal against the result of your grievance at the SECOND STEP and will be regarded as the THIRD STEP in the Grievance Procedure. A decision will be given in [. . .] days or as soon as reasonably practicable.

6) If you remain dissatisfied you may refer your grievance to a director who has been nominated to deal with grievances. This is effectively a second appeal and shall be permitted in the absolute discretion of the Company.

7) At STEPS TWO and THREE your grievance will be dealt with by way of a hearing where it concerns a complaint on your part about something that the Company has done or is contemplating doing to you or where it is alleged that the Company is in breach of obligations to you (whether imposed by legislation or contract) Where your grievance is about another matter (for example scope of duties or relationships at work) the Company will normally follow the three step process but may, in its absolute discretion consider that a hearing is not necessary. You may in the latter case request a hearing. If you request a hearing it will be at the discretion of the person dealing with the grievance.

8) Given that the Company wish to ensure that your grievance is investigated as fully as possible this may entail speaking to other individuals. Any hearing will not take place until the person dealing with your grievance is satisfied that he or she has the necessary information to properly understand your complaints.

9) You are further referred to the rights of representation contained in the disciplinary procedure. You have the same rights of representation

in circumstances where your grievance relates to the performance of the Company of any duty that relates to your employment.

10) The decision of the director who has been nominated to hear the last stage of the grievance procedure will be final

11) The Company may depart from its procedure or treat it as having been complied with where:

- Your conduct (whether through threats or harassment on your part of those involved in the process or of witnesses) causes the Company to decide that it will not complete the procedures.

- It has become impracticable to complete the procedure, whether through long-term sickness or otherwise.

- The grievance is a disclosure under the Public Interest Disclosure Act 1998, as incorporated into the Employment Rights Act 1996, and is more appropriately dealt with as such rather than as a grievance.

12) The Company aims at all times to act as a reasonable employer so that if you have any concerns about the way in which these procedures are being operated in relation to your grievance you should address them to [   ].

Precedent S2: Grievance Procedure Form intended to comply with standard statutory requirements

---

This is the first stage of the formal Grievance procedure

STEP ONE.

If you have not been able to resolve your Grievance by informal means you are entitled to make a formal Grievance. For your convenience the Grievance may be made on this form though you can set out your Grievance *in writing* as you consider to be appropriate. The next stage of the Grievance will be a meeting and this is explained further below.

NAME		ETHNIC GROUP	
POSITION HELD		GENDER	
NAME OF SUPERVISOR		WHETHER SUFFERS FROM DISABILITY	

ONLY COMPLETE THE SECOND COLUMN ABOVE IF YOU WISH

Please set out the nature of your Grievance (continue on fresh sheets if necessary) and provide any supporting documentation.

What actions would you see as acceptable to resolve your Grievance?

Has the Grievance been discussed with your supervisor/line manager?

The Company would normally expect you to discuss your Grievance first with your line manager on an informal basis unless it is about your line manager

---

Do you wish to have a colleague present at the meeting?

It will normally be expected that the Grievance meeting will take place within five days. Are there any times to avoid where you or your colleague will be unable to attend?

DATE OF SUBMISSION	RECEIVED BY

A COPY OF THIS DOCUMENT WILL BE SENT TO HUMAN RESOURCES UPON RECEIPT WHO WILL ACTION THE GRIEVANCE

STEP TWO

Step two of the Grievance Procedure is the meeting that will take place as a result of the Grievance that has been lodged.

THIS SECTION TO BE COMPLETED BY THE MANAGER WHO HELD THE SECOND STEP OF THE GRIEVANCE PROCEDURE

DATE OF GRIEVANCE MEETING _____
ATTENDED BY (AND STATUS)

Please complete this part of the document summarising what happened at the meeting and:

- **If the Grievance was resolved, how it was resolved.**
- **If the Grievance was not resolved, what it was not resolved.**

RESULT OF GRIEVANCE MEETING

- **Grievance rejected – if so, why?**
- **Grievance resolved, if so how?**

SIGNATURE

A COPY OF THIS DOCUMENT WILL BE PROVIDED TO THE AGGRIEVED EMPLOYEE WHO WILL BE ASKED TO COMPLETE THE NEXT PART OF THIS DOCUMENT

MEMBER OF STAFF WHO BROUGHT GRIEVANCE TO COMPLETE

I have read the above summary and agree that it accurately reflects the meeting [or] I have read the above summary and have added my comments on a separate sheet of paper, attached.

(Cross out as appropriate and complete the following)

MY GRIEVANCE HAS BEEN RESOLVED

I DO NOT WISH TO PROCEED FURTHER AND MY GRIEVANCE HAS BEEN WITHDRAWN

SIGNED BY PERSON WHO BROUGHT GRIEVANCE

THIRD STEP

The Third Step of the Grievance Procedure is that you will be entitled to appeal to a more senior manager. In your case it will be _____ . This is likely to be the last stage of the procedure and will normally take place within seven days of receipt of notification that Step 2 has not resolved your Grievance. Please complete the next section and return this document to Human Resources.

I am not satisfied with the results of Step 2 of the Grievance procedure and wish to appeal. The Grounds on which I wish to appeal are:

(continue on fresh sheets if necessary) and provide any supporting documentation.

Do you wish to have a colleague present at the appeal meeting?

It will normally be expected that the appeal meeting will take place within seven days. Are there any times to avoid where you or your colleague will be unable to attend?

DATE OF SUBMISSION	RECEIVED BY

A COPY OF THIS DOCUMENT WILL BE SENT TO HUMAN RESOURCES UPON RECEIPT WHO WILL ACTION THE APPEAL

DATE OF APPEAL MEETING

PERSON WHO HEARD THE APPEAL:

OTHER PERSONS PRESENT (AND STATUS):

THE NEXT SECTION TO BE COMPLETED BY PERSON WHO HEARD THE APPEAL.

Please complete this part of the document summarising what happened at the appeal meeting and:

- **If the appeal was allowed, how the Grievance was resolved.**

- **If the Appeal was not allowed, why it was not allowed**

RESULT OF APPEAL (TO BE SENT TO THE AGGRIEVED EMPLOYEE)

MEMBER OF STAFF WHO BROUGHT GRIEVANCE TO COMPLETE

I have read the above summary of the appeal meeting and agree that it accurately reflects the meeting [or] I have read the above summary and have added my comments on a separate sheet of paper, attached.

(Cross out as appropriate and complete the following)

SIGNED BY PERSON WHO BROUGHT GRIEVANCE

RECEIVED BY HR ON _____ AND FURTHER ACTION TO BE TAKEN?

COMMENTARY ON S: GRIEVANCE PROCEDURES

A failure to investigate an employee's grievance may amount to a breach of an implied term that the employers will reasonably and promptly afford a reasonably opportunity to their employees to obtain redress of any grievance that they may have. In **W A Goold (Pearmark) Limited v McConnell** [1995] IRLR 516 two salesmen suffered a substantial loss of salary as a result of a re-organisation. Although they raised this on a number of occasions nothing was done. There was no written grievance procedure. It was held that they had been constructively dismissed. The right to have a grievance dealt with was a fundamental one. Nevertheless, there may be circumstances where the employer may be justified in delaying the grievance process, such as where the employee is absent due to sickness (**Harlow v General Healthcare Group** [EAT 0436/01]; 4 October 2002 where the procedures provided for speedy resolution but it was reasonable to wait for an employee to return to work so that there was no constructive dismissal).

Where the employee does not utilise any grievance procedure in circumstances where there has been a fundamental breach of contract on the part of the employer the fact it is has not been implemented will not affect the issue of breach of contract (**Fruscher v Mycalex Motors Limited** [EAT 182/80]) but it will now prevent the employee from bringing tribunal proceedings in accordance with the reforms contained in the Employment Act 2002.

By section 3 of the Employment Rights Act 1996 an employer must provide a note specifying (by description or otherwise) a person to whom that employee can apply for the purpose of seeking redress of any grievance and the manner in which any application should be made. The duty is limited to identifying the person and, if there if any setting out "the manner in which any such application should be made". Section 36 of the Employment Rights Act 1996 removes the small employer exemption of employers that employ 20 employees so that from 1 October 2004 the requirement to provide the name of the person to whom the grievance should be addressed and the manner in which it should be made will apply to all employers. Moreover, all employers will have to comply with the statutory procedure.

The ACAS Code suggests that grievance procedures should be there for employees to address issues with management about their work or their employers, clients or fellow workers' actions that affect them. Some examples are listed:

- terms and conditions of employment;

- health and safety;

- relationships at work;

- new working practices;

- organisational change and equal opportunities.

Precedent S1 contains a standard procedure that distinguishes between the statutory requirements and other grievances.

Precedent S2 sets out a grievance procedure which is intended to emulate the suggestions in the ACAS Code.

The basic position

There are two types of statutory grievance procedure: the standard and the modified procedure, the latter applying where the employee has already been dismissed. The basic requirement is set out in paragraphs 6 and 9 of Schedule 2 to the Employment Act 2002, which is that the employee must set out the grievance in writing and send a copy of it to the employer (in the case of the modified procedure paragraph 9 states that the basis for the grievance must also be set out). This is step 1 of the procedure.

In the case of the standard procedure, step 2 is to hold a meeting which should not take place until the employee has informed the employer of the basis for the grievance and the employer has had a reasonable opportunity to consider his response to "that information". The modified step 2 procedure, where the employee has already been dismissed is to set out the response in writing and send the statement or a copy to the employee.

In the case of the standard procedure step 3 is an appeal meeting if the employee wishes to appeal.

The effect of the statutory grievance procedure

Section 32 of the EA 2002 provides that the statutory grievance procedures apply to the jurisdictions listed in Schedule 4. (See the end of Part R, which lists the jurisdictions.)

By section 32(2) an employee shall not present a complaint to an employment tribunal under a jurisdiction set out in Schedule 4 if it concerns a matter in relation to which the requirement in paragraph 6 or 9 of Schedule 2, to send a Grievance Letter applies, and the requirement has not been complied with.

By section 32(3) an employee shall not present a complaint to an employment tribunal under a jurisdiction set out in Schedule 4 if it concerns a matter in relation to which the requirement in paragraph 6 or 9 of Schedule 2 has been complied with, and less than 28 days have passed since the day on which the requirement was complied with.

By section 32(4) an employee shall not present a complaint to an employment tribunal under a jurisdiction set out in Schedule 4 if it concerns a matter in relation to which the requirement in paragraph 6 or 9 of Schedule 2 has been complied with, and the day on which the requirement was complied with was more than one month after the end of the original time limit for making the complaint. The Secretary of State may specify by regulations that an employment tribunal may direct that subsection (4) shall not apply in relation to a particular matter.

By section 32(6) an employment tribunal shall be prevented from considering a complaint presented in breach of subsections (2) to (4), but only if—

(*a*) the breach is apparent to the tribunal from the information supplied to it by the employee in connection with the bringing of the proceedings; or

(*b*) the tribunal is satisfied of the breach as a result of his employer raising the issue of compliance with those provisions in accordance with regulations under section 7 of the Employment Tribunals Act 1996 (c 17) (Employment Tribunal procedure regulations).

Sections 32(7) and (8) confer considerable rule making powers on the Secretary of State including amending the section.

Definition of Grievance and application of the Grievance Procedures

By the definition part of the Regulations:

> "grievance" means a complaint by an employee about action, which his employer has taken or is contemplating taking in relation to him;

> "grievance procedures" means the statutory procedures set out in Part 2 of Schedule 2;

The regulations define a grievance as "a complaint by an employee about action which his employer has taken or is contemplating taking in relation to him" which will also cover the actions of a third party (e.g. a colleague) in cases where the employer could be vicariously liable for those actions. The Precedents cover this definition but go further in that grievances about other matters may be pursued under the procedures. Though the statutory definition is limited in scope, there is still a need for procedures relating to matters such as working environment as there will be a danger of the employer breaching the implied term of mutual trust and confidence if there is no mechanism for the employer to listen to and deal with employees' concerns.

Regulation 6 provides that the grievance procedures apply in relation to any grievance about action by the employer that could form the basis of a tribunal claim under one of the jurisdictions set out in Schedules 3 or 4 to the Act.

The statutory grievance procedures do not apply where an employee makes a protected disclosure within the meaning of the Public Interest Disclosure Act 1998, unless the employee actually intended the making of the disclosure to constitute the raising of a grievance. The provisions in PIDA will always take precedence. This effectively gives the employee the right to choose whether to raise a concern as a grievance or as a protected disclosure.

In the ACAS Code of Practice, under the section "What is a grievance hearing?" it is stated:

> "For the purposes of this right, a grievance hearing is a meeting at which an employer deals with a complaint about a duty owed by them to a worker, whether the duty arises from statute or common law (for example contractual commitments).

For instance, an individual's request for a pay rise is unlikely to fall within the definition, unless a right to an increase is specifically provided for in the contract. Equally, most employers will be under no legal duty to provide their workers with car parking facilities, and a grievance about such facilities would carry no right to be accompanied at a hearing by a companion. However, if a worker were disabled and needed a car to get to and from work, they probably would be entitled to a companion at a grievance hearing, as an issue might arise as to whether the employer was meeting their obligations under the Disability Discrimination Act."

Regulation 6(1) provides that the grievance procedures apply, in accordance with the paragraphs (2) to (7) of the regulation, in relation to any grievance about action by the employer that could form the basis of a complaint by an employee to an employment tribunal under a jurisdiction listed in Schedule 3 or 4, or could do so if the action took place. The GPs are therefore very much limited to actions that may be taken by the employer in relation to the employee and which may amount to a breach of the legislation set out in the Schedules. It should be noted that this will include breach of contract as the Employment Tribunal Extension of Jurisdiction (England and Wales Order 1994 is included within the Schedule.

The Standard Procedure

By regulation 6(2) subject to paragraphs (3) to (7), the standard grievance procedure applies in relation to any grievance, as defined above.

The Modified Procedure

By regulation 6(3), subject to paragraphs (4) to (7), the modified grievance procedure applies in relation to a grievance where the employee has ceased to be employed by the employer; the employer was unaware of the grievance before the employment ceased, or was so aware but the standard grievance procedure was not commenced or was not completed before the last day of the employee's employment; and the parties have agreed in writing in relation to the grievance, whether before, on or after that day, but after the employer became aware of the grievance, that the modified procedure should apply.

The Standard (three-step) grievance procedure

The Standard Procedure is contained in Schedule 2 Part 2 of the 2002 Act.

The ACAS Code of Practice on Disciplinary and Grievance Procedures recommends that employees should aim to settle most grievances informally with their line manager.

Where the grievance cannot be settled informally, then the employee should turn to the statutory procedure to raise a formal grievance if the grievance is about something that the employer proposes to do in relation to the employee and one of the jurisdictions in the Schedule applies.

The standard grievance procedure is initiated by the employee writing a letter to the employer. In response, the employer will be required to arrange a meeting to discuss the issue, and to provide an opportunity for the employee to appeal if the meeting fails to resolve the matter.

The DTI Guidance contains the following table in relation to the standard procedure:

Standard (three-step) grievance procedure	
Step One	The employee must set down in writing the nature of the alleged grievance and send the written complaint to the employer.
Step Two	The employer must invite the employee to at least one hearing at a reasonable time and place at which the alleged grievance can be discussed. The employee must inform the employer what the basis for the grievance is. The employee must take all reasonable steps to attend. After the meeting, the employer must inform the employee about any decision, and offer the employee the right of appeal.
Step Three	If the employee considers that the grievance has not been satisfactorily resolved, he/she must inform the employer that he wishes to appeal against the employer's decision or failure to make a decision. Where possible, a more senior manager should attend the appeal hearing. After the meeting, the employer's final decision must be communicated to the employee.

The Standard procedure will apply where the employee is aggrieved about an action taken by an employer in relation to him where the employee asserts that the action was taken wholly or mainly by reason of *something other than conduct or capability*. Such actions may *include* warnings (written and oral), investigatory suspensions and those actions giving rise to constructive dismissals, but will *exclude* other dismissals and "collective" actions. It is clear that the procedure will also apply when an employee wishes to complain about actions taken by colleagues. If the employer fails to address the issue, then the employee should initiate the standard grievance procedure.

It is to be noted that the Schedules include the discrimination legislation. If the employee has a complaint that he is being discriminated against, for example by being harassed by a colleague on the ground of his colour, this will be a matter that triggers the statutory grievance procedure if he wishes to make a complaint.

The standard (three-step) procedure applies in *all* cases where the employee is still in the employer's employment but there are exemptions where the employee is no longer employed.

The Modified (two-step) grievance procedure

The modified grievance procedure is contained in Schedule 2, Part 3, Chapter 2 of the Act. The DTI Guidance contains the following table:

Modified (two-step) grievance procedure	
Step One	The employee must set down in writing the nature of the alleged grievance and send the written complaint to the employer.
Step Two	The employer must set out his or her response in writing and send it to the employee.

As noted above, by regulation 6(3), the modified (two-step) grievance procedure will apply in circumstances where the standard grievance procedure would otherwise apply but where the employment has ended and *either*:

• the employer was not aware of the grievance before the employment ended; or

• if the employer was so aware, the standard grievance procedure had not started or had not been completed by the time the employment ended; and

• the parties must have agreed in writing that the modified, rather than the standard, grievance procedure shall apply.

The modified procedure does not require a meeting to take place as the view was taken that it would be unreasonable to oblige the parties to follow the standard procedure, including attending meetings, where there is no ongoing employment relationship and the parties have no interest in following the procedures, and where they are in mutual agreement on this point.

General requirements which apply to the procedures

Part 3 of Schedule 2, (set out in the section on Disciplinary Procedures), Part R regulates the timetable for meetings and the nature of the meeting that should take place. The basic criterion is that of reasonableness.

By Part 4 of Schedule 2 it is confirmed that there is a right to be accompanied and it is stated that, where the matters raised could amount to a protected disclosure under Part 4A of the ERA 1996, the information shall only be treated as the raising of a grievance where it is it is intended by the employee that the disclosure should constitute the raising of the matter with his employer as a grievance. Thus a public interest disclosure will not be a grievance unless it is clearly intended to have that effect.

Questionnaires

Regulation 14 provides that issuing a questionnaire under the discrimination legislation will not count as a Step One grievance letter as the view was taken that using one document for both purposes would be confusing for employers.

General exemptions from the grievance procedures

A number of exemptions exist for all the statutory procedures and these have been considered in the section on Disciplinary Procedures.

There are a number of exemptions that apply only to the grievance procedures. Where this is the position the extended time limits will not apply and the admissibility requirements of section 32 of the Act will not come into play.

By regulation 6(4), neither of the grievance procedures applies where –

• the employee has ceased to be employed by the employer;

• neither procedure has been commenced; and

- since the employee ceased to be employed it has ceased to be reasonably practicable for him to comply with paragraph 6 or 9 of Schedule 2.

By regulation 6(5) neither of the grievance procedures applies where the grievance is that the employer has dismissed or is contemplating dismissing the employee.

By regulation 6(6) neither of the grievance procedures applies where the grievance is that the employer has taken or is contemplating taking relevant disciplinary action against the employee unless one of the reasons for the grievance is a reason mentioned in regulation 7(1) in which case the parties will then be treated as having complied with the grievance procedures even though the procedure has not taken place.

The grievance procedures *will* generally apply if the employer has taken or contemplates taking conduct or capability related disciplinary action, and the employee feels either that it is, or would be, unlawfully discriminatory basis or that, contrary to the employer's assertion, it is not being taken on conduct or capability grounds. For example, the employee might feel the disciplinary action is being taken because of a personality clash with the line manager, rather than his or her ability to do the job.

By regulation 6(7) neither of the grievance procedures applies where regulation 11(1) applies; that is there have been threats or harassment or the employer reasonably believes that such is likely to occur – see Part R.

Circumstances in which parties are treated as complying with the grievance procedures

Regulation 7 provides for circumstances where the parties will be treated as complying with the procedures.

By regulation 7(1) where the grievance is that the employer has taken or is contemplating taking relevant disciplinary action against the employee and one of the reasons for the grievance is:

- that the relevant disciplinary action amounted to or, if it took place, would amount to unlawful discrimination; or

- that the grounds on which the employer took the action or is contemplating taking it were or are unrelated to the grounds on which he asserted that he took the action or is asserting that he is contemplating taking it, the standard grievance procedure or, as the case may be, modified grievance procedure shall apply but the parties shall be treated as having complied with the applicable procedure if the employee complies with the requirement in regulation 7(2).

Regulation 7(2) requires the employee to set out the grievance in a written statement and send the statement or a copy of it to the employer a) where either of the dismissal and disciplinary procedures is being followed, before the meeting referred to in paragraph 3 or 5 (appeals under the dismissal and disciplinary procedures) of Schedule 2, or b) where neither of those procedures is being followed, before presenting any complaint arising out of the grievance to an employment tribunal. Thus the parties will treated as having complied with the grievance procedure in full as long as the employee writes to the employer setting out his grievance before the appeal meeting under the applicable dismissal and disciplinary procedure. This will give the parties a chance to address this new element in the context of the dismissal and disciplinary procedure. If the employee fails to write to the employer before the appeal meeting under the dismissal and disciplinary procedure, he will have to raise the grievance separately under the applicable grievance procedure before being entitled to complain to an employment tribunal under a Schedule 4 jurisdiction.

By Regulation 7(3) "unlawful discrimination" means an act or omission in respect of which a right of complaint lies to an employment tribunal under any of the following tribunal jurisdictions (specified in Schedules 3 and 4) –

- section 2 of the Equal Pay Act 1970;

- section 63 of the Sex Discrimination Act 1975;

- section 54 of the Race Relations Act 1976;

- 17A of the Disability Discrimination Act 1995;

- regulation 28 of the Employment Equality (Religion or Belief) Regulations 2003;

- regulation 28 of the Employment Equality (Sexual Orientation) Regulations 2003.

Grievance procedure not completed because it is not reasonably practicable

By regulation 8, the parties shall be treated as having complied with the grievance procedure where the standard procedure would normally apply, but employment has ended and, since the end of employment, it has ceased to be reasonably practicable for one or both of the parties to comply with the remainder of the procedure If the parties have already had the first meeting, the employer has to inform the employee in writing of his or her decision.

Collective grievances

By regulation 9, the parties will be treated as having complied with the relevant grievance procedure if the grievance is raised in writing on behalf of at least two employees (including the complaining employee) by an "appropriate representative". The "appropriate representative" is defined in regulation 9(2) as an official of an independent trade union recognised by the employer for the purpose of collective bargaining or an employee of that employer who was elected or appointed to represent employees and has authority to do so under an established procedure to resolve grievances.

This provision is intended to allow grievances to be dealt with collectively where more than one employee has the same grievance in order to save the time and resources of both employer and employees.

Alternative collectively agreed dispute resolution procedure

The employer and trade union may have jointly developed sophisticated dispute resolution procedures which allow the employee to raise a grievance with this joint body. By regulation 10 the procedure has to be agreed by two or more employers or an employers' association and at least one independent trade union, and the employee is entitled to raise his or her grievance with this body and if he does so, then the parties will be treated as complying with statutory procedures. This avoids any risk that agreed procedures can no longer be used because the parties have to comply with the statutory procedures.

The following matters also need to be considered in the context of Grievance Procedures and are outlined in Part R on Disciplinary Procedures:

(1) The effect of failure to comply with a procedure and when this failure will be attributed to one of the parties.

(2) The effect of non-commencement of Grievance procedures (see below for admissibility).

(3) The effect of non-commencement or failure to carry through the procedures where one of the exemptions applies.

(4) The relationship between the procedures and other procedures, in particular discrimination questionnaires.

(5) Additional awards that may be made where procedures have not been complied with and other compensation that may be paid.

(6) Extension of time limits in order for procedures to be carried out.

(7) The requirement for Written Particulars (See Chapter 4).

(8) Overlapping procedures i.e. where disciplinary procedures and grievances procedures have been commenced.

Admissibility

If an employee wishes to submit an employment tribunal claim based on a grievance, he *must* write the Step One letter and allow 28 days (unless otherwise exempt from going through the procedures) or the complaint will not be admitted (section 32 of the 2002 Act). This applies both to current employees and to employees who are no longer in the employer's employment.

Once this requirement has been met, the employee will be able to bring a claim, as long as it is not out of time. If the procedures as a whole have *not* been completed, then any award may be subject to adjustment (section 31).

The employee is free to complain to an employment tribunal about any breach of his employment rights arising from an action where the statutory *dismissal and disciplinary procedure* applies. There are no admissibility requirements for claims arising from dismissal and other disciplinary action.

It is apparent that the reasonable employer will also wish to have in place grievance procedures to deal with the position where the employee has a grievance about his workplace. This has been encouraged by the Employment Relations Act 1999 and the provisions of the revised ACAS Code on

Disciplinary and Grievance Procedures. The philosophy behind the provisions are stated in the Code:

> "in any organisation workers may have problems or concerns about their work, working environment or working relationships that they wish to raise and have addressed. A grievance procedure provides a mechanism for these to be dealt with fairly and speedily, before they develop into major problems and potentially collective disputes."

The precedents address this point and, though it is not necessary in such cases to hold meetings, it is advisable that some formality is now adopted in relation to such cases. This is particularly so where there is a risk of construtcive unfair dismissal being claimed. For example, the employee may allege that there has been a breach of trust and confidence which had led to the employee terminating his employment. The safest course is simply to follow the same procedure in relation to all grievances.

PART T: EQUAL OPPORTUNITIES

Precedent T: Equal Opportunities

T1:	**Equal Opportunities Policy**	**985**
T2:	**Company Policy against Harassment**	**988**
T3:	**Equal Pay Policy Recommended by the Equal Opportunities Commission in its Code of Practice**	**993**
T4:	**Disability Policy**	**995**
Commentary:	**Equal Opportunities**	**998**

Useful Websites

- Equal Opportunities Commission

  http://www.eoc.org.uk/

- Code of Practice on Equal Pay

  http://www.eoc.org.uk/cseng/legislation/law_code_of_practice.pdf

---

Useful Websites *(continued)*

- Code of Practice on Discrimination

  http://www.eoc.org.uk/cseng/legislation/law_code_of_practice_-_sex_discrimination.asp

- Commission for Racial Equality

  http://www.cre.gov.uk/

  There is a revised draft Code out for consultation:

  http://www.cre.gov.uk/gdpract/employment_code.html

- The Disability Rights Commission

  http://www.drc-gb.org/

- Code of Practice in Employment

  http://www.drc-gb.org/publicationsandreports/publicationdetails.asp?id=227&section=emp

---

Precedent T1:   Equal Opportunities Policy

1   The Company is an equal opportunities employer and is committed to opposing all forms of discrimination in the workplace. The Company will not tolerate discrimination based upon age, disability, marital status, race (which means colour, race, nationality, ethnic or national origins), sex discrimination, sexual orientation or religion. The aim of this policy is that all members of staff know that they are able to work in an environment that is free from discrimination and you are able to achieve your full potential in your job. The Company will make decisions without reference to discriminatory criteria. All members of staff must be aware of this equal opportunities policy and should abide by its terms at all times.

The Definition of Discrimination

2 In a number of areas the law protects employees and discriminatory conduct or omissions are prescribed by Government legislation. There are specific concepts of discrimination which make it clear what is unlawful.

Direct Discrimination

3 The first area, which has become known as direct discrimination, occurs when an individual is treated less favourably than another person on the grounds of their disability, marital status, sex, sexual orientation, religion or race. [Although age is not yet covered by legislation the Company will treat discrimination on the ground of age in the same manner as other areas of discrimination.] It does not matter that you may believe you are acting in the interests of the individual or the employee if your less favourable treatment is on one of these grounds. This is because if you would not have treated a person who did not possess that characteristic in the same way this is direct discrimination.

Indirect Discrimination

4 Indirect discrimination occurs when a provision, criterion or practice is applied to an employee which is applied equally to persons not of the same group but that the employee finds he/she is not able to meet because of one of a particular ground of marital status, sex, sexual orientation, religion or race; which has a disproportionate effect on that particular group as compared with other groups and which cannot be shown to be objectively justified.

5 Whilst this concept may appear technical it is of importance since the Company may incur liability if you, in the scope of the duties entrusted to you, apply provisions, criteria or practices that are discriminatory against a particular group.

Harassment

6 The Company has a separate harassment policy to which reference should be made. Harassment is defined as unwanted conduct that violates an employee's dignity or creates an intimidating, hostile, degrading, humiliating or offensive work environment for the employee. In considering whether conduct amounts to harassment, regard will be had to all the circumstances and this will include the perception of the employee who complains of harassment.

7 Harassment will be treated very seriously by the Company and will be dealt with under the Harassment and/or Disciplinary Policy.

Disability: Reasonable adjustments

8 Disability discrimination does not have a concept of indirect discrimination because it has a concept that goes further and requires the Company to make a reasonable adjustment to seek to take away the disadvantage a disabled person may have in the workplace because of the disability. This means that the Company will consider alternative means by which a disabled person may be able to carry out the job or alternatively whether other steps may be possible.

Victimisation

9 Victimisation involves treating an individual less favourably than others because that individual has, in good faith, made allegations of discrimination, brought proceedings under the relevant legislation or grievances procedures, given evidence or information in connection with any proceedings or done anything under or by reference to such proceedings.

COMPANY POLICY STATEMENT

The Company will not tolerate discrimination on any grounds and operates an active equal opportunity policy. However, it cannot operate to stamp out discrimination unless it is made aware that this is happening

Discrimination may be treated as part of the disciplinary procedure, grievance procedure or sexual harassment depending upon its nature. The equal opportunities policy will apply at all stages from recruitment, throughout employment to issues of termination of employment.

Policy

8   All recruitment procedures followed by the Company will be on the basis of fair and objectively justified criteria that do not apply any requirements or conditions that are not necessary for the needs of the post or the business. Where job applicants have a disability the position of the Applicant will be reviewed and all possible steps will be taken to ensure that the Applicant does not suffer from any disadvantage in the recruitment process.

9   Throughout your employment you are expected to conduct yourself in a manner that is not discriminatory and the Company will take all possible steps to ensure that equal opportunity is maintained. This will include:

1.   Ensuring that job specifications relate to the requirements for the performance of the job.

2.   Providing equal opportunity training as the Company considers it is appropriate to enable you and other staff to implement equal opportunities. Where you consider that it is appropriate for you to receive equal opportunities training then you may contact the Personnel Department to discuss this matter.

3.   Monitoring the ethnic and gender composition of the workforce. This will be done in accordance with accepted practice as recommended by Equal Opportunities bodies or good human resources practice. All monitoring will be used only for the purpose of equal opportunity monitoring and will be anonymous.

4.   In the case of disability, considering what steps may be taken to ensure disabled individuals are not disadvantaged in the Company's workplace.

The Company Policies are drafted taking into account the above principles.

Precedent T2:   Company Policy against Harassment

Policy Statement

The Company is an Equal Opportunities Employer and does not permit any form of harassment in its workplace, whether it be based upon sex, race, disability, sexual orientation, age or personality. Harassment will be regarded most seriously and will be treated as gross misconduct under the Company's Disciplinary Procedure. The following Policy sets out the steps that you may take if you feel that you are the victim of harassment and the steps that the Company will take in relation to complaints of harassment.

The Definition of harassment

Harassment in the relevant legislation is defined as unwanted conduct which has the effect of violating the individual's dignity or creating an intimidating, hostile or offensive environment for the individual. The Company will consider all the circumstances in considering whether there has been harassment including the perception of the individual who alleges that he or she has been harassed. Harassment will include unwanted conduct whether verbal or not, which is of a sexual or racial nature or is based upon age, religion or sexual orientation, or other behaviour that is based on race, gender, religion, sexual orientation or age, and in this respect:

- Sexual, racial or religious banter or comments about sexual orientation may amount to harassment and should be avoided;

- the Company will not tolerate the display of any material that has sexual, racist or homophobic connotation;

- Verbal or non-verbal conduct or other behaviour that is directed to someone because of their disability and which could affect the dignity of the individual in the workplace. By way of example comments about an individual's ability to carry out the job because of disability may amount to harassment.

- Any form of verbal or non verbal conduct which could be regarded as bullying or intimidatory behaviour will fall within this harassment policy. By way of example comments made to junior staff that demean them in the workplace may amount to harassment.

Any of the above committed outside the workplace or outside working hours will be regarded by the Company as harassment if it affects the working environment.

A single act or incident can amount to harassment;

The issue is whether the recipient of the conduct could take the view that he or she was being harassed; it does not make any difference if you consider your conduct to be acceptable where the recipient does not.

Harassment Procedure

1   Stage 1: Informal procedures

In the first instance, the recipient of conduct that is considered by the employee to amount to harassment may seek to resolve the complaint on an informal basis. This may involve three stages:

1. If you consider that you are the recipient of such conduct you may prefer to resolve the matter by speaking to the individual concerned and pointing out that the conduct is not acceptable because it is unwanted and is interfering with the working environment. This is acceptable to the Company but you should not feel that this step must be taken if you feel uncomfortable about speaking to the harasser.

2. You may seek confidential advice from [Human Resources/ Counselling etc.]. Any staff from whom advice is sought have been fully trained to assist and will give advice about how a re-occurrence of the conduct may be prevented. Any advice will be confidential and will not be reported to anyone in the Company without your consent.

3. You may take the matter up with [set out who] if you prefer and an informal meeting can be arranged between yourself and the individual about whom you have a complaint at which an attempt may be made to resolve matters. Alternatively, the individual may be approached and informal discussions held if you request.

4. No disciplinary action will arise at this stage as this is intended to be an informal procedure which will enable you to resolve the matter without any further action by the Company.

5. However, if you consider that a criminal offence has been committed (i.e. assault or a sexual offence) you may seek the assistance of [...] to make a formal complaint to the police. Where a serious criminal offence is alleged [...] will discuss with you whether reconsideration should be given to a report to the police.

6. You may be offered compassionate paid leave in certain circumstances or, if you feel that you need such leave, you should not hesitate to request it.

2   Formal Complaint

If you have not been able to resolve matters on an informal basis or you consider the outcome to be unsatisfactory, you are entitled to make a formal complaint. The procedure that will be adopted is as follows:

> You should make your formal complaint in the first instance to [set out]. This may initially be oral but you will be asked to put your complaint in writing so that the nature of the complaint is clear. It is recognised that complaints may be sensitive and difficult to formulate and you may seek assistance from [set out] in formulating such complaint.

3   Investigation

The next stage will involve the investigation of your complaint. This will be carried out with sensitivity and with respect to you and the person against whom the complaint is made. The investigation will remain confidential and everyone who is interviewed will be told that they are not to discuss the matter with anyone and that breach of confidentiality is a disciplinary matter. The investigation will be carried out as follows:

1) The investigation will be carried out as expeditiously as possible. It will be conducted by someone who is not connected with any of the allegations and who is at least a grade above the person against whom the complaint is made;

2) The investigator will carry out the investigation as he considers most appropriate. This is likely to involve interviewing all concerned. Anyone who is interviewed will be permitted to be accompanied by a friend, colleague or trade union representative;

3) Notes will be taken of the interviews and those interviewed will receive copies to ensure that they agree with the notes. The investigator will concentrate on the facts of the complaint and will avoid, wherever, possible, embarrassing or intimate details. The complainant and harasser's witness statements will not be provided to any other party;

4)   At all stages you will be kept informed of the progress of the investigation and are entitled to ask how the investigation is progressing.

3   During the investigation consideration will be given, wherever possible, to the complainant and harasser being kept apart at work. You will not be moved to any position that is detrimental to you or if you object to being moved. You are entitled to ask for compassionate leave but this will not be required of you.

4   Report after investigation

Once the investigating officer has carried out his investigation he will prepare a report. This will be submitted to [...] who will decide whether the complaint has been made out. [...] may wish to make further inquiries or hold a meeting in order to come to his conclusion. A decision will normally be issued within [...] days of receipt of the investigator's report

5   The Disciplinary Procedure

Once the Investigation has been completed and a report has been provided by the Investigator, the Company may be of the view that the conduct warrants the implementation of its Disciplinary Procedure. This procedure will have to be invoked where sanctions are being considered against the alleged harasser and reference should be made to the procedure.

6   The sanctions

Once the Disciplinary procedure has been carried out and if the complaint is upheld, consideration will be given to the wishes of the complainant as to what should be done. This may involve:

•   Moving the harasser to another post. It should be noted that the question of disciplinary action against the harasser is separate matter.

•   If the complainant so wishes, moving him/her to a different place or post. The complainant will not be required to move if this is not acceptable.

- The complainant may be offered counselling and will be given leave or financial assistance to enable the complainant to recover from the effect of the harassment.

If the complaint is not upheld, because there is insufficient evidence and the parties cannot work together consideration may still be given to any steps that can be taken to resolve the situation.

Complaints that are malicious, known by the complainant to be unfounded or made in bad faith may result in disciplinary action.

As an Equal Opportunities Employer, the Company monitors and keeps records of any complaints to ensure that harassment is being dealt with effectively and eradicated from the workplace.

Precedent T3: Equal Pay Policy recommended by the Equal Opportunities Commission in its Code of Practice

A model equal pay policy

We are committed to the principle of equal pay for all our employees. We aim to eliminate any sex bias in our pay systems.

We understand that equal pay between men and women is a legal right under both domestic and European law.

It is in the interest of the organisation to ensure that we have a fair and just pay system. It is important that employees have confidence in the process of eliminating sex bias and we are therefore committed to working in partnership with the recognised trade unions. As good business practice we are committed to working with trade union/employee representatives to take action to ensure that we provide equal pay.

We believe that in eliminating sex bias in our pay system we are sending a positive message to our staff and customers. It makes good business sense to have a fair, transparent reward system and it helps us to control costs. We recognise that avoiding unfair discrimination will improve morale and enhance efficiency.

Our objectives are to:

- Eliminate any unfair, unjust or unlawful practices that impact on pay

- Take appropriate remedial action.

We will:

- implement an equal pay review in line with EOC guidance for all current staff and starting pay for new staff (including those on maternity leave, career breaks, or non-standard contracts)

- Plan and implement actions in partnership with trade union/employee representatives

- Provide training and guidance for those involved in determining pay

- inform employees of how these practices work and how their own pay is determined

- Respond to grievances on equal pay as a priority

- In conjunction with trade union/employee representatives, monitor pay statistics annually.

Precedent T4: Disability Policy

Disability Policy

This policy sets out the Company's policy with regard to disability. The Company recognises that disabled workers can make a positive contribution to the Company's Business and Society. This policy should be read in conjunction with the Company's Equal Opportunity and other relevant policies. No discrimination on the ground of disability will be tolerated. In addition the Company will, in certain circumstances, be under an obligation to make reasonable adjustments to its working practices to facilitate the employment of disabled workers. Where workers become disabled during employment similar duties will arise. All employees of the Company are expected to be familiar with the terms of this policy.

---

1. The Company is under a legal obligation not to discriminate against disabled persons by subjecting or allowing them to be subjected to less favourable treatment. In addition the Company may be under a duty to take positive steps to ensure that disabled persons are not disadvantaged in the workplace. If you consider that you are disadvantaged as a disabled person or have any concerns then you should contact Personnel [a Director of the Company]. These concerns will be discussed and positive steps may be taken to remedy the problem. Where steps cannot be taken the reasons for this will be explained.

2. The Company through [Personnel/ Director] will monitor the position with regard to disability in the workplace and will ensure that policies are implemented that ensure equal opportunities for disabled individuals.

3. Where there are employee representatives they will be kept fully informed of current policies and will co-operate with the Company to ensure that policies are fairly applied.

4. It will be the duty of employee representatives to ensure that employees are informed of current developments and any issues will be discussed in

joint consultative meetings. If you have any concerns you may address them to your employee representative or to [Personnel/your Line Manager/Director].

Recruitment Policies

5. The Company's **Recruitment and Selection Policy** sets out the procedure for the recruitment and selection of staff and reference should be made to the Policy. It should be noted that:

    (1) All recruitment advertisements, job descriptions and specifications will make it clear that (1) applicants may inform the Company if they have a disability and (2) steps will be taken to ensure that they are not disadvantaged in the recruitment process by making reasonable adjustments to the process or to the job, where possible, to accommodate the needs of the disabled person.

    (2) The process will be carried out with the **Equal Opportunity Policy** in mind.

    (3) The Company encourages applications from disabled persons.

6. Personnel will maintain close liaison with management responsible for the interview process and consideration will be given to help that may be required in the interview process. Those involved will be informed (for example reception will be informed on a confidential basis about any assistance that may be given).

7. Consideration will be given to trial periods where possible in order to ascertain whether the disabled person can carry out the job.

8. Consideration will be given to adapting premises or equipment or changing working practices where appropriate and possible and these may be considered during the interview process.

9. The Company will liase with external bodies where appropriate with a view to obtaining guidance, advice and assistance.

Terms of employment and the working environment

10. The Company will seek to ensure that those with a disability are offered terms that are not less favourable than other persons though in some cases

(for example where rate of pay is dependent upon the employee's productively) there may be differentials but the Company will ensure that these are objectively justified and will be prepared to consider any representations made in relation thereto.

11. All employees are expected to give consideration towards disabled colleagues and it may be a disciplinary offence to treat disabled employees less favourably.

12. Training and promotion is available to all employees regardless of disability and consideration will be given to reasonable adjustments that may be made. Where appropriate, trial periods may be given to assist the disabled employee in considering whether the position may be carried out.

13. Where an employee becomes disabled during the course of his or her employment consideration will be given to whether any reasonable adjustments may be made or are appropriate. This may include changing terms and conditions of work, re-deployment or retraining. The Company will ensure that the employee's capabilities are assessed with a view to considering whether any alternative work is suitable.

14. The Company's **Grievance Procedures** may be utilised by anyone who has a disability and considers that there is a problem arising out of the way the employee is being treated by colleagues or by the Company. Disabled persons will be treated in the same manner if a grievance is made against them but the Company will take into account the circumstances of disability where relevant.

Termination

14. Disabled persons are subject to the same **Disciplinary Procedures** in the same way as all members of staff. Account may be taken of disability in assisting disabled persons. Where:

(1) A capability issue arises because of disability, especially in relation to performance of an unacceptable standard, consideration will be given to whether reasonable adjustments may be made, which may include alternative employment or changes in terms and conditions. Where the disabled person cannot continue in employment because of the nature of the disability, no steps will be taken before discussion at appropriate directorate level.

(2) A disabled person will be disciplined in the same way as other employees for misconduct. The Company will be careful to distinguish between misconduct and disability.

(3) In considering candidates for redundancy the circumstances of the disabled person may be taken into account.

15. The usual appeals procedures may be followed in relation to dismissals.

SIGNED

DIRECTOR

COMMENTARY TO T: EQUAL OPPORTUNITIES

It is necessary for employers to have an equal opportunities policy, which covers all those areas in which discrimination has been outlawed, namely:

(1) Sex Discrimination and equal pay;

(2) Race Discrimination;

(3) Disability Discrimination;

(4) Religious Discrimination;

(5) Discrimination based upon sexual orientation.

(6) Age discrimination when it comes into force.

The general concepts were considered in Chapter 1. Equal Opportunities is a constant theme of this book so that consideration is given to the relevant issues in the appropriate chapter (see for example, Recruitment at Chapter 3 holidays and time off at pages 820–821, dress and appearance at pages 839–842).

The approach to be taken by employers may be viewed in two parts; that of *preventing* unlawful discrimination and ensuring liability does not arise on the part of the employer through its own acts or the acts of its employees by way of vicarious liability. To this end, the employer should have an equal opportunity policy, which may be comprehensive, or separate policies, which cover specific areas such as harassment, disability discrimination and equal pay as well as the general law.

The second aspect is that of *promoting* equal opportunities though the ability of employers to take positive or affirmative action in this country is very limited. Although the recent Sexual Orientation Regulations and Religion or Belief Regulations refer to positive action they make it clear that it is unlawful to extend more favourable treatment to the minority where there may be less favourable treatment of someone who does not fall within that group. There is a distinction between good practice and acts that amount to less favourable treatment.

However, as part of the culture of *promoting* equal opportunity the Government is seeking to foster through its advocacy of the 'work/life' balance (See the Governments site at *http://164.36.164.20/work-life balance/* and family friendly policies (see the DTI site at *http://www.dti.gov.uk/er/workingparents.htm*). One of the main planks of this reform is to give parents the young children the opportunity to request flexible working and this is covered in some detail at pages 786–804.

An Equal Opportunity Policy

The model Equal Opportunities Policies set out at T1 are largely self-explanatory. They set out the definitions of discrimination and the approach that will be taken by the employer if there is discrimination in the workplace. The Policies contain a company policy statement and make it clear that positive steps that will be taken by the employer to promote good relations. The employer should ensure that employees are aware of the statement and that active steps are taken to promote and implement equal opportunities. It is important that employers put the policy into practice; the courts have made it clear that the mere existence of a policy is not sufficient. In **Balgobin and Francis v London Borough of Tower Hamlets** [1987] IRLR the EAT upheld an Industrial Tribunal finding that the employers were not liable for proven sexual harassment of the appellant women by a male colleague because the employers had made out the defence under s.41(3) of the Sex Discrimination Act by establishing that they "took such steps as were reasonably practicable to prevent the employee from doing" the acts which the employees complained about. Management had not been aware of the acts but the employer has shown that there was proper and adequate staff supervision, and that the employers had made known their policy of equal opportunities. The existence and positive implementation of a procedure may thus provide a defence in discrimination cases under various legislation, which adopts the same defence as that in section 41(3) of the SDA 1975 where the employer may otherwise be vicariously liable.

Harassment

The issue of harassment in the workplace has come to the fore in recent years and the recent legislation provides a definition of harassment, which is set out in Chapter 1. Harassment may found a claim at common law as well as under the legislation.

Implied terms

There is, generally speaking, an implied term that an employer will give its employees reasonable support so that they can carry out their duties without harassment or disruption from other workers. In **Wigan Borough Council v Davies** [1979] IRLR 127; ICR 411 Ms Davies received 'cold shoulder' treatment from fellow employees arising out of a dispute where she had sided with management and, despite giving an undertaking to support her, her employer did nothing when she made a number of complaints. The ET and EAT held that the employer was in breach of the express undertaking and in breach of an implied term that the employer would give reasonable support. The onus of showing that there was nothing that could be done was on the employer. This may be compared with **McCabe v Chicpack Limited** [1976] IRLR 38 where there was nothing further an employer could do other than make it is clear to employees that conduct was not acceptable in circumstances where a disabled employee had been bullied but refused to name the culprits.

However, employers should treat bullying and harassment allegations as failure to do so is likely to breach the implied term of trust and confidence and may lead to claims of constructive dismissal. Bad language coupled with criticism is likely but will not always be a breach of the implied term. In **Palmanor Limited v Cedron** [1978] IRLR 303 Mr Justice Flynn stated that the test is whether:

> "in a case of this kind the Tribunal is required to ask itself the question whether the conduct was so unreasonable, that it really went beyond the limits of the contract. [and] ... although it is quite right that in these cases Tribunals have to be careful not to attach too great importance to words used in the heat of the moment or in anger,...nonetheless there comes a time when the language is such that even if the person using it is in a state of anger, an employee cannot be expected to tolerate it"#

(See also **A Garner v Grange Furnishings Limited** [1977] IRLR 206.) The employer ignores complaints at its peril (see **W A Goold (Pearmark) Limited v McConnell** [1995] IRLR 516).

Failure to do anything about bullying may also amount to a breach of the duty to provide a safe place of work.

The Protection from Harassment Act 1997

The Protection from Harassment Act 1997, by section 1 provides that

> "**1.**–(1) A person must not pursue a course of conduct–
>
> > (a) which amounts to harassment of another, and
> >
> > (b) which he knows or ought to know amounts to harassment of the other "

The person whose course of conduct is in question ought to know that it amounts to harassment of another if a reasonable person in possession of the same information would think the course of conduct amounted to harassment of the other. By section 3(1) an actual or apprehended breach of section 1 may be the subject of a claim in civil proceedings by the person who is or may be the victim of the course of conduct in question. Damages may be awarded for (among other things) any anxiety caused by the harassment and any financial loss resulting from the harassment (s 3(2)).

The Act also creates a criminal offence of harassment and there is provision for restraining orders to be made by the courts.

The Act was designed to deal with stalking but there is no reason why it could not be used by an employee against a co-employee where harassment occurs.

Sexual Harassment

Sexual harassment is not defined in the Sex Discrimination Act 1975 but is defined in the Recommendation on the Protection of the Dignity of Men and Women at Work (91/131) as an " unwanted conduct of a sexual nature, or other conduct based on sex affecting the dignity of men and women at work. This may include unwelcome physical, verbal or non verbal conduct".

Sexual harassment includes behaviour that is "unwanted, unreasonable and offensive to the recipient" and which is regarded at creating "an intimidating, hostile or humiliating work environment for the recipient". In **Insitu Cleaning Co Limited v Heads** [1995] IRLR 4 the EAT held that a one off act may be discriminatory and that it will be obvious in certain circumstances that conduct is unwanted. The lay members also gave guidance as to the procedure that an employer should follow:

> "1. The appellants [should] adopt a separate procedure which deals exclusively with complaints of sexual harassment.
>
> 2. Such a procedure should contain an informal first step which will enable complaints to be dealt with sympathetically before matters get out of hand. The experience of the lay members is that many women just want the harassment to stop and are not concerned to have the offender disciplined.
>
> 3. Any complaint should be dealt with 'from the perception of the person aggrieved'."

It was held in **Reed & Bull Information Systems Limited v Stedman** [1999] IRLR 299 that such conduct is unwanted if it is unwanted to the recipient regardless of what the harasser thought. General guidance was also given on the way that harassment cases should be approached:

> "For the sake of brevity only, we will take the more usual case where a woman makes a complaint of sexual harassment against a man, whilst accepting that there may be cases where a man complains of a woman's conduct towards him. The sort of questions which appear to have been of concern may be summarised thus:
>
> 1. If a woman regards as a harassment of a sexual nature words or conduct to which many women would not take exception or regard as a harassment, has her claim been made out?
>
> 2. If a man does not appreciate that his words or conduct are unwelcome, has her claim been proved?
>
> 3. Is a 'one-off' act (words or conduct) sufficient to constitute harassment?

It seems to us important to stress at the outset that 'sexual harassment' is not defined by statute. It is a colloquial expression which describes one form of discrimination in the workplace made unlawful by section 6 of the Sex Discrimination Act 1975. Because it is not a precise or defined phrase, its use, without regard to section 6, can lead to confusion. Under section 6 it is unlawful to subject a person to a 'detriment' on the grounds of their sex. Sexual harassment is a shorthand for describing a type of detriment. The word detriment is not further defined and its scope is to be defined by the fact-finding tribunal on a commonsense basis by reference to the facts of each particular case. The question in each case is whether the alleged victim has been subjected to a detriment and, second, was it is on the grounds of sex. Motive and intention of the alleged discriminator is not an essential ingredient, as in any other direct discrimination case, although it is will often be a relevant factor to take into account. Lack of intent is not a defence.

The second question must always be asked, but in a sexual harassment case, the answer will usually be quite clear without resort to a comparator, actual or hypothetical.

The essential characteristic of sexual harassment is that it is words or conduct which are unwelcome to the recipient and it is for the recipient to decide for themselves what is acceptable to them and what they regard as offensive. A characteristic of sexual harassment is that it is undermines the victim's dignity at work. It is creates an 'offensive' or 'hostile' environment for the victim and an arbitrary barrier to sexual equality in the workplace.

Because it is for each individual to determine what they find unwelcome or offensive, there may be cases where there is a gap between what a tribunal would regard as acceptable and what the individual in question was prepared to tolerate. It does not follow that because the tribunal would not have regarded the acts complained of as unacceptable, the complaint must be dismissed. It is seems to us that there will be a range of factual situations which may arise, in relation to which there may be difficult problems of proof. It is particularly important in cases of alleged sexual harassment that the fact-finding tribunal should not carve up the case into a series of specific incidents and try and measure the harm or detriment in relation to each. As it is has been put in a USA Federal Appeal Court decision (eighth circuit) (**USA v Gail Knapp** [1992] 955 Federal Reporter, 2nd series at p.564):

> 'Under the totality of the circumstances analysis, the district court [the fact-finding tribunal] should not carve the work environment into a series of incidents and then measure the harm occurring in each episode. Instead, the trier of fact must keep in mind that "each successive episode has its predecessors, that the impact of the separate incidents may accumulate, and that the work environment created may exceed the sum of the individual episodes.

Thus, for example, as here, a blatant act of a sexual nature, such as the deliberate looking up of the victim's skirt whilst she was sitting down, may well make other incidents, such as asking to be shown personal photographs, which the victim was looking at in work, take on a different colour and significance. Once unwelcome sexual interest in a female employee has been shown by a man, she may well feel bothered about his attentions which, in a different context, would appear quite unobjectionable.

As to whether the conduct is unwelcome, there may well be difficult factual issues to resolve. In general terms, some conduct, if not expressly invited, could properly be described as unwelcome. A woman does not, for example, have to make it clear in advance that she does not want to be touched in a sexual manner. At the lower end of the scale, a woman may appear, objectively, to be unduly sensitive to what might otherwise be regarded as unexceptional behaviour. But because it is for each person to define their own levels of acceptance, the question would then be whether by words or conduct she had made it is clear that she found such conduct unwelcome. It is not necessary for a woman to make a public fuss to indicate her disapproval; walking out of the room might be sufficient. Tribunals will be sensitive to the problems that victims may face in dealing with a man, perhaps in a senior position to herself, who will be likely to deny that he was doing anything untoward and whose defence may often be that the victim was being over-sensitive. Provided that any reasonable person would understand her to be rejecting the conduct of which she was complaining, continuation of the conduct would, generally, be regarded as harassment. But at all times, the tribunal should not lose sight of the question at issue: was the applicant subjected to a detriment on the grounds of her sex? The answer to that question does not depend upon the number of incidents. A one-off act may be sufficient to damage her working environment and constitute a barrier to sexual equality in the workplace, which would constitute a detriment."

The EAT adopted and expanded on the statements in *Reed* in the case of **Driskell v Peninsula Business Services Limited** [2000] IRLR 151 where the EAT stated:

"the tribunal's approach should be as follows:

(a) The tribunal hears the evidence and finds the facts. As has already been pointed out, it is desirable not to include in this exercise judgments as to the discriminatory significance, if any, of individual incidents, judgment thus far should be limited to the finding of all facts that are prima facie relevant. If ad hoc assessments 'discrimination or no' are made the result is a fragmented and discursive judgment; more importantly, there is the potential noted in Reed and Bull for ignoring the impact of totality of successive incidents, individually trivial.

(b)   The tribunal then makes a judgment as to whether the facts as found disclose apparent treatment of the female applicant by the respondents as employers in one or more of the respects identified in section 6(2)(a) and (b) that was less favourable than their treatment, actual or potential, of a male employee.

(c)   The tribunal further considers any explanation put forward on behalf of the respondent employers. In the light of any such explanation is the discrimination so far potentially identified real or illusory?

(d)   In making judgments under (b) and (c) above (and in practice these two stages may elide together) the following guidance is applicable:

1.   Sexual harassment is helpfully categorised in Reed and Bull, op cit. At 302:

(The passage from Reed beginning "It seems to use important..." was then set out.

2.   The finding of less favourable treatment leading to 'detriment' is one of fact and degree so that a single act may legitimately found a complaint, c.f. Insitu Cleaning Co Ltd, op cit.

3.   The ultimate judgment, sexual discrimination or no, reflects an objective assessment by the tribunal of all the facts. That said, amongst the factors to be considered are the applicant's subjective perception of that which is the subject of complaint and the understanding, motive and intention of the alleged discriminator. Thus, the act complained of may be so obviously detrimental, that is, disadvantageous (see Insitu, op cit) to the applicant as a woman by intimidating her or undermining her dignity at work, that the lack of any contemporaneous complaint by her is of little or no significance. By contrast she may complain of one or more matters which if taken individually may not objectively signify much, if anything, in terms of detriment. Then a contemporaneous indication of

sensitivity on her part becomes obviously material as does the evidence of the alleged discriminator as to his perception. That which in isolation may not amount to discriminatory detriment may become such if persisted in notwithstanding objection, vocal or apparent. The passage cited from the judgment of the US Federal Appeal Court is germane. By contrast the facts may simply disclose hypersensitivity on the part of the applicant to conduct which was reasonably not perceived by the alleged discriminator as a being to her detriment _ no finding of discrimination can then follow.

4. In making its judgment a tribunal should not lose sight of the significance in this context of the sex of not just the complainant but also that of the alleged discriminator. Sexual badinage of a heterosexual male by another such cannot be completely equated with like badinage by him of a woman. Prima facie the treatment is not equal: in the latter circumstance it is the sex of the alleged discriminator that potentially adds a material element absent as between two heterosexual men.

5. Throughout the tribunal should remain conscious of the burden and standard of proof. That said, the notion that discrimination may well be covert and is not readily admitted is as applicable in the context of sex as in the context of race. The passage cited from **King v Great Britain China Centre**, op cit, consistently proves authoritative guidance on these aspects.

The SDA 1975 differs from the other legislation in that it does not contain a specific definition of harassment so that one has to consider whether the conduct amounted to less favourable treatment. The following have been considered in the case law:

- Remarks of a sexual nature or unwanted physical contact: **Insitu Cleaning Co Ltd v Heads** [1995] IRLR 5; **Reed**; **Driskell** above.

- Display of offensive literature (nude photographs) was not considered to be discriminatory in **Stewart v Cleveland Guest (Engineering) Ltd** [1994] IRLR 440 because a man could equally be offered. However, the EAT did state that it was crucial that complaints not be treated as trivial but that "They shoudl be taken up, investigated and dealt with in a sympathetic and sensible fashion."

The employer should protect the employee against the acts of third parties where it is forseeable that acts may occur that amount to less favourable treatment (**Burton and Rhule v De Vere Hotels** [1996] IRLR 596 but query whether this case would be decided the same today because of comments made in **Macdonald v Advocate General of Scotland and Ors** [2003] UKHL 34 [2003] IRLR 512).

The employer may be liable where the harassment takes place at a social gathering, such as the office party where the social occasion may be regarded as an extension of employment (compare **Chief Constable Lincolnshire Police v Stubbs** [1999] IRLR 81 where harassment at a leaving do in a public house "were connected with work and the workplace" with **Waters v Commissioner of Police of the Metropolis** [1997] IRLR 589 and **Sidhu v Aerospace Composite Technology Limited** [2000] IRLR 602).

The harassment procedure set out in Precedent T2 seeks to implement the guidance given in these cases. However, the procedure has been extended to areas other than sex discrimination where harassment may occur.

Racial harassment, religion or belief harassment and harassment based on sexual orientation

These areas all contain the same definition of harassment, namely where a person "he engages in unwanted conduct which has the purpose or effect of—

(a) violating that other person's dignity, or

(b) creating an intimidating, hostile, degrading, humiliating or offensive environment for him."

In deciding whether conduct has this effect it is necessary to consider all the circumstances, including the perception of the person who alleges that they have been harassed. The test is objective but it takes account of the subjective perception of the person harassed as one of the factors.

Disability harassment

From October 2004 the DDA 1995 will contain a specific definition of harassment (see Chapter 1) It was in any event possible for a disabled person to bring a claim of less favourable treatment when he or she is subjected to behaviour which would not be directed at a non disabled person. In one tribunal case, **Cox v Rentokil Services Limited** [2002/ case no 2405154/00] an employee with severe hearing difficulties was subjected to comments such as "have you got your ears switched on". This was found to be disability discrimination and the employee was awarded damages for injury to feelings.

The Employers Forum on Disability (*http://www.employers-forum.co.uk/ www/index.htm*) produces briefing guides on dealing with disabled persons.

Devising and implementing a harassment policy

It is essential that the employer has some form of harassment policy and it will be very difficult to rely upon the defence to vicarious liability if there is no such procedure. There should be:

- A Policy statement that all employees have the right to be treated with dignity and that any form of harassment will not be condoned.

- The policy will define the forms of harassment that are covered.

- The policy should set out the sanctions that may be applied. In the case of possible dismissal the statutory dismissal and disciplinary procedures may be engaged.

- The Harassment policy should set out the positive duty of managers. The *Commission Recommendation and Code Of Practice* No 2/131/EE of 27 November 1991 on the protection of the dignity of men and women at Work states at Annexe 1 notes managers (including supervisors) have a particular duty to ensure that sexual harassment does not occur in work areas for which they are responsible. It is recommended that managers explain the organisation's policy to their staff and take steps to positively promote the policy. Managers should also be responsive and supportive to any member of staff who complains about sexual harassment, provide full and clear advice on the procedure to be adopted. maintain confidentiality in any cases of sexual harassment and ensure that there is no further problem of sexual harassment or any victimisation after a complaint has been resolved."

- There should be a separate procedure because of the sensitive nature of the allegations. The policy should be made clear to everyone and distributed to all employees. Part 5 of the EC Code referred to above sets out procedures which have been adopted in the Precedent at T2.

Disability and Equal Opportunities

It is sensible to have a separate disability policy since issues of disability are likely to raise matters that are unique to this legislation, particularly, in regard to reasonable adjustments. A draft policy is contained at T4. The Company may wish to include specific examples of what can amount to reasonable adjustments and this is particularly helpful where the Company has already made adjustments in the past so that it can point to these in order to illustrate that it takes its duties seriously. The Act is considered in Chapter 1 and issues of disability have been referred to at the relevant parts of the Book.

Religious or Other Belief and Sexual Orientation

The concepts of discrimination based upon Religious or Belief and on Sexual Orientation are considered in detail in Chapter 1 and the General Equal Opportunities Policy refers to discrimination on these Grounds. Again, the issues are considered throughout the book. One particular issue that may arise in the future is the tension between the two sets of Regulations where those with strong religious beliefs take exception to working with employees of a particular sexual orientation. The two ACAS Guides deal with this by reference to the following question:

> **"Q I am concerned that on the grounds of religion, some of my staff may refuse to work with their gay or lesbian colleagues.**
>
> **A** Some religions do have strong views concerning sexual orientation but most do not advocate persecution of people because of their sexual orientation. Everyone has the right to be treated with dignity and respect in the workplace whatever their sex, race, colour, disability, age, religion or sexual orientation. You should include this over-riding premise in your Equality Policy and show that you take a robust view when this principal is not adhered to. Your workers do not have to be friends but you can insist that they treat each other professionally."

It is suggested that this answer does not get to grips with the problem. Where an employee refuses to work with someone because of their sexual orientation or the workplace is disrupted because of the attitude of such an individual this should be a matter that is dealt with under the Disciplinary Policy as it is precisely this type of conduct that the Equal Opportunities Policies are aimed at outlawing.

An American Court took such a view in **Richard D. Peterson, Plaintiff-Appellant, No. 01–35795 v. D.C. No. _CV–00–00068–LMB HEWLETT-**

PACKARD CO., a corporation, Defendant-Appellee. United States Court Of Appeals For The Ninth Circuit Appeal from the United States District Court for the District of Idaho (see *http://caselaw.lp.findlaw.com/data2/circs/9th/0135795p.pdf*) and employment lawyers are recommended to read this decision, which contains the approach which, it is suggested, should be taken in relation to the Regulations.

Examples of issues that may arise under the Sexual Orientation Regulations, as referred to in the ACAS Guides, include:

- Taking care when inviting partners to social functions so that same sex partners are not excluded.

- Avoiding homophobic jokes and comments.

- Ensuring confidentiality of procedures so that individuals are not 'outed' against their wishes.

- Avoiding stereotyping; i.e., in relation to HIV.

Examples under the Religion or Belief Regulations include giving consideration to:

- times within work schedules for religious observance. ACAS notes that the regulations do not say that employers must provide time and facilities for religious or belief observance in the workplace. However, ACAS states that employers should consider whether their policies, rules and procedures indirectly discriminate against staff of particular religions or beliefs and if so whether reasonable changes might be made. It may be reasonable to provide a prayer room if the employer has the facilities or to re-arrange rest breaks so that prayers can be said.

- special dietary requirements, for example kosher, halal and vegetarian food. It may be necessary to ensure that food can be stored separately in sealed containers where a vegetarian cannot store lunch in a fridge next to meat.

- avoiding ice breakers and training activities that use language or physical contact that might be inappropriate for some beliefs

- avoiding exercises which require the exchange of personal information.

- ensuring related social activities do not exclude people by choice of venue

- significant religious festivals such as Ramadan. ACAS states at paragraph 4.2. of its Guide that:

> "...A worker may request holiday in order to celebrate festivals or attend ceremonies. An employer should sympathetically consider such a request where it is reasonable and practical for the employee to be away from work, and they have sufficient holiday entitlement in hand. While it may be practical for one or a small number to be absent it might be difficult if numerous such requests are made. In these circumstances the employer should discuss the matter with the employees affected, and with any recognised trade union, with the aim of balancing the needs of the business and those of other employees. Employers should carefully consider whether their criteria for deciding who should and who should not be granted leave may indirectly discriminate."

Rules on personal appearance may be of significance in the context of the Religion and Belief Regulations (see Part T).

There is much practical Guidance in the ACAS Guides and they are to be commended.

Equal Pay

The Equal Pay Act 1970 which came into force at the same time as the Sex Discrimination Act 1975 outlaws discriminatory terms and conditions of employment, including pay, unless differences can be justified by a "genuine material factor" defence where the difference is not related to sex (section 1(3)). The Act operates by implying an equality clause into every contract (section 1(1)) breach of which is a breach of contract. The clause will apply where a man and woman are engaged on 'like work', 'work rated as equivalent ' or 'work of equal value' (section 1(2)). It is necessary for the complainant to identify a comparator even if not employed at the same time (**Kells v Pilkington PLC** [2002] IRLR 693) and a comparator does not have to be from the same employer provided the relationship is sufficient close (as where the terms and conditions derive from the same source); See **South Ayrshire Council v Morton** [2002] ICR 956; **Allonby v Accrington & Rossendale College** ECJ case C–256/01 on 13th January 2004).

The policy at T4 is taken from the Equal Opportunities Code of Practice.

U. HEALTH AND SAFETY

<table>
<tr><td>Precedent U:</td><td>Health and Safety</td><td></td></tr>
<tr><td>U1:</td><td>Policy statement</td><td>1012</td></tr>
<tr><td>U2:</td><td>Fire policy</td><td>1015</td></tr>
<tr><td>Commentary:</td><td>Health and Safety</td><td>1016</td></tr>
</table>

Precedent U1: Health and Safety at Work Policy Statement in Accordance with the Health and Safety at Work etc. Act 1974

The Company is committed to providing a safe working environment and to care for the health and safety of its employees. The Company has a strict policy that it will comply with the provisions of the Health and Safety at Work Act 1974 and all associated regulations and codes of practice that are made and may come into force under it from time to time. The Company co-operates with the Health and Safety Executive and takes into account all recommendations that it may make. The Company will comply with what is regarded as best practice in relation to the work that it carries out.

The following is a general policy statement. Detailed matters relating to Health and Safety can be found in [*SET OUT*].

Company Responsibility

1 The Directors have ultimate responsibility for Health and Safety matters and are committed to ensuring that standards are upheld and that sufficient funding and training is made available.

2 At all times the Company will conduct its activities in such manner as to ensure that the health and safety of its employees are not affected and that they are not exposed to risk to heath and safety. The nature of the industry means that there may be risks and where they exist the Company will do everything that is reasonable to reduce these risks. In this respect there are two broad areas that the Company will seek to ensure mean that the health and safety of its employees will be placed first.

Lines of Responsibility

3 It is important that there is clear recognition of the lines of responsibility in relation to health and safety matters so that areas of health and safety are not ignored or neglected. In this respect the general lines are:

1. Overall and final responsibility for health and safety policy rests with [. . . . .] [*A DIRECTOR*].

2. Overall responsibility for the day to day implementation of health and safety policy rests with [. . . . .].

3. The Company takes its duties of consultation very seriously and responsibility for consultation with employees on health and safety issues rests with [. . . .]. Where appropriate this consultation will take place through trade unions or staff representatives.

4. On a day to day basis, managers have responsibility for implementing health and safety policies and employees must ensure that they comply with all rules, regulations, instructions or other measures to ensure health and safety at work and they must co-operate with their managers in this respect.

5. On a day to day basis there are set procedures should an accident occur and employees should be fully acquainted with these procedures, which can be found [. . . . .]. There are also rigorous reporting procedures in relation to accidents, which can be found [.

. . . .]. The person to whom any queries should be directed in relation any accident you may have at work is [. . . . .].

The Company's responsibilities

4   The Company carries out the following in order to ensure that health and safety standards are complied with:

1.   Assessment of risks in the workplace to the health and safety of employees and identification of measures that need to be implemented to comply with all health and safety obligations. Periodic risk assessments are carried out for this purpose.

2.   The provision of:

   a)   a safe place of work by ensuring that all equipment, machinery and safety devices thereon, locations and means of access and egress to the workplace are such that the environment is safe;

   b)   all necessary safety equipment and clothing;

   c)   instruction and training to ensure safety standards are complied with.

3.   The establishment of clear emergency procedures.

4.   Regular consultation with the workforce to ensure that they are fully aware of safety matters, are able to air their concerns and that there is full co-operation between the Company and the workforce.

5.   The establishment of appropriate committees for consultation.

The Employee's Responsibilites

5   In order to assist the Company in ensuring safety standards are met the employee has a responsibility to ensure that he is fully conversant with all requisite standards and any failure to comply with health and safety standards may amount to a disciplinary offence. As part of this duty the employee should:

1.   Actively co-operate with the Company to ensure that this health and safety policy is met by complying with all safety instructions or

directions that are issued, ensuring that the health and safety of other persons are taken into account by complying with all health and safety requirements and by using all safety equipment or clothing that has been provided.

2.   Ensure that any equipment or machinery is used in accordance with safety instructions and immediately report any malfunction or other difficulty with machinery or equipment that could be a risk or health hazard.

3.   Report any accidents that occur and co-operate in any investigation.

This policy is for your own good and must be adhered to. If there are any queries about the policy or training you may contact [. . . . .].

Precedent U2:   Fire Policy

You should be fully conversant with this fire policy which is for you own safety.

1   The Workplace

You should make yourself fully aware of your nearest fire exit and alterative exits and you should be aware of the details of the procedures and assembly points in the event of a fire. These are posted on notice boards and you should be familiar with them. A Fire Warden is appointed to [your area][floor] and his name is on your notice board.

Regular drills will be carried out to ensure everyone knows the procedure.

2   If you witness a fire

Operate the nearest fire alarm immediately and make known the location of the fire to reception or to the most appropriate person [*i.e.* Head of Department, *etc.*]

Do not attempt to tackle a fire yourself unless it is very minor and you have been trained and are able to do so. The Company wants Healthy staff not Heroes!

3 In the event of a fire

In the event of a fire the Fire Warden will be responsible for the evacuation of your floor. You should follow the Fire Warden's instructions. You should in any event make your way to the nearest exit. You should leave immediately in a calm and orderly manner and should not stop to collect personal possessions or any other items. Do not use any lifts. Assemble at your assembly point.

Do not go back into the building unless you are instructed that it is safe to do so.

COMMENTARY TO U: HEALTH AND SAFETY

The two precedents contain model statements of (1) general health and safety policy and (2) a model fire procedure. They are statements of general practice since there is a myriad of statutory provisions that the employer has to comply with in this field and a complete overview of health and safety cannot be achieved in a book of this size. The employer has both common law and statutory duties that are onerous.

At common law there is an implied term that employers will take all reasonable care for the safety of their employees whilst they are carrying out their duties (**Matthews v Kuwait Bechtel Corporation** [1959] 2 QB 57) which will include transferring employees to work that may be detrimental to safety (**Jagdeo v Smiths Industries Limited** [1982] ICR 47). Employers should deal promptly with matters of safety that are drawn to their attention as part of their general duty to take reasonable care for the safety of employees (**BAC v Austin** [1978] IRLR 332).

There is an implied term that employees will not be expected to work in unreasonable working conditions (**Concord Lighting International v Willis** [EAT 343/800] where the employee had to work in a cold draft in winter; **Graham Oxley Tool Steels Limited v Firth** [1980] IRLR 135 — cold temperatures; **Keys v Shoefayre Limited** [1978] IRLR 476 — where the employer failed to do anything about staff safety after armed robberies).

Risk to health

A term in a contract which requires the employee to carry out work that is injurious to health is likely to be unenforceable. The Court of Appeal refused to strike out an action as disclosing no reasonable cause of action in **Johnstone v Bloomsbury Health Authority** [1991] IRLR 118 where a trainee doctor claimed that a requirement he work 48 hours overtime in addition to a 40 hour week was injurious to his health and therefore unlawful. See further Part W which refers to the latest cases on stress. Where it is known that the employee is suffering from depression, anxiety or other psychological illness as a result of the stressful nature of the job the employer may be in breach of contract by failing to give sufficient support or training (**Walker v Northumberland County Council** [1995] IRLR 36; **Lancaster v Birmingham City Council** (*IDS Brief* 648 page 7 — and see *Work Related Injury – XPL Publishing*). However, in **Morrison v West Lothian College and Lothian Regional Council** [Court of Session 21.7.1999 *IDS Brief* 655] it was held that the employer will only be liable in relation to a stress related illness, caused by the working environment, where they have a recognised psychiatric illness or disorder and it is reasonably foreseeable to an ordinary bystander that stress or anxiety is likely to be suffered to the extent that it will cause such disorder.

Duties at common law include:

- A duty to provide a safe place of work (**General Cleaning Contractors v Christmas** [1953] AC 180) which cannot be delegated and includes providing a safe means of access.

- A duty to provide a safe system of work (see section 2 of the Health and Safety at Work Act 1974 and *Christmas.*)

- A duty to provide safe equipment plant and materials.

- A duty to ensure that fellow workers do not indulge in dangerous horseplay when it is known that they have such a propensity (**Hudson v Ridge Manufacturing Co Limited** [1957] 2 QB 348).

- A duty to protect from risk of injury.

Notable statutes include:

- The Management of Health and Safety at Work Regulations 1999, SI 1999/3242 dec99015.txt which replaced the Management of Health and Safety at Work Regulations 1992. See also:

  - HSE Guidance for employers on welfare provision, INDG293, dated 5/99 reproduced at the end fo this chapter.

- The Health and Safety at Work Act 1974 and related statutory instruments;

- The Occupiers Liability Act 1957;

- The Fire Precautions Act 1971 and related statutory instruments;

- The Management of Health and Safety at Work Regulations 1992;

- The COSHH Regulations;

- The Workplace (Health, Safety and Welfare) Regulations 1992.

Reference must be made to specialist health and safety texts for a detailed outline of their effect.*

The note below shows the level of detail given by the Health and Safety Executive and reference should be made to their Website for assistance and for detailed forms/books on the topic. (See *http://www.hsebooks.com/*.)

---

*   See further, for the legal context *Health and Safety: A Modern Guide*, EMIS Professional Publishing, 2002.

Introduction

If you employ anyone (however short the period) you must 'so far as reasonably practicable', provide adequate and appropriate welfare facilities for them while they are at work. This means you must provide such facilities unless it is clearly unreasonable in terms of time, trouble, cost and physical difficulty.

'Welfare facilities' are those that are necessary for the well-being of your employees, such as washing, toilet, rest and changing facilities, and somewhere clean to eat and drink during breaks.

WHAT TOILET AND WASHING FACILITIES DO I NEED TO PROVIDE?

You have to provide adequate toilet and washing facilities for your employees. 'Adequate' means you have to provide:

-   enough toilets and washbasins for those expected to use them – people should not have to queue for long periods to go to the toilet;

-   where possible, separate facilities for men and women – failing that, rooms with lockable doors;

-   clean facilities – to help achieve this walls and floors should preferably be tiled (or covered in suitable waterproof material) to make them easier to clean;

-   a supply of toilet paper and, for female employees, a means of disposing of sanitary dressings;

-   facilities that are well lit and ventilated;

-   facilities with hot and cold running water;

-   enough soap or other washing agents;

-   a basin large enough to wash hands and forearms if necessary;

-   a means for drying hands, e.g. paper towels or a hot air dryer;

– showers where necessary, i.e. for particularly dirty work.

You must always consider the needs of those with disabilities.

DO I NEED TO PROVIDE DRINKING WATER?

Yes. The law requires that you provide drinking water and ensure that:

– it is free from contamination and is preferably from the public water supply – bottled water dispensers are acceptable as a secondary supply;

– it is easily accessible by all employees;

– there are adequate supplies taking into consideration the temperature of the working environment and types of work activity;

– cups or a drinking fountain are provided;

– taps and containers are clearly and correctly labelled as drinking water.

WHAT IF STAFF WORK IN REMOTE WORKPLACES WITHOUT SUITABLE PLUMBING AND A WATER SUPPLY?

You may need to provide chemical toilets and washing facilities, such as water containers.

WHAT IF MY EMPLOYEES ARE WORKING AT TEMPORARY WORKSITES?

'So far as is reasonably practicable' you need to provide flushing toilets and running water. Portable cabins converted into toilet facilities are available from hire companies. If this is not possible consider alternatives such as chemical toilets and water containers.

Use of public toilets and washing facilities should be a last resort and not used just because they are the cheaper option! This would not be acceptable where the provision of better facilities would be reasonably practicable.

WHAT FACILITIES DO I NEED TO PROVIDE FOR CHANGING AND STORING CLOTHING?

If the work activity requires your employees to change into and wear specialist clothing (overalls, a uniform, thermal clothing etc.), then you must provide enough changing rooms for the number of people expected to use them.

Where a changing room is provided it should:

- be readily accessible;

- contain, or lead directly to, clothing storage and washing facilities;

- provide seating;

- provide a means for hanging clothes – a hook or peg may be sufficient;

- ensure the privacy of the user.

Try to prevent employees' own clothing coming into contact with work-soiled clothing or getting dirty or wet. Provide separate storage for clean and contaminated clothing which:

- allows wet clothing to be hung up to dry out during the course of the day;

- is well ventilated.

Separate guidance is available from HSE Books on the provision of personal protective equipment

WHAT ARRANGEMENTS SHOULD I MAKE FOR MEAL BREAKS?

There should be a suitable seating area for workers to use during breaks

- it needs to be clean and located where food will not get contaminated.

There should be washing facilities nearby, and a means of heating food or water for hot drinks. You must maintain good hygiene standards.

DO I HAVE TO PROVIDE A ROOM FOR THOSE WHO SMOKE?

No. However, you must provide a working environment where people can work without being irritated by tobacco smoke – the most effective way of doing this may be to prohibit smoking in all but a few designated rooms.

DO I NEED TO PROVIDE REST FACILITIES FOR PREGNANT WOMEN AND NURSING MOTHERS?

Yes, if it is 'reasonably practicable' for you to do so. You may need to provide a room for pregnant women/nursing mothers to rest or lie down.

IF I DO ALL THIS, HAVE I DONE ENOUGH?

No. You must also ensure that the facilities are kept clean and in good condition, and that there is always an adequate supply of toilet paper, soap etc.. This means that you need to put in place an effective system to maintain them to a high standard, including regular cleaning.

Ask yourself – would you be happy to use the welfare facilities you provide for your employees?

HOW MANY FACILITIES DO I NEED TO PROVIDE?

The following tables show the minimum number of toilets and washbasins that should be provided.

Table 1: Number of toilets and washbasins for mixed use
        (or women only)

People at work	1–5	6–25	26–50	51–75	76–100
Toilets	1	2	3	4	5
Washbasins	1	2	3	4	5

Table 2: Toilets used by men only

Men at work	1–15	16–30	31–45	46–60	61–75	76–90	91–100
Toilets	1	2	2	3	3	4	4
Urinals	1	1	2	2	3	3	4

WHERE CAN I GET MORE INFORMATION AND ADVICE?

This leaflet summarises the requirements of the Workplace (Health, Safety and Welfare) Regulations 1992. You can find more information in:

– Workplace health, safety and welfare. Workplace (Health, Safety and Welfare) Regulations 1992. Approved Code of Practice and guidance L24 HSE Books 1992 ISBN 0 7176 0413 6

– A short guide to the Personal Protective Equipment at Work Regulations 1992 INDG174 HSE Books 1996

You may also find it useful to discuss your needs with manufacturers and suppliers of welfare facilities, services and consumables.

PART V: TERMINATION

Precedent V: Termination

V1:	Termination of employment and notice	1024
V2:	Payment in lieu	1025
V3:	Accrued holiday pay	1025
V4:	Sick pay during the notice period	1026
V5:	Garden leave	1026
V6:	Summary termination	1027
V7:	Retirement	1028
Commentary:	Termination	1028

Precedent V1: Termination of Employment and Notice

You are entitled to the following notice from the Company:

1. Less than two years' continuous employment: One week

2. After two years' continuous service: One week for every year of such continuous employment up to a maximum of 12 weeks.

You must give four weeks' notice to terminate your employment. Notice, once given by you, cannot be retracted unless the Company agrees in writing.

The above notice periods are subject to the Company's right to terminate your employment without notice where it is entitled to do so.

V2: Payments in lieu of notice

Precedent V2.1: The Company may decide in its absolute discretion to pay you salary *in lieu* of the notice period that would otherwise be given by making payments to you during the notice period at the time you would have otherwise been paid your salary. However, during the notice period you will use your best endeavours to obtain other employment and should you obtain such employment you will provide details of all benefits to the Employer who shall be entitled to offset such payments against any salary otherwise due.

Precedent V2.2: Upon notice having been given to terminate by either party the Company reserves the right to make a payment *in lieu* of notice for the whole or any unexpired period (which it may make at any time during the notice period) and such payment shall consists solely of basic salary [*LIST ANY OTHER ITEMS THAT MAY BE INCLUDED*] and shall be subject to such deductions as the Company is required or authorised to make.

Precedent V3: Accrued Holiday Pay on Termination

Your holiday entitlement is as provided for [in the contract of employment]. Upon the termination of your employment:

1. You will not be entitled to any holiday pay for holiday that would otherwise have accrued save as is required by the Working Time Regulations 1998.

[You will be paid accrued holiday pay at your basic rate of salary].

2. If you have taken more days holiday than your entitlement would have been at the date of termination of your employment you will be responsible for re-paying holiday pay that you have already received in respect of this excess and, for this purpose the Employer will be entitled to deduct from your final salary such excess.

Precedent V4: Sick Pay during the Notice Period

During your notice period, given by either party, the Company may withhold payment for sickness absence, other than any statutory entitlement.

Precedent V5: Garden Leave

Upon notice being given by either party the Company shall have the absolute right to require you not to attend work during your period of notice but to remain available for work during normal working hours should you be required. If the Company exercises this right:

1. You must not attend at your workplace or at any Company or group premises unless required.

2. You must not without the written permission of the Company contact or make any attempt to contact any client, customer supplier or employee of the Company or Group and must not make any representation or statement in this regard. You are also not permitted to contact any professional advisers of the Company or group (such as solicitors and accountants) nor its bankers.

3. The Company may require you to return all Company equipment and other property to it during the notice period.

4. The Company may require you to resign any Company directorships or other positions during your notice period.

5. You will continue to receive your full salary and benefits during your notice period.

As a matter of contract, the Company shall not be under any obligation to provide you with work.

Precedent V6: Summary Termination

The Company will be entitled to dismiss you without notice if you commit any of the following acts:

1. You are guilty of conduct set out in the Company's Disciplinary Procedures which warrants dismissal without notice.

2. You commit any act of negligence, neglect of duty which is serious or any act which causes the Company to lose trust and confidence and which justifies dismissal without notice.

3. You are in serious or repudiatory breach of this agreement.

4. You commit any act outside your employment which is liable to bring the Company [or Group] into disrepute.

5. You are declared bankrupt or otherwise enter into any arrangement with creditors.

6. You are convicted of a criminal offence and in the case of a motoring offence this results in disqualification or imprisonment.

7. You suffer from mental disorder which makes it unable to carry out your duties.

8. You are persistently absent from work for a period of [.....] days in any [....] months.

Precedent V7: Retirement

The normal retirement age is [....] years and your contract will automatically terminate on your [....] birthday. The Company may permit early retirement and may permit you to work after normal retirement age. Enquiries should be made of ....

COMMENTARY TO V: TERMINATION

Precedent V1: Notice

This precedent sets out the statutory entitlements to notice under section 86 of the Employment Rights Act 1996. Notice, once given, cannot be retracted without the agreement of the parties (see **Riordan v The War Office** [1959] 3 All ER 552 and Duggan, *Wrongful Dismissal and Breach of Contract* at page 285).

Precedent V2: Payment in lieu

Where there is a provision that the employer may give notice to the employee or may make a payment *in lieu* of notice this may have two effects. First, the employer may lawfully bring the contract to an end by summarily terminating the employment and making a payment *in lieu* of notice. If the money is not paid then it may be claimed as a debt. Second, there will be no duty to mitigate as the payment may be characterised as liquidated damages.

In **Abrahams v Performing Right Society Limited** [1995] ICR 1028; IRLR 486, Mr Abrahams was employed under a five year fixed term contract which was amended to give two years' notice or an equivalent payment *in lieu* of notice. Shortly before the fixed term was due to expire it was sought to agree a new fixed term but this could not be agreed and on 12 March 1992 it was agreed that two years' notice would be worked out to 31 March 1994. He was summarily dismissed on 14 October 1992. The Court of Appeal held that the employer had brought the contract to an end lawfully by summarily terminating the contract but had neglected to pay money *in lieu* and the claim was for a contractual sum in respect of which no duty to mitigate arose.

In **Morran v Glasgow Council of Tenants Association & Ors** [1998] IRLR 67 the employee was entitled to four weeks' notice and the contract provided that he was not entitled to a notice period if he was summarily dismissed for gross misconduct or if a payment *in lieu* of notice was made. He was dismissed just before the qualifying period for unfair dismissal but was not given any payment *in lieu*. The Court of Session had to decide the sole question of whether or not he was entitled to the loss of the right to bring an unfair dismissal claim. The Court of Session held that the employee was entitled to damages that would put him in the position he would have been if the employer had performed the contract in the least burdensome manner to themselves. If they had done so they could have brought the contract to an end by making a payment *in lieu* and the employee would not then have been employed for two years. The employee was therefore only entitled to payment based upon two years' payment *in lieu* and not to damages for loss of the chance of claiming unfair dismissal.

The Court of Appeal construed a differently worded clause in **Gregory v Wallace & Anor** [1998] IRLR 387. The contract provided that (1) the contract could be terminated by giving two years' written notice (2) in the event of two years' written notice being given the employee was free to take other employment during the period (3) upon the giving of two years' written notice the employer would be entitled to terminate the agreement henceforth ('forthwith') and could at their election pay monthly instalments over a two year period or the aggregate sum discounted to reflect early payment. Administrators were appointed and Mr Gregory was summarily dismissed. The Court of Appeal held that the administrators had not given two years' notice so that the option of paying two years *in lieu* never arose as two years' notice was required to be given before the employer could terminate the employment forthwith. This was the effect of the contract so that there was a breach of contract and the employee's claim was for damages for breach and not liquidated damages. However, the contract entitled the employee to do other full time work in addition to receiving the sums due to him during the notice period so that the employee was entitled to receive the full damages.

In **T & K Home Improvements Limited v Skilton** [1999] IRLR 375 the employee's contract provided that he failed to achieve his performance target in any quarter he could be dismissed with immediate effect. The EAT held that this did not entitle the employer to dismiss without contractual notice pay. In order for the employer to be entitled to do this the clause must be clear and unambiguous so that the requirement of notice is negated.

The case of **Cerebus Software Limited v Rowley** [1999] IRLR 690
highlights the difficulties of drafting clauses relating to payment *in lieu*. The
contract provided that the employee was entitled to six months' notice. It
also provided that the employer could make a payment *in lieu* of notice to
the employee. Mr Rowley was summarily dismissed and not paid *in lieu* of
notice with effect from 26th June. He obtained a job at a higher salary from
1st August. An ET held that he had been entitled to six months' salary and
was not under any duty to mitigate his losses. In the EAT the employer
argued that it had three options: to give notice; to give no notice but to pay
money *in lieu* of notice or to give no notice and make no payment. It argued
that the third option was a breach of contract so that there was a duty to
mitigate. The EAT held that the employee was entitled to full payment as the
employee was given the right to notice or to a payment *in lieu* of notice. The
employer was in breach of contract by not making the payment so that the
employee was entitled to claim the monies without any deduction for
mitigation. The same result was achieved whether the claim was regarded as
being one under the contract or a claim for damages for breach which put
the employee in the position he would have been if the contract had been
performed. However, the EAT questioned whether the employee should be
entitled to the statutory minimum notice period but considered itself bound
by the authorities.

Reversing the decision of the EAT, the Court of Appeal at [2001] IRLR 160
held that the EAT had erred in construing a clause which provided that the
employer "may make a payment in lieu of notice to the employee" as giving
the employee a contractual entitlement to be paid in lieu where no notice
was given and in holding, therefore, that when he was dismissed summarily
for no good cause, the employee was entitled to assert a right to payment in
lieu of notice as a sum due under the contract without giving credit for
earnings received in new employment obtained within the notice period.

A provision in a contract which provides that the employer may make a
payment in lieu of notice gives the employer the choice whether or not to
make a payment in lieu of notice and is totally inconsistent with the
employee having a contractual right to insist on such a payment being made.

The contract expressly provided that employment would continue unless and
until determined by either party giving the other not less than six months'
notice of termination. In ignoring that and choosing to terminate summarily,
the employers were in breach of the contractual obligation to give six months'
notice. Accordingly, the employee's claim was for damages for breach of
contract, i.e. damages for wrongful dismissal, and the measure of damages was
the amount that the employee would have earned had the employment

continued according to contract, subject to the ordinary rule that the employee must minimise his loss by using due diligence to find other employment. The case was distinguished from **Abrahams v Performing Rights Society Ltd** [1995] IRLR 486 where the Court of Appeal held that a contractual clause which provided that "in the event of termination of your employment ... you would be entitled ... to a period of notice of two years or an equivalent payment in lieu", gave the employee a right to payment in lieu which was a contractual entitlement, not in the nature of a claim for liquidated damages and, therefore, not subject to a duty to mitigate.

A payment *in lieu* is taxable under Schedule E as an emolument if made pursuant to the express contractual right to bring the contract to an end by making such a payment (**EMI Group Electronics Limited v Coldicutt (Inspector of Taxes)** [1997] British Tax Cases 540). See also **Richardson (HMI) v Delaney** [2001] IRLR 663).

The law relating to PILON clauses is fully considered in Duggan, *Wrongful Dismissal and Breach of Contract* at pages 338–442.

Precedent V3: Accrued Holiday Pay

This precedent sets out whether or not there is an entitlement to accrued holiday pay on termination of employment. It should be read in conjunction with **Part I** on holidays.

Precedent V4: Sick pay

This further precedent should be read in conjunction with **Part J** on sickness. Where the contract provides for notice period in excess of the statutory minimum and entitlement to sick pay has ended it will not revive on notice being given (**The Scotts Company (UK) Limited v Budd** [2003] IRLR 145). Where the notice is for the statutory minimum the right to sick pay revives upon an employee who is absent due to sickness being given notice (see sections 87–88 of the Employment Rights Act 1996).

Precedent V5: Garden leave

Garden leave clauses are common in contracts with executives and directors and a model is contained at V5 (see also the contracts for precedents). There may be an implied right to order garden leave or it may be express. For a consideration of the law see Duggan, *Wrongful Dismissal and Breach of Contract* at Chapter 10.

Implied terms

In **William Hill Organisation Limited v Tucker** [1998] IRLR 313 Mr Tucker was employed as a senior dealer in the field of spread betting, which was a specific form of betting pioneering by CI Limited. His contract of employment provided for six months' notice and contained a clause that prevented him from undertaking any employment that conflicted with the interests of the company. He decided to leave and to work for CI Limited. He was told that his six months' notice was required but that he was not expected to attend work during the notice period, would be paid and that he could not start work elsewhere during this period. There was no express term permitting garden leave and the High Court and Court of Appeal held that the failure to provide work was a breach of contract so that Mr Tucker was entitled to leave forthwith. The Court of Appeal stated that the employer had no express or implied right to insist that the employee stay at home. The Courts have been increasingly ready to recognise the importance of work to the employee and of exercising his skills. This was a case where it could be said that the employee's job was unique and the skills necessary for carrying it out required frequent exercise for their preservation and enhancement. The employer was not obliged to provide work if there was none that could be done with profit or to allocate work to the employee in preference to others, but it was not allowed to exclude him from the position. Morritt LJ stated that "..the court should be careful not to grant interlocutory relief to enforce a garden leave clause to any greater extent than would be covered by a justifiable covenant in restraint of trade previously entered into by an employee."

Express terms

In **Evening Standard Co Limited v Henderson** [1987] ICR 588; IRLR 64, Mr Henderson was employed as a production manager. His contract provided that he had to give twelve months' notice and he was not allowed to work anywhere else during the notice period without permission. He was offered a job with a competitor and gave two months' notice. The Court of Appeal held that the balance of convenience was in favour of granting an injunction. It was not possible to quantify the damage to the employer if the employee went to work for a competitor. Lawton LJ stated:

"The injunction must not force the defendant to work for the plaintiffs and it must not reduce him, certainly, to a condition of starvation or to a condition of idleness, whatever that may mean on the authorities on this topic. But all that, in my judgment, is overcome by the fact that the plaintiffs have made the offer they have. The defendant can go back to work for them. If he elects not to go back...he can receive his salary and full contractual benefits under his contract until such time as his notice would have expired had it been for the proper period."

A different result was reached in **Provident Financial Group PLC v Hayward** [1989] IRLR 84 where there was a twelve months' notice period with a provision that the employee could be required to remain at home on 'garden leave'. On the facts of that case there was no damage to the employer if the employee took up new employment as it was not in competition with the employer and there were no elements of confidential information so that the employer could not be caused any damage.

In **Euro Brokers Limited v Rabdy** [1995] IRLR 206 the employee intended to work for a rival firm in breach of a six months' notice requirement in a case where customer connection was important. He offered to go on garden leave for three months. The High Court held that a six month period was enforceable given that the customer connection had been built up at the employer's expense, even if this meant that he remained idle for a period.

Where the employee is paid *in lieu* of notice this may have the effect of relieving the employee from being required to stay at home on garden leave and enable her to undertake work for another employee. In **Hutchings v Coinseed Limited** [1998] IRLR 190 Miss Hutchings' contract provided that: "During any period of notice the company is under no obligation to provide you with work and may require you to stay at home and do no work for the company or for anyone else." She gave one month's notice on 29th March and was told that she would be paid *in lieu* of notice. On 2 April, Miss Hutchings started work in a new job at a higher basic salary. Soon afterwards, her former employers discovered that the new job was with a competitor and, as a result, they refused to pay her the promised salary. The Court of Appeal held that a district judge had been wrong in holding that she was not entitled to her salary for her notice period on grounds that she had repudiated her contract of employment by starting a new job with a competitor, notwithstanding that she had been told by the defendants that she was not required to work for them during the period of notice. The mere fact that an employee takes another job during the notice period does not necessarily amount to a repudiatory breach entitling the employer to elect to bring the contract to an end, even where the employee goes to work for a "competitor". Whether there is a repudiatory breach depends upon whether taking the new job was wholly inconsistent with the employee's obligations to the employers at that time. In the present case, there was no express obligation that the plaintiff should not take another job and an obligation that she should not do so could not be implied, given that she had been released from further work and told that she would be paid *in lieu* of notice.

Restrictive covenants and garden leave

For consideration of the period and scope of restraint and whether the period can be reduced see: **GFI Group Inc v Eaglestone** [1994] IRLR 119 and **Euro Brokers Ltd v Rabey** [1995] IRLR 206.

Where there is a restrictive covenant as well as a garden leave clause, a combination of the two may mean that the employee is kept out of the industry for a lengthy period. The Court of Appeal considered the interrelationship between the two in **Credit Suisse Asset Management Limited v Armstrong** [1996] IRLR 450. Employees were placed on garden leave for a six month period after they resigned. There was a non-competition clause for six months after termination of employment in the contracts. The Court of Appeal held that the restrictive covenant, being valid, was enforceable notwithstanding the garden leave clause. The Courts are entitled to exercise their discretion as to the period that it considers a garden leave clause should apply. If the restrictive covenant is valid the employer is entitled to have it enforced but the existence of a garden leave clause at the time the contract is entered into may be taken into account in determining the validity of the covenant. Neill LJ stated that he would "leave open the possibility that in an exceptional case where a long period of garden leave had already elapsed, perhaps substantially in excess of a year, without any curtailment by the court, the court would decline to grant any further protection based on a restrictive covenant."

Duties during garden leave

In **Symbian Limited v Christensen** [2001] IRLR 77 it was the view of the Vice Chancellor that the duty of fidelity and fiduciary duties no longer applied when an employee was required to go on garden leave. He stated:

> "There are obligations of good faith and fidelity both ways, as the BCCI employees have succeeded in establishing in the House of Lords. The origin of these obligations is the relationship of employer and employee. What a garden leave notice does, in effect, is to put an end to the contractual relationship. It is expressed to continue only for so long as the notice period terminating the contract continues. But since the garden leave not only requires the employee not to attend for work but forbids him to attend for work, not only absolves him from carrying out

employment duties, but forbids him to take any part in the work of his employer or to enter upon his employer's premises, or to approach any of his co-employees, it seems to me that it fundamentally and irretrievably undermines the employment relationship between the parties. The contractual relationship continues but the employment relationship is destroyed as it seems to me, by the garden leave notice. I do not think that thereafter there can subsist any implied obligation of good faith and fidelity between the parties."

The Court of Appeal did not think it necessary to address the point, though Counsel for the employee, Andrew Stafford QC, conceded he would have difficulty in putting forward the proposition. It is submitted that it is wrong and that the duties do continue, otherwise the employee would be free to do what he wanted during the garden leave period.

Precedent V6: Summary Termination

These clauses are a variation on the provisions contained in **Part R** and should be read in conjunction with them. There is a vast amount of case law on summary termination and this is considered in detail at Duggan, *Wrongful Dismissal and Breach of Contract* Chapter 7 and *Unfair Dismissal.*

Precedent V7: Retirement age

Note that the contractual stipulation as to retirement age in the contract is likely to be regarded as the normal retirement age for unfair dismissal purposes: In **Wall v British Compressed Air Society** [2004] IRLR 147, it was held that normal retirement age may be that stipulated in the contract, even where there is only one employee.

PART W: STRESS POLICIES

Precedent W: **Stress Policies**

    W1: **A Model Stress Policy**   **1037**

  Commentary: **Stress Policies**   **1038**

Useful Websites

- ACAS have a site that deals with Stress at work:

  http://www.acas.org.uk/publications/b11.html#7

  Advisory Booklet on Health and Employment.

- The HSE Guide on Work related stress:

  http://www.hse.gov.uk/pubns/indg281.pdf

- See Business link which sets out common causes of stress and has links to other useful sites:

  http://www.businesslink.gov.uk/bdotg/action/detail?type= RESOURCES&itemId=1074428029

Precedent W1:   A Model Stress Policy

The company recognises that its staff are its most important asset and it is committed to providing the support to assist its staff to undertake their work and develop their skills in an environment that is as stress free as possible. It is recognised that all staff are subject to stress in their daily lives and that if it reaches debilitating levels then work performance can suffer.

Stress is a matter of legitimate concern, be it physical or mental, and the Company is committed to assisting by providing a support system that will help minimise and alleviate stress within the workforce.

Where work suffers because of stress related matters the Company will not normally treat this as a disciplinary matter but may treat it as a capability/sickness issue.

If you feel that your work is suffering because of stress related matters occurring outside the workplace you may raise this informally with your line manager who will do everything in his power to assist. This may include referring the matter to more senior management who will consider what they can do to assist and will handle matters in a sympathetic and helpful way. Remember: if you do not tell the Company that you have a problem, they cannot help you.

The same applies where stress is caused by matters within the working environment. It you consider there to be a problem you may take the same approach as set out above. Alternatively if you think it more appropriate you may invoke the grievance procedure. Where you believe that stress is caused as a result of the way that you are being treated by others you may invoke the bullying/harassment policy.

The Company will ensure that management have the necessary training in stress awareness.

Where appropriate the Company is prepared to provide professional counselling at its own expense.

STRESS POLICIES: COMMENTARY

Precedent W contains a general statement about how stress will be dealt with in the workplace. However, the policy will be of no use unless it is actively implemented (to that end see the Management Strategy checklist below). Employers are at risk if they do not provide a safe working environment (see Part U on Health and Safety).

There is potential liability as follows:

- Personal injury claims caused by stress;

- Constructive and unfair dismissal claims;

- Claims under the Disability Discrimination Act 1995;

- Breach of contract claims;

- Claims in negligence.

In **Walker v Northumberland County Council** [1995] IRLR 35; [1995] ICR 702; [1995] 1 All ER 737 the claimant claimed damages arising out of stress and anxiety due to increased pressure of work. In 1995 he produced reports stressing the need to alleviate the work pressures of himself and his team. His proposals were not accepted. At the end of November 1986 he suffered a nervous breakdown. He was told that he would be given assistance when he returned to work but, in the event, this only lasted for a month. His stress symptoms returned and on 16th September 1987 he was advised to go on sick leave. He had a second mental breakdown and was dismissed on the grounds of permanent ill health in February 1988. He claimed damages for breach of care in that the employer failed to take steps to avoid exposing him to a health endangering environment, contending that the Council ought to have appreciated the effect of the workload given his warnings and his first breakdown. Colman J held that the defendant County Council was in breach of the duty of care it owed to the plaintiff as his employer in respect of the second mental breakdown, which he suffered as a result of stress and anxiety occasioned by his job as Area Social Services Officer responsible for an area with a very heavy workload, including an increasing incidence of child abuse cases.

The judge stated that an employer owes a duty to his employees not to cause them psychiatric damage by the volume or character of the work that they are required to perform. Although the law on the extent of the duty on an employer to provide an employee with a safe system of work and to take reasonable steps to protect him from risks which are reasonably foreseeable had developed almost exclusively in cases involving physical injury to the employee, there was no logical reason why risk of injury to an employee's mental health should be excluded from the scope of the employer's duty. The judge was of the view that the standard of care required for performance of that duty must be measured against the yardstick of reasonable conduct on the part of a person in the employer's position.

He decided that what is reasonable depends upon the nature of the relationship, the magnitude of the risk of injury which was reasonably foreseeable, the seriousness of the consequences for the person to whom the duty is owed of the risk eventuating, and the cost and practicability of preventing the risk. The practicability of remedial measures must take into account the resources and facilities at the disposal of the person or body who owes the duty of care, and the purpose of the activity which has given rise to the risk of injury.

The case is a warning for employers who ignore stress related illness brought on by the working environment. Mr Walker eventually received over £200,000 (c.f. **Fraser v The State Hospitals Board for Scotland** [Court of Session 11.7.2000] where there was no liability when the employer could not foresee that the employee would suffer psychiatric illness as a result of disciplinary action). The issue of work related stress has been considered by the Higher Courts in several recent cases (see Duggan, *Wrongful Dismissal and Breach of Contract* at 6.21 and 14.20 for more detailed consideration).

In **Chairman of the Governors of Thomas Becket RC v Hatton & Ors** [2002] ICR 613; IRLR 263, [2002] EWCA Civ 76] Hale LJ summarised the principles as follows:

> "the following practical propositions emerge:
>
> (1) There are no special control mechanisms applying to claims for psychiatric (or physical) illness or injury arising from the stress of doing the work the employee is required to do (para. 22). The ordinary principles of employer's liability apply (para. 20).
>
> (2) The threshold question is whether this kind of harm to this particular employee was reasonably foreseeable (para. 23): this has two components, (a) an injury to health (as distinct from occupational stress), which (b) is attributable to stress at work (as distinct from other factors) (para. 25).

(3) Foreseeability depends upon what the employer knows (or ought reasonably to know) about the individual employee. Because of the nature of mental disorder, it is harder to foresee than physical injury, but may be easier to foresee in a known individual than in the population at large (para. 23). An employer is usually entitled to assume that the employee can withstand the normal pressures of the job unless he knows of some particular problem or vulnerability (para. 29).

(4) The test is the same whatever the employment: there are no occupations which should be regarded as intrinsically dangerous to mental health (para. 24).

(5) Factors likely to be relevant in answering the threshold question include:

   (a) The nature and extent of the work done by the employee (para. 26). Is the workload much more than is normal for the particular job? Is the work particularly intellectually or emotionally demanding for this employee? Are demands being made of this employee unreasonable when compared with the demands made of others in the same or comparable jobs? Or are there signs that others doing this job are suffering harmful levels of stress? Is there an abnormal level of sickness or absenteeism in the same job or the same department?

   (b) Signs from the employee of impending harm to health (paras. 27 and 28). Has he a particular problem or vulnerability? Has he already suffered from illness attributable to stress at work? Have there recently been frequent or prolonged absences which are uncharacteristic of him? Is there reason to think that these are attributable to stress at work, for example because of complaints or warnings from him or others?

(6) The employer is generally entitled to take what he is told by his employee at face value, unless he has good reason to think to the contrary. He does not generally have to make searching enquiries of the employee or seek permission to make further enquiries of his medical advisers (para. 29).

(7) To trigger a duty to take steps, the indications of impending harm to health arising from stress at work must be plain enough for any

reasonable employer to realise that he should do something about it (para. 31).

(8) The employer is only in breach of duty if he has failed to take the steps which are reasonable in the circumstances, bearing in mind the magnitude of the risk of harm occurring, the gravity of the harm which may occur, the costs and practicability of preventing it, and the justifications for running the risk (para. 32).

(9) The size and scope of the employer's operation, its resources and the demands it faces are relevant in deciding what is reasonable; these include the interests of other employees and the need to treat them fairly, for example, in any redistribution of duties (para. 33).

(10) An employer can only reasonably be expected to take steps which are likely to do some good: the court is likely to need expert evidence on this (para. 34).

(11) An employer who offers a confidential advice service, with referral to appropriate counseling or treatment services, is unlikely to be found in breach of duty (paras. 17 and 33).

(12) If the only reasonable and effective step would have been to dismiss or demote the employee, the employer will not be in breach of duty in allowing a willing employee to continue in the job (para. 34).

(13) In all cases, therefore, it is necessary to identify the steps which the employer both could and should have taken before finding him in breach of his duty of care (para. 33).

(14) The claimant must show that that breach of duty has caused or materially contributed to the harm suffered. It is not enough to show that occupational stress has caused the harm (para. 35).

(15) Where the harm suffered has more than one cause, the employer should only pay for that proportion of the harm suffered which is attributable to his wrongdoing, unless the harm is truly indivisible. It is for the defendant to raise the question of apportionment (paras. 36 and 39).

(16) The assessment of damages will take account of any pre-existing disorder or vulnerability and of the chance that the claimant would have succumbed to a stress-related disorder in any event (para. 42)."

In three of the four conjoined cases, including *Barber* the Court of Appeal concluded that the employer had not been in breach. Mr Barber was the only party who appealed further to the House of Lords (see below).

The High Court applied *Hatton* in **Pratley v Surrey County Council** [2002] EWHC 1608; [2003] IRLR 794 where it held that depression triggered by work related stress had not been foreseeable. The Council had not been under any duty to take steps as there had been no reason to anticipate any injury to the employee's health (c.f. **Young v Post Office** [2002] IRLR 660, referred to in *Wrongful Dismissal* at page 427). Other cases where stress claims have failed because the injury to health was not reasonably foreseeable are **Barlow v London Borough of Broxbourne** [2003] EWHC 50 and **Morland v London Borough of Tower Hamlets** (High Court 1.5.2003).

The Court of Appeal followed *Hatton* in **Bonser v RJB Mining (UK) Ltd** [2004] IRLR 164 in which it took a strict approach to the test for recovering damages for stress. In *Bonser*, the manager was subjected to an ever-increasing workload by an overbearing superior and eventually had a nervous breakdown. The Court of Appeal held that the claimant was required not simply to establish that it was reasonably foreseeable that overwork would result in the employee suffering from stress but also that it would lead to psychiatric illness. The Court of Appeal held that there was no basis upon which the judge could properly have reached the conclusion that the risk that the claimant would suffer a breakdown should have been apparent to her employers. The claimant did not manifest by her conduct or complaint anything which sufficiently put her employers on notice that she was vulnerable to imminent risk of injury to her health. The only visible sign was of her being tearful on a single occasion some months before her eventual breakdown. That event did not sufficiently foretell the breakdown that was to occur. To the knowledge of her employers she may have become vulnerable to the stress of overwork but not of psychiatric breakdown. Had the claimant not in fact been particularly vulnerable to stress-induced health breakdown, there was no reason to think that she would have succumbed to suffering it. The employers knew nothing of that vulnerability and therefore were not liable for the breakdown when it occurred.

The House of Lords heard the appeal against the Court of Appeal decision of **Sutherland v Hatton** [2002] IRLR 263 in the case named **Barber v Somerset County Council** [2004] IRLR 475 (Mr Barber being the only appellant).

The claimant's appeal was allowed but the case may be seen as primarily turning on its own facts. Lord Walker stated that Hale LJ's analysis, set out above, was "a valuable contribution to the development of the law". However, Lord Walker emphasised that *Sutherland* "should not be read as having anything like statutory force" and that in determining whether an employer was in breach of the duty of care owed to an employee in respect of psychiatric illness caused by work-related stress, "the best statement of general principle" remains that of Mr Justice Swanwick in **Stokes v Guest Keen and Nettlefold (Bolts and Nuts) Ltd**, which sets out the dictum:

> "the overall test is still the conduct of the reasonable and prudent employer taking positive thought for the safety of his workers in the light of what he knows or ought to know."

So that "where there is developing knowledge, he must keep reasonably abreast of it and not be too slow to apply it".

There is some uncertainty as to the status of the *Sutherland* guidelines given Lord Scott's dissent from the majority decision, in which he stated that he preferred Lady Justice Hale's statement of general principle to the propositions set out in *Stokes*.

The trial judge's finding that the employers were in breach of their duty to take reasonable care from the time when they became aware that the employee had returned from work after an absence due to stress and did nothing to help him was restored by the majority though the case was stated to be "close to the borderline".

The House of Lords held that at the very least, once the employee had been off work for three weeks due to stress and depression, the senior management team at the school should have made "sympathetic inquiries" about his problems, and should have made some reduction in his workload, instead of brushing him off unsympathetically or sympathising but simply telling him to prioritise his work. The House of Lords make it clear that it is not just for the employee to draw the employer's attention to the problem but that it will be necessary for the employer to be proactive where it has become aware the employee is suffering from stress.

The EAT considered a different issue in **Paul v National Probation Service** [2004] IRLR 190, namely where the employer believes that the job may be too stressful for an employee because the employee already suffers from depression, is it permissible to refuse the position on this basis or should some adjustment be made. The employee had chronic depression for which he was under the care of a consultant psychiatrist. An offer of employment to him was withdrawn after an occupational health adviser wrote to his GP and, on the basis of that report, decided that the employment might be too stressful. The employment tribunal focused on whether the applicant had been placed at a disadvantage by the employer's requirement that all appointments were subject to occupational health clearance. The EAT, however, pointed out that in many cases, having a disability will not adversely affect an individual's general health. Cox J stated that:

> "the existence of a disability does not of itself therefore substantially disadvantage a disabled person who is subject to this general requirement."

The tribunal should have considered whether there were reasonable steps that the employers could have taken to comply with its duty to prevent disadvantage to the applicant. These included obtaining specialist advice from the applicant's consultant on his fitness for the post, and taking steps in relation to adjusting the job they had offered, for example increasing his period of induction and/or the training or supervisory periods.

It is thus clear that where an employer is concerned that a position may be too stressful for an employee because of a disability it should take steps to assess whether the position will have that impact, by speaking to the relevant medical experts, and it should also consider whether adjustments can be made to the job in order to reduce or obviate the stressful aspects of the position.

The employer should have a management strategy for its senior employees, for which the checklist below may provide a starting point.

Management Strategy Checklist

Aims	Actions
Introduce a staff development and review scheme that takes account of stress	• Ensure that all employees are aware of the stress policy • Make clear to employees that stress is not a sign of weakness • Be prepared to discuss stress at appraisals • Ensure stress is taken into account when job descriptions are prepared or altered, including the hours and quantity of work

Aims	Actions
Ensure that all individuals are aware of the harassment policies	• Make sure there is a harassment policy and it is properly implemented • Make sure employees are aware of the policy
Ensure equal opportunity policies are applied	• Make sure there is an equal opportunities policy and it is properly implemented • Make sure employees are aware of the policy
Be aware of the effect of management styles on employees	• Ensure that management have proper training in relation to stress in the workplace
Ensure health and safety requirements are complied with	• Make sure that proper consideration is given to the working environment, taking into account such matters as accommodation, noise, security and other such matters that may cause stress • Ensure that employees know that they are also responsible for their own well being and that of their co-employees
Regularly review the workload of staff	• Ensure that the workload is not excessive leading to stress
Ensure employees have a current job description and are clear about their roles and responsibilities	• Ensure that employees are clear about what is expected of them and that they can cope
Where roles are changed make sure this is done with proper consultation and sympathetically	• Ensure that there is no uncertainty about roles as this can lead to additional stress

Aims	Actions
Ensure that employees are aware of the options open to them if they are suffering from stress because of work or no work related matters	• Ensure that all employees are aware of the stress policy • Ensure that employees know that stress is not treated as a sign of weakness • Ensure all employees know the procedures to be followed if they are having problems

SECTION FOUR
DIRECTORS

SECTION FOUR
DIRECTORS

Precedents: **Director's Contract of Employment**

7.1: **Director's Contract of Employment**   **1049**

7.2: **Non Executive Director, Letter of Appointment**   **1066**

Commentary: **1073**

Precedent: Director's Contract of Employment

Precedent 7.1: Director's Contract of Employment

SERVICE AGREEMENT BETWEEN . . . .

('The Company') and

. . . . ('The Director').

1.	Employer and Employee	The Company is . . . . of . . . . Company Registration No . . . . The Employee is . . . . of . . . . The execution of this Service Agreement was approved at a meeting of the Board of Directors on . . . . by a minute number . . . .
2.	Definitions	The Board: The Board of Directors of the Company. Associated Company: Any Associated Company as defined in the Employment Rights Act and the Companies Act. Group: The Associated Companies and any Holding Company.
3.	Date employment began, continuous employment and hours of work	The Director's employment as an Employee began on . . . . and the Director's date of continuous employment began on . . . . [The Director's employment began on . . . . and will continue for a [. . . .] year fixed period. The employment may be terminated during the fixed period as provided for hereafter, and, subject to termination as set out hereafter, after the end of the fixed term period by the giving of [. . . .] months' notice.] If the Service Agreement is not terminated earlier it will end automatically on the Director reaching retirement age as defined in the Company [Group] Pension Scheme. *Hours of work* The Director's normal hours of work are . . . . . a.m. to . . . . . p.m. However, the nature of the Director's position is such that he will be expected to work such hours as are necessary in order that he can fully carry out his duties. There is no additional pay for overtime. The provisions of the Working Time Regulations in relation to hours of work are not applicable.

4. Job title and duties	Director [ADD IN IF MANAGING DIRECTOR, ETC.]
	The Company may change the Director's job title in its absolute discretion and as it considers necessary. It may also appoint a Director to act in a joint capacity.
	Description
	The Director's job description [was provided with the Letter of Appointment][is appended to this contract].
	Duties and flexibility
	During the period of his Employment:
	1. The Director will diligently, well and faithfully serve the Company [and Group] and will do all in his powers to promote the interests of the Company [and Group].
	2. The Director will not accept or take up any other employment nor will he accept, whether indirectly or directly, any form of paid or unpaid Consultative or other work whilst employed by the Company [or any Group Company].
	3. The Director agrees that he will carry out such duties as may from time to time be assigned to him by the Board, or instructed by [. . . . . . .], whether or not those duties fall within the job title or description, provided that they are consistent with his status and position with the Company.
	4. The Company is part of the Group and the Director agrees that he will carry out duties for other Companies in the Group if so instructed.
	5. The Director will endeavour at all times to promote the interests of the Company [and the Group].

5.	Remuneration and other benefits	*Salary*
		1. The Director will be paid the sum of £ . . . . per annum.
		2. The Salary will be calculated and accrue on a daily basis and will be paid by credit transfer on the . . . day of each month, provided that the Director acknowledges that the salary may be paid at a later date if, for reasons beyond the control of the Company salary was not paid on the above date and such late payment shall not be regarded as any breach of this Service Agreement. Salary will be paid once the Director has provided details of the bank to which it is to be transferred.
		3. The Salary will be reviewed by [the Managing Director/ Board /Remuneration Committee, etc.] [on . . . . . /by end of the . . . . . month] each year and a Salary rise may be awarded in the absolute discretion of the [the Managing Director/Board /Remuneration Committee, etc.]. There is no guarantee of any Salary rise [but the Salary will not be adjusted downwards].
		Bonus
		4. The Company may award a bonus at the [set out when]. The bonus is based upon [set out how — e.g. profitability of the Group, Division, turnover brought in by the Director]. The bonus is paid at the absolute discretion of the Company [and the Director acknowledges that he has no set expectation that he will be paid a bonus].
		Commission
		5. Commission is paid as follows: [SET OUT HOW IT IS CALCULATED].
6.	Share options	The Company [Group] operates a Share Option Scheme. If the Director is entitled to participate in the Scheme he will have been advised in his Letter of Appointment. The Options are subject to the Rules of the Scheme to which reference should be made.

7. Company car	1. The Director will be provided with a Company car, which shall be not less than [SET OUT . . . . . .] [suitable for the Director's duties and status]. The Company will tax, insure, pay for maintenance and repairs [provided they were not caused by the Director's negligence].
	2. The car may be replaced when the Company considers it appropriate.
	3. The car may be used for private purposes as well as Company business. The Company will pay for petrol used for business purposes which may be claimed as part of expenses.
	4. The Director warrants that he has a clean driving licence and he will bring to the attention of the Company any matter that may affect his continued ability to drive the car.
	5. The Director agrees that he will not do anything that may invalidate the insurance policy.
	6. Upon termination of this Agreement, for whatever reason, the Director agrees that he will immediately deliver up the car or make it available for collection [and acknowledges that he will no longer be insured to drive the car from the date of termination].
	[ALTERNATIVELY: The Company operates a car policy which the Director agrees he has read and signed. See MANUAL PRECEDENT F10 & COMMENTARY]
8. Pension	The Director is entitled to join the [Group] Company's Pension Scheme and the terms of the Scheme are incorporated into this Agreement.
	There is [is not a] contracting out certificate in relation to the Pension Scheme.
9. Expenses	The Company will reimburse the Director expenses incurred in the course of his employment which were incurred in the furtherance of his duties. The Director should acquaint himself with the procedure for reclaiming expenses.

10. Holidays and other absences	*Holiday*
	1. The Director is entitled to [. . . . .] days' holiday per year on full salary, in addition to the normal statutory holidays.
	2. The Director must agree holiday in advance with [. . . . .] by giving at least twice the number of working days' notice of the number of days he intends to take on holiday and this will be subject to the Agreement of the Company. The Company may stipulate the days that the Director must take as paid holiday.
	3. Holidays not taken in the calendar year which runs from [. . .] to [. . .] and cannot be carried over [save with the written agreement of . . . .].
	4. For the purposes of termination of employment, holidays accrue on a daily basis and the Director will be entitled to any accrued holiday pay on the termination of his employment.
	Other absences
	The Company operates a maternity and paternity policy to which reference should be made.
	[SEE MANUAL PRECEDENT K1 & COMMENTARY]
11. Sickness absences and benefits	*Sickness*
	1. Where the Director is absent due to sickness he must, as soon as is possible, inform or cause to be informed [STIPULATE WHO — e.g. THE BOARD] of the Company.
	2. Self certificates must be provided for periods of up to [. . .] days and medical certificates must be provided for any longer periods.
	3. The Company will continue to pay full salary whilst the Director is absent due to sickness for a period of [. . . .] days. However, the Company has the right not to pay salary where:
	(1) The Director is absent for more than [. . . .] days in any one period or [. . . .] days during the calendar year.

11. Sickness absences and benefits	(2) The Director does not provide certificates as required.
	(3) The Director fails to respond to any reasonable request from the Company about his condition and prognosis.
	(4) The Director has repeated spells of short absence that cumulatively amount to [. . . .] days in any six month period.
	(5) The functions of the Director become impossible of performance due to the absence of the Director.
	4. The Director will give credit for any statutory or other benefits he receives arising out of his absence due to sickness and which do not arise out of any private insurance taken out by the Director.
	5. The Director's employment may be terminated for sickness in the circumstances set out herein.
	Medical examination
	The Company may require the Director to undergo a medical examination and refusal to do so may result in non payment of salary or in dismissal.
	[SEE MANUAL AT J FOR FURTHER EXAMPLES OF THE ABOVE PRECEDENTS]
	Private Health Insurance
	The Director [and his family which shall consist of spouse and children] are entitle to membership of the Company's Private Health Insurance Scheme, on the terms that may from time to time exist. If the Director chooses not to join the Scheme he is not entitled to any sums by way alternative.
	Third Parties
	Where the Director's absences arise out of the action of a third party which entitles him to claim damages the Director agrees that any sums advanced to him by way of salary will be regarded as sums that must be refunded out of any damages recovered for loss of earnings.
	[SEE ALSO MANUAL PRECEDENT F11 & COMMENTARY]

12. Place of work	The Director's place of work will be as set out above [OR SET OUT ADDRESS, ETC.]. However, the Director agrees:
	1. Should the Company decide to relocate, he may be required to move to anywhere within the United Kingdom upon such relocation, provided that the Company will pay the reasonable costs of removal and other incidental expenses to be agreed beforehand.
	2. The Director will be required, as part of his duties, to travel in the United Kingdom and abroad (for which he confirms he has a valid passport) and the Company [or Group] may so instruct him in the proper furtherance of his duties [provided that he will not have to spend time abroad for more than [. . . .] days at any one time without prior mutual agreement]. The Director can claim expenses in relation to such travel.
	[FOR AN OVERSEAS CONTRACT SEE 5.10]
	[FOR A RESIDENTIAL REQUIREMENT SEE 5.12]
13. Disciplinary and other procedures	The Director's attention is drawn to the Company's Disciplinary and Grievance Procedures which are applicable with appropriate modifications. They do not form part of this Service Agreement.
	For the purposes of any disciplinary matter, the following persons are responsible:
	• Warnings: . . . .
	• Dismissal: . . . .
	• Appeals against warnings: . . . .
	• Appeals against dismissal: . . . .
	For the purposes of the Grievance procedure, the following individuals:
	• Initial informal Grievance: . . . .
	• Formal Grievance: . . . .
	• Further complaint where not satisfied with outcome: . . . .
	[SEE MANUAL PARTS R AND S FOR FURTHER DETAIL AND COMMENTARY]

14. Standard of work and other duties during employment	The Director acknowledges that his title, position and the nature of his work require a high standard and breach may cause the Company or Group [irremediable] harm. He therefore warrants that he has the requisite qualifications and abilities to perform the full functions of his job and will drawn to the attention of the Company any matter that may affect his ability to carry out his job.
	Because of the nature of his Employment, the Director recognises that, in addition to those matters set out in the Disciplinary Policy as constituting grounds for dismissal, any act of negligence or act that may bring the Company or Group into disrepute or that undermines the trust and confidence of the Company or Group may lead to summary dismissal.
	The Director also expressly acknowledges that he will draw to the attention of the Company any act by any Director, employees or third party, that is a breach on their part or may harm the interests of the Company or Group.
	[ALTERNATIVELY:
	The Director undertakes that he will disclose to the Company [Board], forthwith upon it coming to his knowledge, any of the following information or matters:
	• Any activities on the part of other Directors or employees that may be harmful to the interests of the Company, including but not limited to:
	(1) any plans of employees to leave the Company [or Group] or to join a Competitor or to take any steps to set up or establish a business that is or may be in competition;
	(2) any steps taken by employees to carry out such plans;
	(3) any use of confidential information or other property or assets of the Company [or Group] by Directors or employees for the furtherance of such plans;
	(4) any other matters that may adversely affect the business of the Company.]

15. Scope of duties	*Whole Employment*
	The nature of the Director's employment is such that the Director cannot be engaged in any activity that may mean he cannot give his full attention to his duties with the Company [or Group] or which may place him in a position of conflict. The Director therefore agrees that he will not accept or take up any employment whilst employed by the Company nor will he accept, whether indirectly or directly, any form or paid or unpaid Consultative or other work [without the prior permission in writing of the Managing Director Board of the Company, which will not be unreasonably withheld]. The Director may however, purchase shares in [set out the extent of the interests that may be permissible or any other interests].
	Implied Duties
	The Director further acknowledges that the nature of his employment creates implied fiduciary duties and duties of fidelity and any and all covenants herein are subject to those implied duties where they be wider.
16. Covenants during employment	*Directors and Employees*
	The Director will not at any time during his employment solicit or seek to recruit any current Directors or employees of the Company [or Group] to be engaged to work for the Director or any other person, firm, company or organisation, and will not make any comment, representation or statement that may facilitate, induce, persuade procure, or howsoever cause any Director or employee to leave the employment of the Company [or Group].
	[ALTERNATIVELY:
	The Director shall not at any time during his employment with the Company, whether directly or indirectly, and for his own behalf or that of any company, firm, person or other third party, seek to encourage or entice any employee of the Company [or Group] to leave the employment of the Company [or Group].]

	Other activities The Director will not during the period that he is employed by the Company: 1. take any steps to seek work with any competitor which will be regarded as a breach of his fiduciary obligaitons; 2. canvass solicit or otherwise make any represent-ation or statement to any customer or supplier which may cause harm or adversely affect the Company/Group's business or entertain any offers from customers or suppliers, and in the event of the latter shall immediately inform the Company of any offers. *Secret Profits* The Director agrees that he will not take any money or other benefit from any client of the Company and will immediately advise the Company if any such money or other benefit is offered to the Company and he will not make any benefit from his position other than his agreed remuneration without the prior agreement of the Board. [SEE ALSO MANUAL PRECEDENT Q5 & COMMENTARY]
17. Intellectual property	[SHORT FORM CLAUSE] Where the Director's duties will involve him in formulating and dealing with [LIST e.g. marketing, etc.] these duties will involve the production of designs, manufacturing methods, plans, processes or techniques in which any copyright or other intellectual property rights will subsist. The Director agrees that any such rights vest absolutely in the Company and he will take all steps and carry out all acts that may be necessary to ensure that the intellectual property is lawfully vested in the Company, including signing all applications and any other documents that may be necessary to apply for any Patent rights or other form of application in the United Kingdom and Worldwide, and that this obligation will continue to exist when the Director's employment has ended.

	[ALTERNATIVELY: Because of the nature of the employment the Director has signed an Intellectual Property Agreement. [It is a condition of your employment that you sign the Company's Intellectual Property Agreement]] [SEE MANUAL PRECEDENT Q4 FOR AN AGREEMENT AND Q5 FOR A FURTHER CLAUSE & COMMENTARY]
18. Confidentiality	The Director agrees that he will not at any time during his Employment and after the termination of his employment without restriction in time comm-unicate, disclose or divulge to any third person or in any way make use of the Company/Group's Confidential Information or Trade Secrets [which, without prejudice to the generality of the foregoing include [LIST] relating to the Company, the Group, its customers or Suppliers provided that once the Director has left the employment with the Company this restriction shall not apply where such information has been ordered to be disclosed by a Court or otherwise by law and the Director shall not be prevented from using his own skills and experience. [FOR MORE DETAILS PROVISIONS SEE MANUAL PRECEDENTS Q2 AND Q5 AND COMMENTARY]
19. Post termination covenants: non solicitation, non dealing and non poaching	The Director agrees that for a period of [. . . .] months from the termination of his Employment he will not: 1. Canvass, solicit or otherwise in any way seek to procure, the business or business opportunities from any customer or client of the Company [or Group], where the customer or client of the Company [or Group] has been a customer or client [. . . .] months immediately preceding the termination of employment of the Director and with whom the Director has had, or is aware of, business dealings within the previous [. . . .] months.

2. Canvass, solicit or otherwise in any way seek to procure, orders from any supplier of the Company [or Group] where the supplier has supplied the Company [or Group] within the previous [. . . .] months and the Director has had dealings with the supplier or is aware of any agreement between supplier and the Company [or Group].

3. Deal with any customer or client of the Company [or Group], where the customer or client of the Company has been a customer or client [. . . .] months immediately preceding the termination of employment of the Director and with whom the Director has had business dealings within the previous [. . . .] months.

4. Deal with any supplier of the Company [or Group] where the supplier has supplied the Company [or Group] within the previous [. . . .] months and the Director has had dealings with the supplier or is aware of any agreement between supplier and the Company [or Group].

5. Seek to persuade or solicit or provide work, whether directly or indirectly, or by self employment or consultancy, to any person who was an employee of the Company [or Group] [. . .] years prior to the termination of the Director's employment, or was engaged in any capacity, and who would be in a position to harm the business of the Company [or Group] were he to accept any employment or engagement.

6. Accept, whether through himself or a third party, indirectly or indirectly and whether of his own or a third party's benefit any orders for any products or services with which the Director was concerned whilst he was working for the Company [or Group] or which fell within his responsibilities as a Director and which the Company [or Group] would have been in a position to supply.

[SEE MANUAL PRECEDENT Q5 FOR A MORE DETAILED COVENANT & COMMENTARY]

20. Post termination: working for competitors	The Director agrees that for a period of [. . . .] months from the termination of his Employment he will not:
	1. Hold any material interest in any business which is or is likely to be in competition with the Company [or Group].
	2. Hold any material interest in any business which may require or might reasonably be considered by the Company [or Group] to require the disclosure of Confidential information belonging to the Company [Group] in order to properly discharge his functions in such business.
	3. Accept employment or take any engagement, whether self employed or otherwise and whether directly or indirectly, from any competitor of the Company [Group] which is likely to adversely affect the business of the Company [Group].
	[SEE MANUAL PRECEDENT Q5 FOR A MORE DETAILED CLAUSE & COMMENTARY]
	[SEE SALESMAN AT 5.13 FOR A TERRITORIAL COVENANT]
21. Company's property	Upon the termination of the Director's contract for whatever reason, the Director shall immediately return to the Company all property that belongs to the Company [Group], including:
	1. Any computer, printer or other such equipment, and all computer discs and other software. If the Director has a password on any computer, the detail of the password.
	2. All documents in whatever form, including any copies or summaries of the same and including the Director's working notes.
	3. The Company car and keys.
	For the purpose of this Agreement the Director irrevocably gives the Company the right to enter any property where the Company's property is held and remove the same.

22. Directorships	The Director agrees that upon the termination of his employment for whatever reason he will immediately resign all Company directorships in the Company or any Group Company and will sign all necessary forms for such purpose.
23. Severability of covenants	The Director agrees that the each of the covenants contained in this Agreement are reasonable and are necessary for the protection of the Company's business. However, each provision of this Agreement is independent and severable and if any of them should be found by a Court of Law to be unenforceable or ineffective for whatever reason that shall not affect the validity of the separate covenants. If any covenants would become valid if any wording was deleted then the covenant shall be deemed to be applicable with such deletions and shall apply as so amended as to make the same enforceable.
24. Termination of contract	*Notice* Save as set out below, the Company must give the Director [. . . ..] months' notice to terminate this Agreement and the Director must give [. . . . .] months' notice. *Payment in lieu* The Company will have the right in its absolute discretion to terminate the Director's employment by paying in lieu of notice, on the following terms: 1. The payment will be the basic salary of the Director and no account shall be taken of any bonus, pension contributions or any benefits in kind. 2. The payment shall be subject to deductions for income tax and national insurance contributions. 3. The Director has no right to payment in lieu of notice. [CONSDER THE ISSUE OF MITIGATION — SEE MANUAL AT PART V]

	Earlier Termination
	The notice period is subject to the Company's rights to dismiss the Director without notice if:
	1. He is guilty of conduct set out in the Company's Disciplinary Procedures which warrant dismissal without notice.
	2. He commits any act of negligence, neglect of duty which is serious or does any act which causes the Company to lose trust and confidence and which justifies dismissal without notice.
	3. He is in serious or repudiatory breach of this agreement.
	4. He commits any act outside his employment which is liable to bring the Company [or Group] into disrepute.
	5. He is declared bankrupt or otherwise enters into any arrangement with his creditors.
	6. He is convicted of a criminal offence and in the case of a motoring offence this results in disqualification or imprisonment.
	7. He suffers from mental disorder.
	8. He is persistently absent from work for a period of [. . . .] days in any [. . . .] months.
	9. He is guilty of any serious or repudiatory breach of this Agreement.
25. Garden leave	Where notice has been given by either side to this Agreement, or the Director purports to leave the employment in breach of the notice that he is required to give
	The Company:
	1. shall no longer be under any duty to provide work to the Director and the Director shall have no right to carry out any work or services for the Company [but the Director may be required to make himself available during normal working hours should the Company [or Group] require his services];

	2 may direct that the Director cease all contact with any customers or Suppliers or employees of the Company [or Group];
	3. shall be entitled to exclude the Director from the Company [or Group]'s premises; provided that
	4. the Company shall continue to have the right to suspend the Director in the circumstances provided for in the Disciplinary Policy;
	5. during the notice period the Director will continue to receive all his contractual benefits.
26. Whole Agreement	This Agreement forms the Whole Agreement between the parties, save that it is subject to any further terms contained in the Letter of Appointment and the Director acknowledges that he has read the Letter, this Agreement and any Company Policies that are referred to in the Letter of Appointment. [CONSIDER WHETHER EXPRESS REFERENCE SHOULD BE MADE I.E. TO EQUAL OPPORTUNITY POLICIES, ETC.]
27. Disputes	[CONSIDER WHETHER AN ARBITRATION/ MEDIATION CLAUSE SHOULD BE INCLUDED — SEE Duggan on Wrongful Dismissal]
SIGNATURES	[CONSIDER WHETHER THE DOCUMENT SHOULD BE SIGNED AS A DEED]

Precedent 7.2: Non-Executive Director Letter of Appointment

[Thanks to Rob Bryan of Darbys for contributing this precedent]

[name and address]

[date]

Dear [name]

I am writing to record the terms on which you have been appointed non-executive director of [name] ("the Company") with effect from [date]. This is not a contract of service.

1. Definitions

In this letter, the following terms shall have the following meanings:

1.1 "the Board" means the board of directors for the time being of the Company;

1.2 "Associated Company" means a subsidiary and any other company which is for the time being a holding company (as defined by section 736 of the Companies Act 1985) of the Company or another subsidiary of any such holding company.

2. Term of Office

2.1 Your appointment as a non-executive director will continue, subject to the terms of this letter, for an initial period of [insert] years expiring on [date]. At or before the end of that period, the Board may resolve to re-appoint you for a further term. Any such further appointment will be on the terms of this letter, subject to any variation to be agreed between the parties.

2.2 Your appointment is subject to rotation under the provisions of the Articles of Association of the Company. Your appointment will automatically cease if you are not re-elected as a director.

2.3 Your appointment will also terminate automatically without entitlement to compensation if you are disqualified from acting or you are required to vacate your office as a director for any reason either under the Companies Acts or under the provisions of the Articles of Association of the Company.

2.4 Save as aforesaid, your appointment is terminable on [3] months' written notice from either party.

3. Fees

3.1 You will be entitled to a fee at the rate of [£   ] per annum payable in monthly instalments in arrears. Your fee will be subject to deductions for income tax and National Insurance contributions which the Company is by law obliged to make.

3.2 The terms of this letter do not cover any arrangements under which you perform any special duties (outside your ordinary duties as a non-executive director). These are matters which will be dealt with, should they arise, in separate documentation, and will be separately remunerated.

4. Expenses

You will be entitled to be reimbursed reasonable and proper travelling, subsistence and accommodation expenses for attendance at Board meetings and other meetings which the Company requires you to attend or which you reasonably believe that you should attend for the proper performance of your duties. You should not incur any other expense without clearing the matter with [name] before it is incurred.

5. Duties

5.1 As a non-executive director you will be expected to perform your general fiduciary duties and exercise the skill and care expected of every director. In particular, your role will be to make suggestions about, advise on and monitor matters relating to:

5.1.1 the strategy of the Company;

5.1.2 the Company's performance;

5.1.3 present and future availability and use of resources;

5.1.4 standards of conduct, compliance and control on the Board and in the Company generally;

5.1.5 the appointment of key employees and officers.

Your role as a non-executive director in maintaining good corporate governance is vital. You will be primarily responsible for the working of the Board, for its balance of membership (subject to Board and shareholder approval), for using your best efforts to ensure that relevant issues are on the agenda, and for ensuring that all directors, both executive and non-executive, are encouraged and enabled to play their full part in the activities of the Board. You should be able to stand back sufficiently from the day-to-day running of the business to ensure that the Board is in full control of the Company's affairs and alert to its obligations to shareholders.

5.2 You may also be required to serve as a member of the Remuneration and Audit Committees of the Board and to serve on any other sub-committees of the Board and/or to accept additional appointments in or on behalf of the Company where best practice requirements dictate that your presence as a non-executive presence is required.

5.3 You will be required to accept responsibility for matters relating to the Company, normally together with other directors, when required to do so by the Companies Acts, the rules of any regulatory authority, the Listing Rules published by the UK Listing Authority, the practice or rules of the London Stock Exchange, or the terms of the City Code on Takeovers and Mergers; and in any event, in the terms set out in the Statement of Adherence to Directors' Responsibilities which will be printed in the Company's accounts.

5.4 You will be expected to attend at all scheduled Board meetings and the meetings of the Remuneration Committee and Audit Committee whilst you sit on them unless your absence from any such meeting has been excused in advance by [name].

5.5 Whilst you hold office in the Company, you should not without the prior consent of the Board hold other directorships or have a material interest in shares in, nor should you be interested in any contracts with, any company or concern in the field(s) in which the Company or any Associated Company is involved to a material extent. For the purposes of this Clause a material interest in shares of a company is one which either amounts to 3% or more of the issued share capital of that company.

5.6 You will be subject to the Model Code for dealings by directors in shares of the Company. A copy of the Model Code is available from the Company Secretary together with a note of the approved procedures currently in force. Your obligations in this regard will also be regarded as extending to all other companies of which you are, or may from time to time be, a director and which is a shareholder in the Company. It is therefore a term of your appointment that you will ensure, so far as lies within your power, that such company is also bound by the provisions of the Model Code in respect of dealings in the Company's shares as if it were a person connected with you as a director, as defined in the Model Code.

5.7 Save as set out in this letter, your appointment does not involve the acceptance of any other specific responsibilities, outside the general duties of any director of a company.

6   Access

6.1 The Company confirms that:

6.1.1   you will be given full access to all information in or about the Company or any Associated Company and its affairs which is available to the executive directors of the Company or its subsidiaries;

6.1.2   agendae for Board meetings and all relevant papers will be provided to you in good time to allow you to consider them in advance of the meetings (and likewise for the proceedings of committees); and

6.1.3   you will be given access to the Chief Executive, the Finance Director and to any other directors of the Company whenever you reasonably request the same.

6.2 The Company will hold computer records and personnel files relating to you (which may, where necessary include sensitive data in relation to your health and data held for ethnic monitoring purposes) for personnel, administration and management purposes. Your right of access to this data is as prescribed by law. By signing this letter you will be taken to agree that the Company may process personal data relating to you (including such sensitive data) for such personnel, administration and management purposes and may, when necessary for those purposes, make such data available to its advisers, to parties providing products and/or services to the Company, to regulatory authorities (including the Inland Revenue), to potential purchasers of the Company or its business (on a confidential basis) and as required by law. Further, the Company may transfer such data to and from any Associated Company including any Associated Company located outside the European Economic Area.

7 General

7.1 As a non-executive director, you should note that you do not have authority to commit the Company in any way, nor should you make any statements on the Company's behalf or concerning the Company to the media, financial institutions or anyone associated with the stock market or investor community, in each case without the express authorisation of the Board.

7.2 Save as required by law or by a competent regulatory authority, you will not disclose or permit to be disclosed to any person, firm or organisation outside the Company any confidential information relating to the Company or any Associated Company nor shall you use to the detriment of the Company any information relating to the Company or any Associated Company, save that you shall not be restricted from making a "protected disclosure" pursuant to Part IVA of the Employment Rights Act 1996. For this purpose "confidential information" excludes both information which you have been authorised to disclose to the recipient and information which is already in the public domain (other than by your own unauthorised disclosure of it).

7.3 You will be entitled to the indemnity afforded to directors by the Company's Articles of Association, and you will also be covered by and required to participate in any directors' and officers' liability insurance scheme which is established by the Company. In this regard the Company agrees that it will maintain and continue to maintain such cover for a sum not less than [£   ].

7.4 On the termination of your appointment for whatever reason, you will:

7.4.1 at the request of the Company, resign from office as a director of the Company and all offices held by you in any company in the Group. Should you fail to do so, the Company is hereby irrevocably authorised to appoint some person in your name and on your behalf to sign any documents or do any things necessary or desirable to give effect to such resignation(s); and

7.4.2   return all property belonging to the Company which you used or acquired during the course of this appointment (whether or not containing confidential information) and not retain any such property in whatever form.

Kindly confirm your agreement to the terms and conditions set out above by signing the enclosed duplicate copy of this letter and returning it to me at the above address.

Yours sincerely

....

Director
for and on behalf of the Company

I agree to the terms and conditions set out above.

....

[name]

Date:........................

The detailed contract of employment at 7.1. contains model clauses that one would expect to find in a Director's Service Agreement and has been cross referenced with many of the earlier parts of this book. A detailed commentary on each clause is not therefore necessary and the checklist in relation to managers (see page 1072) is also a useful guide in considering what clauses to include. There are, however, a number of issues that are very specific to directors.

COMMENTARY

The position of a company director is an office but a director may also be an employee. This is not automatic and a director may or may not be an employee (**Secretary of State for Trade and Industry v Bottrill** [1999] IRLR 326; **Connolly v Sellers Arenascene Ltd** [2001] ICR 760). The above contract is drafted on the basis that the director is an employee.

It is also possible for a person to be a shadow director where he is a person in accordance with whose directions the directors of a company are accustomed to act (Companies Act section 741(2)) and such person may be an employee.

There is a distinction between executive and non-executive directors, the latter usually being an officer but not an employee. Non-Executive Directors will play a part in fixing remuneration for Executive Directors. However, the duties of a director mean that he owes a fiduciary duty to the company and there are also restrictions on the type of contract that may be entered into. A non Executive Director will normally be appointed under a Letter of Appointment and do not normally provide full time services to the company but merely attend meetings for which they may receive a fee. They will normally be subject to the PAYE scheme. They may also act as a consultant (See Chapter 5). (See further *www.frc.org.uk/combined.cfm* at page 63).

The Service Agreement

The following points may be made about the nature of the Service Agreement of a Director.

–   A director cannot be given a fixed term appointment of more than 5 years without the shareholders' approval (section 319, Companies Act 1985).

–   In the case of listed companies the Combined Code of the London Stock Exchange recommends that approval should be sought for a fixed contract of more than one year.

–   Directors of public companies may not be appointed after the age of 70 unless the shareholders have voted on a resolution of which special notice has been given (section 293, CA 1985).

- Directors may be required to hold shares and if they are not acquired within two months the office will be regarded as vacated (section 291, CA 1985).

- The company must keep a copy of the contract of employment available for inspection by shareholders (section 318, CA 1985).

- The listing rules of the London Stock Exchange have more onerous requirements for inspection. They must be available for inspection by any party and there are a number of requirements of disclosure that must be contained in them, particularly relating to remuneration, profit sharing, commission or compensation on termination.

Fiduciary Duty

The following points may be made.

- Executive Directors owe a fiduciary duty to the company. By section 317 of the CA 1985 they must avoid any conflicts of interest and declare any interests in transactions or contracts discussed by the Board. The requirement to disclose interests in contracts or proposed contracts with the company at the appropriate board meetings applies to directors' contracts and to variations of the contracts. The requirements must be strictly met; See **Neptune Ltd v Fitzgerald** [1995] 3 All ER 811 though a variation may not make a contract or variation unenforceable (**Runciman v Walter Runciman PLC** [1992] BCLC 1084) but a failure to comply with any general duty of disclosure may make the transaction voidable (**Guinness PLC v Saunders** [1990] 2 AC 663).

- If a director makes a profit from his position he will have to account to the company for all the profits (**Regal (Hastings) Limited v Gulliver** [1942] 1 All ER 378) and he will have to account for any damage caused by activities that were not the company's (**Bishopgate Investment Trust Limited v Maxwell** [1994] 1 All ER 262). See also **CMS Dolphin Ltd v Simoner** [2001] 2 BCLC 704 which reviews most of the authorities. (**British Midland Tool Limited v Midland International Tooling Limited** [2003] All ER(D) 174; [2003] 2 BCLC 523).

- If a director puts his interests before the company the court will not enforce the transaction (**Wilton Group PLC v Abrams** [1991] BCLC 315).

- A director cannot take part in any discussions about his salary and, in the case of listed companies it is recommended that a remuneration committee be set up, with a majority of non-executive directors to decide terms and conditions.

–   A director must disclose his and his family's interests in the shares and debenture holding in the company (section 324, CA 1985).

–   He may also not exploit inventions and discoveries made in the course of his employment even if he would have been able to claim copyright were he not a director.

–   Any provision that a director will not be liable for negligence or other breaches of duty is void (section 310, CA 1985) but he may be insured against certain liabilities.

    •   A director may be liable where he has not acted in the best interests of the company: See **Criterion Properties PLC v Stratford UK Properties LLC** [2003] 1 WLR 2108; **ExtraSure Travel Insurance Ltd v Scattergood** [2003] BCLC 598; **Colin Gwyer Associates Limited v London Wharf (Limehouse) Ltd** [2003] 2 BCLC 153.

Termination

Payment of compensation for loss of office must be approved by the shareholders (section 312 CA 1985). There are a range of grounds on which the director's contracts may be terminated

–   by resignation provided proper notice is given (**Glossop v Glossop** [1907] 2 Ch 370;

–   by failure to attend, which may be provided for in the Articles of Association and should be considered when drafting the Clauses relating to sickness and sick pay;

–   if he is disqualified from holding a directorship;

–   if he is removed by ordinary resolution on special notice (section 303 CA 1985). This will not prevent the director from bringing a claim for breach of contract or a claim in the Employment Tribunal (see **Schindler v Northern Raincoat Co. Ltd** [1960] 2 All ER 239; 1 WLR 1038 and Duggan, *Wrongful Dismissal, Law, Practice and Precedents* for a full consideration of the principles);

– upon retirement. The articles may provide for the directors to retire by rotation. A director of a public company must retire at the annual general meeting on his seventieth birthday. He may be reappointed only by a shareholders' special resolution, of which special notice has been given, that states his age (section 293 CA 1985

Remuneration and information in accounts

The Companies Act 1986, schedule 6, requires certain information regarding directors remuneration to be stated in the notes of company accounts. The Directors Remuneration Report Regulations 2002 (SI 2002/1986) replaces the requirements of Schedule 6 with regard to listed companies for financial years ending on or after 31st December 2002.

INDEX

Precedents or clauses are indicated in bold

Absences *see* Dependants, Holiday,
  Incapacity for work, Jury Service,
  Marriage, Public duties, Religious
  holidays, Sickness, Special leave
ACAS induction checklist, 174
Acceptance of offer, 201
Accidents outside work, absence and,
  693, 724
Adoption
  Flowchart, 782
  Leave, 781
  Letter stating date of return, **754**
  Letter requesting leave, **753**
  Paternity, 779
  Pay, 784
Advertising, recruitment, 181–186
  Discrimination, 47, 181
Age discrimination *see* Discrimination
Agencies, 186, 222–287
  Agreement with Hirer, **233**
  Charges to hirers, 281
  Conduct, 261
  Definition, 259, 260, 261–264, 269
  Industrial disputes, 281
  Information from hirer, 275
  Information from work-seeker, 276
  Information to be given, 277
  Liabilities, 286
  Obligations, 279
  Payment, 262, 272, 279, 281
  Terms of business, 270, 272, 273, 274
Agency workers, **222**, **229**, 259–287
  Discipline and grievance procedures,
    286

Employer, identity of, 34, 259,
  264–287
Holiday entitlement, 287, 673
Indemnities, 287
Minimum wage and, 285
Restrictive covenants, 280, 287
Statutory intervention, future, 287
Working time and, 281
Alcohol, **824**, 833
  Unfair, dismissal, sickness, 833
Annual leave *see* Holiday
Annualised hours, **311**, 317
Ante-natal care, 757
Appearance *see* Dress
Application forms, 188
Application letters, 188
Appraisals **844** *and see* Staff
  development
  Checklist, 847
Area covenant, 898

Bank holidays *see* Holiday
Basic salary, **594–598**, 598–604
  Collective Agreement, **596**
  Deductions from *see* Deductions
  Implied term, 600
  Minimum Wage, 598, 600–603
  Salary review, **597**
  Salesman, 485
  Varying, 598, 600
Belief, discrimination, *see*
  Discrimination
Benefits, *and see* Remuneration
  Cars, 23
  Employer's duty to inform, 12
  Loans, 24

Office workers, 433
Varying, 598
Betting workers, 288–294
    Definition, 291
    Dress and appearance, 294
    Protected status, 291
    Shortfall of takings, 294
    Sunday working, **288**, 291
        Duty of employer, 293
        Effect of opting out notice, 293
        Opting in notice, 293
        Opting out, 292
        Remedies, 293
Bonus, **607**, 615–619
    Implied terms, 618
    Managers, 423
Breach of contract,
    Fixed term contracts, 347
    Varying pay, 598

CCTV, checklist, **103–105**
Car allowance, 628
Cars, 23, **612**, 628–629, **646**
    And see Driving licence
    Managers, 424
Casual staff *see* Temporary staff
Change of heart, 203
Childcare costs, 469
Client, entertaining, **830**, 842
Clocking in *see* Timekeeping
Clothing *see* Dress
Collective agreements, 9, 214
    Bonus scheme, 618
    Express terms, and, 9
        Employees deemed aware, 10
        Improvement in terms,
            consideration, 11
        Local agreements, 10
        National agreements, 10
        Restraining orders, 11
        Statutory rights, and, 10
        Union authority to negotiate, 10
    Fixed term contracts and, 346
Commission, **608**, 619
    Change of status, and, 620
    Implied terms, 620
        Advances on termination, 620

Provision of work, 620
    Managers, 424
    Salesman, 485
Computers, **109–110**, **828**, 838
Concluding the contract, 201
Conduct, 23
    And see Standard of work
    Office workers, 433
Confidential information, **882**, 889
Confidentiality agreement,
    Managers, 429
    Office workers, 434
Consultants, **318**–326
    Independence of, 323
    IR35, 324
    Restrictive covenants, 323
    Services, contract for, **318**
    Services, standard of, 323
Continuity of employment
    Homeworkers, 384
    Managers, 422
    Temporary staff, 316
Contract for services *see* Consultants
Contracts of employment,
    Agency workers, 34, **222**, **229**,
        258–287
    Betting workers, **288**–294
    Casual staff, **295**
    Concluding, 201
    Consultants, **318**
    Employee status and, 31, 264–287
    Employer, control and, 33
    Exclusivity, 35
    Express terms, 9
    Factors in assessing whether in
        force, 34
    Factory workers, 327–328, 588
        Clocking in, 327, **525**, 588
        Closure, 328, **525**
        Hours of work, 328, **525**, 588
        Layoff, 328, **526**, 588
    Fixed term contracts, **330–337**
    Frustration, through long term
        absence, 715
    Homeworkers, **349–375**
    Implied terms, 11

Intention of the parties, 35
Managerial staff, **386–420**
   Checklist for drafting, 421
Mutuality, 32
Office staff, **431–432**
Overseas employment, **435–439**
Particulars and, 207–218
Personal performance, 31
Salesman, **473–484**
Shiftworkers, **524**
Shop workers, **487**, **527**
Sources of, 9–40
Substitutes, 35
Temporary staff, **298**
Tools of the trade, provision of, 35
Wages and, 35
Written, need for, 5
Covenants,
   and see Restrictive covenants,
     Confidentiality agreement
Convictions, spent, 155
   Employment exceptions, 156
Criminal Records Bureau,196
   Code of Practice, 155

Data controller, 113
Data processing, 118, 132–133
Data processor, 114
Data protection, 91–149, **828**, 838
   Absence recording, 702
   CCTV, policy, **103–105**
   Codes of Practice, 142
   Computers, **109–110**, **828**, 838
   Definitions, 112–123
   E-mail policy, **108–109**, **827**, 838
   Eighth principle, 137
   Employment records,
     Keeping, 143
     Policy, **93–98**
   First principle, 124
   Fifth principle, 134
   Fourth principle, 133
   Guidance, 120
   Monitoring, 144
     Checklist on impact, **106–108**
     Policy, **98–103**
     Sickness, 702

Non-EEA, 122, 137
Processing personal data, 111, 133
Recruitment, 125–131,
   Policy, **162**
Request for personal data, **110**, 141
Second principle, 132
Security, 135
Sensitive personal data, 122
Seventh principle, 135
Sixth principle, 134
Subject access rights, 140
Third principle, 133
Data subject, 114
   Access rights, 140
   Consent, 127
Deductions from wages or salary, 24,
   595, **608**, **609**, 620–624
   Enforcement, 624
   Exception, 622
   Payments to the employer, 623
   Shop work, **609**
   Shortfall of takings
     Betting workers, 294
     Shopworkers, 623
   Unauthorised, 621
Dependants, time off for,
   Entitlement, 814
   Policy, 8, **806**
Development, staff *see* Staff
   development
Differences, contract, interview,
   between, 202
Directors, 1047, **1049–1073**, 1073–1076
   Fiduciary duty, 1074
   Non-executive, appointment
     1066–1073
   Remuneration, accounts and, 1076
   Service agreement, 1073
   Termination, 1075
Disability discrimination *see*
   Discrimination
Disability
   Absence, 727
   Policy, **700**, 1009
Disciplinary procedures *see* Dismissal
   and disciplinary procedures

Discrimination, 40–90
  Advertising, recruitment, 181–186
  Age, 88
  Application forms, 188
  Application letters, 188
  Concept, 41
  Contract, pre-existence of, 40
  Disability
    Advertising, 76
    Comparator, 71
    Definition, 64
      Long term, 65, 715
      Mental or Physical
        impairment, 64
      Normal day-to-day activities,
        68
      Substantial adverse effect, 66
    Direct discrimination, 69
    Equal opportunities, 1009
    Harassment, 75, 1007
    Knowledge of, 75
    Policy, **995**
    Reasonable adjustments, 72
      Policy, 173
    Recruitment, and, 76, 160
  Failing to offer employment, 202
  Homeworkers, 384
  Hours of work, 592
  Human rights and, 90, 821
  Interviews, 161, 192
  Job descriptions, 187
  Job specifications, 160, 187
  Maternity, 770
  Part-time workers, 466
  Personal execution of work,
    requirement, 40, 41
  Qualifications, 191
  Race
    Advertising, 57
    Definition, 56
    Direct, 51
    During employment, 58
    Exceptions, 59
    Harassment, 56, 1007
    Indirect, 53
    Recruitment, and, 57, 160

    Victimisation, 55
  Recruitment, and, **160**
  Refusing to offer employment, 202
  Religion or belief, 82, 1009
    Concepts, 83
    Direct, 83
    Employment, 86
    Harassment, 84, 1007
    Indirect, 83
    Occupational requirement, 85
    Positive action exceptions, 86
  Religious holidays, 820, 1011
  Selection criteria, 190
  Sex, 42–50
    Advertising, 47
    Bonus, 618
    Concepts, 43
    Direct, 43
    Equal pay, 50
    Exceptions, 48–49
    Hours of work, 592
    Indirect, 46
    Recruitment, and, 47, 160
    Victimisation, 47
  Sexual orientation, 77
    Concepts, 77
    Direct, 76
    Employment, 81
    Harassment, 76, 1007
    Indirect, 76
    Occupational requirement, 76
    Positive action exceptions, 80
  Terms and conditions, of offer, 199
  Work permits, 195
Dismissal and Disciplinary procedures,
    8, 215, **901–914**, 921–961
  ACAS Code, 711
  Agency workers, 286
  Agreement, procedures, 938
  Application of, 926
  Business, sudden closure, 938
  Collective redundancies, 936
  Complying, both parties, 941
  Conduct, 215
  Constructive, 939
  Contravening a duty, 938

Exempt dismissals, 935, 939
    Failure of a party to comply, 944
    Modified dismissals only, 939
Fixed term contract, 929
Grievance procedures and, 931
Homeworkers, 379
Industrial action, 937
Jurisdiction, 923
Letters, **915–921**
Managers, 427
Meetings, 931
    Rearranging, 934
Minimum standards, 925
Modified procedure, 929
National security, 941
Overlapping disputes, 951
Overseas employment, 443
Re-engagement, 936
Retirement, 929
Right to be accompanied to hearing,
    932
Scope, 925
Short form, **901**
Standard procedure, 927
Statutory terms, 924
    Awards, and, 945
    Effect, 943
    Failure of a party to comply, 944
    Other procedures and, 945
Timetable, 931
    Extension, 947
Unfair dismissal, 921
    Changes, Polkey and, 953
    Fairness generally, 954
Written particulars, 951
Dress and appearance, **829**, 839
Betting workers, 294
Driving licence, 169, 205, **646**, 649
Drugs, **824**, 833
Unfair, dismissal, sickness, 833
Duties *see* Scope of duties, Job
    description
Duty of trust and confidence *see* Trust
    and confidence

E-mail policy, 108–109, 827, 838
Interception, 838

Employee,
    Definition, 29
    Individual not an, **26–27**
Employee liability, standard of care and,
    516, **824**
Employee representation, 851–854
    Policy, 7
    Staff Association representation, **852**
    Trade Union representation, **851**
Employer, control by, 33
Employer/employee, mutuality, 32
Employer protection, contract as,
    Essential documentation, 7
Employment records, policy, data
    protection, **93–98**
Employment Health Check, 14
Employment status, 26–40
    Agency staff, 264–287
    Casual workers, 314
    Discrimination, and, *see*
        Discrimination
    Homeworkers, 376
Entertainment, client, **830**, 842
Equal opportunities, **984–998**, 998–1011
    And see Disability, Equal pay,
        Harassment
    Harassment policy, **988**, 1000
        Implied term, 1000
    Monitoring forms, **172**
    Policy, **985**
Equal pay, 50, 1011
    Policy, **993**, 999
Equipment, homeworkers, 380, 384
Essential terms and conditions *see* Terms
    and Conditions
Expenses,
    Homeworking, 380
    Managers, 424
Express terms, 9
    Collective agreements, and, 9
    Hours of work, 531, 586
    Scope of duties, 511

Factory workers, 327–328
    Health and safety, 328
    Hours, 328, **525**
    Layoff, 328, **526**, 588

Shiftworking, 327, **525**, 588
Shutdown, 328, **525**
    Holiday, 328, **661**
    Timekeeping, 327, **525**, 588
    Working time, 328, 588
Filing system, relevant, 118–121
Financial sector, *and see* Office staff
Fixed term contracts, 329, **330–337**,
    337–348
    Collective agreements, 346
    Comparators, 342
    Definition, 338, 341
    Dismissal procedure, 929
    Extension of, **336**
    Maternity leave cover, offer of, **336**
    Objective justification defence, 344
    Offer of, **335**
    Pension schemes, 344
    Permanent employees, and, 342
    Pro rata principle, 344
    Rights and remedies, 343
    Successive, 345
    Unfair dismissal, 347
    Workforce agreements, 346
    Written statement, right to, 345
Flexible working, 786
    Application, 790, 791
        Decision, 794
        Employer acceptance, 792
        Meeting, 793
    Contractual issues, 790
    Disposal by agreement, 803
    Entitlement, 788
    Extensions of time, 803
    Latest age of child, 789
    Nature of, 788
    Refusal, 794
        Appeals, 802
        Grounds, **795–802**
    Remedies, 804
Flexibility,
    Clauses, limits of, 515–516
    Clauses, notice in introduction to
        company, 496
    Homeworkers, 384
    Office workers, 433

Part-time workers, 466
Flexitime, **522**, 585

Garden leave, **1026**, 1031
    Duties during, 1034
    Express terms, 1032
    Implied terms, 1032
    Restrictive covenants and, 1034
Grievance procedures, 215, **962–971**,
    971–982
    Admissibility, 982
    Agency workers, 286
    Basic position, 972
    Collective grievances, 981
    Compliance, deemed, 979
    Definition, 974
    Dispute resolution procedure, 981
    Exemptions, 978
    General requirement, 978
    Managers, 427
    Modified procedure, 975, 977
    Not reasonably practicable, 981
    Policy, 8, **962–971**
    Questionnaires, 978
    Standard procedure, 975, 976
    Statutory procedure, effect of, 973

Harassment,
    Disability discrimination, 75
        Policy against, **988**, 1000
    Race discrimination, 56
    Religion or belief, 84
    Sexual, 1001
    Sexual orientation, 78
Health and safety, **1012–1016**,
    1016–1023
    And see Smoking
    Factory and shiftwork, 328
    Fire policy, **1015**
    Policy, 8, **1012**
    Risk to health, contractual term, 1017
Health insurance *see* Permanent Health
    Insurance and Medical Insurance
Health records, data and, 123, 144–145
Hirer, agency workers and, **233**, 269
    Charges to, 281
    Information from, 275

Information to, 277
Letter to agency, **258**
Terms, 274
Holiday
    See, further, Working time
    Accrual methods, **659**
    Agency workers, 287
    Contract of employment, proof of, 35
    Entitlement, **659**, 664, 673
    First year, 666
    Managers, 425
    Notice to take leave, 667
    Overseas employment, 442
    Part-time workers, 463, 673
    Payment, 667
    Public, **661**, 665
    Request form, **662**, 667
    Rolled up holiday pay, **662**, 668
    Salesman, 486
    Shutdown, factory, **661**
    Summary, 674
    Temporary staff, 317
    Termination, and, 671
    Variation, 675
    Working time, 663–676
Homeworkers, **349–375**
    Continuity, 384
    Disciplinary code, 379, 384
    Discrimination in pay, 384
    Employee status, 376
    Expenses, 380–383
    Equipment, 380, 385
    Flexibility, 384
    Guidance, 385
    Holiday, 384
    Minimum wage, 376
    Piece work, 377–378
    Place of work, 384
    Tax, 380
    Travel, 382
    Whistleblowing, 379
Hours of work, **518–530**, 530–593
    Discrimination, 592
    Express terms, 531, 586, 589
    Factory workers, 588
    Flexibility, **522**
    Flexitime, 585
    Implied terms, 532, 586
    Managers, 424
    Normal, **518**
    Office workers, 433
    Overtime **521**, 585 *and see* Overtime
    Part time workers, 458
    Retail, 592
    Shiftworking, 588
    Time keeping, **524**, 588
    Varying, 585
    Working time *see* Working time
Human Rights Act, 88
    Discrimination, 90, 821
    Expression, 90
    Fair trial, 88
    Monitoring telephone calls, 835
    Privacy and, 89
    Religious holidays and, 89, 820, 821

Implied duties, managers, 428
Indemnities, agency staff, 287
Induction checklist, 174
Industrial disputes, agency workers
    and, 281
Informal recruitment, 186
Information Commissioner, Guidance,
    120, 142–149
Injury, *and see* Sickness
Intellectual property, **883**, 894
    Managers, 429
    Protection of, 894
Internal appointments, recruitment,
    187
Interviews, 192
Introduction to the Company,
    495–499, 499–501
    Importance of bringing attention to
        key clauses, 499
IR35, 324

Job description, 187
Job offers, 162, **168**
    and see, Offers of employment
Job specifications, 187
    Discrimination, 187

Job title, **502–504**, 504–506
  Relationship to duties, 504
Jury Service, 809

Layoff, 328
  Express terms, 589
  Implied terms, 588, 590
Liability of employee, standard of care, 516
Loans, 24, **611**, 627
  Educational, **611**, 627
  Season ticket, **611**
Long term sickness, **690**
Luncheon vouchers, **614**

Malingering, 720
Managerial staff, **386–420**
  Checklist for drafting, 421
    Bonus, 423
    Car, 424
    Commission, 424
    Confidentiality, 429
    Continuity, 422
    Disciplinary procedures, 427
    Expenses, 424
    Flexibility, 423
    Grievance procedures, 427
    Holidays, 425
    Hours of work, 424
    Identity of parties, 422
    Implied duties, 428
    Intellectual property, 429
    Maternity and paternity, 425
    Mobility, 426
    Nature of employment, 423
    Overseas employment, 426
    Overtime, 424
    Payment in lieu, 430
    Pensions, 424
    Period of employment, 422
    Place of work, 426
    Probationary periods, 422
    Proper law, 430
    Remuneration, 423
    Residential accommodation, 427
    Restrictions during employment, 428

Secret profits, 428
Share options, 424
Sickness, 425
Standard of work, 428
Termination, 429
Variation clause, 427
Whistleblowing, 428
Whole employment, 428
Company Group, **403–420**
No Company Group, **386–402**
Manual, 8
Marriage, **807**, 817
Maternity, 429, 757
  Additional, 761
  Ante-natal care, 757
  Compulsory, 758
  Discrimination, 770
  Dismissal, 770
  Fixed term contracts as cover, **336**
  Flowchart, 763
  Letter to employer, **750**
  Ordinary, 758
    Terms and conditions, 761
  Part-time workers, 462, 463
  Policy, 7, **730–747**
  Return to work, 765
    Notice, 766
    Sickness in the last four weeks, 752
    Terms and conditions during absence, 761, 762
Medical examination, 162, 169, 205
Medical insurance, **610**, 625, 629–630
Medical reports, sickness, **695–700**, 707
Method of payment *see* Remuneration
Minimum wage, 598, 600–603
  Agency workers and, 285
  Homeworkers, 376
  Output work, 602
  Salaried hours work, 602
  Time work, 602
  Unmeasured work, 602
Mobile phones, 23, **831**, 842
Mobility clause, **632**, 639–644
  Express terms, 642
  Implied terms, 639
    Nature of work, 640

Territory changes, 641
  Managers, 426
  Overseas working, 439
  Temporary transfer, breach of
    contract, as, 643, 644
Model terms and conditions, *see* Terms
  and conditions
Monitoring of data, 145–149
  Policy, 98–103
Mutuality, 32

Nature of employment, managers, 423
Nil hours contract, **313**, 317
Non-competition covenant, 897
Non-dealing covenant, 898
Non-solicitation covenant, 897
Normal hours *see* Hours of work
Number of employees, effect of
  More than 5, pensions, 214

Objective justification defence,
  Fixed term workers, 344
  Part-time workers, 465
Occasional staff *see* Temporary staff
Occupational pensions *see* Pensions
Offences, criminal, 196
  Records of, 123
Offer letter, 7, 162, **168**
Offers of employment, 18–25, 162, **168**
  Ability to accept, 169
  Acceptance, 201
  Covenants, 170
  Driving licence, 169, 205
  Medical examination, 162, 169, 205
  Place of work, 170
  Probationary period, 24, 170, 205
  Qualifications, 191
    Conditional on, 169
  References, 162
    Conditional on, 168
  Restrictive covenants, 169
  Right to work, 168, 650
  Salary and benefits, 170
  Terms, 199
  Withdrawing, 205
    Letter, **171**
  Work permits, 169

Office staff, 431–432
  Benefits, 433
  Conduct, 433
  Confidential information, 434
  Flexibility of duties, 433
  Hours of work, 433
  Office policies, 434
  Overtime, 433
  Standard of work, 433, **824**
Oral terms, 5
Overseas employment, **435–439**
  Additional benefits, 439
  Applicable law, 441
  Currency of payment, 439
  Disciplinary procedures, 443
  Discrimination, 440
  Managers, 426
  Period of work, 439
  Sickness, 443
  Statutory holidays, 442
  Terms of return, 439
Overtime, **521–522**, 585, **606**, **607**, 615
  See also Remuneration
  Managers, 424
  Obligatory, **607**
  Office staff, 433
  Part-time workers, 461, 465
  Working time, 585

Parental leave, 772–778
  Adoption
    Paternity, 779
  Entitlement, 772, 774
  Letter stating reason for
    postponement, **756**
  Managers, 429
  Part-time workers, 463
  Policy ,**730–747**
  Reasons for absence, 775
  Terms and conditions during
    absence, 777
Part-time workers, **444–455**, 455–469
  Definition, 456
  Discrimination law, 466
  Holidays, 463, 673
  Hours of work, 458
  Letters, **449–454**

Maternity leave, 463
Maternity pay, 462
Overtime, 461, 465
Paternity leave, 463
Pensions, 462
Policy, **444**
Pro rata principle, 458, 464
Rate of pay, 460
Redundancy, 464
Remedies, 459
Returning after absence, 458
Sick pay, 462
Training, access, 462
Transferring, 458
Unfair dismissal, 466
Written statement, 466
Paternity leave, 778 *and see* Parental
leave
Pay, 780
Paternity policy, 7, **730–747**
Payment in lieu of notice, 430
Pensions, **609–610**, 625
Fixed term contracts, 344
Managers, 426
Part-time workers, 462
Stakeholder, 610
Period of employment, 422
Permanent health insurance, **614**,
629–630, **694**
Absence and, 629, 724
Personal data, 111, 114–117, 133, 134
Accuracy, 133
Keeping, 134
Security, 135
Personal telephone calls, **827**, 834
Piece work, 377–378
Place of work, 170, **632**, 639–644
And see Mobility
Homeworkers, 384
Implied terms, 639
Territory changes, 641
Managers, 424
Political beliefs, data and, 122

Preconditions of employment, 645–657
And see References, Probationary
Period, Driving licence,
Qualifications
Pregnancy, letter to employer, **749**
Pro rata principle, 344, 458, 464
Probationary periods, 24, 170, 205, 422,
646, 648
Proper law clause, 430
Public duties, **807**, 817
Public interest disclosure *see*
Whistleblowing

Qualifications, 169, 191, **647**, 649
Discrimination, 191

Race discrimination *see*
Discrimination
Racial origins, data, 122
Rate of pay, *see* Remuneration
Recruitment, 151–205
ACAS, 205
Advertising, 160, 181–186
Agencies, 186
Application forms and letters,
188–189
Appointment, letter of, 7, 8 *and see*
Offer letter
Change of heart, 203
Concluding the contract, 201
Criminal Records Bureau Code of
Practice, 155
Data processing and, 125–132
Information Commissioner's
Code, 143
Differences, contract, interview,
between, 202
Equal opportunities *see* Equal
opportunities
Failing to offer employment, 202
Informal, 186
Internal appointments, 187
Interviews, 161, 192, 201
Job descriptions, 187–188
Job offers, 201
Job specifications, 160, 187–188
Methods, 186

Qualifications, 191
Policy, **160**
    Prevailing documents, 205
Promotions, 160
Reference check, consent to, **152**
Reference, letter requesting, **153**
Reference, letter responding, **154**
Refusing to offer employment, 202
Rehabilitation of Offenders, spent
    convictions, 155, 196
Selection criteria, 190–191
Sex discrimination, 47
Unsolicited letters, 187
Word of mouth, 186
Work permits, 205
Redundancy
    Layoff, 589
    Mobility, 642
    Part-time workers, 464
References, 162, 168, **645**, 648
    Accurate, duty of employer to
        give, 648
    Check, consent to, **152**
    Letter of request for, **153**
    Letter responding, **154**
    Rehabilitation of Offenders, spent
        convictions, 155
Relationships, personal, **829**
Relevant filing system, 118–121
Religion, discrimination, *see*
    Discrimination
Religious beliefs, data and, 122
Religious holidays, **809**, 820
    Discrimination, 820, 1011
Relocation, 639–644 *and see* Mobility
    Application form, **636**
    Policy, **633**
Remuneration
    Managers, 423
    Other than basic salary, **605–614**,
        615–630
        Bonus, **607**, 615–619
        Cars, **612**, 628
        Commission, **608**, 619–620
        Deductions from salary, **608**, **609**,
            620–624

        Loans, **611**, 627–628
        Luncheon vouchers, **614**
        Medical insurance, **610**, 625, 629
        Overtime, **521**, **606**, **607**, 615
        Pension schemes, **609**, **610**, 625
        Permanent health insurance, **614**,
            629–630
        Share schemes, **611**, 625–627
        Vehicles, **612**
    Part-time workers, 460
    Varying, 598
Request for personal data, **110**
Residential accommodation, 471–472
    Cessation of employment, 471
    Managers, 427
Residential staff, **470**
Responsibilities *see* Scope of duties
Restrictions after employment, *see*
    Restrictive covenants
Restrictions during employment, 24,
    428, 881–899
    Confidential information, **882**, 889
    Employment, conflict with duties,
        881, 889
    Intellectual property, protection of,
        883, 894
Restrictive covenants, 169, 205
    Ability to accept work, 169
    Agency workers, 287
    Blue pencilling, 899
    Breach by the employer, 899
    Consultants, 323
    Garden leave and, 1034
    Model, **881–884**, 895
        Area covenant, 898
        Non-competition covenant, 897
        Non-dealing covenant, 898
        Non-poaching, 897
        Non-solicitation covenant, 897
    Severing the clause, 898
Retail *see* Shopworkers
Retirement, 929
    Termination, **1028**, 1035
Right to work in the UK, **647**, 650–657

Sabbatical leave, 811
Salary, 170 *and see* Remuneration

Salesman, **473–484**
  Basic salary, 485
  Commission, 485
  Holiday, when entitled, 486
  Product, link to, 485
  Restrictive covenants, 486, 889–892
  Targets, achieving, 485
  Territory, 485, 641
Scope of duties, **507**–517
  Express terms, 9, 511
    How construed, 512–514
    Job content, 512
    Status, change of, 512
  Flexibility clause, and, 515–516
  Implied terms, 509
    Conduct, 510
    Duties, 510
    Intolerable conduct, no, 510
    Job content, 510
    Status, 509–511
    Trust and confidence, 510
Season ticket loans, **611**
Seasonal worker, **314**
Secret profits, managers, 428
Section 1 statements, *see* Terms and
  conditions
Selection criteria, 190
Service agreements, 421, 1073
Sex discrimination *see* Discrimination
Sexual harassment, 1001
Sexuality, records, 123
Share options, 617 *and see* Share
  schemes
  Managers 424
Share schemes, **611**, 619, 625–627
Shiftworkers, 328
  Hours, **524**, 588
  Implied terms re premium rates, 619
Shop workers, **487**, 488
  Deductions from salary, 488, **609**,
    623
  Dress and appearance, 488
  Hours, **526**, 592
  Sunday working, 488
    Hours, **527**, 592

Shortfall of takings, betting workers,
  294
Shutdown, factory, 328
Sickness, 677–728
  Absence, **689**, 716
    Calculating rate of, 704
    Persistent short term, 717
    Recording, 702
  Abuse of, **683**, **689**
  ACAS Code, 711
  Accidents outside work, absence and,
    693, 724
  Disability
    Adjustments, 716, 727
    Discrimination, 713, 727
    Policy, **700**, 727
  Insurance, **694**, 724
    Scope of, 725
  Length of service, dependent on, **692**
  Letters, 685–688
  Long term, **680**, **690**, 715
    Frustration, 715
  Malingering, 720
  Managers, 425
  Measuring, 701
  Medical reports, **695–700**, 707
    Exemptions, 709
    Individual rights, 708
    Retention of, 709
  No payment, **692**
  Overseas working, 443
  Part-time workers, 462
  Payment, **688**, **692**, 716
    In notice, 1026
  Permanent health insurance, **694**
  Policy, **679**
  Return to work, **691**, 722
  Short-term absence, persistent, 717
  Statutory Sick Pay, **693**, 722
  Suspension, **692**, 721
  Unauthorised absence, 720
  Warnings, 719
Skills *see* Standard of work
Smoking policy, **824**, 832
Social functions, **830**
Special leave, **807**, 816

Staff appraisal *see* Staff development
Staff Association representation, **852**, 853
Staff development, 23, **844**
Standard of work, **824**, 831
  Agency workers, 317
  Employee's liability for, 516
  Managers, 428
  Office workers, 433
  Temporary staff, 317
Statement of particulars, **208–213**
  See also Terms and conditions
  Betting workers, **289**
  Fixed term workers, **330**
Status *see* Employment status
Statutory Sick Pay, **693**, 722
Stress policy, **1036–1038**, 1038–1048
  Management checklist, 1044
  Model, **1037**
Student loans, **611**
Sunday working
  Betting workers, **288**, 291
    Duty of employer, 293
    Effect of opting out notice, 293
    Opting in notice, 293
    Opting out, 292
    Remedies, 293
  Shop workers, 488
    Catering, 488
    Definition, shop, 488
    Entertainment, and, 488
    Hours, **527**
    Premises, divided, 488
    Provisions, when apply, 488
Summary termination, **1027**
Suspension, sickness, **692**, 721

Tax
  Homeworking, 380
Telephone calls
  Monitoring, 835
  Personal, **827**, 834
Teleworking, **356–363**
  Application to, **373**
  Policy, **363–373**
  Tax, 380

Temporary staff, 222–287 *and see* Work-seekers
  Annualised hours contract, **311**
  Continuity, 316
  Employees, **303**, 314
  Holiday, 317
  Letter to agency from hirer, **258**
  Nil hours contract, **313**
  Not employees, **295**
  Permanent, conversion to, 281
  Seasonal worker, **314**
  Self-employment, 316
  Standard of work, 317
  Status, employment, 259–287, 314
  Working time, 316
Termination, 25, **1024–1035** *and see* Disciplinary and dismissal procedures
  Accrued holiday pay, 671, **1025**, 1031
  Directors, 1075
  Fixed term contracts, 929
  Garden leave, **1026**, 1031
    Duties during, 1034
    Express terms, 1032
    Implied terms, 1032
    Restrictive covenants and, 1034
  Holiday pay, **1025**, 1031
  Managers, 429
  Notice, **1024**, **1025**, 1028
  Payment in lieu of notice, **1025**, 1028
  Retirement, 929, **1028**, 1035
  Sick pay during notice, 1028, 1031
  Summary, **1027**, 1035
Terms and conditions, 6, A–Z, 219–489
  Additional maternity leave, 762
  Betting workers, 289
  Cars, 23
  Essential, section 1, 6, 7, 16–23, **207–213**, 213–218
    Changes, 216
    Collective agreements, 9, 20, 214
    Date continuous employment started, 18
    Date employment began, 18

Disciplinary procedure, 20, 21, 215
Disciplinary rules, 20
Grievance procedure, 21, 215
Holidays, 19, 214
Hours of work, 18
Incapacity for work, 19
Intervals remuneration paid, 18
Name of employee, 18
Name of employer, 18, 213
Notice, 19
Overseas employment, 20, 439
Pensions, 19, 21, 214
Period of employment, 19
Place of work, 19
Remuneration, 18, 213
Timing, 216
Title, 19, 504
Express, 9
Implied, 11
Introduction to the Company, **495–499**, 499–501
Introduction to the Manual, *see* Introduction to the Company
Maternity leave, 761, 762
Parental leave, 777
Statement of, particulars, **208–213**
Trust and confidence, operation of terms and, 13
Terms of engagement, **502** *and see* Job title
Time off, statutory rights, 25
Timekeeping, **524**, **525**, 588
Tips, 600, 602
Title, 502–506
Trade Union representation, **851**
Trade unions
  Data and, 122
Training, **844**
  Access to, part-time workers, 462
Trust and confidence, 13

Unfair dismissal
  Alcohol and drugs, 833
  Disciplinary procedures, 921
  Fixed term contracts, 347
  Maternity leave, 770

Sickness, 714, 723
  Part-time worker, remedy, 466
Unpaid leave, **810**
Unsolicited letters, recruitment, 187

Variation clause, 428
  Clauses, notice in introduction to company, 499
Vehicles, **612** *and see* Cars
Victimisation
  Race discrimination, 55
  Sex discrimination, and, 47

Wages, payment of and contracts, 35
Whistleblowing, 8, 23, 856–880
  Contractual prohibition void, 872
  Disclosure, definition, 863
  Employer, 868
  Exceptionally serious failure, 871
  Good faith, 867
  Homeworkers, 379
  Legal adviser, 869
  Managers, 428
  Minister of the Crown, 870
  No duty to report wrongdoing, 860
  Policy, 8, **856–860**
    Small employers, **858**
  Prescribed person, 870, 874–880
  Qualifying disclosure, 864
    Exclusions, 867
    Requirements, 868–872
  Worker, definition, 872
Whole employment, managers, 428
Withdrawal of offer, **171**
Work-finding services, 269 *and see* Agencies
Work permits, 170, 195, 205
Work-seeker, 270, 276 *and see* Agency workers
  Information to, 277
  Payment of, 283
  Protection, 278
  Right to seek work, 280
Workers, **26–27**, 36
  Checklist, 28
  Definitions, 36,
  Employees, distinction, 36,

Part-time, 444
Temporary, 264
Whistleblowing, 872
Workforce agreement, working time,
   528–530
   Fixed term contracts, and, 346
Working time, 25, 36, **527–530**,
   532–593
   Adult, 535
   Agency worker, 286, 579
   Agricultural workers, 583
   Annual leave, 555
   Applicability – chart, 557
   Armed forces, 578
   At a glance guide, 557–567
   Aviation workers, 570
   Calculating 48 hour week, 538
   Casual workers, 316
   Children, 575
   Crown employment, 580
   Daily rest periods, 547, 562
      Young workers, 547, 563
   Day, split, 577
   Definition, 532–536, 557
   Different occupations, 568–584
   Doctors, 550, 555, 575
   Domestic servants, 552, 576
   Exceptions, 548–551
   Excluded sectors, 548
   Exclusion clause, 527, 555
   Factory and shiftworkers, 328, **524**
   Freelance workers, 580
   Holiday, 663–676
      Entitlement, 664, 673
      Notice, 667
      Payment, 667
      Summary, 674
      Termination, 671
   Houses of Parliament, 581
   Inland waterways, 549, 571
   Maximum weekly, 536
      Nightworkers, 535, 540, 559,
         560–561

Minimum wage and, 602
Mobile worker, 535, 551, 569
Night time, 535
Nightworker, 535, 540, 559, 560, 575
   Adequate breaks, 561
   Health assessment, 544, 560
   Health questionnaire, **545**
   Special hazards, 560
   Transfers to daily work, 561
Non-mobile workers, 568
Opt-out agreement, **528**, 556
Police, 582
Rail workers, 570
Reforms, 556
Regulations, 534–584
Rest breaks, 548, 566
   Young workers, 548, 567
Road transport, 550, 569
Seafarers, 549, 571, 572
Security workers, 576
Self employment, 580
Shift workers, 554, 577
Special cases, 553
State workers, 580
Temporary staff, 316
Unmeasured, 553, 577
Untrained workers, 582
Weekly rest periods, 547, 564
   Young workers, 547, 565
Work patterns, 547
Workforce agreement, **528–530**, 535
Young worker, 547, 548, 563, 567,
   572, 573, 574, 579
Workplace monitoring of data, policy
   98–103
Written terms, need for, 5
   Fixed terms workers, 346
   Part-time workers, 466

Zero hours contracts *see* Nil hours
   contracts

Michael Duggan's Employment Books

Throughout these volumes there are cross-references to three other works in the series of major employment law texts published by xpl and written by Michael Duggan.

We recommend that you obtain a copy through our website to ensure that you have information on the latest edition: *www.xplpublishing.com*.

Wrongful Dismissal and Breach of Contract: Law, Practice and Precedents

Sets out the complexities of the common law, and examines the rules to be followed by practitioners in assessing compensation, the tax position and much more.

ISBN 1 85811 232 X

Unfair Dismissal – Second Edition

The leading work on *Unfair Dismissal*, now being thoroughly updated. Coverage is extensive and fully cross-referred to this edition Contracts of Employment.

ISBN 1 85811 339 3

Family Friendly Policies

This first guide to the Government's Family Friendly Policies is invaluable for legal practitioners and HR professionals alike. Well laid out and hugely comprehensive.

ISBN 1 85811 319 9

xpl ... law explained.

XPL Publishing
www.xplpublishing.com
sales@xplpublishing.com

Printed in the United Kingdom
by Lightning Source UK Ltd.
102859UKS00001B/25-204